# The Atonement

*The Congregational Union Lecture for 1875*

By R. W. Dale

Published by Pantianos Classics

ISBN-13: 978-1-78987-641-3

First published in 1875

# Contents

# *Advertisement*

By the Committee of the Congregational Union of England and Wales.

---

The Congregational Union Lecture has been established with a view to the promotion of Biblical Science, and Theological and Ecclesiastical Literature.

It is intended that each Lecture shall consist of a course of Prelections, delivered at the Memorial Hall, but when the convenience of the Lecturer shall so require, the oral delivery will be dispensed with.

The Committee hope that the Lecture will be maintained in an unbroken Annual Series; but they promise to continue it only so long as it seems to be efficiently serving the end for which it has been established, or as they may have the necessary funds at their disposal.

For the opinions advanced in any of the Lectures, the Lecturer alone will be responsible.

18, South Street, Finsbury,
*January*, 1874.

# Preface

These Lectures were prepared at the request of the Committee of the Congregational Union of England and Wales, and were delivered in the Memorial Hall, Farringdon Street, during the months of February, March, and April in the present year.

Concerning the method which I have followed, there is little to be added to the explanations contained in the Lectures themselves. It may, however, be well to state that in illustrating the testimony of our Lord Jesus Christ and of His Apostles to the Fact of the Atonement, my intention is simply to show that the Death of Christ is conceived and described as being the objective ground on which we receive the Remission of sins. The premature attempt to construct a Theory of the Atonement on the basis of those descriptions of the Death of Christ which represent it as a Ransom for us, or as a Propitiation for the sins of the world, or on phrases in which Christ is described as dying for us, or dying for our sins, has been the mischievous cause of most of the erroneous Theories by which the glory of the Fact has been obscured.

Until we have considered the actual relations of the Lord Jesus Christ, both to the eternal Law of Righteousness which the sins of men have violated, and to the human race, — and until we have discovered what light these relations throw upon the Fact that His Death is the ground on which sin is forgiven, — it appears to me that we are in no position to determine with any confidence to what extent the Death of the Lord Jesus Christ, which is described as a "Ransom," is analogous to other ransoms, or to what extent the Death of Christ, which is described as a "Propitiation," is analogous to the propitiatory acts by which men are accustomed to allay the anger of those whom they may have offended, or to the propitiatory sacrifices by which the heathen have attempted to avert the displeasure of angry gods. These descriptions cannot be made the foundation of a theory of the Atonement, but they are sure tests by which we may ascertain the accuracy of a theory. Unless our conception of the Death of Christ gives a natural explanation of all the forms in which it is represented by our Lord Jesus Christ and by the writers of the New Testament, our conception is either false or incomplete.

The series of Lectures of which this is the third, may be regarded as taking the place of another series, known as the **Congregational Lecture,** which commenced in the year 1833, and which was suspended about 1860. The third Lecture in the earlier series was also on the Atonement. It was delivered in the Congregational Library, exactly forty years ago, by the late Rev. Joseph Gilbert, of Nottingham, who was one of the most learned and thoughtful theologians among the Congregational ministers of his time. I read and re-read Mr. Gilbert's Lectures at a time when my own theological convictions were unformed. How much I am indebted to them it would be difficult to say. They always seemed to me singularly judicious and able.

To my friends the Rev. Dr. Henry Allon, the Rev. J. G. Rogers, the Rev. Professor Simon, and Professor Massie, I am under obligations of various kinds. That Dr. Allon and Mr. Rogers, notwithstanding their own heavy engagements, should have been good enough to assist me in the irksome task of revising the proofs of this volume, calls for my most grateful acknowledgments.

Three or four paragraphs which appeared in two articles on the Atonement, published in the British Quarterly Review for October, 1866, and October, 1867, have been transferred to the text of these Lectures. Should any of my readers notice this fact, they must be good enough to accept my assurance that, in making use of the *British Quarterly* articles, I am not guilty of plagiarism.

R. W. DALE.

Birmingham,
*May* 6, 1875.

# Lecture One - Introductory

Francis Turretin, — the greatest of Calvinistic theologians — in the first of his celebrated dissertations on the Satisfaction offered by our Lord Jesus Christ for the sins of men, speaks of the doctrine of the Atonement as "the chief part of our salvation, the anchor of Faith, the refuge of Hope, the rule of Charity, the true foundation of the Christian religion, and the richest treasure of the Christian Church." "So long," he says, "as this doctrine is maintained in its integrity, Christianity itself and the peace and blessedness of all who believe in Christ are beyond the reach of danger; but if it is rejected, or in any way impaired, the whole structure of the Christian faith must sink into decay and ruin." [1]

Such words as these are true only of the Atonement itself; they cannot be justly used concerning any doctrine or theory of the Atonement. There are large numbers of Christian men who have never been able to discover any direct relation between the Death of Christ and the forgiveness of sin, and who sometimes protest with vehement moral indignation against the doctrine which alone explains the power of the Cross over their own conscience and heart. It remains true that Christ's Death — though they know neither how nor why — has done more than either His teaching or His life to constrain and enable them to trust in the mercy of God for the pardon of sin; and because Christ is the Propitiation for the sins of the world, God has responded to their trust, and they are eternally saved. For it is not the doctrine of the Death of Christ that atones for human sin, but the Death itself; and great as are the uses of the doctrine in promoting the healthy and vigorous development of the spiritual life, the Death of Christ has such a wonderful power, that it inspires faith in God, and purifies the heart, though the doctrine of the Atonement may be unknown or denied.

Even among those who accept, in their direct and obvious sense, the explicit declarations of Holy Scripture, that "Christ once suffered for sins, the Just for the unjust, to bring us to God," there are very many — and perhaps their number is rapidly increasing — who shrink from the attempt to determine the precise function of the Death of Christ in human redemption. Reverence restrains their speculation. In the presence of the Son of God, dying for the sins of men, they can only acknowledge with penitence the greatness of their guilt and adore the infinite tenderness and strength of the Divine Love. Or they believe that the mystery of His Death transcends the limits of human intelligence, and belongs to provinces of the Divine life and thought which are altogether inaccessible to us. Or the history of theological doctrine has convinced them that the attempt to form a theory of the Atonement is not only presumptuous but perilous, and will inevitably introduce into our conception of the supreme manifestation of the Divine Mercy elements derived from human imperfection, by which its moral and spiritual power will be diminished and its original glory obscured. It is even feared, and not without reason, that we may so speculate on the relations between the Death of Christ and the Divine government of the human race, as to provoke men to deny that, in any sense, the Lord Jesus Christ died to atone for the sins of the world. We are warned that the fact may be rejected, because our explanations of it are incredible.

No one who has thought much on this doctrine can be insensible either to the difficulties which encompass it, or to the grave and complicated evils which a false conception of it may inflict on the life of the Church. The difficulties are obvious. In the present condition of theological thought many of them are insoluble; and it is more than doubtful whether some of them will ever disappear until we have the open vision of God on the other side of death.

For any complete theory of the Atonement must include a definition of the eternal relations between the Son of God and the Father. It is the habit of some modern theological thinkers to say that the names by which we know the several Persons of the Trinity are derived from their revealed relations to mankind. This may be conceded; but surely these relations are conditioned by relations deeper than themselves. We cannot imagine that He whom we know as the God and Father of our Lord Jesus Christ could have laid aside His glory and assumed the same relationship to the Son that the Son assumed to Him: if this were possible, then the relationship as known to us between the Lord Jesus Christ and the Father would be purely contingent and arbitrary, and would rest on no eternal fact in the nature of God. What may be described as the internal and mutual relations of the Trinity must contain the ultimate solution of some of the questions suggested by the relation of Christ in His redemptive work to the Father. But the development of the doctrine of the Trinity has been practically arrested for thirteen or fourteen hundred years; and in those early centuries when that doctrine absorbed the theological thought of the Church, the theory of the Atonement had as yet assumed so rudimentary and imperfect a form that it was impossible for theologians to appreciate the close and profound relations between these two great provinces of Christian speculation. During the Athanasian controversies the construction of the doctrine of the Trinity suffered very seriously through the absence of a just theory of the Atonement; and until the doctrine of the Trinity has received a much richer and fuller development, there are questions relating to the theory of the Atonement to which we can give no reply.

Nor, on the other hand, has the thought of the Church ever reached a firm, coherent, and permanent conception of the original relation of the Eternal Word or Son of God to the created universe, and especially to our own race — a relation which appears to underlie the possibility of the Incarnation of our Lord Jesus Christ, and to involve the solution of some of the severest speculative difficulties connected with the theory of Redemption. It cannot, indeed, be alleged that the question has never been seriously investigated. It was forced upon the consideration of the early Church by the wild dreams of Gnosticism; it was partially illustrated by the profound thought of Athanasius; it was not overlooked by the schoolmen of the Middle Ages; it has occupied a prominent place in the noblest theological speculation of Germany during the last half century. But the question has never passed out of the province of speculation into the province of faith. It belongs to theologians, and not to the commonalty of the Church. The great words of St. Paul — "For in Him were all things created that are in heaven and that are in earth, visible and invisible, whether they be thrones or dominions or principalities or powers; all things were created by Him and for [εἰς unto] Him: and He is before all things, and in Him all things consist" [2] — give us a glimpse of vast and fruitful provinces of truth which are almost unknown to us. They have been traversed from time to time by the solitary path of adventurous speculation, but the Church has never made her home there: the golden harvests are unreaped; not even a wandering sect has pitched its tents and fed its flocks on those rich and boundless plains. They belong to a remote and glorious realm lying far beyond the frontiers of familiar truth — a realm whose mountain ranges and whose rivers are laid down in no theological survey which the Church has accepted as authentic, and whose wealth has never enriched the common thought of Christendom. All things were created "in Him," "by Him," "for Him;" "in Him all things consist,"— these wonderful words are still "dark with excess of light." They affirm the existence and define the character of relations between the Divine personality of the Lord Jesus Christ and the universe which we have never been able to grasp; but a clear conception of these relations is indispensable to a satisfactory theory of the Atonement.

There are some other preliminary questions lying on the border land of philosophy and of theology, of which at present we appear to have discovered no final and generally accepted solution, although the solution has been repeatedly attempted both in ancient and in modern times. How, for instance, are we to conceive of the law of righteousness, which we have violated by the sins for which Christ died? Is the law the expression of God's arbitrary will, or is it necessary and eternal? If necessary and eternal, is God so related to it that His freedom is determined and controlled by the law, so that the law is supreme and God only its minister? Or is there a sense in which, even in relation to the eternal law of righteousness, He is "God over all, blessed for evermore"?

These questions, again, involve the nature and necessity of Punishment. Are we to think of Punishment as a stern but benignant expedient for the discipline of God's moral creatures? Or are the penalties which vindicate the authority of the Divine law rooted in principles as necessary and immutable as those which are expressed in its precepts?

In the presence of questions like these, which confront us on the very threshold of any serious inquiry into the doctrine of the Atonement, the hardihood of speculation must be abashed; and it may appear to many devout minds that the inquiry is not only presumptuous and perilous, but profane. Some of these problems are confessedly insoluble in the present condition of theological science; some of them appear to lie beyond the farthest range of our intellectual powers. We can find peace and strength and consolation in the certainty of the remission of sins for Christ's sake. Is it not safer to cease to speculate on the mode in which His Death is related to the Divine government and to the redemption of our race? To confess the limitations of human knowledge is the part not only of devout humility, but of the highest wisdom. When God descended in clouds and fire and glory on the mountain in the desert, the people were commanded to stand afar off, and were warned that if they ventured, at the impulse of a daring curiosity, to "break through unto the Lord to gaze," they would perish. Are we not guilty of a similar offence in attempting to penetrate a more august and awful mystery? The words of Richard Hooker express the temper which we should cherish in all our thoughts on the ways of God, and never is that temper more necessary than when we are contemplating the very crisis and agony of the Divine struggle with the sins and miseries of mankind, the supreme act of the Divine love, the central mystery towards which all other mysteries converge: "Dangerous it were for the feeble brain of man to wade far into the doings of the Most High, whom, although, to know be life, and joy to make mention of His name, yet our soundest knowledge is to know that we know Him not as, indeed, He is, neither can know Him; and our safest eloquence concerning Him is our silence, when we confess without confession that His glory is inexplicable. His greatness above our capacity and reach. He is above, and we upon earth; therefore it behoveth our words to be wary and few." [3]

We may accept the caution, but it is doubtful whether it lies within our power to remain neutral in the presence of conflicting theories of the Atonement. The fundamental question. Whether the Death of Christ has a direct relation to the remission of sins, or whether it was simply a great appeal of the Divine love to the human race — "God's method of conquering the human heart" — determines the whole attitude of the Christian soul to Christ. One of these two conceptions we must accept, one we must reject, not merely as theologians, but as Christians. One of these two theories is implicated in every devotional act, in every confession of sin, in every prayer for forgiveness, in every thanksgiving for redemption.

If we say that we are sure that the Death of Christ reveals the infinite love of God, but that we cannot tell whether it has a direct relation to human sin and human forgiveness, and that we must be satisfied to remain in doubt, we do not liberate ourselves from the responsibility of a decision. Our election between the rival theories is made, even when we think that we have refused to make it. What we relegate to the shadowy region -of uncertainty forms no spiritual habit and quickens no spiritual affection; what we regard as true, becomes one of the active forces of our spiritual life.

If we go so far as to acknowledge that there are parts of our Lord's teaching, and of the teaching of His Apostles, which are perfectly conclusive in favour of one of these alternatives — the alternative which represents the almost unanimous faith of Christendom from the earliest times to our own — it is hardly possible for us to escape a conception of the Sacrifice of Christ which will amount to a theory of the Atonement. We may refuse to speculate on the necessities of the Divine government or of the Divine nature, which the Death of Christ has been supposed to satisfy, or on its precise relation to the exercise of the Divine mercy in the remission of sin; but if there is habitual trust in the Lord Jesus Christ, as the Propitiation for the sins of the world, we shall have a theory, spite of ourselves.

It seems very difficult to attribute any religious authority to the New Testament writers and yet to refuse to accept a theory of the Atonement. The rudiments of a theory are contained in all the terms by which they describe the nature and purpose of the Death of Christ. "Christ died for the ungodly;" He "suffered,...the Just for the unjust;" these words must either remain non-significant for us, or else we must make our choice between interpreting them as meaning that the Death of Christ had a vicarious, or perhaps a representative, character, or as meaning nothing more than that in some general way His death was intended for our advantage; and if we accept the last hypothesis we have still to determine the kind of benefit that we derive from it.

The Apostles often represent the Death of Christ as a "ransom," and speak of its effect as "redemption." We can, of course, practically obliterate these expressions by declining to attach any meaning to them; but if we feel that to cancel isolated passages in the mere text of the apostolic writings is a less presumptuous offence than to cancel ideas which are wrought into the whole substance of apostolic teaching, we shall endeavour to discover what conception of the Death of Christ underlies expressions in which it is represented as being analogous to the price that is paid for the ransom of slaves.

That the Apostles believed in the existence of a very intimate relation between human sin and the Sacrifice of Christ, is indisputable. Not in set and uniform phrases, but under a considerable variety of forms, they affirm that it was for our sins that Christ suffered. It is not easy — it is, perhaps, impossible — for those who are constantly reading the New Testament to leave this relation vague and indefinite. We shall incline either to the theory that Christ suffered for our sins, because suffering came upon Him instead of coming on us, or that in the depth and perfection of His sympathy with us our guilt seemed to become His own, or that His Death was simply the natural result of the antagonism of the human heart to perfect goodness, and that He therefore "suffered for sins," just as all good men have suffered who elected to endure the worst that malice and wickedness could inflict upon them rather than be unfaithful to God. In any case, we adopt a theological theory.

There are other forms under which the Death of Christ is represented in the New Testament which make it still more difficult to practise a severe abstinence from all speculation on this great mystery. When, for instance, St. John affirms that our Lord Jesus Christ "is the Propitiation for our sins; and not for ours only, but also for the sins of the whole world," the Apostle does not simply affirm that in some undefined way the Lord Jesus Christ secures for us the Divine pardon: he expresses a definite conception of the way in which Christ secures it. We may refuse to analyse this conception; we may pronounce it impossible to determine whether a Propitiation was necessary before God could forgive us, or how, and in what sense, Christ was a Propitiation; but if we admit this conception of the work of Christ into our minds at all, we surrender ourselves to a theological theory. The results of refusing to make the theory a definite object of reflection may be most mischievous. We may come almost unconsciously to ascribe to God those blind movements of passion which, among ourselves, are sometimes exhausted by the infliction of cruel suffering, and sometimes placated by ignominious submission or by still more ignominious intercession: our idea of God may be corrupted, and we may involve the Sacrifice of Christ in the deepest dishonour. To speculate is perilous; not to speculate may be more perilous still.

It is very possible for our theory of the Atonement to be crude and incoherent, but it is hardly possible to have no theory at all. Some conception, however vague, of the relations between human sin and the Death of Christ, and between the Death of Christ and the Divine forgiveness, will take form and substance in the mind of every man who is in the habit of reading the New Testament, and who believes that the teaching of Christ and of His Apostles reveals the thought of God.

Further, to insist that a due reverence for the awful greatness of God requires us to accept the fact that we are forgiven for Christ's sake, but to make no attempt to discover the principles of the Divine government or the perfections of the Divine nature which the fact illustrates, appears to be inconsistent with the characteristic spirit of the Christian revelation and a renunciation of the prerogatives which belong to the sons of God. "The entrance of Thy words giveth light:" this is the testimony of one who lived in those early times when God dwelt apart, when "clouds and darkness" were round about Him, and the hearts of saints were longing for that clearer vision of His glory which was to be the joy and wonder of later and happier generations. Even then the Divine Word was something more than a dark formula in an unknown tongue. It was not an incantation or a spell. When it came to men even as a definite law the underlying principle shone through.

It was necessary, no doubt, in the earlier stages of the history of our race that the Will should be chastened and disciplined by authoritative commandments; for men must be formed to the practice of the elementary virtues before it is possible for them to recognise the beauty and nobleness and eternal obligation of Righteousness. But commandments which at first seemed arbitrary were so transfigured that to devout souls the Divine "statutes" became "songs" which filled with music the house of their pilgrimage.

13

When the heir differed nothing from a servant, though he was lord of all, God relaxed the bonds of mere external authority for those who had the spirit of children, and treated them not as slaves, but as sons. Now that "the fulness of time has come" it is at once our duty and our blessedness to accept complete emancipation, and to "stand fast in the liberty wherewith Christ hath made us free."

This liberty is something more than exemption from the mere inconveniences imposed by the irksome restraints of the ancient law. It is one of the noblest prerogatives of that higher and more intimate relationship to the Father into which we have entered through our union with Christ. It determines the spirit and form of the whole revelation of God's character and will, and it should determine our own attitude in the presence of that revelation.

The precepts of the Lord Jesus Christ are all of a kind to enlighten the conscience, and not merely to control the will. They are useless so long as the principles of which they are the expression do not shine in their own light. They are positively mischievous to those who try to obey them as rules instead of using them freely as aids to the apprehension of great ethical and spiritual laws. "Give to him that asketh thee, and from him that would borrow of thee, turn not thou away;" "Take no thought for your life, what ye shall eat, or what ye shall drink; nor yet for your body what ye shall put on;" "Judge not, that ye be not judged;" — these commandments and many others are unavailable as mere rules of conduct. They fulfil a higher purpose, and are intended so to exalt and purify our ideal of perfection that every Christian man may become a law to himself.

The revelation of Truth in the New Testament conforms to the same method. It comes to us not as dogma, but as doctrine. We are "taught of God," and are not merely required to profess our faith in the articles of a creed. There are, no doubt, positive declarations that the Lord Jesus Christ was God manifest in the flesh, — declarations which have been built up by theologians into massive arguments for the defence of the great truth of our Lord's divinity. But the reverence and worship with which we bow down before Him who is seated at God's right hand, "far above all principality, and power, and might, and dominion, and every name that is named, not only in this world, but also in that which is to come," the loyal homage that we offer to "the King of kings and Lord of lords" are not the answer of a blind submission to the "prooftexts" of dogmatic theology. We, too, have seen "His glory, the glory as of the only-begotten of the Father," "we have heard Him ourselves, and know that this is indeed the Christ, the Saviour of the world."

"He that followeth Me" — this was His own promise — "shall not walk in darkness, but shall have the light of life." He has declared that if we "continue" in His "Word," we "shall know the Truth." What we receive at first on His bare authority, we shall come to know for ourselves — as He knew it; not, indeed, with the same fulness and completeness of knowledge, but with the same directness of intuition.

14

If it should be said that this immediate knowledge of spiritual truth is transcendental, and that even those to whom it comes in largest measure may be unable to translate it into the forms of the logical understanding; that the vision of God which is promised to "the pure in heart" is one thing, and the theory of God which is attempted by the theological or philosophical intellect a different thing altogether, I admit it. This admission, however, can be of little service to those who contend that the Death of Christ as the Propitiation for the sins of the world is a mystery of which we can know nothing, and which we cannot attempt to penetrate without presumption. All theological theories, which are anything more than empirical classifications of Scripture texts, are imperfect attempts to express in the language of the intellect what has been immediately revealed to the spirit; as all scientific theories are attempts to express in the language of the intellect what has been immediately revealed to the senses. We are related to two worlds — the world of physical phenomena and the world of spiritual facts and persons. Of both we have an immediate and direct, though limited, knowledge. The function discharged by science for the knowledge which comes to us, we know not how, of the boundless and incessant flux of colour, and sound, and form in the material universe, is discharged by theology for the knowledge which comes to us, we know not how, of the universe of spiritual life and action. That there should be presumption in the attempt of sinful creatures like ourselves to look on the very face of God, I could understand. I could understand the humility and dread with which devout men might warn us that so long as the imperfections of this mortal condition are still upon us, it must be presumptuous to invoke the illumination of the Holy Ghost to reveal to us the very thought and life of God as expressed in the redemptive work of Christ; but such warnings cannot be listened to, for it was of this immediate revelation that our Lord was speaking when He said, "This is life eternal, that they might know Thee, the only true God, and Jesus Christ whom Thou hast sent." And since we are encouraged to hope and to pray for this transcendent knowledge, it is difficult to perceive how we can be guilty of presumption in attempting to give to what has been revealed to us accurate intellectual expression. And this is what I mean by a theory of the Atonement.

I propose, therefore, in this series of Lectures to show that there is a direct relation between the Death of Christ and the remission of sins, and to investigate the principles and grounds of that relation. I have first to establish a Fact, and then to attempt the construction of a Theory.

The proof that in the New Testament our Lord's Death is represented as the objective ground on which God absolves us from sin and delivers us from eternal destruction has been exhibited with great elaboration and with a large amount of exegetical learning in many treatises on the Atonement. All the passages have been classified and carefully analysed which affirm that our Lord died for sinners, that He died for our sins, that He bore our sins, that He was made sin for us, that He was made a curse for us, that we have remission of sins and deliverance from wrath through Him, that He gave His life as a ransom for us, that His death was a Sacrifice, that He is the Propitiation for the sins of the world. [4] The collection of passages seems to be very complete, and I do not know that the classification can be improved. Nor is there much to be added to the criticism and illustration of the separate texts on which the argument is built, for since the days of Socinus these texts have been investigated and reinvestigated in the interests of hostile schools of theology.

It is not my intention, therefore, to present the argument precisely in this form. The proof as it stands appears to me to be conclusive, and within the narrow limits of this series of Lectures it may not be possible for me to add anything to its cogency. But I propose to adopt a somewhat different method, which, if it were properly handled, might, I think, greatly strengthen the argument.

It must be obvious to every reader of the New Testament that a mere catalogue of texts in which any great truth is definitely taught can never give a just impression of the place which that truth held in the thought and faith of the Apostles. This observation has a special application to texts selected from the apostolic epistles. For these epistles were for the most part *occasional* writings. They were suggested by accidental circumstances. The space which is given to the illustration of particular doctrines or duties was determined, not by the intrinsic and permanent importance of the doctrines or duties themselves, but by the perils which threatened the Christian faith or the Christian integrity of the Churches to which they were written, and by many other circumstances of a temporary character. The exhortations addressed to the Church at Corinth to contribute liberally to the relief of the distressed Christians in Judaea fill as many columns in the Second Epistle to the Corinthians as the discussion of the doctrine of the Resurrection in the First Epistle. The moral scandals and disorders in the Corinthian Church occupy as many pages in the two epistles to that Church as the doctrine of Justification in the Epistle to the Romans; and these disorders and scandals were of a kind which are never likely to occur except in the transition from a heathen to a Christian life.

The frequency and distinctness with which a doctrine is asserted in the apostolic writings is, therefore, no test of its importance. It might even be contended with considerable plausibility that the importance of a doctrine is likely to be in the inverse ratio of the number of passages in which it is directly taught; for the central and most characteristic truths of the Christian Faith are precisely those which the Churches were least likely to abandon. These truths were safe, and the Epistles generally deal with the truths which were in danger. Even in writing to Churches largely composed of converts from heathenism, it was not necessary for St. Paul to dwell at length on the unity of God and to denounce idolatry, for if a man was a Christian at all, he had finally abandoned the altars and the divinities of his heathen countrymen. Nor was it necessary to reiterate that Jesus of Nazareth is the Son of God and the Saviour of men, for unless men had acknowledged His claims they would have had no place in the Churches to which the Epistles were addressed. From the very nature of the apostolic writings those truths which belong to the essence of the Christian creed are, for the most part, implied rather than explicitly taught; they are appealed to and taken for granted as the recognised motives to Christian living and the recognised sources of Christian hope and consolation; they are frequently the inspiration of rapturous thanksgiving, and they frequently constitute the substance and the argument of a prayer.

To make collections of "proof-texts" is therefore an unsatisfactory means of arriving at a knowledge of apostolic faith. We must resort to less easy and less direct methods. Some of the passages which are most decisive in the determination of what the Apostles believed could find no place in such arrangements of "proofs" as are common in theological treatises.

An illustration of what I mean occurs in the well-known passage on the Lord's Supper in the First Epistle to the Corinthians. Its direct intention is to rescue the Lord's Supper from dishonour and to secure its reverential celebration. St. Paul uses words which have caused many devout persons to approach the Lord's Table with dread. But that in a Church founded by the Apostle himself a very short time before the Epistle was written, it should have been possible for the Lord's Supper to be associated with the disgraceful excesses which he rebukes, and that in rebuking them he makes no use of the awful argument which would have come at once to the lips of a priest of the Church of Rome or a Ritualistic priest of the Church of England, is a proof, from which there can be no appeal, that St. Paul had never taught and did not believe that the consecrated bread and wine are changed into the body and blood of Christ.

To take another illustration. There is no passage in the New Testament which is more destructive of the humanitarian theory of our Lord's person than that in which St. John says that "every spirit that confesseth not that Jesus Christ is come in the flesh is not of God; and this is that spirit of Antichrist, whereof ye have heard that it should come; and even now already is it in the world." [5]

As a "proof-text" these words would be alleged in support of the truth that our Lord was really man; but that it should have been necessary for the apostle to assert His humanity with such vehemence is an absolute demonstration that the Church had been taught to regard Him as being infinitely more than man. In our times the philosophical difficulties of the Incarnation are often solved by the denial of the superhuman dignity of our Lord; but this was impossible in the first century. His superhuman dignity had so filled the imagination of the Church, that the solution was sought in the denial of His humanity.

No catena of quotations can adequately represent the overwhelming evidence that the Apostles believed in the Divinity of our Lord Jesus Christ. If all the "proof-texts" usually alleged from the apostolic epistles in support of this doctrine were cancelled, the proof would remain almost as strong as before. There is hardly a page in which it is not clear that to the founders of the Christian Church, Christ was infinitely more than an inspired teacher or an example of perfect holiness. He is never out of their thoughts. All their teaching centres in Him, and in Him they find the sanction of every duty and the foundation of every hope. To the saved He is wisdom and righteousness, sanctification and redemption; and when He is revealed from heaven with His mighty angels, and in flaming fire, the lost are to be punished with eternal destruction. The history of the world before His Incarnation was a long and weary waiting for His coming, and with His second advent the history of the world is to come to a close. In Him all earthly relations are transfigured, and those who are one with Him have already passed into the kingdom of heaven. He is the object of a reverence which cannot be distinguished from worship, and of a love as fervent as that which glows in the anthems of the cherubim and seraphim that surround the throne of God. In Him the Apostles "live and move and have their being." His will is their supreme law; His glory their supreme end; His approbation their supreme reward. To select a score of passages in which it is affirmed that Christ is God, or in which divine attributes, divine prerogatives, or divine works are ascribed to Him, and to treat these quotations as though they constituted the evidence that, to St. Paul, St. Peter, and St. John, the Lord Jesus Christ was God manifest in the flesh, is to do injustice to the argument. The real proof lies in the absolute sovereignty in which Christ is enthroned over their moral and spiritual life; and the illustrations of this can hardly be subjected to logical analysis and arrangement.

What is true of the Divinity of our Lord is also true of His Atonement for human sin. That the Apostles regarded the Death of Christ as a Sacrifice and Propitiation for the sins of the world appears in many passages which yield no direct testimony to the doctrine. It sometimes determines the form and structure of an elaborate argument, which falls to pieces if this truth is denied. At other times it gives pathos and power to a practical appeal. It accounts for some of the misconceptions and misrepresentations of apostolic teaching. It explains the absence from the apostolic writings of very much that we should certainly have found in them if the Apostles had not believed that for Christ's sake, and not merely because of the effect o-n our hearts of what Christ has revealed, God grants us remission of sins. It penetrates the whole substance of their theological and ethical teaching, and is the very root of their religious life. If, instead of selecting passages in which it is categorically affirmed that Christ died for us — died that we might have remission of sins, died as a Propitiation for sin — we selected those which would lose all their force and all their significance if this truth were rejected, it would be necessary to quote a large part of the New Testament. For reasons which I shall attempt to explain in the next Lecture, it is equally impossible to exhibit the testimony of the four Gospels to this truth by the mere enumeration of those passages in our Lord's teaching in which He speaks of the nature and purpose of His Death.

It may appear to some persons that the questions which I propose to discuss have no longer any real interest to mankind. It can hardly be said indeed that the temper of our times is not favourable to theological investigation. But in this country, at least, the great race of dogmatic theologians has disappeared, and purely doctrinal controversies, which once created fierce excitement, and in which the noblest intellects of Christendom revealed the wealth of their learning and the splendour of their genius, have come to be regarded with indifference. But surely the question whether the original teachers of the Christian Faith represented the Death of Christ as a Propitiation for the sins of mankind, is invested, at least, with the greatest historical interest by the vast and enduring influence which their writings have exerted, not only on the religious thought, but on the civilization and political fortunes of the foremost races of the modern world.

The questions we are to investigate have an interest of another kind; for in the whole range of problems which have exercised the genius of men from the very dawn of philosophy to our own times, there are none which transcend in majesty, in difficulty, or in speculative importance, the problems of which a true theory of the Atonement ought to contain a partial if not a complete solution.

But it is neither the historical nor the speculative interest of this subject that has induced me to undertake to discuss it. The Christian Faith, in the judgment both of its enemies and its friends, is at this moment threatened by dangers as formidable as any which it has ever had to confront during the whole course of its history. For myself I am unable to discover any signs that its power is decaying, much less that its glory is destined to early extinction. In our own days, and after the lapse of eighteen centuries, its influence is gradually extending among the civilised populations of Asia; it is redeeming the races of Central and Southern Africa from barbarism; it is giving intellectual culture and a higher morality, as well as a purer faith, to the scattered tribes of the Pacific Ocean; and, notwithstanding all adverse appearances, it is, I believe, maintaining its power over the kindred nations of Europe and America. The very bitterness and vehemence, the anger and the scorn, the infinite variety of argument, and the inexhaustible energy of hostility with which Christianity is assailed, demonstrate how strongly it is entrenched in the common faith and common traditions of Christian nations, and demonstrate, too, the intensity of the devotion and the depth of the reverence with which it is cherished in the hearts of innumerable Christian men.

There were times, indeed, when the Christian priesthood exerted an authority in the States of Europe which they have happily lost. The science and learning of the West were in the hands of the doctors of the Church, and the priests of Rome inherited the great traditions and the principles of policy which had made the Eternal City the mistress of the world. They laid a strong hand on the vigorous but uncultivated and superstitious nations which over-ran the dislocated provinces of the fallen empire, and governed them by their sagacity, by their courage, by their knowledge of the science of legislation, by their general intellectual superiority, by the compactness of their organiza-tion, and by their lofty pretensions to be the representatives of the august authority of God and the channels of His infinite mercy. Those were the days when the wealth and power of princes were at the command of the Church; and majestic cathedrals and stately monasteries, enriched with costly mar-bles, with curious sculpture, with shrines of silver and of gold, rose towards heaven in every country of Europe from the North Sea to the shores of the Mediterranean; and bishops were the chancellors and ambassadors of mighty kingdoms, and great priests outshone the splendour and defeated the ambition of great nobles. They were "Ages of Faith;" but the Faith was not the Faith which listens for itself to the voice of God, and finds in Him absolution from guilt, consolation in sorrow, and the hope which triumphs over death and exults in the vision of an immortality of glory. It clung to the priest ra-ther than to Christ, and was filled with awe and wonder by the power and magnificence of the Church rather than with devout fear and perfect joy by the majesty and love of the living God. [6] And so, when the rulers of the Church became luxurious, feeble, and corrupt, and when the great resources of the races which they had disciplined and civilised began to be developed, the Ages of Faith gradually vanished away.

Many causes contributed to that great revolution. The orators, philoso-phers, and poets of the ancient world rising from the tomb of centuries wrested from priests and monks the intellectual supremacy which had been a principal element of their power. Statesmen and kings, who had learnt the art and principles of government from the Church, began to desire to govern for themselves, and they chafed under the pretensions of ecclesiastical con-suls deriving their authority from Rome. The schism widened; the revolt went on; every new generation added new elements of bitterness to the con-flict; and now that a great part of Europe has finally broken away from the control of the Church, it has become apparent that though Christendom had submitted to the ascendency of the priesthood, it had never really submitted to the authority of Christ.

The irreligion and the unbelief which were once suppressed by the power of a vast ecclesiastical organization, are suppressed no longer; and the sullen moral resistance which was offered for centuries to the true Faith, and which revealed itself in the violent passions, the coarse vices, and the rude supersti-tions of an ignorant population, reveals itself now in an active and energetic intellectual antagonism.

There may, however, be as much living Faith in God in these days of open revolt against the throne of Christ as in the days when the Church ruled the nations with an uncontested authority. But the revolt is general. Unbelief has become not only articulate, but eloquent. It is rich in the old learning, and it claims for its own the new sciences. It has the audacity of youth and the restless energy of genius. Its hostility to the characteristic truths and claims of the Christian revelation is relentless and uncompromising. I prefer the new conditions of the conflict to the old. We are stripped of every adventitious advantage. Henceforth the triumphs of the Church will be real — the triumphs of the truth of Christ and of the power of the Holy Ghost.

In this hour — not of peril, but of fierce struggle — the Church must use all her varied and boundless resources — her science, her learning, her logic, her eloquence — and must use them with a patience, a courage, and an energy corresponding to the great issues of the strife.

But our true strength lies in those moral and spiritual forces by which, in all ages, the victories of the kingdom of heaven have been won. We must not be satisfied with an attempt to demonstrate the authority of the Christian Faith; we must so preach it that, even apart from demonstration, its authority shall be confessed. The consciences of men must be made to apprehend the reality of sin, and their hearts must be filled with dread and with hope by the anger and the mercy of the living God. The mysterious instinct, suppressed but not destroyed, which bears witness to the kinship of the human soul to the Father of spirits, must be quickened into activity; and then, without any argument of ours, men will recognise in the voice of Christ an august sovereignty to which they cannot refuse to do homage, and will discover for themselves that in dying, the Just for the unjust, to bring us to God, He has met the deepest wants of their spiritual life as well as revealed the infinite wealth and tenderness of the Divine love.

The power of the Spirit of God is with us, and He, in wonderful ways, finds direct access to the innermost life of man, piercing through intellectual difficulties and antagonisms which seemed to create invincible obstacles to the Truth. The human conscience and heart are also with us. There is an indestructible conviction in the human soul that God must be on the side of righteousness, and that all sin must be intolerable to Him. There are vague fears of His displeasure which cannot be dissipated; there is a restless craving for access to Him; there is a sense of loneliness and desolation so long as the soul has not found Him, which no intellectual or sensual excitements can permanently stifle; there is a hope, faint and faltering, yet with strange vitality in it, that although God seems no longer "nigh at hand," He cannot have forsaken and forgotten us altogether, and that in some way He will surely return to us.

It is because the great truths and laws, of which the Atonement of Christ is the highest and most perfect expression, appeal directly to these central and enduring elements of the moral life of man, and because the Atonement satisfies what .in every age, and through all the changes of his intellectual and social condition, is man's chief necessity, that we in our times should rely upon the power of the Death of Christ for the triumph of the Divine Righteousness and Love over the doubt as well as the sins and sorrows of mankind. We ourselves may derive inspiration and energy from the truths which we must preach to others, for the zeal of the Church has always been kindled into intensest fervour at the Cross of the Lord Jesus Christ; and the Cross has always been the symbol of her strength and the prophecy of her victories.

I may be unable to contribute any additional force to the evidence that the Death of the Lord Jesus Christ was an Atonement for sin, and I may fail to illustrate its relations to the life of God, the life of man, and the laws of the spiritual universe; but if any of those who listen to these Lectures, and any of those who read them, are drawn to deeper and devouter thought upon the mystery and glory of His great Sacrifice, I shall not have written or spoken in vain.

[1] Note A.
[2] Col. i. 16, 17.
[3] *Ecclesiastical Polity*, bk. i. cap. 2; Works, vol. 1. p. 201.
[4] Note B.
[5] 1 John iv. 3.
[6] Les évêques avoient remplacé, pour lui [Clovis], non point les prêtres de la Germanie, mais les idoles dans le culte desquelles il avoit été élevé. C'etoient les évêques qu'il servoit, qu'il adoroit, et il pactisoit avec eux comme un homme accoutumé à encenser des fétiches. — Sismondi, *Précis de l'Historie aes Français*, vol. i. page 39.

# Lecture Two - The History of Our Lord Jesus Christ in Relation to the Fact of the Atonement

It is assumed in this series of Lectures that the Lord Jesus Christ was "God manifest in the flesh." The revelation which has come to us through Him is, therefore, different in kind from that which has come to us through the Prophets of the Old Testament and the Apostles of the New.

It is said of Moses that the Lord spake to him "face to face, as a man speaketh unto his friend," [1] and that Isaiah "saw His glory." [2] St. Paul declared that the gospel preached by him was "not of man;" — "I neither received it of man, neither was I taught it, but by the revelation of Jesus Christ." [3] And St. John describes his own function, and that of the other Apostles, when he says, "The life was manifested, and we have seen it, and bear witness, and show unto you that eternal life which was with the Father, and was manifested unto us." [4]

But the Lord Jesus Christ was Himself the "brightness of [God's] glory, and the express image of His person." [5] And to one of the Apostles, who was longing for the immediate vision of God, and who said to Him, "Show us the Father, and it sufficeth us," our Lord replied, "He that hath seen Me hath seen the Father." [6] When Prophets have told us their visions and Apostles their

22

gospel, their work is done. They are weak, erring, sinful men like ourselves. They have seen the Divine glory, and they tell us what they have seen. They have been taught of God, and they tell us what they have learnt. But the revelation is over when they cease to speak. Their personal character and history, their relations to their friends and to their enemies, their occupations, their sorrows and their joys — all these have only a secondary and human interest. It is not so with our Lord Jesus Christ. Far more of God was revealed in what He was, in what He did, and in what He suffered, than in what He taught.

The resources of human language had been almost exhausted, before Christ came, in the attempt to celebrate the majesty, the holiness, and the mercy of God; and although, as a Teacher of religious truth, the Lord Jesus Christ had a unique power, we misapprehend the character of the supremacy which He claims, if we suppose that it is to be illustrated and vindicated by placing His mere words side by side with the words of Prophets who preceded Him. I doubt whether He ever said anything about the Divine compassion more pathetic or more perfectly beautiful than had been said by the writer of the hundred-and-third Psalm: "Like as a father pitieth his children, so the Lord pitieth them that fear Him. For He knoweth our frame; He remembereth that we are dust." It is not in the words of Christ that we find a fuller and deeper revelation of the Divine compassion than in the words of the Psalmist, but in His deeds.

"There came a leper and worshipped him, saying, Lord, if thou wilt, thou canst make me clean. And Jesus ["moved with compassion," Mark i. 41] put forth His hand and *touched* him" — touched the man, from whom his very kindred had shrunk; — "touched him," — it was the first time that the leper had felt the warmth and pressure of a human hand since his loathsome disease came upon him; — "touched him, and said, I will, be thou clean." [7]

And when the heart of Christ was filled with sorrow by the news of John the Baptist's death, and He went into "a desert place apart," He did not, in the weariness of His grief and the solemn anticipation of His own end, turn away, vexed and annoyed, from the people that followed Him into His solitude; but when He saw the great multitude. He "was moved with compassion, and he healed their sick." [8]

Every form of human sorrow affected Him. "He came nigh to the gate of the city [of Nain], and, behold, there was a dead man carried out, the only son of his mother, and she was a widow." She was a stranger, and made no appeal to His pity. But "when the Lord saw her. He had compassion on her, and said unto her. Weep not. And He came and touched the bier; and they that bare him stood still. And He said. Young man, I say unto thee. Arise. And he that was dead sat up, and began to speak." Nor is this all. The story is completed by the simple words, which suggest a scene of ineffable tenderness: "And He delivered him to his mother." [9]

Still more affecting is the narrative of the death and resurrection of Lazarus. Our Lord had finally left Galilee, and had come to the neighbourhood of

23

Jerusalem, to remain there till He was betrayed, condemned, and crucified. The dark succession of sorrows through which He was to pass was near, and He knew it; but when He saw Mary "weeping, and the Jews also weeping which came with her, He groaned in spirit, and was troubled." They asked Him to come with them to the grave, and "Jesus wept." He was about to raise His friend, but the actual grief of those whom He loved, almost broke His heart, and He wept; wept too, perhaps, as has been suggested, "in pure sympathy with the sorrows of humanity, for the myriad myriads of desolate mourners who could not, with Mary, fly to Him, and say, 'Lord, if Thou hadst been here, my mother — brother — sister had not died!'" [10] When we read these narratives, and remember His own declaration, "He that hath seen Me hath seen the Father," even the words of the Psalmist seem to lose all their tenderness and power.

The point on which I am insisting is so important, and is so often forgotten in this controversy, that, obvious as it is, I must venture to illustrate it still more fully.

It is acknowledged even by those who not only reject the doctrine of the Atonement but deny our Lord's Divinity, that He revealed the infinite mercy of God as it had never been revealed before. It is certain that since His coming, and as the result of His coming, the Divine mercy has attracted a stronger and a deeper trust, and that sinful men have had more perfect rest in God.

But how was the nobler revelation made? Is it possible to quote from the discourses of our Lord any more thrilling representations of the mercy of God than can be quoted from the Old Testament? Did He say more than Nehemiah said: "Thou art a God ready to pardon, gracious and merciful, slow to anger and of great kindness"? [11] Or more than Jonah said, who shrunk from threatening Nineveh with the Divine judgments, because he feared that the threatenings might, after all, never be fulfilled: "Therefore I fled unto Tarshish; for I knew that Thou art a gracious God, and merciful, slow to anger, and of great kindness, and repentest Thee of the evil"? [12] Did our Lord say more than Isaiah said: "Though your sins be as scarlet, they shall be as white as snow; though they be red like crimson, they shall be as wool:" "Let the wicked forsake his way, and the unrighteous man his thoughts, and let him return unto the Lord, and He will have mercy upon him; and to our God, and He will abundantly pardon"? The passages of Scripture which come to our lips when we wish to acknowledge in nobler and richer words than our own the longsuffering of God and His readiness to pardon sin, are rarely taken from the discourses of Christ; they are the words of Psalmists, Prophets, and Apostles.

If it is objected that there is nothing in the Old Testament, and nothing else in the New, comparable to the three great parables of the Lost Sheep, the Lost Piece of Money, and the Prodigal Son, the very objection sustains the position for which I am contending. These parables were spoken by our Lord in self-defence. They explained and vindicated what the Pharisees charged

Him with as a crime: "This man receiveth sinners and eateth with them;" and to me even these wonderful parables are a less affecting illustration of the energy and tenderness of the Divine mercy than the freedom with which the Son of God, the Creator of the heavens and the earth, the Holy One and the Just, sat at table with irreligious and sinful men, spoke to them as a friend, and encouraged them to forsake sin and win eternal life and glory. It was by His assumption of our nature, by the gentleness and kindness with which He treated those who were guilty of the worst sins, by His merciful words to repenting harlots and publicans, by the look of love and sorrow which broke the heart of the Apostle who had just denied Him, and by the large and generous promise, with which, in the very act of dying, He responded to the prayer of the penitent thief, and, above all it was by shedding His blood for the remission of our sins that He revealed, as Prophets and Apostles could never reveal, the infinite mercy of God; for, written in light under every line of the narrative of His earthly history, we should recognise His own words: "He that hath seen Me hath seen the Father."

To say, therefore, that "the words of the Lord Jesus Christ must ever be regarded by His disciples as the central glory of the Bible and the most precious heritage of humanity;" [13] to describe a classification of the Sayings of our Lord as "a complete guide on the great subjects of Christian faith and practice," and as comprehending "the clear, complete, and authoritative teaching of the Divine Head of the Church," [14] implies a very imperfect conception of the manner in which Christ has revealed the Father. It is true that He spake as never man spake, and His words are "spirit and life;" but what He revealed cannot be exhibited in a catena of quotations from His teaching. To quote His words only is to leave out the larger half of the revelation which has come to us through Him. He himself is the truth, the light, as well as the life of men; the very Word of God.

It is this which constitutes the glory of the Four Gospels; they contain the history as well as the teaching of Him whom we acknowledge as God manifest in the flesh. They stand alone. They admit neither of comparison nor contrast with any other books either in the Old or the New Testament. St. Paul develops the Christian idea of Faith as it is not developed in any of our Lord's discourses; but the power and mercy and authority of Christ attract and command the Faith whose nature and functions the Apostle only illustrates. Cancel every passage in the Gospels in which our Lord insists on the necessity of Faith in Himself, and you neither impair the harmony between His teaching and the teaching of St. Paul, nor do you so impoverish the theological wealth of the Gospels as to make them inferior in value to the Epistles. St. Paul insists that in order to be saved I must trust in the Lord Jesus Christ, but when I see Christ, and know who He is, I cannot help trusting in Him for salvation. It is not necessary that He should tell me to believe; before He speaks of Faith my heart clings to Him for the pardon of sin and for the gift of eternal life.

St. John tells us that "God is love." I do not know that there are any words of our Lord in which this truth is expressed with such simple and lofty sublimity. But shall we, therefore, conclude that the disciple is greater than his Master? Any such conclusion would be strangely illegitimate. St. John had learnt the truth from Christ. Christ may never have uttered it in words, but His whole life was the expression of it. He came to manifest God, and this is the concise summary and ultimate result of what was revealed in His personal character, in His mighty and merciful works, and in His fastings, temptations, sufferings, and death — "God is love."

The principle which I wish to maintain, — that the Truth which Christ revealed is to be found in His history as well as in His teaching, is of great importance, not only in relation to the doctrine of the Atonement, but in relation to the whole Faith and Life of the Church. It seems to have been overlooked by some modern writers; among the rest by the late Rev. Frederick Robertson, of Brighton. [15] After a very just protest against the opinion of those "who would not scruple to assert that, in the highest sense of the term, it [the Sermon on the Mount] is not Christianity at all, but only preparatory to it — a kind of spiritual Judaism; and that the higher and more developed principles of Christianity are to be found in the writings of the Apostles," he proceeds to remark that "it seems extremely startling to say that He who came to this world expressly to preach the Gospel, should in the most elaborate of all His discourses omit to do so: it is indeed something more than startling, it is absolutely revolting to suppose that the letters of those who spoke *of* Christ should contain a more perfectly developed, a freer and fuller, Christianity than is to be found in Christ's own words." It would be hardly fair to Mr. Robertson to criticise too closely statements which appear to express a vehement indignation rather than a deliberate theological judgment, or else I might observe that our Lord does actually omit "in the most elaborate of all His discourses" some of the highest and most characteristic elements of His own teaching. The Sermon on the Mount is not "a kind of spiritual Judaism;" it is, to use Mr. Robertson's own words, "deeply and essentially Christian; "but though it contains very much of the gospel it does not contain the whole. It is silent on the New Birth, concerning which our Lord spoke to Nicodemus; it is silent on the living and enduring relation between our Lord and His disciples, which He illustrated in the parable of the Vine; it does not explicitly insist on the necessity of Faith in Himself as the condition of eternal redemption. But the whole passage rests on a grave misconception of our Lord's mission. It is implied not only that Christ "came to this world expressly to preach the gospel," but that this was the chief if not the only purpose of His coming. The real truth is that while He came to preach the gospel, His chief object in coming was that there might be a gospel to preach.

To me there would be nothing "startling," much less "revolting," in supposing that there might be in the writings of the Apostles "a more perfectly developed, a freer and fuller, Christianity than is to be found in Christ's own words," any more than in supposing that there might be a clearer and richer exposition of the aesthetic truths and principles illustrated in the Apollo Belvedere, in a treatise written by a critic who never handled a chisel than in the recorded conversations, if we had them, of the great sculptor himself; or in supposing that a military critic who never commanded a regiment might give us a more scientific explanation of the victories of Napoleon than is contained in Napoleon's own despatches and letters. I am very far, indeed, from believing that the Epistles are actually richer in Christian truth than the discourses of our Lord. The Apostles came very slowly to the apprehension of some of the simplest and clearest parts of His teaching; and I cannot doubt that there are treasures of wisdom in His words which the Apostles never exhausted, and which remain unexhausted still.

But there is nothing "revolting," nothing even "startling," in supposing that the Life of Christ may contain revelations of truth, and revelations of infinite value, to which He himself never gave a definite form in language. Much less can there be anything either "revolting" or "startling," in supposing that when His great work was finished the Apostles may have discovered that truths of which their Master had rarely spoken, and to which they had listened unintelligently and reluctantly, were invested by His Passion and Death with exceptional and even supreme importance.

The Lord Jesus Christ did not translate all that He was and all that He did into words. As "the heavens declare the glory of God, and the firmament showeth his handiwork," as "day unto day uttereth speech, and night unto night showeth knowledge," though "there is no speech nor language," and "though their voice is not heard" — so, even in the silence of Christ there is a revelation transcending all that is contained in the raptures of Psalmists, the visions of Prophets, and the wisdom of Apostles.

The highest achievements even of human genius — paintings, poems, great buildings — must speak for themselves; "notes and comments" may sometimes obscure instead of revealing their perfection. Heroic deeds and the courageous endurance of martyrs, are also beyond the reach of the most philosophical and eloquent exposition. The virtues they express are expressed more perfectly in action and in suffering than in words. And when God was living among men He was not always explaining Himself. Complete explanation was impossible. You cannot translate the Alps into a series of propositions: and there is no formula for the purple and golden pomp of a sunset, or for the majesty of a thunderstorm.

If there are any in our own times who would contend that there is a sense in which the writings of the Apostles "contain a more perfectly developed, a freer and fuller, Christianity than is to be found in Christ's own words," they only mean to assert that what appears in the Gospels as History reappears in the Epistles as Doctrine; that what appears in the Life of Christ as Fact appears in the teaching of the Apostles as Theory. And this assertion is only a partial statement of a principle which lies at the very root of a living and noble and generous theology — that since the Lord Jesus Christ was the Eternal Word of God, the brightness of the Father's glory, and the express image of His person, the revelation of Truth contained in His Life and Death is infinite: it transcended the thought of Apostles; it was not exhausted in the discourses by which our Lord Himself illustrated the character of His work and the purposes of His mission: it remains, and will remain for ever, a perpetual fountain of light and glory. The words of Christ are great, but Christ Himself is greater still.

I propose, therefore, to consider, first of all, what the History of our Lord suggests concerning the unique character of His Death. Even if He had said nothing — and happily He said much — about the relation of His Death to the guilt and the redemption of the human race, it seems to me that the doctrine of the Atonement developed in the Epistles would be the only satisfactory explanation of some of the most remarkable phenomena recorded in the Four Gospels.

It is not undeserving of notice that all the four Evangelists were agreed about the exceptional importance and significance of our Lord's last sufferings. Only two of them relate the circumstances of His Birth, which we might have supposed none of them would have omitted. Only two tell the story of the Temptation. [16] The Sermon on the Mount appears neither in the second Gospel nor in the fourth. St. John says nothing about the Transfiguration, the Agony in the Garden, or the institution of the Lord's Supper. The story of the Resurrection and of the appearances of the risen Christ to His Disciples occupies only twenty verses in St. Matthew's narrative; only twenty — perhaps only nine [17] in St. Mark's; and St. John appears to have said in thirty verses all that he intended to say, and to have added another five and twenty at the request of his friends. St. Matthew tells us nothing of our Lord's Ascension into heaven, nor does St. John; and even if the closing verses of St. Mark's Gospel came from his own hand, he tells us nothing more than the bare fact that the Lord "was received up into heaven, and sat on the right hand of God." The time and the place are left indefinite, and our Lord's parting words to His Disciples and the vision of angels are passed over in silence. But the Betrayal, the Arrest, the appearance before Caiaphas, Peter's denial, the cry of the people for the release of Barabbas and the crucifixion of our Lord, Pilate's judgment, the inscription fixed on the cross, are contained in all the four Gospels; and they all bring the story to a close with words which indicate that to the very moment of our Lord's Death there was no loss of consciousness or exhaustion of strength.

The Evangelists found no precedent for this elaborate account of the Death of our Lord in the Old Testament. The death of Moses, of Aaron, of David, is told with a severe simplicity and brevity; the writers of the ancient Scriptures felt that it is to the life of prophets and saints — not to the circumstances of their death — that the enduring interest of their history belongs. St. Luke dismisses in one brief sentence the martyrdom of an Apostle — "And

[Herod] killed James the brother of John with the sword." And if the martyr-dom of Stephen is told at greater length, it is plainly for the sake of what Stephen said, rather than for the sake of what he suffered.

It may be suggested that the deep and reverential love with which the Evangelists regarded our Lord constrained them to dwell on the mournful hours in which His earthly sufferings culminated; or that they narrated at great length all that happened in connection with His Death in order to illustrate the deliberation and unanimity with which the Jews rejected the Messiah, for whose coming so many centuries had been hoping; or that it was necessary to emphasise the circumstances of His Death in order to invest His Resurrection with reality and glory. But a careful examination of the four Gospels will lead us to prefer a different explanation. In the importance which the Evangelists attach to the Death of our Lord, they are but following the line of His own thought.

To Him, His Death — whatever may have been its significance — was distinctly present from the very commencement of His ministry, and He constantly spoke of it as necessary to the accomplishment of His mission.

I wish to illustrate this statement with some fulness. The manner in which He anticipated His Death when it was still remote, the increasing terror which it created in His mind as it gradually drew nearer, and the mystery of His moral sufferings while on the cross, appear to require some such explanation as is supplied by the doctrine of the Atonement.

It seems more than probable that in the hours which He spent with John the Baptist, about the time of His Baptism, He had spoken of the Death by which He was to atone for the sins of men, and that what He had said suggested the form of John's testimony to Him: "Behold the Lamb of God that taketh away the sins of the world." [18] At the first Passover after His public ministry began He prophesied that, by putting Him to death, the Jewish people would destroy the sanctity of their Temple, and that henceforth the true Home of God would be in Himself and in those who are spiritually one with Him. [19] A few days later He told Nicodemus that, "as Moses lifted up the serpent in the wilderness, so must the Son of man be lifted up." [20] To the people that thronged the synagogue at Capernaum, and who the day before had wanted to "take Him by force and make Him King," He spoke of His Death as necessary to the life of the world. [21] It was "a hard saying," especially in the form in which He uttered it, and "from that hour many of His disciples went back, and walked no more with Him."

Peter made his great confession: "Thou art the Christ, the Son of the living God;" and "from that time forth began Jesus to show unto His Disciples how that He must go unto Jerusalem, and suffer many things of the Elders and Chief Priests and Scribes, and be killed and be raised again the third day." [22] He was Transfigured, and Moses and Elias "spake of the decease which He should accomplish at Jerusalem;" [23] and as He came down from the mountain He charged Peter and James and John to "tell no man what things

29

they had seen till the Son of man were risen from the dead." [24] While they were in Galilee, after the Transfiguration, Jesus repeated the prophecy of His Death. [25] When He described Himself as the Good Shepherd, He repeated no less than three times, in the course of a very few sentences, that He was to lay down His life for the sheep. As He was going up to Jerusalem for the last time. He "took the twelve disciples apart in the way," and told them again that he was about to be put to death. [26] When the mother of Zebedee's children asked that her sons might sit, the one on the right hand and the other on the left, in the kingdom of heaven, His Death rose immediately to His thoughts: "Ye know not what ye ask. Are ye able to drink of the cup that I shall drink of, and to be baptised with the baptism that I am baptised with?" [27] After His great discourse on the Judgment, He said to His Disciples, "Ye know that after two days is the Passover, and the Son of man is betrayed to be crucified." [28] When Mary of Bethany broke the alabaster box and poured the costly perfume on His head, He justified her against the murmuring of His Disciples by saying: "She is come aforehand to anoint my body to the burying." [29]

It cannot, I think, be fairly said that these repeated intimations of His approaching Death show nothing more than our Lord's desire to prepare His Disciples for the catastrophe which seemed for the time to be the destruction of all their hopes. They indicate that from the very first His Death had taken possession of His own mind, that the anticipation of it was constantly recurring to Him, that He lived almost always under its shadow.

He not only spoke of it: He looked forward to it with anxiety and fear. There are passages in which this is very plainly indicated. It was of His Death that He was thinking when He said, "I have a baptism to be baptised with, and how am I straitened till it be accomplished." [30] This was while he was still in Galilee, twelve months before the final crisis; but He saw it afar off, and — if we may venture to say it — was eager to have it over. When it came near, it filled Him with agitation and, at last, with terror. In the week which preceded His crucifixion, some Gentiles, who had come up to Jerusalem to celebrate the Passover, wished to see the great Teacher whose miracles and bold antagonism to the ecclesiastical rulers had created so much excitement in the city. When He saw them His heart was thrilled with a sudden joy. They were the representatives of the "great multitude that no man can number of all nations and kindreds, and peoples and tongues," who, through Him, would be rescued from sin and eternal perdition, and restored to the life and light of God, and He exclaimed, "The hour is come that the Son of man should be glorified." [31] But there rose up at once between Him and that great glory the dark presence of death. "Verily, verily, I say unto you, Except a corn of wheat fall into the ground and die, it abideth alone; but if it die, it bringeth forth fruit." [32] And the vision of death sunk upon Him like a vast and gloomy cloud, obscuring all the splendour. His heart was shaken with fear, and He said, "Now is my soul troubled, and what shall I say? Father, save me from this hour." And yet He could not turn aside, for He adds, "But for this cause came I to this hour." [33]

At the Last Supper the agitation returned. "He was troubled in spirit," [34] and troubled because the traitor was sitting with Him at the table, and He knew that the deed of treachery was about to be consummated, and that in an hour or two He would be in the hands of His enemies. As soon as Judas left, the agitation seems to have passed away for a time, and the heart of our Lord recovered its calmness.

He delivered a discourse, in which He revealed all the tenderness and depth of His love for His disciples (whom He now called His friends, instead of His servants), and a wealth of spiritual thought which is unsurpassed and hardly equalled in any other passage of His teaching. His whole nature rose to its loftiest activity. Not a solitary intellectual power was latent; not a solitary affection slumbered. The discourse was followed by a prayer, which is the evidence that He was in full and conscious communion with the Father. It is the prayer of One on whom the full glory of heaven has descended.

He then passed out of the city, crossed the ravine through which the Kedron flows, and entered into an olive-orchard, not far, probably, from the garden now called Gethsemane. The Paschal moon must have been filling the valley with its light, resting tranquilly on the olives and palm-trees which then clothed the sides of Olivet, and making the towers of the Temple and the walls of the city, on the other side of the ravine, shine like silver. The whole scene was suggestive of perfect peace.

But suddenly a great terror came upon Him. Matthew tells us that "He began to be sorrowful," [35] and Mark, that "He began to be sore amazed." [36] And He said to Peter, James, and John, "My soul is exceeding sorrowful, even unto death." [37] He had chosen these three to be with Him in the trouble which was becoming darker every moment, and which He felt would soon become almost too terrible for Him to endure. He clung to the relief and support which the mere presence of those we love affords us in times of great distress. But He could not remain with them. Matthew says, "He went a little further." [38] Luke uses a word which implies that He was restless, and was unable to stay where He was [39] — that He tore Himself away from them. Then followed a succession of prayers, which were uttered in what we may, perhaps, venture to call successive spasms of spiritual anguish and effort. He was like a great tree, bending and almost broken under a storm. His resolution to endure the worst was rooted too deeply and securely for Him to be torn away from it; but again and again it almost seemed as though He must yield to the tremendous strain. His Death was near; the woe which had been present to Him from the beginning of His ministry was descending upon Him, and He shrank from it, and cried, "O My Father, if it be possible, let this cup pass from Me; nevertheless, not as I will, but as Thou wilt." [40]

It is not thus that good men have been accustomed to confront death. St. Paul speaks several times of his own approaching end, but never with an agitation like this. He had a desire "to depart, and to be with Christ;" and vast numbers of Christian men have confronted cruel torments for Christ's sake with unshaken fortitude, and have forgotten the sharp pain of the axe and the sword, and the rage of wild beasts, and the fierce heat of the fires of martyrdom, in the triumphant energy of their faith and their passionate longing to see the face of Christ. But to Christ death rose up in appalling terror between Himself and His return to God. He said to His disciples that, if they loved Him, they would rejoice because He had told them that He was going to the Father; [41] but He Himself could not rejoice. Even before He was nailed to the cross, He was overwhelmed with a sorrow which nearly crushed His strength, and under which He felt that He must die.

I cannot believe that His terror was caused by His anticipation of the physical tortures of crucifixion. Crucifixion was a very painful form of death, but while these indications of our Lord's dismay in anticipation of His last hours are recorded by the Evangelists, it is significant that not one of them dwells upon the physical anguish which He must have endured upon the cross. Their ample narratives say nothing of the throbbing pain which He must have suffered from the nails which were driven through His hands, nothing of the sharp pangs which must have shot through every fibre of His frame, nothing of the fever which must have been kindled in His blood. But they speak of a mysterious spiritual sorrow which forced Him to utter the most bitter cry that can ever break from a human heart; and it was into the dark shadow of this sorrow that He seems to have come as soon as He entered into Gethsemane.

The agony of the garden is, indeed, inexplicable until we see Him on the cross. It was an awful death — a death of great physical suffering, but the physical suffering was the least terrible element of its complicated woe. He had come into the world to restore men to righteousness and to God, but during the few hours which preceded His crucifixion there had been committed a series of atrocious sins, and it must have seemed to Him that He had been led to His Death by a dark procession of the basest crimes of which wicked men can be guilty, and their evil and malignant forms surrounded Him in His agony, mocking His sufferings and exulting in His shame. Corrupt and ambitious priests, whose power He imperilled, had conspired and plotted against His life; lying witnesses had charged Him — Him, the Son of God! — with blasphemy; He had been betrayed by a false friend; the people who a few days before had rent the air with cries of "Hosanna," who had brought to Him their sick, their blind, their deaf, their dumb, and He had healed them all, and to some of whom He had given their dead children alive again — the people, maddened with resentment because He refused to satisfy their hopes of secular greatness and glory, savagely cried for His blood; the Roman governor, after pronouncing Him innocent of the crime that was charged against Him, gave Him up to sacerdotal hatred and popular fury. Those few brief hours had revealed the infirmity of His friends as well as the relentless wickedness of His enemies. His very Disciples, as soon as He was arrested, "all forsook Him and fled." Peter, who had been most vehement in his protestations of devotion, denied Him thrice with oaths and cursings. As He hung on the cross between two criminals, the object of heartless jests and insults, it seems as though only a solitary Apostle and a few faithful women remained near Him.

All this He could have endured; but there came another and still more appalling sorrow. His fellowship with the Father had been intimate and unbroken. He had lived in the life of God. Till now He could always say, "I am not alone, for the Father is with me," but He can say it no longer. The light of God's presence is lost. He is left in awful isolation, and He cries, "My God, My God, why hast Thou forsaken Me?" [42] In the "hour of great darkness" which has fallen upon Him He still clings to the Father with an invincible trust and an immeasurable love, and the agony of being deserted of God is more than He can bear. His heart is broken. Death comes upon Him from within as well as from without; and He dies as much from the loss of the sense of God's presence as from the exhaustion of crucifixion. [43]

This is not martyrdom.

What is it? He has never sinned. He is the Son of God, and inherits the infinite love of the Father. In the hour of His anguish He is consummating the work which is dearest to the Father's heart; but He endures that loss of fellowship with the Divine blessedness, that exile from the joys of God's presence, which is the effect of the Divine wrath in the case of the impenitent.

What is the explanation of this mysterious anguish? He has come to make known to sinful men the love of God, and He Himself, who has never sinned, is forsaken of God. He has declared that He is the way to the Father, and that no man cometh to the Father except through Him — and now, even to Him, access to God is closed. The Son of God, the only-begotten Son, in whom the Father is well pleased, is not only the victim of human malignity; in the very extremity of His woe. He is deprived of all Divine consolation; He declares that God has forsaken Him!

I decline to accept any explanation of these words which implies that they do not represent the actual truth of our Lord's position. There are times when great suffering may force from our lips words about God of which, when the suffering is over, we repent. We think, we say, that He has forsaken us, and we charge Him unjustly. Did Christ repent that He had uttered this cry? Impossible. There are times when we mistake depression and gloom, which are the effect of purely physical causes, for the effect of the withdrawal of God's presence. Did Christ commit that mistake? I say, again, Impossible.

I take the words in their clear and unqualified meaning. It is only by taking them in this way that very much that is contained in the previous history of our Lord becomes intelligible. He knew that He was to die this awful death; that He was to be forsaken of God in His last hours. This explains why it was that his mind was filled with the thought of His Death from the very first, and why, as it approached, it filled Him with dismay.

Surely this supreme anguish must have a unique relation to the redemption of mankind. If not, why was it that the anticipation of His Death was associated with some of the greatest moments in His history? Why did He speak of it to Peter, when Peter confessed that He was the Christ, the Son of the living God? Why did it occur to Him when the Greeks came to speak to Him at the Feast? Why did He institute a religious rite to commemorate it?

When I try to discover the meaning of the sorrow of Christ on the cross, I cannot escape the conclusion that He is somehow involved in this deep and dreadful darkness by the sins of the race whose nature He has assumed. If the dread with which He anticipated His Death, and if the Divine desertion which made His Death so awful, are to pass into Doctrine, I can conceive of no other form in which they can appear than that which they assume in the Apostolic Epistles — "He was delivered for our offences." [44] "He died for our sins;" [45] He "suffered,...the Just for the unjust;" [46] "He was made a curse for us." [47]

As I look, as I listen, I am driven to exclaim, "Surely He hath borne our griefs and carried our sorrows. He was wounded for our transgressions and bruised for our iniquities. The Lord hath laid on Him the iniquity of us all." [48] In no other way are His sufferings explicable. To fulfil these words of ancient prophecy, He can endure no greater, no keener anguish. If this is not the explanation of His desertion on the Cross, then the Cross, instead of declaring that God has not forsaken the human race, notwithstanding all its crimes, seems to be an appalling testimony to all nations and to all centuries, that not even the purest goodness can secure for One who has assumed our nature the strength and the peace which come from the perpetual manifestation of God's presence and love. Instead of revealing the infinite love of God refusing to forsake those who have sinned, it is an awful proof that He may forsake in the hour of their utmost and sorest need those who have perfectly loved and perfectly obeyed Him. Either the Death of Christ was the Atonement for human sin, or else it fills me with terror and despair.

[1] Exod. xxxiii. 11.

[2] John xii. 41.

[3] Gal. i. 12.

[4] I John i. 2.

[5] Heb. i. 3.

[6] John xiv. 9.

[7] Matt. viii. 2, 3; Mark i. 40, 41; Luke iv. 12, 13. It is remarkable that every one of the Synoptical Gospels notices the fact that our Lord "touched" the man.

[8] Matt. xiv. 14.

[9] Luke vii. 11-15.

[10] Henry Rogers: Defence of the Eclipse of Faith, p. 143.

[11] Neh. ix. 17.

[12] Jonah iv. 2.

[13] Preface to The Divine Teacher; being the Recorded Sayings of our Lord Jesus Christ during His Ministry on Earth.

[14] Preface to The Sure Resting-Place; being Selected Sayings of our Lord Jesus Christy arranged as a Manual of Faith and Practice.

[15] Sermons, Third Series, p. 144.

[16] St. Mark simply states the fact that "He was there in the wilderness forty days, tempted of Satan; and was with

the wild beasts." — Chap. i. ver. 13.

[17] The last eleven verses of St. Mark's Gospel being of doubtful genuineness.

[18] John i. 29. Note C.

[19] John ii. 19-21.

[20] Ibid. iii. 14.

[21] Ibid. vi. 51-56.

[22] Matt. xvi. 16, 21.

[23] Luke ix. 31.

[24] Mark ix. 9.

[25] Matt. xvii. 22.

[26] Ibid. xx. 17-19; Mark x. 35-45; Luke xviii. 31-34.

[27] Matt. xx. 22.

[28] Ibid. xxvi. 2.

[29] Mark xiv. 8.

[30] Luke xii. 47.

[31] John xii. 27.

[32] Ibid xii. 24.

[33] Ibid. xii. 27.

[34] Ibid. xiii. 21.

[35] Matt xxvi. 37.

[36] Mark xiv. 33.

[37] Matt. xxvi. 38; Mark xiv. 34.

[38] Matt. xxvi. 39.

[39] Καὶ αὐτὸς ἀπεσπάσθη ἀπ' αὐτῶν. Luke xxii. 41. The same word occurs in St. Luke's account of St. Paul's departure from the elders of the Ephesian Church, who met him at Miletus (Acts xxi. i).

[40] Matt. xxvi. 39.

[41] John xiv. 29.

[42] Matt. xxvi. 46; Mark xv. 14.

[43] Note D.

[44] Rom. iv. 25.

[45] I Cor. xv. 3.

[46] I Pet. iii. 18.

[47] Gal. iii. 13.

[48] Isa. lv. 4-6.

# Lecture Three - The Fact of the Atonement: The Testimony of our Lord

We have now to inquire whether our Lord gave any account of His Death which at all explains the mysterious facts which we considered in the previous Lecture, and to which the Evangelists give so much prominence.

Had He been silent on the relation of His sufferings to human redemption, it would have remained true that His Death was present to His mind from the very commencement of His ministry; that when it came near, it filled Him with dismay; and that on the cross He was forsaken by the Father. But He was not silent. Nor are we left to discover His inner thought concerning His Death from obscure allusions to it of ambiguous meaning, or from words spoken incidentally and suggested by circumstances which we might call accidental, or from parables which might be of doubtful interpretation, or from illustrations derived from Jewish institutions about whose precise significance there might be interminable controversy. It was of infinite importance that there should be no misapprehension of His meaning, and He therefore selected for the full and final explanation of the nature and intention of His Death an hour of pathetic solemnity. The explanation was not drawn from Him by any request of His disciples or by any taunts of His enemies: it came altogether from Himself, and as -the result of a deliberate purpose. It was veiled under no metaphor. It was expressed plainly, directly, explicitly. As if to save it from all the chances and perils which are inseparable from the transmission of thought to remote countries and remote generations. He connected it with the institution of a new and peculiar sacred rite, which was to be celebrated by His disciples to the end of time.

We have four accounts in the New Testament of the institution of the Lord's Supper, St. Matthew's, St. Mark's, St. Luke's, and that given by St. Paul in the First Epistle to the Corinthians. The variations between them are neither uninteresting nor unimportant, but it is unnecessary that I should discuss them.

It was the night before His Passion, the night, as St. Paul reminds us, in which He was betrayed. Our Lord and His disciples were celebrating the Passover, [1] and as they were eating, Jesus took bread and gave thanks, and brake it, and gave unto them, saying, "Take eat, this is My body which is given [or broken] for you: this do in remembrance of Me." And He took the cup and gave thanks, and gave it to them, saying, "Drink ye all of it; for this is My blood of the New Testament [or covenant], which is shed for many [or for you] for the remission of sins: this do ye as oft as ye drink it in remembrance of Me." [2] It appears, therefore, that our Lord declared that His Death is in some way related to "the remission of sins."

He declared, indeed, that it was for the remission of sins that He was about to die. Other ends might be accomplished by His Death, but at a time when we might reasonably suppose that His mind would be filled with the chief and direct objects of His Passion, this is the only one of which He speaks. His blood was shed "for the remission of sins."

He never says that He was tempted "for the remission of sins;" or that He endured hunger, thirst, weariness, and poverty, "for the remission of sins;" or that it was for this that He was transfigured, or that it was for this that He endured the agony of Gethsemane, or that it was for this that He spoke to men about the powers and laws and mysteries and glories of the kingdom of heaven. The whole of His ministry is a revelation of the righteousness and of the love of God, an authoritative appeal to the heart and conscience of the human race, a mighty force constraining men to repent of sin and to trust in the infinite love of the Father. And if His Death contributed to our eternal redemption only by producing in us those dispositions which render it right and possible for God to forgive us, it would be no more intimately related to the remission of sins than every part of His public ministry. Men have been filled with terror by His awful declarations concerning judgment to come and the final doom of the impenitent, and have entreated Him to deliver them from "the worm that dieth not and the fire that is not quenched." The parable of the Prodigal Son has broken their hearts with sorrow for sin, and inspired them with trust in the Divine mercy. I suppose that there is hardly a word of His recorded in the four Gospels that has not drawn some man nearer to God. His miracles. His tears — tears shed at the grave of His friend and over the city of His murderers — all the incidents of His earthly life, are charged with the same wonderful power. In an indirect way, it might be said that His teaching from first to last, all that He did, all that He endured, was intended to secure for us the remission of sins. But never, even incidentally — never, even by implication — does our Lord affirm that it was for this that He wrought miracles, or revealed truth, or submitted to the sorrows and pains which preceded the cross. He does affirm that it was for the remission of sins that He died. He must have believed that the relation between His Death and the remission of sins is different in kind from that which exists between His teaching or His example and the remission of sins.

There is another peculiarity in our Lord's manner of speaking about His Death. As I have said already, the four narratives contained in the New Testament of the institution of the Lord's Supper vary: no two of them have preserved our Lord's words in precisely the same form, but the same fundamental conception of His death appears in them all. St. Matthew and St. Mark do not tell us that when our Lord broke and distributed the bread He said that He was about to die for others; but they both tell us that when He took the cup He said, "This is My blood of the New Testament [or covenant], which is shed for many." St. Paul does not tell us that when He took the cup He said that His blood was to be shed for others; but he tells us that when our Lord took the bread He said, "This is My body which is broken for you." St. Luke alone represents our Lord as declaring that His Death was a death for others, both when He broke the bread and when He passed the wine. The preservation of this central idea, notwithstanding the variations of the four narratives, is very impressive.

This was not the only time that He described His Death as a death for others. That same night, after the institution of the Supper, He said to His disciples, "Greater love hath no man than this, that a man lay down his life for his friends. Ye are My friends if ye do whatsoever I command you." [3]

Three months before, He had claimed to be the Good Shepherd, and in illustration of His claim He emphasised in the most remarkable manner His readiness and His *intention* to die for His flock. He does not say that He will lead His sheep to the greenest and most abundant pastures, and to streams which are not dried up by the summer's heat or swollen by the rains of winter into dangerous torrents; but He declares again and again that He will die for them. "I am the good Shepherd; the good Shepherd giveth his life for the sheep." "As the Father knoweth Me, even so know I the Father: and I lay down My life for the sheep." [4] Up to this point, however, it remains uncertain whether He was to die for the flock of God in any other sense than many faithful shepherds have died for it. Jewish prophets, Christian apostles, many reformers and missionaries, and many courageous ministers of the gospel in evil times, have died rather than betray their trust. Had our Lord said nothing more, it might have been possible to interpret His words as meaning that He was to die as they have died. The shepherd may lose his own life while he is struggling with the wolf; the wolf may be killed, or, even if not, the struggle may give the flock time to escape, though the shepherd perishes. To prevent any misconception, He breaks up His illustration. The shepherd that dies defending his flock does not die voluntarily; he dies because the wolf is too strong for him: but our Lord declares that it is not to be so with Him: "I lay down my life...No man taketh it from Me, but I lay it down of Myself. I have power to lay it down, and I have power to take it again." [5] His devotion to men is as great as that of the shepherd who imperils and actually loses his life in protecting his flock against the wolf; He, too, dies for the sheep; but He lays down His life deliberately and of set purpose: "no man taketh it from (Him)." Our Lord's Death is unique. The parallel fails. He died for men in some other sense than those have died who have shrunk from no dangers in the service of the Church and of God. Words of our Lord, which we have already considered, suggest a partial explanation of the peculiarity of His death: His blood was shed "for the remission of sins."

There are other words of His which contribute additional illustration to the sense in which He laid down His life "for the sheep." On His way to Jerusalem, and a very short time before His death, He had spoken to Peter and the other Apostles about the greatness of their future position in the kingdom of heaven: "Verily I say unto you. That ye which have followed Me, in the regeneration when the Son of man shall sit in the throne of His glory, ye also shall sit upon twelve thrones, judging the twelve tribes of Israel." [6] After this, indeed. He had warned them that a great crisis in His personal history was very near, and that He was going up to the holy city to die. His words were very distinct, and so terrible that we might have supposed that all personal ambition in the hearts of the disciples would have given place to anxiety and distress about the sufferings which menaced their Lord. He had said: "Behold, we go up to Jerusalem; and the Son of man shall be delivered unto the chief priests, and unto the scribes; and they shall condemn Him to death, and shall deliver Him to the Gentiles; and they shall mock Him, and shall scourge Him, and shall spit upon Him, and shall kill Him; and the third day He shall rise again." [7] But they do not seem to have believed that He meant exactly what He said. There was something in His manner which "amazed" them, and "as they followed [Him] they were afraid;" [8] but that these terrible words were to be literally fulfilled was incredible. They knew that He was accustomed to speak in parables. His commonest sayings had often a hidden sense. His thoughts had always transcended theirs. More than once they had missed His meaning because they had mistaken the form for the substance: and now, whatever He meant, He could not mean that He was to be actually betrayed to His enemies by one of themselves, and put to death. Heavy storm-clouds might be gathering about Him, but He would break through them with victorious splendour; and if the final struggle was at hand, the kingdom of God would immediately appear, and the "thrones" He had promised them would be theirs. They thought it no harm to speculate about how the honours of His kingdom would be distributed among them. James and John might have felt that their rank was secure but for those ominous words with which the Lord had closed what He had said to them about their coming glory: "Many that are first shall be last, and the last shall be first." [9] To make their position certain, they came to Him, or rather their mother came for them, and asked that He would reserve for one of them the throne on His right hand, and for the other the throne on His left hand, in His kingdom. [10] In reply. He spoke of His sufferings, and said that they, too, would suffer; but He gave no promise that their request would be granted. The rest of the Apostles, naturally enough, were "moved with indignation," and "much displeased with James and John." But Jesus called them to Him, and told them that the law of greatness in the kingdom of God was unlike that which determined the rank and power of princes in earthly states: "Whosoever will be great among you, shall be your minister: and whosoever of you will be the chiefest, shall be servant of all. For even the Son of man came not to be ministered unto, but to minister, and to give His life a ransom for many." [11]

As the ethical idea of Sacrifice has become vague and indefinite to us because we are not familiar with the original institution, so the ethical idea of Redemption has lost very much of the sharpness of its outline because we are not in the habit of paying ransoms. But to the people of our Lord's time the payment of ransoms was a familiar custom, and under the Jewish law ransoms were the subject of very definite regulations. Some of these regulations were probably obsolete, but they were not unknown. To a Jew a ransom was the money which a man paid to recover possession of his inheritance when he had parted with it; [12] it was the price he paid when he purchased the freedom of any that was "nigh of kin to him" who had become a slave to a stranger; [13] it was what he gave in exchange for the life of the first-born of an unclean animal which he wanted to keep, and which the law required him either to redeem or to destroy; [14] it was the five shekels which he had to pay for the life of his first-born child; [15] it was the half shekel which every man over twenty years of age had to pay at the census, to avert Divine judgments — "atonement money" — a price which every man paid for his life; [16] it was the money which the parent, wife, child, or brother of a man who had been killed by an ox, known to be vicious or dangerous, claimed from the owner, and on the payment of which the owner was permitted to live; [17] it was what the murderer, in accordance probably with ancient custom, might offer to "the revenger of blood," to prevail upon him not to inflict the penalty of death, but which the Mosaic law in its just severity forbade him to accept, so that for the life of the murderer no ransom was possible. [18] A ransom, when given for persons, rescued them from slavery or from death; it averted Divine judgments; it cancelled the claims which deprived them of freedom, or the crime by which they had forfeited life. It was in money that the ransom was usually paid, but there was one large class of cases in which, by the sacrifice of the life of one creature, another was redeemed from death. [19] And our Lord had come to "give His life a ransom for many." It was in this sense, then, that He was to "lay down His life for" those who were no longer His servants, but "His friends;" and in this sense that the Good Shepherd was to give His life for the sheep.

The explanations which our Lord gave of His Death are coherent. He gave His life a ransom for us, and therefore it is that through the shedding of His blood we receive the remission of sins, and escape eternal destruction.

The passages which I have quoted, if they stood alone, would be sufficient to demonstrate that to our Lord's own mind His Death was something more than the incidental or even the inevitable consequence of His fidelity to the truth, and of His antagonism to the corrupt ambition, the hypocrisy, and the evil passions of the ecclesiastical rulers of the Jewish people; that He did not die as martyrs die, because He chose death rather than apostasy; that His Death has a unique relation to the redemption of our race; that whatever may be effected for the restoration of mankind to God by His Incarnation, by the fulfilment in Him of the Divine ideal of human perfection, by the revelation in His life and character, in His miracles and teaching, of the Divine holiness and love, the remission of sins is rendered possible by His Death. But these passages do not stand alone, there are others which sustain the general argument.

Why was it that in His conversation with Nicodemus our Lord insisted on His Death with such singular emphasis, and ascribed to it such great results? The conversation opens with a declaration of the necessity of the New Birth. To enter the kingdom of God, a man must receive the life of God. But to whom is this Divine and eternal life given? How is it to be brought within the reach of those who have transgressed the Divine laws and provoked the Divine anger? Is it enough that the holiness and grace of the Son of God should fill the hearts of men with shame and grief for their sin? that the blessedness of His communion with the Father should make them passionately desire to receive the life which dwells in Him, that His blessedness may become theirs? that His compassion. His mercy, His "exceeding great and precious promises" should inspire them with trust in the infinite love of God, and give them courage to appeal to Him for that supreme gift by which they are to be "made partakers of the Divine nature," and rendered capable of entering the Divine kingdom? This is not the impression that we receive from our Lord's words. That the Divine life may become ours, the Son of God must die.

"As Moses lifted up the serpent in the wilderness, so must the Son of man be lifted up" — His Incarnation is not enough, His Ministry is not enough, He must die — "that whosoever believeth in Him should not perish, but have eternal life." [20] It is this conception of His Death that gives form to the words which follow: — "God so loved the world, that He gave" — did not merely send, but gave — "His only begotten Son" — surrendered Him up to all that was involved in the great work of saving mankind, delivered Him over to the death which has just been illustrated by a reference to the lifting up of the brazen serpent — "that whosoever believeth in Him should not perish, but have everlasting life." [21]

I reminded you in the previous Lecture of the conflicting joy and dread which agitated the heart of Christ when certain Gentiles, who had come up to

Jerusalem to celebrate the Passover, wished to see Him just before the close of His public ministry; but I did not quote all that He said to them. The time was approaching when men of every race would be attracted to Him, but as yet the nations He had come to save belonged to "this present evil world," and the power of "the prince of this world" was unbroken. His Death, which was now so near, was to establish a new and Divine order. "Now shall the prince of this world be cast out. And I, if I be lifted up from the earth, will draw all men unto Me." [22] His Death, not His birth, was to be the great crisis in the history of mankind. His Death, not His living ministry, was to reverse the evil fortunes of the human race. His apparent and temporary defeat was the condition of His real and enduring victory; He must die on the cross in order to become the Prince and Saviour of the world. Discourses richer in spiritual truth than the Sermon on the Mount, and more pathetic than His address to His disciples on the night before His Passion; parables of diviner beauty than that of the Lost Sheep and the Prodigal Son; manifestations of sympathy with human suffering more tender than His tears at the grave of Lazarus; manifestations of mercy for human sin more generous and more touching than His lament over the city of His murderers — all these would be in vain: He must die, if all men are to be drawn to Him. Other explanations of the necessity of His Death may be given. I prefer His own. He gave His life a ransom for many; His blood was shed for the remission of sins.

There is a discourse of our Lord's in which His direct intention is to illustrate the relation of His Death to the gift of eternal life rather than to the remission of sins, but which is not without value in this argument. It was delivered in the synagogue of Capernaum, in the very synagogue, perhaps, whose ruins are still to be seen at Tell Hum, and on a lintel of which is sculptured the pot of manna, the visible symbol and memorial to the modern traveller of the discourse delivered within its walls eighteen centuries ago. On the previous day He had fed five thousand men, besides women and children, on five barley loaves and two small fishes. The miracle was wrought on the other side of the lake of Galilee, but the crowd had followed Him to Capernaum. They wanted Him to repeat the great historical miracle of the wilderness. "What sign showest Thou, then, that we may see and believe Thee? What dost Thou work? Our fathers did eat manna in the desert" — not mere barley loaves and fish miraculously multiplied — "as it is written. He gave them bread from heaven to eat." [23] Our Lord replied that He was the true bread from heaven, the bread of God, the bread of life, and that "if any man eat of this bread he shall live for ever." [24] But He went on to speak of His Death as necessary to the eternal life of mankind. "The bread that I will give is My flesh, which I will give for the life of the world... Verily, verily, I say unto you, except ye eat the flesh of the Son of man, and drink His blood, ye have no life in you. Whoso eateth My flesh and drinketh My blood hath eternal life, and I will raise him up at the last day." [25]

The people were confounded and the disciples perplexed. He at once removed the impression that they were literally to eat His flesh; for He said that "the Son of man" was to "ascend up where He was before;" and He added that "it is the spirit that quickeneth, the flesh proliteth nothing;" and the spirit was in a sense and in a measure already theirs. "The words that I speak [or have spoken] to you, they are spirit and they are life." [26]

But the startling form under which He had represented His Death as the necessary condition of the life of the world, He leaves unexplained. The explanation is suggested by the words of the Evangelist at the commencement of the narrative: "The passover, the [great] feast of the Jews, was nigh." [27] From the manna which fell in the wilderness, our Lord's mind passed to the lamb that was killed on the night of the Exodus. When the angel of the Lord smote the first-born of Egypt, "from the first-born of Pharaoh that sat on the throne, unto the first-born of the captive that was in the dungeon," his terrible sword had not smitten the first-born of the Jews. They had been delivered because, in obedience to the command of God, the blood of the paschal lamb was on the lintel and door-posts of every house. The lamb was slain, and the first-born were saved. The blood of the lamb was sprinkled on the outside of the house, the family within ate the flesh. And Christ was the true Passover Lamb; His Death averted death from the true Israel of God, "the church of the first-born;" and His flesh was to give new life and strength to those who received Him.

At the time these words were spoken His meaning was hidden even from the Apostles. Another passover came, and He celebrated it with them on the night before He was crucified; and then "He took bread and blessed it, and brake it; and said, Take, eat; this is My body. And he took the cup, and gave thanks, and gave it to them, saying. Drink ye all of it; for this is My blood of the new covenant, which is shed for many for the remission of sins." Even then they probably failed to grasp His meaning. But after He had risen again, and when they discovered that He had accomplished for them a greater deliverance than Moses had accomplished for their fathers, then doubtless they recognised the same wonderful truth in the "hard saying" which had troubled them in the synagogue at Capernaum, and in the new rite which He had instituted in the upper chamber in Jerusalem. Our Lord was the true paschal lamb; His blood, "shed for many for the remission of sins," saved them from death; His flesh was to be the perpetual support of their new and free and happy life. [28]

There is another consideration which appears to have some force. The silence of a great Teacher like our Lord is often as expressive as His speech. He came to a people that claimed to stand in a nearer relation to God than the rest of mankind, and He acknowledged the claim. He recognised the Divine commission of Jewish prophets, and the Divine authority of Jewish institutions. He called the temple His "Father's house." He kept the feasts. He told the leper whom He healed to go to the priest and to offer the gift that Moses commanded. Even when conversing with a Samaritan, He asserted the prerogatives of the Jewish race: "Ye worship ye know not what: we know what we worship: for salvation is of the Jews." [29] He said that the Jewish Scriptures testified of Him. He declared that He had not come to destroy the law or the prophets, but to fulfil them; the fundamental ideas of the national institutions and the national life were to reappear, developed and perfected, in the kingdom of heaven.

Now among the institutions of Judaism, sacrifices were the most conspicuous; they stood at the very centre of the religious thought and service of the nation. To offer them was the special function of a numerous and powerful priesthood. The ritual of sacrifice was governed by the most minute and elaborate regulations. All the offerings were not of one kind. Some of them were intended to express, as their chief idea, the perfect surrender of the soul to God; others were intended to be the expression of happy fellowship with God and hearty thanksgiving. But there was one class of sacrifices— a class separated into two groups — which were specifically intended to atone for certain kinds of offences against the Mosaic law. The offender brought his sacrifice to the priest, and the offering of the sacrifice secured forgiveness. Whatever theory we may form of the Divine idea underlying this symbolic institution, the Law appeared to affirm that the relation between the offering of the sacrifice and the remission of the sin was immediate and direct; [30] and this was obviously the belief of the Jews in the time of our Lord.

It is true that no sacrifices secured forgiveness for specific moral offences: a Jew who had broken one of the Ten Commandments could not bring a sheep or a lamb to the priest, and atone for his sin. But every year there was a great ceremonial at which all the sins of the nation were confessed, and in some sense atoned for. Those who had been trained to connect the remission of a ceremonial offence with the offering of the sacrifice required by the Law, were certain to connect the remission of graver offences with the offering of the sacrifices on the Day of Atonement. The disproportion between the sacrifices of that day and the guilt of the whole nation prevented the consciences of those who were troubled by the sense of sin from finding perfect rest in the ritual; but the idea of remission of sins was inseparable from the idea of a sacrifice for sins.

Sacrifices for the sins of the whole nation were also offered at other times — at the beginning of every month and at the great festivals. Nor was the idea of expiation altogether excluded from the burnt-offerings which were presented in the temple every day. [31]

That the Jewish people believed that sacrifice and remission were directly related to each other, is clear from the Epistle to the Hebrews.

The writer takes this belief for granted when he illustrates the greatness of the sacrifice of Christ by contrasting it with the sacrifices of the ancient law. "Under the law, without shedding of blood, is no remission;" [32] "where remission [of sins and iniquities] is, there is no more offering for sin." [33] "Christ was once offered to bear the sin of many," [34] and "after He had offered one sacrifice for sins. He for ever sat down on the right hand of God." [35]

It may be alleged that the whole argument of the anonymous writer of this epistle is nothing more than a concession to Jewish habits of thought, a kindly and skilful endeavour to facilitate the transition of Jewish believers from the old faith to the new; that it was necessary to invest Christ with sacerdotal functions, and to express the significance of His Death by sacrificial symbols, because the Jews had been so long accustomed to find access to God through a priesthood, and to connect the remission of sins with the shedding of blood. Let this hypothesis be granted; for the moment I have no occasion to dispute it. Whether they were true or false, the ideas which determine the whole argument of the Epistle to the Hebrews were firmly rooted in the mind of the Jewish people. If they were true — if the relation created by the institutions of Judaism between the remission of sins and sacrifice for sins was the symbolic expression of a Divine law — there is an end of the controversy: our Lord's Death is the objective reason on the ground of which God pardons human transgressions. But if these ideas were false, how was it that our Lord did not protest against them? If the Jewish people had misinterpreted their national institutions, if God never intended to train them to the recognition of a direct relation between the offering of sacrifices and the remission of sin, how can His silence be explained? More than once He came into violent collision with the faith and customs of the nation. The Scribes and the Pharisees found fault because His disciples omitted to wash their hands before eating bread. In itself the custom was not only harmless, but decent and cleanly: the only harm was that it had been made a religious obligation. Our Lord defended His disciples with an unusual vehemence of indignation, and charged the authoritative religious teachers of the nation with making the word of God of none effect through their traditions. [36] Again and again He deliberately provoked the most bitter hostility by working miracles on the Sabbath day: the healing of the impotent man at the pool of Bethesda on the Sabbath was indeed the origin of that unrelenting antagonism which at last culminated in the conspiracy to put Him to death.

But surely mere ceremonial superstitions, and excessive rigidity in keeping the Sabbath, however inconsistent with the true idea of a perfect life, were harmless compared with the error — if it were an error — involved in the Jewish conception of the functions and powers of an atoning sacrifice. Those who deny that remission of sins is granted on the ground of an objective sacrifice for sins, maintain that the theory against which they protest obscures the glory of the Divine mercy, rests on false ideas of the Divine justice, and exerts a most pernicious influence on the whole development of religious thought and life. If the theory which they reject is false, they are right in the earnestness and energy with which they denounce it. But this theory penetrated the whole substance of Jewish thought, and I ask again. How is the silence of our Lord to be explained? His silence! It is no ordinary silence which has to be accounted for. At the very commencement of His ministry He received without a protest the testimony of John the Baptist — "Behold the Lamb of God that taketh away the sin of the world." [37] His silence was a definite acceptance of the testimony; it was an acknowledgment that He had come to fulfil the idea of the sin-offering of the Jewish law, and to secure for men the remission of their sins.

But He came to "fulfil" "the prophets" as well as "the law." Demonstrations of Christian doctrine resting on isolated passages selected from the Jewish Scriptures are, no doubt, unsatisfactory and inconclusive. Nothing can be more uncritical than the use which theologians have made of the Old Testament. To discover richer treasures of evangelical truth in the book of Leviticus than in the four Gospels, in the minor prophets than in the Epistles of St. Paul, betrays not only intellectual perversity, but an utter ignorance of the principles which have determined the whole course of the Divine procedure in accomplishing human redemption. There is great interest, indeed, in watching the gradual brightening of the great hope of a Deliverer, the development of the Messianic idea in richer and richer forms, forms suggested as much by the vicissitudes of Jewish history as by the direct revelations which were made to Jewish prophets. The institutions and Scriptures of the ancient faith have not become obsolete; but Truth as well as Grace came by Jesus Christ our Lord; history is better than prophecy; and facts are greater than symbols.

It is certain, however, that to our Lord Jesus Christ the law of Moses, the prophets, and the psalms were full of Himself. [38] He found in the literature and institutions of Judaism, the hopes which He had come to fulfil, the cravings which He had come to satisfy, the ideas which were to be illustrated in His personal history. Could we have listened while He expounded to the two disciples who were on their way to Emmaus "the scriptures...concerning Himself," or have sat with the larger company that same evening, assembled together with shut doors for fear of the Jews, and heard Him when He "opened their understanding, that they might understand the scriptures, and said unto them, Thus it is written, and thus it behoved Christ to suffer, and to rise from the dead the third day: and that repentance and remission of sins should be preached in His name among all nations;" [39] we should have received large accessions to our knowledge concerning the thought of Christ about His own work and His relation to the history and faith of the Jewish people.

But on the night preceding His Death He had definitely connected His last sad hours with a very memorable passage of Old Testament prophecy. Whatever maybe our interpretation of the direct and original reference of the fifty-third chapter of Isaiah, our Lord declared that in Him the idea of that chapter was to be fulfilled: "This that is written must yet be accomplished in Me, And He was reckoned with transgressors: for the things concerning Me have an end." [40]

The representations of our Lord's Death which we have considered in this Lecture throw an intense light on the sense in which He intended that the prophecy would be fulfilled in Himself. Our Lord spoke of laying down His life for His sheep and for His friends; and the prophet declares that the Servant of Jehovah, whose sufferings he is describing, "was wounded for our transgressions, was bruised for our iniquities: the chastisement of our peace was upon Him...He was cut off out of the land of the living: for the transgression of My people was He stricken" (vv. 5, 8). Our Lord said that He had come to give His life a ransom for many: the prophet says, "He hath borne our griefs and carried our sorrows;...with His stripes we are healed" (vv. 4,5). John the Baptist pointed to Him as the Lamb of God that taketh away the sin of the world: the prophet declares that Jehovah will make the soul of His Servant "an offering for sin." The prophet says, "All we like sheep have gone astray, and the Lord hath laid on Him the iniquities of us all....He bare the sin of many...By His knowledge shall my righteous servant justify many, for He shall bear their iniquities" (vv. 6, 12, 11); and Christ told His disciples that His blood was to be "shed for the remission of sins." The whole prophecy, in all its separate parts, finds its parallel in various sayings by our Lord, in which He describes the character of His sufferings and their relation to the redemption of mankind. [41]

The results of this investigation of our Lord's testimony concerning His Death are these: —

1. His Death was neither the incidental nor the inevitable consequence of His collision with the passions and prejudices of the Jewish people.

2. The laying down of His life was a voluntary act.

3. To lay down His life was one of the ends for which He came into the world.

4. His Death is immediately related to the deliverance from condemnation of those who believe in Him, to the remission of sins, and to the establishment of His sovereignty over the human race.

5. He accepted the testimony of John the Baptist that He was the Lamb of God that taketh away the sin of the world, and He associated His Death with the sacrifice of the passover lamb on the night of the Exodus.

6. He described His Death as a death for others, and more specifically He said that He gave His life a ransom for others.

In any adequate theory of the purpose of the Death of Christ, these various statements must find a place and an explanation. It is further necessary, in any theory of His Death, to account for the extent to which it filled His mind from the commencement of His ministry, the increasing fear with which He anticipated it as it came nearer, and the mysterious sorrow He endured on the cross, a sorrow which compelled Him to cry, "My God, My God, why hast thou forsaken Me?" [42]

Dr. Jowett, in his essay "On Atonement and Satisfaction," referring to the alleged absence from our Lord's teaching of any clear and unambiguous pas-

sages which can be quoted in support of this doctrine, says: "It is hard to imagine that there can be any truer expression of the Gospel than the words of
Christ Himself, or that any truth omitted by Him is essential to the Gospel.
'The disciple is not above his master, nor the servant greater than his lord.'
The philosophy of Plato was not better understood by his followers than by
himself, nor can we allow that the Gospel is to be interpreted by the Epistles,
or that the Sermon on the Mount is only half Christian, and needs the fuller
inspiration or revelation of St. Paul, or the author of the Epistle to the Hebrews." [43] I will not stay to insist on the fundamental error involved in the
suggestion that our Lord's relation to His Apostles has even the remotest
analogy to the relation between Plato and his followers. What Plato taught
contained nearly everything that Plato contributed to the development of the
intellectual and moral life of mankind; but whatever may be our theory of the
Death of Christ, the larger part of what Christ revealed of God is contained in
His personal character, in the relations which He sustained to various descriptions of men, in the sufferings to which He Himself submitted, and in the
miracles by which He relieved the sufferings of others. [44] But Dr. Jowett's
reference to the relation between Plato and his followers suggests the relation between Plato and his master.

We have two representations of the teaching of Socrates — one in the
Memorabilia of Xenophon, the other in the Platonic Dialogues — and the differences between them are not altogether unlike those which are alleged to
exist between the teaching of the historical Christ, as it may be ascertained
from the Gospels, [45] and the theological theories developed in the Apostolic Epistles. Now, if in the Memorabilia it had been recorded that Socrates referred to his approaching martyrdom in terms at all like those in which it
appears that our Lord spoke of His Death; if — forgive me if the hypothesis
appears strained and forced — we had learnt from Xenophon that when Socrates was beginning to discuss philosophy with the sophists and young men
of Athens, he had accepted testimony which implied that he was to be sacrificed to the gods for the sins of the Athenians'; if we learnt that his mind was
oppressed from the very first by the anticipation of the sorrows of his last
hours; if to those who came to him inquiring about the Supreme Good he had
said that he must die in order that the Supreme Good might be theirs; if he
had spoken again and again of laying down his life for others; if he had said
that his life was not to be taken from him by the power of his enemies, but
that he would lay it down of himself; if he had declared that the δαίμων, to
whose voice he always listened, had revealed to him that the very purpose
for which he had been born was that he might give his life a ransom for
many; if he had deliberately connected the idea of his own death with expiatory sacrifices which his countrymen were accustomed to offer to the gods; if
he had declared that the lines of an ancient poet, predicting that the sins of
the Athenians were to be laid upon the head of one of the greatest of Atheni-
an citizens, were to be fulfilled in himself; and if during his last day in prison,

and just before the slave brought him the hemlock, instead of discoursing on immortality, he had instituted a religious rite to be celebrated by his friends in commemoration of his death, and said that he was about to die that his disciples and his fellow-citizens might receive the remission of sins; - if, I say, all these things had been told us of Socrates by Xenophon, and if we believed that they were the true expression of his own conception of his martyrdom, Xenophon's testimony alone would have been sufficient to assure us that Socrates himself believed that his death was an atonement, a satisfaction, a sacrifice for the crimes of Athens. Plato might then have written another dialogue; under the lofty and beautiful cypresses of the woods consecrated to Jupiter, he might have assembled Phaedo, Apollodorus, Crito, Critobulus, Hermogenes, and the other friends of Socrates who were with him on the day of his martyrdom; and he might have developed a theory of the expiatory power of the death of Socrates even more elaborate than that which Christian theologians have found of the Death of Christ in the Epistles of St. Paul and the Epistle to the Hebrews; and we might have claimed the authority of Socrates for the theory of Plato without incurring the reproach which Dr. Jowett directs against evangelical theology, when he reminds us that "the disciple is not above his master, nor the servant greater than his lord."

Let the Gospels stand alone, let the testimony of the Epistles be completely suppressed, and the strong foundations of that conception of the Death of Christ which has been the refuge of penitents and the joy of saints for eighteen hundred years will remain unshaken. The words of Christ, and the words of Christ alone, are a sufficient vindication of the ancient faith of the Church.

[1] The force of the argument in the text is not really affected if it is contended that the Lord's Supper was celebrated on the night before the true Passover night. I believe, however, that the traditional view of the Church is sound, and that our Lord celebrated the Passover with His disciples at the time appointed by the Law, and that during the celebration He instituted the great feast of the Church, which has taken its place. The question is discussed at length by all the critical commentators. There is a useful summary of opinions in Lange's *Commentary on St. John's Gospel*, vol. iii. p. 347, and an elaborate discussion of the subject in Wieseler's *Synopsis of the Four Gospels*, p. 308, seq.

[2] Matt. xxvi. 26-28; Mark xiv. 22-24; Luke xxii. 19, 20 I Cor. xi, 23-25. In the text the four narratives are combined.

[3] John xv. 13.

[4] John x. 11, 15.

[5] John x. 17, 18.

[6] Matt. xix. 28.

[7] Mark x. 33, 34.

[8] Ibid. x. 32.

[9] Matt. xix. 30.

[10] Ibid. xx. 20, 21.

[11] Mark x. 43-45. "This price of redemption He gave $\grave{\alpha}\nu\tau\acute{\iota}$, and not merely $\acute{\upsilon}\pi\acute{\epsilon}\rho$, in the wider sense, *i.e., instead of,* in exchange of, or as a substitute, Matt. xvii. 27; Heb. xii. 16. This redemption at the price of His life was made $\grave{\alpha}\nu\tau\acute{\iota}$ $\pi o\lambda\lambda\tilde{\omega}\nu$. The expression *many* is not intended to indicate a smaller number as compared with *all,* — the latter expression occurring in Rom. v. 18; 1 Tim. ii. 4. In the opinion of the author, the term is intended by way of antithesis to the *One* whose life was the ransom of the *many*.

At the same time the expression undoubtedly indicates not only the objective bearing, but also the subjective efficacy of the ransom, by which many are in reality redeemed. Comp. Rom. v. 15; Matt, xxvi. 28."—Lange's *Gospel of Matthew*, vol. ii. p. 254.

[12] Levit. xxv. 25-27.

[13] Ibid, xxv. 47-49.

[14] Num. xviii. 15; Exod. xiii. 13, xxxiv. 20

[15] Num. xviii. 16.

[16] Exod. xxx. 12, 13, 16.

[17] Exod. xxi. 29, 30.

[18] Num. xxxv. 31.

[19] Ibid, xviii. 15; Exod. xiii. 13; xxxiv. 20.

[20] John iii. 14, 15.

[21] Ibid. iii. 16.

[22] John xii. 32.

[23] John vi. 30, 31.

[24] Ibid. vi. 51.

[25] Ibid. vi. 51, 53, 54.

[26] John vi. 62, 63.

[27] Ibid. vi. 4. See GODET: *Commentaire sur l'Evangile de S. Jean*, vol. ii. 79, 132, seq.

[28] "As much as to say the blood of the lamb was shed in Egypt for the salvation of the first-born of the Israelites. This my blood is shed for the remission of sins." — Chrysostom: *Catena Aurea*, Matt. xxvi. 28.

[29] John iv. 22.

[30] Lev, iv.

[31] Note E.

[32] Heb. ix. 22.

[33] Ibid. x. 18.

[34] Ibid. ix. 28.

[35] Ibid. x. 12.

[36] Mark vii. 1-13.

[37] John i. 29.

[38] Luke xxiv. 44.

[39] Luke xxiv. 26, 27, 45, 46.

[40] Ibid. xxii. 37.

[41] Note F.

[42] Note G.

[43] *The Epistles of St. Paul*, ii. 555.

[44] See Lect. ii. pp. 37-49.

[45] The differences between the Synoptists and St. John are of inconsiderable importance in relation to this argument. The statement of the case would have been only slightly enfeebled if all allusions to the Fourth Gospel were cancelled. Further, the characteristic theology of the Fourth Gospel is not of a kind to create distrust of any testimony it may contain to the Doctrine of Expiation.

# Lecture Four - The Fact of the Atonement: The Testimony of St. Peter

In the present Lecture I propose to consider the testimony to the Atonement contained in the discourses and the First Epistle of St. Peter.

But it may be alleged that the attempt to establish this doctrine by an appeal to apostolic testimony is premature, and that the moral objections which have been urged against the theory that the Death of Christ was in any sense a Propitiation or Sacrifice for the sins of the world, ought first to be discussed, and, if possible, dissipated. The moral objections to the doctrine of the Atonement are felt by many persons to be far too grave to be overborne by mere apostolic authority. These objections may even impair the force of the argument from the testimony of our Lord in the previous Lecture. With many who confess that the Lord Jesus Christ was "a Teacher sent from God," and who even acknowledge that He was "God manifest in the flesh," the repugnance to the idea of expiation is so strong, that while they receive the Four Gospels as containing a fairly authentic account of our Lord's life and teaching, they believe that the Apostles could not have received this idea from Christ Himself, and they are perplexed that the writers of the Gospels should have attributed to Him language which appears to sanction it.

The tendency to discriminate between apostolic teaching and the teaching of the Lord Jesus Christ is, I believe, very general. To *His* words — when we are sure that we have them — absolute authority is conceded; but there are many who hesitate to concede the same authority to the words of St. Peter or of St. John. The hesitation does not often assume a very definite form. It is the result of a spiritual instinct, or of what seems to be a spiritual instinct, rather than of a theological theory. Men feel that if Christ were still visibly present among us, accessible in all hours of difficulty and doubt, they would infinitely rather trust Him than trust themselves. If at any time His words seemed to be in conflict with their own highest conceptions of moral and spiritual truth, they would feel sure that He must be right and that they must be wrong. But if it were only an Apostle that was still living in the world the case would be different; they are not quite clear that the same submission would be due.

If, therefore, we can be certain that Christ Himself taught the doctrine of the Atonement, it is acknowledged that however strong the objections to the doctrine may seem to us, we cannot challenge it, and can only confess that we are in the presence of a great mystery. But the objections are of such a kind, that those who feel their force are not willing to accept the doctrine if it is sustained by apostolic testimony alone; and they are half inclined to believe that the words in which our Lord is represented as teaching this doctrine, must have been attributed to Him by mistake. For the theory of the Atonement is declared to be inconsistent with all our conceptions of the Divine Justice, and a travesty of the Divine Mercy, and to be irreconcilable with the moral and spiritual nature both of God and man.

I am not about to make any attempt to remove these objections in the present Lecture. Just now, for a reason which will appear presently, I am rather anxious that their full force should be recognised. Perhaps I have not stated them with sufficient clearness and energy, and it may therefore be well to quote the most concise and vigorous statement of them with which I am familiar. The Rev. James Martineau has expressed with perfect accuracy, the position not only of those who, with himself, deny the deity of our Lord, but of very many who, while rejecting the idea of Atonement, regard the Incarnation as the central and characteristic fact of the Christian religion.

"Faith in the human conscience," he says, "is necessary to faith in the Divine perfection, and *this* again is the needful prelude to the belief in any special revelation...This Moral Perfection of God being assumed as a postulate in the very idea of a Revelation, no system of religion which contradicts it can be admitted as credible *on any terms*. But," he proceeds to say, "the doctrine of the Atonement involves a plain denial of God's moral excellence. Theologians speak as if there were some crime, or at least some weakness in the clemency which freely receives a repentant creature into favour."....But "how is the alleged immorality of letting off the sinner mended by the added crime of penally crushing the sinless?" [1]

Something, perhaps, of the energy of this protest was inspired by certain theological theories, for which I have no occasion to offer apology or defence; but the objection is directed against every theory which affirms that in any sense our iniquities were laid upon Christ; that there is a direct relation between His Death and the remission of sins; that it is for Christ's sake that the penitent is received back again into the light and joy of God. It is the Idea of an objective Atonement which provokes repugnance, no matter what may be the form in which that Idea is represented. The repugnance is so deep that no system of religion in which the Idea is present "can be admitted as *credible on any terms."*

In the course of these Lectures I trust it will become apparent that in the Death of the Lord Jesus Christ as a Sacrifice and Propitiation for the sins of the world, the Moral Perfections of God find their highest expression, and the deepest necessities of man's moral and spiritual life their only complete satisfaction; but I have been anxious to state thus early the principal objection to the doctrine which I hope to establish, because that objection seems to suggest a practical solution of the difficulty with regard to the authority of apostolic teaching.

Let me re-state the difficulty. With those persons to whom these Lectures are addressed, the authority of the Lord Jesus Christ is absolute. He is God manifest in the flesh, and in Him the very truth of the Divine character has been revealed to mankind. But it is maintained that the Apostles may have misapprehended very much of His teaching. It is clear that they did not easily liberate themselves from the influence of Jewish habits of thought and Jewish traditions. Their inspiration, whatever it may have been, did not make them omniscient. There were many things of which they knew nothing; there were some things which they thought they knew, about which, for a time at least, they were mistaken. Their authority, therefore, is not decisive. When we are sure that *Christ* is speaking, we are sure that we have the very thought of God, but we cannot determine the extent of the inspiration of the Apostles; and it is alleged that when *they* are speaking we are not sure whether what they are telling us came to them from the teaching of the Holy Ghost, or from their own erring thoughts about the will and work of their Master, or even from the common and untrustworthy conceptions of Divine truth which prevailed among their fellow-countrymen. It is probable that even in reporting the words of Christ their report may have been coloured by religious errors of their own; it is still more probable that these errors may have misled them when they attempted to illustrate and develop Christian facts and doctrine. Even, therefore, if it can be shown that the apostles taught that in some sense the Death of Christ is the ground on which God forgives human sin, it does not follow that they had learnt it from Christ Himself, or by a special revelation from heaven.

I wish to show that on this particular question we cannot reject the authority of the Apostles — whether they were inspired or uninspired — without rejecting the authority of Christ Himself, and the moral objections to the Idea of Atonement suggest the proof.

For in the judgment of those who reject this Idea, as well as in the judgment of those who receive it, our reception or rejection of it determines our whole conception of the Divine character. When reading the impassioned denunciations of the Idea of the Atonement which are to be found in the pages of some modern writers, it is hardly possible to resist the conviction that in their opinion those who receive it and those who reject it worship different Gods, and belong to forms of religion which, in their fundamental principles and essential spirit, are mutually antagonistic and destructive.

If there is any measure of truth in this representation of the gravity of the controversy, it is quite unnecessary to consider to what extent the inspiration granted to the apostles secured them from religious error." It is unnecessary to raise the question whether they received any supernatural inspiration different in kind or degree from that which is granted to the commonalty of the faithful. The original Apostles were the friends of Christ, and they were entrusted by Him with the task of propagating the Faith of which He was the Founder. I believe that they had an exceptional form of spiritual illumination to qualify them for their work; but in the present argument I need not insist on this. Let it be conceded, if the concession is asked for, that beyond their personal intimacy with the Lord Jesus Christ — whom I assume to have been the Son of God — they had no special prerogatives, no surer access to Divine Truth than any of ourselves, no greater immunity from religious error. Let it be conceded that the substance as well as the form of their writings bears traces of their Jewish training, and, if you will, of their Jewish narrowness, their Jewish prejudice, and their Jewish superstition. Still there must have been some limits to their possible mistakes. If St. Peter and St. John, while professing to deliver to mankind the revelation which had come to them through Christ, gave representations of His Death and of its relations to human redemption, which, to quote the words of Mr. Martineau, are "an outrage upon the first principles of rectitude," and betray a "reckless disregard of all moral considerations," from the thought of which it is a just matter of astonishment "that all good men do not recoil," [2] He who "spake as never man spake" must have been the most inefficient of moral teachers.

On a question of such magnitude and of such broad and practical interest as this, a question vitally affecting the character of God and determining the whole attitude of the soul in relation to Him, I should be satisfied to learn what Christ taught from the testimony of any two or three men of fair intelligence who were in moral sympathy with Christ, and who had had sufficient opportunity of learning His mind.

That on this point the teaching of the original Apostles must have been in harmony with the teaching of our Lord, is still further demonstrated by the fact that it was their special commission to fulfil His intention "that repentance and remission of sins should be preached in His name among all nations, beginning at Jerusalem." [3]

It is incredible that He should have invested men with such a commission as this, who were capable of associating with the infinite mercy of God in the remission of sins an idea which justly revolts the conscience of mankind, and ascribes to God Himself a gross, deliberate, and systematic violation of the principles of eternal righteousness. If the idea of Atonement rests upon so appalling a misconception of the Divine character and of the principles of the Divine government, and if that idea is present in the teaching of the Apostles, we have to explain — not how so grave and fatal an error is consistent with the theory that they had received supernatural inspiration to qualify them for becoming the religious teachers of mankind — but how it was possible for men of the most ordinary capacity so grievously to pervert and corrupt the teaching of their Master. You cannot elude the argument founded on their testimony by distinguishing between His teaching and theirs. On a subject of such gravity, a subject involved in the very substance of the commission they received from Christ, such distinctions are unavailing. Whatever moral objections may be urged against their teaching on a point like this, are an impeachment of the authority of Christ.

It is unnecessary, for the purposes of the present argument, to discuss the nature or the limits of apostolic inspiration. The varying forms in which the Apostles state the relation between the Death of Christ and the forgiveness of sin may be their own; but if their varying statements are harmonious expressions of the same idea — that the Death of Christ is the immediate ground on which God grants to the penitent remission of sins — the Apostles must have received the idea from Christ Himself.

In our times the doctrine of inspiration is in a very unsettled and even chaotic condition, and many devout men are unable to determine to what extent the supernatural illumination of the Holy Ghost protected the Apostles from religious error. The inquiry has considerable speculative interest, but the solution of it is practically unimportant in relation to the chief articles of the Christian Faith. Whether Jesus of Nazareth died on the cross and rose from the dead, whether He wrought miracles, whether He appealed to the Jewish nation with the authority of a Teacher sent from God, whether He claimed a unique relation to God, whether He condemned sin and taught the necessity of repentance, whether He asserted the necessity of a supernatural life as the condition of entrance into the Kingdom of Heaven, whether he affirmed that the forgiveness of sin and escape from eternal condemnation depend upon faith in Himself — these are questions on which the concurrent testimony of His personal friends is decisive. There are some points on which, apart from special inspiration, it is quite conceivable that they may have mistaken their Master's meaning; there are others, and these the greatest, on which, even apart from inspiration, mistake was impossible. The importance of the inspiration of the original Apostles may be said to vary in an inverse ratio with the importance of the religious doctrines on which they are writing.

In considering, therefore, the testimony of St. Peter, St. James, and St. John, to the doctrine discussed in these Lectures, I do not think it necessary to claim for them any such spiritual illumination as would have saved them from all religious error. The argument does not require it. Whatever errors they may have fallen into, it is inconceivable that they should have taught that the Death of Christ is the objective ground on which God forgives human sin, unless they had learnt it from Christ Himself.

We will consider, first, the discourses of St. Peter contained in the early chapters of the Acts of the Apostles; his address on the day of Pentecost to the great multitude, composed of devout Jews from many lands, and speaking many tongues; his address delivered in Solomon's porch to the crowd assembled by the healing of the lame man who had been accustomed to ask alms "at the gate of the temple which is called Beautiful;" his reply to Annas and Caiaphas, when the miracle was challenged, and he was asked "by what power or by what name" it had been wrought; his speech when he was brought a second time before the Council; and his explanation of the gospel to Cornelius the centurion, and the kinsmen and friends gathered in his house. These discourses are especially interesting, because they are among the very few apostolic addresses preserved to us which were delivered to persons who were not believers in Christ.

The substance of them all is the same. Peter declared that Jesus of Nazareth, as the Jewish people knew, was "a man approved of God by miracles and wonders and signs which God did by Him," in the midst of them; [4] that He was the Christ of whom Moses and the prophets had spoken, and for whose coming they and their fathers had been waiting and longing for centuries; [5] that in crucifying Him the people and their rulers had committed a great crime; [6] that God had raised Him from the dead; [7] that He was now reigning in heaven, and was appointed by God to be the Prince and Saviour and Judge of men; [8] that it was the immediate duty of men to repent of the sin of rejecting Him, to be baptized into His name, to acknowledge His authority, and to rely on Him for salvation; [9] that if they repented and believed in Him they would receive remission of sins and the gift of the Holy Ghost; [10] and that "through His name," and only through His name, was remission of sins possible to men. [11]

But St. Peter does not tell the people that our Lord's Death was an expiatory sacrifice. Dr. Young thinks that on our theory the omission is inexplicable. He says: —

"The personal friends and companions of Jesus, who had been most intimately and affectionately associated with Him for three years,.... who had witnessed His Death, and had seen Him, and had intercourse with Him after His resurrection; who, after His departure, had, at His command, waited in solemn prayer to God during seven days for that Holy Ghost whom He had promised to send forth, and on whose souls at last an extraordinary Divine power had descended, — they certainly must have known what their Master intended should be preached as

54

His gospel, and above all must have known that which was most essential and Divine in it. And when only seven weeks after His Death, on the day of Pentecost, they assembled in Jerusalem, it is impossible to doubt that their minds and their hearts must have been full of Christ, of His teaching, His thoughts, His spirit, and His very words A noble occasion of disburdening their full hearts was presented. Jerusalem was crowded with multitudes from all corners of the known world; a mighty audience was prepared, and they were not only expected, but invited to speak. And they did speak. Thoroughly instructed as they were in the life and death and doctrine of the Lord, glowing with love of Christ and love of their yet blinded countrymen, specially entrusted with the message of salvation, and specially endowed to proclaim it, they did speak, and with great freedom and fervour and fulness. But their theme, what was it? The expiation of human sin, and satisfaction to Divine justice, by the sacrifice and sufferings of Jesus on the cross? Pardon obtained from God through means of that sacrifice and these sufferings? If ever there was an occasion, whether we look to the speakers or to the hearers or to the circumstances, when these announcements, supposing them to be fundamental and vital, must have been made, this was that occasion. But they were not made, and nothing like them was once uttered. Peter's sermon on the day of Pentecost to the crowding, eager multitudes at Jerusalem, the first Christian sermon ever preached in this world, contains from beginning to end nothing of this kind." [12]

The substance of this criticism is repeated in Dr. Young's observations on the other discourses and addresses of St. Peter contained in the early chapters of the Acts of the Apostles.

The clearness and force with which it is maintained that the original Apostles "must have known what their Master intended should be preached as His gospel, and above all must have known that which was most essential and Divine in it," are admirable, and confirm what has been already said on that subject in the earlier part of this Lecture. But the criticisms on St. Peter's omission of all reference to the expiatory character of the Death of Christ rest partly on a misconception of evangelical doctrine, and partly on what appears to me to be a failure to appreciate the influence which the historical circumstances in which these discourses were spoken must have had on their contents and character.

As directed against those evangelical theologians who maintain that there can be no true faith in Christ where there is not a clear recognition of His Death as the Propitiation for the sins of the world, Dr. Young's argument is conclusive. If that position could be maintained St. Peter's silence would be incapable of explanation; but that position is no essential part of the evangelical creed. There is true Christian faith wherever the Lord Jesus Christ is acknowledged as "Prince and Saviour," the Founder of the kingdom of heaven, the Moral Ruler of mankind, the Author of eternal salvation. That He atoned for sin on the cross is the explanation of the power which He has received to forgive sin; but a penitent heart may rely on Him for forgiveness, and for restoration to holiness and to God, without apprehending the rela-

55

tion of His Death to human redemption. It was St. Peter's immediate object to prevail upon the Jews to repent of the crime of rejecting and crucifying the Lord Jesus, and to persuade them that He was the Messiah of Jewish prophecy and Jewish hope, through whom, and through whom alone, it was possible to obtain the pardon of sin and eternal life and glory. If they repented of their crime, confessed that Jesus whom they had crucified was Lord and Christ, and trusted in Him for salvation, their faith would be true and genuine; and they would receive the redemption which Christ had achieved for them by His Death, though, as yet, they might not know that only through His Death was their redemption made possible.

It was but seven weeks before, as Dr. Young reminds us, that the Jewish people had crucified the Lord Jesus Christ as an impostor. To have spoken of the expiatory power of His Sacrifice to those who had been guilty of that supreme offence, or who had condoned it, would have been useless. It would have been worse than useless. There was one solitary aspect under which, for the time, it was indispensably necessary that they should regard the Death of Christ. In crucifying Him, they had committed an appalling crime. It was their immediate duty to repent of this crime, and to confess its enormity. With startling boldness and relentless severity St. Peter insists on all the circumstances which aggravated their guilt. For a moment he speaks of Christ as having been "delivered by the determinate counsel and foreknowledge of God" [13] — words which show that already the Apostle regarded the Death of Christ not as an accidental event, but as entering into the Divine conception of His mission — but he instantly returns to his immediate practical purpose, and adds: "Him ye have taken, and by wicked hands have crucified and slain." To have explained that the Death of Christ was a Propitiation for the sins of the world would have perplexed the minds of those to whom he was speaking, and broken the force of those terrible denunciations by which he endeavoured to awaken their consciences and alarm their fears.

On the evangelical theory of the Atonement this seems to me an adequate explanation, both of the contents and omissions of the Apostle's discourses. But how are these discourses to be explained on Dr. Young's own theory? He, too, acknowledges, what indeed it is impossible for any one who admits in any sense the authority of the New Testament to deny, that the Death of the Lord Jesus Christ has even a greater place in the moral and spiritual redemption of our race than His life.

"On the cross," he says, "Christ presses into the very centre of the world's heart, takes possession of it, and there in that centre preaches, as nowhere else was possible, the gospel of God's love! 'Be ye reconciled to God,' He cries. 'Come back to your Father! He hath sent Me to call you back! Inflexibly righteous as He is, He pities, He loves you, and only waits to forgive and welcome.'" [14]

True — gloriously true — although it is only part of the truth! But how was it that St. Peter said nothing about it? He and the Apostles had, as we have been reminded, "a noble occasion of disburdening their full hearts" on the day of Pentecost. On Dr. Young's theory, "the cross, symbol of dishonour and weakness, is the mightiest power in the universe;" [15] it is the last and most wonderful revelation of the Divine love. But how was it that the Apostle was as silent about the revelation of the love of God in the Death of Christ as about its expiatory purpose? To Dr. Young the cross is the ultimate demonstration of the Divine compassion and mercy; but of this those who listened to the early discourses of St. Peter heard nothing. He appeals to the cross again and again, not to fill their hearts with hope, but to intensify their anguish and their terror. The recollection of his cowardice in denying his Master on the night before the crucifixion seems to add fire and vehemence to his denunciations: — "Him ye have taken, and with wicked hands have crucified and slain:" "God hath made that same Jesus whom ye have crucified both Lord and Christ:" "Ye denied the Holy One and the Just, and desired a murderer to be granted to you; and killed the Prince of life, whom God hath raised from the dead:" "By the name of Jesus of Nazareth, whom ye crucified, whom God raised from the dead, even by Him doth this man stand before you whole: "We ought to obey God rather than men" — and *you* especially are men whom we cannot obey if we are to obey Him, for "the God of our fathers raised up Jesus, whom ye slew and hanged on a tree." The Apostle never misses an opportunity of representing the crucifixion as the most terrible of sins. He denounces those who had committed it with a persistency and boldness which must have shaken their hearts with fear. He never changes his tone. From first to last, in these early discourses, the Death of Christ is never a revelation of the infinite wealth of the Divine love: it is always a revelation of the enormity of human sin. It is never appealed to in order to awaken hope, but always in order to create dismay.

I ask again, How is this to be explained on the theory of Dr. Young and of those who think with him? It can be explained only by such considerations as those which I have alleged in reply to Dr. Young's criticisms. And these considerations are less available for Dr. Young's theory than for our own. For the expiatory power of the Death of Christ is effective for all who rely on Him for the forgiveness of sins, even though they may know nothing of its expiatory intention; but the power of the Death of Christ as an appeal of the Divine love to the human heart cannot be felt unless the Death is distinctly recognised as a revelation of that love. On our theory, Peter's silence did not prevent those who listened to him from obtaining the remission of sins which the Death of Christ brought within their reach: if they trusted in Him as their Saviour they were forgiven, though they knew nothing of the relation between His Death and their forgiveness. But on Dr. Young's theory the silence of St. Peter was fatal. Dr. Young maintains in common with all evangelical theologians that the Death of Christ has a critical importance in relation to human redemption, but if its whole value lies in its power over the human heart as a revelation of the love of God, the Death is absolutely valueless where that revelation is not seen and understood; and St. Peter, by representing the crucifixion exclusively as a human crime, and saying nothing to suggest that the Death of Christ was a manifestation of the Divine love, made "the cross of Christ of none effect."

But I repeat that it was necessary that those by whom our Lord had been "crucified and slain" should be made to feel and confess their guilt; and therefore whenever St. Peter in these early addresses speaks of the Death of Christ, it is to give intensity and energy to the exhortation to repent. He speaks of it neither as the most wonderful and pathetic revelation of the love of God, nor as the expiation for the sins of the human race.

There are two points, however, in these addresses which require notice — the frequency and earnestness with which the Apostle declares that men may obtain the remission of sins, and the manner in which he connects this great blessing with the Lord Jesus Christ.

It does not appear that either the twelve apostles or the seventy disciples said much about the forgiveness of sins during our Lord's earthly life. They were commissioned to proclaim that the kingdom of heaven was at hand, and to charge men to repent. The promise of the remission of sins, if it formed any part of the substance of their preaching, had only a subordinate place. How was it that it assumed such prominence immediately after our Lord's Death and ascension into heaven? How was it that St. Peter, though he insisted so earnestly on the aggravations of the sin which the Jewish people had committed in crucifying Christ, never threatened them with the Divine judgments for their crime, but repeated incessantly the promise of forgiveness?

Nor does he speak of the infinite mercy of God as the ground on which they might hope for pardon. He invariably connects the remission of sins with the name of the Lord Jesus Christ — "Repent, and be baptized in the name of the Lord Jesus Christ for the remission of sins." [16] The impotent man had been made whole "by the name of Jesus Christ of Nazareth," and "there is none other name under heaven given among men, whereby we must be saved." [17] It was the plain and urgent duty of men to repent of their sins, but forgiveness is not represented as the direct result of repentance or as the immediate expression of the Divine mercy — "Through His name, whosoever believeth in Him shall receive remission of sins." [18] The spiritual order is changed. The old argument of the penitent, "Have mercy upon me, O God, according to Thy loving-kindness; according unto the multitude of Thy tender mercies blot out my transgressions," passes into a new form, and the "name" of Jesus Christ is made the solitary foundation of human hope. To St. Peter this was the fulfilment of ancient prophecy; [19] and henceforth sinful men were to rest their confidence in the power and grace of Him whom the Jews had slain and hanged on a tree, for "Him hath God exalted by His right hand to give repentance...and forgiveness of sins." [20]

These statements do not necessarily imply that by His Death the Lord Jesus Christ had atoned for human sin, but they imply that the relation between

Him and the remission of sins is absolutely unique. He has not simply made a new revelation of the mercy of God, and so strengthened the grounds of human confidence in the Divine readiness to forgive; nor has He simply originated new motives to repentance. He is the channel, and the only channel, of the Divine mercy. For the pardon of sin the faith of the human race is henceforth to rest on Him. Preaching of this kind, so far as I know, has never been associated with a theology which declares that the whole purpose of our Lord's life and sufferings was to produce a moral and spiritual impression on the nature of man. It rests upon another and wholly different conception of His work. It does not necessarily imply the theory of expiation, but it trains the soul to assume precisely that attitude in relation to Christ which the expiatory theory requires. The faith of those who believed the gospel as St. Peter preached it would receive no shock — it would be complemented and perfected — by the discovery that Christ, in whose name they trusted for the remission of sins, had atoned, by His Death, for the sins of the world.

From the early discourses of St. Peter, addressed to persons none of whom had as yet received the Christian faith, and some of whom were the bitter enemies of Christ, we turn to his great epistle, addressed to persons who were not only Christians, but who were suffering persecution for Christ's sake. The epistle is not doctrinal, but hortatory. It was written not to explain the articles of Christian belief, but to inculcate Christian duty, and to strengthen and console its readers in their earthly troubles by reminding them of the great objects of Christian hope.

The omissions of the epistle are hardly less instructive than its contents. St. Peter had been the friend and companion of Christ for three years. Many of our Lord's sayings intended to comfort the sorrowful, and especially to inspire with energy and constancy those who are "persecuted for righteousness' sake," must have been always present to his memory, and must have been the perpetual solace of his heart. He quotes none of them. The Christian people to whom he is writing appear to have been in danger of suffering the loss of all things through their fidelity to Christ. It might have assisted to reconcile them to their misfortunes to be reminded that Christ Himself was poor, and had not where to lay His head. Of the poverty of Christ St. Peter says nothing. They were in great distress, and he must have remembered innumerable scenes in our Lord's earthly history illustrating the tenderness of His sympathy — scenes which to Christian people, in every country, and through eighteen centuries, have been unfailing springs of consolation and hope, sweetening the bitterness of suffering, and sustaining faltering faith in the pity and love of God, and which have touched the hearts of innumerable men to whom the Christian faith was only a beautiful fiction; but to none of these is there any allusion. From the first line of the epistle to the last there is not a single sentence from any of our Lord's discourses, public or private: neither promise nor parable spoken by Him is once quoted. Though His resurrection is mentioned three or four times, there is not a solitary reference to

59

any of His beneficent miracles. But there are no less than eight passages in which the Apostle speaks of our Lord's blood, His Death, or His sufferings. The Spirit of Christ in the prophets "testified beforehand of the sufferings of Christ," [21] and the Apostle describes himself as "a witness of the sufferings of Christ." [22] Those to whom he is writing were "elect ...unto obedience and sprinkling of the blood of Christ." [23] They had been "redeemed... with the precious blood of Christ." [24] They are reminded that Christ "suffered for sins," and "bare our sins in His own body on the tree"; [25] that He "suffered for sins, the Just for the unjust, that He might bring us to God; being put to death in the flesh, but quickened by the Spirit." [26] They are exhorted to "arm" themselves "with the same mind" with which Christ suffered, [27] and to rejoice, inasmuch as they are "partakers of Christ's sufferings." [28] No doubt some of these references to our Lord's sufferings were suggested by the sufferings of the Christian people to whom the letter was written, and have very little if any relation to the doctrine of expiation. But it is significant that St. Peter's whole interest and thought should seem to have been concentrated on the cross and the resurrection.

This subordination — I might almost say suppression — of the ministry of Christ, this elevation of His Death and of His triumph over death into a position of supreme importance, is not peculiar to the Epistle of St. Peter; it is the common characteristic of all the epistles of the New Testament. How was it that when the Apostles were enforcing the duty of submission to human governments, they never appealed to our Lord's great saying, "Render to Caesar the things that are Caesar's, and to God the things that are God's"? How was it that they never spoke to parents of Christ's love for little children? How was it that when they charged children to obey their parents, they never enforced the precept by reminding them that Jesus Himself was "subject" to Joseph and Mary? How was it that His works of compassion, in which He seems to have found relief in His own sorrows, are never mentioned, to confirm by the force of the highest example the duty of doing good to all men? How are we to explain the almost uniform practice of the Apostles in deriving their motives to the discharge of Christian duty, their confirmations of Christian hope, their scla:e for Christian suffering, from the hours of shame and anguish in which our Lord's earthly history closed, and from His resurrection and ascension into heaven? Some explanation is indispensable if we are to reconstruct for ourselves the inner faith of the Apostles, and if we are to interpret their writings accurately. It was not the habit of the Jewish mind to dwell in this way on the death of prophets and saints. It is not the habit of men generally to be silent on the courage and sanctity and wisdom of illustrious religious reformers, and to recur perpetually to their martyrdom.

If it be answered that, on any theological theory, the Death of Christ infinitely transcends in pathos and power the death of the noblest of those who have perished through their fidelity to truth, or their zeal for the good of men, the rejoinder is obvious. His life equally transcends theirs in moral and spiritual interest as being the revelation, at once, of the character of God and of God's idea of human perfection. The question returns, How was it that St. Peter in this epistle said nothing about our Lord's life and teaching, and referred so frequently to His Death?

It also deserves notice that in the Apostle's references to the sufferings and Death of Christ in this epistle there is hardly a trace of the stern and vehement indignation with which, in his early addresses, he had denounced the crime of the crucifixion. When we do honour to the memory of martyrs, we usually condemn the cruelty and injustice of their persecutors. But St. Peter, although he speaks so often of the Death of Christ, expresses no abhorrence — expresses no censure even — of the treachery and ingratitude and malice of the Jewish nation and its rulers. The censure where it is present is only implied; it was no part of his intention to make the memory of those who committed the great offence the object of enduring hatred. In this, too, he illustrates the common spirit and habit of the writers of the New Testament. Very rarely, and even then without any passion and intensity of resentment, do any of them speak of the sin of Judas, or of the high priest, or of the people that clamoured for our Lord's blood. They trusted in the sacrifice of Christ for the remission of their own sins, and when speaking of the cross, it would have been contrary to the habit and temper which the cross encouraged, to say hard things about the sins of others. It almost appears as if the Death of Christ, which expiated before God the sins of the human race, gradually blotted from the memory even of those who loved Him best the crime of His murderers.

The epistle is addressed to Christians who are described as "the elect strangers of the dispersion," living in various countries of Western Asia. It is probable that they were principally Gentiles. If they were Jews they were no longer acknowledged by their countrymen as true children of Abraham: by their apostacy from Judaism, they were regarded as having forfeited the great prerogatives and hopes of the elect race. But to St. Peter, whether they were Jews or Gentiles, they were the heirs of all the ancient promises and the direct descendants of the ancient saints. They were "scattered abroad," and, like the patriarchs, were "strangers and pilgrims" on earth, belonging to no worldly kingdom, but citizens of a "heavenly country." Or, perhaps, and more probably, this description was suggested by the calamities which had driven a great part of the Jewish nation out of the land of their fathers. The "dispersion" was the ordinary name for those Jews who were living in heathen countries, and this is the title which St. Peter gives to the Christians "scattered throughout Pontus, Galatia, Cappadocia, Asia, and Bithynia." *They,* and not the mere descendants of Abraham, Isaac, and Jacob, according to the flesh, were the "children of God scattered abroad," who are ultimately to be brought into an eternal and glorious kingdom. For them is reserved "the inheritance incorruptible and undefiled, and that fadeth not away," [29] of which the land of promise was but a transient prophecy and symbol. They

61

were the "elect race," the "consecrated nation," the "people" that God had made in a special sense His own. [30] All the titles which the Jews had received from God were theirs, and with a nobler meaning; all the sacred institutions and prerogatives of Judaism were theirs, and in a nobler form. They were themselves the very temple of God; [31] they were priests — every one of them — and they had direct access to the Divine presence; priests belonging to a more mysterious and august line than that of Aaron, for they were a "royal priesthood," [32] uniting in themselves the double honours which priestly and regal dignities separately symbolised.

It is in harmony with all these passages that the Christian people to whom the letter is written are described as "elect according to the foreknowledge of God the Father, unto...*sprinkling of the blood of Jesus Christ.*" [33] The Jewish nation was separated from the rest of mankind, and received into a unique relationship with Jehovah at Mount Sinai, by being sprinkled with the blood of sacrifices: half of the blood was sprinkled on the altar, half of it on the people; and St. Peter says that the true elect race was separated from the rest of mankind by being sprinkled with the blood of Christ. The Death of Christ was therefore a sacrifice. What does this mean?

It may be urged that sacrificial language derived' from the institutions of Judaism is extremely uncertain in its meaning, and that it is practically unintelligible to most of us; that some learned scholars and theologians have maintained that the Jewish sacrifices were never supposed to represent the idea of expiation, and that they expressed nothing more than the complete surrender to God of the life of the persons who offered them; that however this may be, it is incredible that our apprehension of the true meaning and purpose of the Death of the Lord Jesus Christ should depend upon our being able to recover the conceptions which v/ere current among the Jewish people in the time of our Lord of the precise intention and character of their peculiar religious services which have now long become obsolete; that if instead of interpreting St. Peter's sacrificial language by the common sacrificial conceptions of his Jewish contemporaries, we are required to interpret it in the light of the original idea of the Jewish institutions, it is unreasonable to insist on our mastering a difficult and obscure province of Jewish learning before we can become simple Christian believers. Or it may be maintained that when a Christian Jew is expressing his conception of the Death of Christ in language suggested by the institutions of Judaism, it is impossible for us to distinguish with any confidence between the Idea and the form under which the Idea is presented, or to be quite sure whether he intends us to understand that all the contents of the temporary symbol reappear in the eternal fact.

Whatever force there may be in these considerations, there are other passages in this epistle to which they do not apply — passages which enable us, without any learned inquiry into the sacrificial institutions of Judaism, to determine in what sense St. Peter used sacrificial language to describe the nature and effect of our Lord's Death.

Like St. Paul, he thought it necessary to exhort slaves [34] to be obedient to their masters. The free spirit of the Christian faith made men resent servitude, and but for the earnestness with which the Apostles protested against any violent and premature attempt to break up the existing social order, might have led to all the useless horrors of a servile revolt. In appealing to them to manifest a spirit of patience and meekness, he reminds them of what Christ endured, and of how He endured it. By charging them to imitate so great an Example, he recognises and vindicates the dignity of which they were conscious, and which made them impatient of their wrongs, while he enforces the duty of submission. "If when ye do well, and suffer for it, ye take it patiently, this is acceptable with God. For even hereunto were ye called: because Christ also suffered for us, leaving us an example, that ye should follow His steps: who, when He was reviled, reviled not again; when He suffered, He threatened not; but committed Himself [rather, delivered over those who inflicted His sufferings] to Him that judgeth righteously: who His own self bare our sins in His own body on the tree, that we, being dead to sins, might live unto righteousness: by whose stripes ye were healed" [35]

What St. Peter affirms in this passage is that Christ suffered, that is, died "for" these Christian slaves. The phrase is certainly a remarkable one. It cannot have been used accidentally and without any particular meaning. It is not a phrase by which the Jewish writers were accustomed to describe the death of their prophets who had perished in the service of God and of the nation. There were martyrs and heroes in their history who "were tortured, not accepting deliverance," who had "trials of cruel mockings and scourgings, yea, moreover, of bonds and imprisonment. They were stoned, they were sawn asunder, were tempted, were slain with the sword; "but the sacred books of the Jews either pass over these sufferings and martyrdoms in silence, or mention them without any extraordinary emphasis. It is never said that any of these illustrious saints "died for" men. But the phrase is constantly used to describe the Death of our Lord. Whether it means that He died in our stead, or as our Representative, or merely, in a more general sense, on our behalf, it is not necessary, as yet, to inquire. Every one of these meanings has been found in the expression; every one of them is a fair representation of the original words when taken separately from the context in which they happen to stand. But we may be quite sure that the fact of the Atonement — if it be a fact — is neither to be established nor imperilled by controversies on the force of a Greek preposition, about whose precise value scholars can have any grave doubt. [36]

In what sense, then, does St. Peter intend to say that Christ died for us? Or, rather — for this is the more exact form of the question which the subsequent part of the passage solves — what was there in the Death of Christ which made it in any sense the words can bear a Death "for us" — a Vicarious Death, or a Representative Death, or a Death on behalf of mankind?

St. Peter appeals to our Lord's sufferings as an example of patience; but if this were all, it is difficult to understand why, like the other writers of the New Testament, he should speak of Christ's suffering, or dying, "for us," and never speak of Christ's living "for us." It, was not in His last hours alone that He translated the Divine law of human perfection into a human history. In His courage as well as in His patience, in His compassion for the sufferings of men as well as in the meekness with which He endured His own sufferings, He left us an example that we should follow His steps.

Again, if all that St. Peter meant by Christ's dying for us, was that we derive a certain religious benefit from the example of His constancy, it is curious that neither he nor any of the other Apostles speak of His having been tempted "for us" in the wilderness; or of His having agonised "for us" in Gethsemane; or of His having been homeless "for us;" or of His having wrought miracles "for us;" or of His having delivered His discourses and spoken His parables "for us." I do not mean to contend that such expressions would have been inadmissible. But they never occur; and the more earnestly it is maintained that when the Apostles speak of Christ's dying "for us," they mean nothing more than that He intended us to receive, from His voluntary submission to death, moral and spiritual advantages the same in kind as those which we receive from His teaching and His life, their non-occurrence becomes only the more remarkable and surprising.

But let the phrase Christ "suffered for us" receive any interpretation that it will bear; exclude from it if you will the remotest suggestion of the Vicarious or Representative character of His Death; and this passage still contains insoluble difficulties for those who imagine that Christ's Death was nothing more than the most illustrious of martyrdoms. For St. Peter defines the cause and describes the nature of the suffering: Christ "bare our sins in His own body on the tree." Every phrase discloses a separate element of the Apostle's conception of our Lord's Death.

"He bare our sins." No language could be less ambiguous. St. Peter was a Jew, and the meaning of the phrase was for ever fixed and determined by its use in the Jewish law. "Whoso curseth his God shall bear his sin. And he that blasphemeth the name of the Lord shall surely *be put to death*." [37] The man who without an adequate reason omitted to keep the Passover was "to be cut off from among his people: because he brought not the offering of the Lord in his appointed season, that man shall *bear his sin*." [38] The meaning of the phrase is further illustrated by the words of God to Moses, declaring that the generation which had sinned in the desert should not enter the Land of Promise. "As for you, your carcases they shall fall in this wilderness. And your children shall wander in the wilderness forty years.... After the number of the days in which ye searched the land, even forty days, each day for a year, shall ye *bear your iniquities*." [39] The expression reappears in the prophets. Ezekiel declares in God's name that if his contemporaries perished it would be for their own sins, and not for the sins of their fathers. "When the son hath done that which is lawful and right...he shall surely live. The soul that sinneth, it shall die...The son shall not *bear the iniquity* of the father, neither shall the father *bear the iniquity* of the son." [40] But what the prophet declares is not to happen between man and man, the Apostle declares has actually happened between us and Christ. "He bare our sins."

"He bare our sins *in His own body*." Had St. Peter meant that Christ "bare our sins" in the sense in which some modern theologians interpret the phrase — that He "bore them on His feeling, became inserted into their bad lot by His sympathy as a friend," [41] — why did he speak of Christ as bearing our sins "in His own body"? It would be contrary to the principles which should govern our interpretation of writings so informal as the apostolical epistles to suppose that he intended to affirm that it was in His body alone that Christ suffered for us; but it is equally contrary to the principles on which writings of any kind should be interpreted to suppose that St. Peter could have written these words had he beheved that Christ suffered for us only in His sympathies. This would be to dissolve all relations between language and thought. [42]

As if protesting unintentionally and unconsciously against the theories of later times, the Apostle adds another clause which ought to have rendered this misapprehension of his meaning impossible: "He bare our sins in His own body on the tree." [43] When we speak of a man ascending the scaffold for crimes which he has never committed, we should be astonished if any one imagined that we were thinking of the moral anguish which a good man must endure when charged with foul and shameful sins. The moral anguish may be more intolerable than the physical penalty, and when he appears on the scaffold to suffer the sentence which has been unjustly pronounced against him, the sense of his disgrace may become most vivid, and his recoil from the terrible charge which has blasted his name most violent; but if we say, without explanation, that with crimes laid upon him of which others were guilty he went up on to the scaffold, our words could never be legitimately interpreted as referring to his mental distress. Nor can it have been merely of any anguish of moral sympathy that St. Peter was thinking when he wrote that Christ "bare our sins in His own body on the tree." If that had been all, his language would have taken an altogether different form.

The force of the passage towards the close of the next chapter — "For Christ also once suffered for sins, the Just for the unjust, that He might bring us to God" [44] — cannot be fully appreciated unless we connect it with the line of thought in which it occurs. In the appeal to the sufferings of Christ which I have already discussed, it was the Apostle's direct purpose to enforce the duty of submitting patiently, as Christ submitted, to undeserved evils. Here, the direct intention is different. St. Peter is thinking now, not of the spirit in which unmerited sufferings should be endured, but of the estimate which Christian people should form of them.

He says that it is the law of the Divine government that well-doing shall be crowned with happiness. "He that will love life, and see good days, let him refrain his tongue from evil, and his lips that they speak no guile: let him eschew evil, and do good; let him seek peace, and ensue it. For the eyes of the Lord are over the righteous, and His ears are open unto their prayers: but the face of the Lord is against them that do evil. And who is he that will harm you, if ye be followers of that which is good?" [45] Under the Divine order, peace, safety, wealth, and honour are the inheritance of righteousness. But that order is disturbed, and for a time the best men may have to endure great trouble. Is this a reason for despondency? Should it discourage the endeavour to keep God's commandments? By no means. St. Peter has said that it is the Divine law that men should be the happier in every way for their righteousness; but he adds, "If ye *suffer* for righteousness' sake," still "ye are blessed. Be not afraid of their terror, neither be troubled.... It is better, if the will of God be so, that ye suffer for well doing than for evil doing." [46] He then reminds them of our Lord Himself. "For Christ also once suffered." Does the Apostle say "for *well*-doing"? This is what we should have expected; this is what the strenuous movement of his previous thought seems to render inevitable; this is what seems absolutely necessary in order to make his appeal to Christ's example effective and even pertinent; but instead of, this he says "Christ also once suffered *for sins*." It seems as though the intimate relation between our sins and Christ's sufferings had taken such complete possession of the Apostle's mind and heart, that to dissolve or suppress that relation even for a moment was impossible to him. Even when he is telling Christian people that it is better, "if the will of God be so," that they should suffer for "well-doing than for evil-doing," he cannot add, "for it was for well-doing that Christ suffered." The habit of his 'mind does not permit it; and he therefore says, "For Christ also suffered *for sins*." [47]

That St. Peter was still thinking, not of the moral anguish which came upon the soul of Christ from the depth of His sympathy with our sinful race, is evident from the words which immediately follow: "Christ also once suffered for sins,...*being put to death in the flesh*." He "suffered for sins" once, and He "suffered for sins" by dying for them.

The "sins" for which He died were not sins with which He was falsely accused by His enemies: this would have brought His death into the category of ordinary martyrdoms for righteousness' sake. We have already learnt that "He bare *our* sins in His own body on the tree;" and it is this truth that St. Peter reaffirms in another form, when, after saying, "For Christ also once suffered for sin," he adds, *"the Just for the unjust,"* He suffered for us because He suffered for our sins.

He suffered "for" us. Those who deny that His Death had anything in it of a vicarious or representative character, are in the habit of changing the preposition. They contend that the meaning of this expression and of others like it is exhausted, when "[Christ] is conceived to simply come into the corporate

66

state of evil, and bear it *with* us, faithful unto death for our recovery." [48] "Bear it *with* us." This is the very symbol of the theory which ascribes the whole power and value of the sufferings of Christ to their moral and spiritual influence on the nature of man. But this is not what St. Peter says; this is not what any of the Apostles are in the habit of saying. How is it that the New Testament writers uniformly avoid the "with" when they are speaking of Christ's sufferings in relation to human sin? They never tell us that in the greatness of His love He came to suffer with us the worst evils which had come upon the race through sin — that He suffered with us as a loyal wife might suffer exile or imprisonment with her husband, or as a philanthropist might suffer the privations and hardships of a savage race, which he could civilize only by sharing the miseries from which he had resolved to rescue them. This was not their way of thinking about the work of Christ. If it had been, it is inexplicable that they should never have expressed it, even by accident. St. Peter — and in this he represents all the Apostles — says that Christ "suffered for us," not "with us;" he does not say that He "suffered for sins, the Just *with* the unjust" — the calamities which had fallen on the guilty being shared by the Innocent; but that He "suffered,..... the Just *for* the unjust," a form of expression which suggests a very different form of thought. [49]

Christ's ultimate object was to "bring us to God." It would be perfectly consistent with the apostolic conception of our Lord's Death, if in these words St. Peter had intended to describe its effect upon our own moral and spiritual life, inspiring us with penitence for sin, and constraining us to trust in the Divine mercy, and to return to our true home in the Divine presence. But I doubt whether this would be a legitimate interpretation of his language. "That He might bring us to God" (ἵνα ἡμᾶς προσαγάγῃ τῷ Θεῷ), suggests the conferring of a new dignity and privilege, rather than the creating of a new disposition. It recalls the idea of St. Paul, in the Epistle to the Ephesians, [50] that through Christ Jew and Gentile "have access (τὴν προσαγωγὴν) to the Father," an idea expressed in another form in the Epistle to the Romans. [51] "By whom...we have access (τὴν προσαγωγὴν) into this grace wherein we stand." The guilt which hindered our access to God has been atoned for, and we are no longer excluded from the honour and blessedness of approaching Him.

Both of these passages illustrate, not only the elements which entered into St. Peter's conception of our Lord's Death, but the great place which that conception held in his religious thought. Most readers of the New Testament probably imagine that the idea of the Atonement controlled the mind of St. Paul more powerfully than the mind of St. Peter; and the whole theory of expiation is supposed by some theological writers to have been constructed by the speculative intellect of the only Apostle who had been trained in the schools of Jerusalem. St. Paul, so it is alleged, first led away the faith of the early Church from the simplicity of Christ.

Yet St. Paul could speak of the sufferings and Death of Christ as an example, without the faintest allusion to the idea of Atonement: St. Peter could not. In that noble passage in the Epistle to the Philippians, in which St. Paul is enforcing "lowliness of mind" and the duty of caring not for our own interests, but for the interests of others, he elaborately develops the successive stages of our Lord's voluntary humiliation. He was "in the form of God" and became man; and "being found in fashion as a man, He humbled Himself" still further, and descended to a lower deep than that which His assumption of humanity rendered inevitable; for He "became obedient unto death, even the death of the cross." [52] But there is not a word about His bearing our sins or suffering "for us." This fact is the more interesting because the conception of our Lord's Death as a vicarious Death, or a Death on behalf of mankind, which is vividly and repeatedly expressed in other parts of St. Paul's writings, seems to lie in the direct line of his thought. He is sustaining, by an appeal to the example of Christ, the exhortation, "Look not every man on his own things, but also on the things of others," as well as the exhortation to cultivate indifference to personal distinction and glory. He would have positively increased the energy of that appeal if He had said explicitly — what he takes for granted — that the humiliation of Christ was "for us," that He "became obedient unto death, even the death of the cross," because He was bearing our sins and achieving our redemption. And yet his mind was so filled with the thought that in His humiliation and Death Christ had left us "an example that we should follow in His steps," that he kept clear of the other purposes which Christ's sufferings accomplished.

But St. Peter, when he was speaking of Christ as an example, could not speak of Him as an example only. He seems to forget his immediate purpose; that Christ "bare our sins," that "He suffered,... the Just for the unjust," constituted no necessary part of his reference to the Death of Christ as illustrating the patience with which it is our duty to suffer wrongfully. It did not lie in his way to speak of the Death of Christ in its relation to our sins, but he cannot help turning aside. This diversion from the line in which His thought and exhortation were running is a proof that the conception of Christ's Death as a sacrifice for the sins of men had such power over his mind and heart that he could not escape from it, even when the subject on which he was writing seemed to require him to represent our Lord's sufferings only under their exemplary aspect. Had the Apostles described the Death of Christ by sacrificial language, only when they were speaking of the remission of sins, the evidence that they regarded it as a real and proper sacrifice would have been greatly diminished. It might have been alleged that, with their Jewish habits of thought, it was almost inevitable that they should connect the remission of sins with a sacrifice; but since they represent the Death of Christ as a sacrifice, even when they appeal to His patience in the endurance of suffering as an example, it is clear that the sacrificial idea was a permanent and essential element in their conception of His Death.

There is an earlier passage in the epistle in which the same characteristic of St. Peter's habit of thought is strikingly illustrated. He tells his readers that they had been "redeemed" from their "vain conversation received by tradition" from their fathers, "not with corruptible things, as silver and gold,...but with the precious blood of Christ, as of a lamb without blemish and without spot." [53] Their former life was a life of moral and spiritual slavery; the ransom by which they had been liberated was the "blood of Christ." This, it may be alleged, is mere rhetoric; and if the passage stood alone it would, no doubt, be illegitimate to insist very strongly on the analogy suggested between the Death of Christ and the price which is paid to purchase the liberty of captives. But the rhetoric is of a very singular kind. The Christian people to whom St. Peter is writing were, at least for the most part, Gentiles; [54] they had worshipped idols instead of the true God, and many of them may have lived in the immoralities of heathenism. It would have been natural to remind them that the preachers of the Christian gospel had taught them "not to think that the Godhead is like unto gold, or silver, or stone, graven by art and man's device;" or that the greatness and goodness of God had been revealed to them in the Life and Ministry of the Lord Jesus Christ; or that the nobler morality and glorious hopes of the new Faith had kindled their imagination, won the homage of their conscience, and touched their hearts; or that they had been filled with fear by what they heard about the wrath to come; or that the power of the Holy Ghost had constrained them to repent of their old sins, and to turn from idols, to serve the living and true God. Language of this kind would represent our own way of thinking about the rescue of heathen people from heathenism. But St. Peter's thought took another form. They had been delivered by a sacrifice. "The blood of Christ" — not the revelation of new truth concerning God, not the gracious aspects of the gospel to the poor and the sorrowful, not the promises of pardon to the sinful and of strength to the morally weak, not the assurances of a blessed immortality — but "the blood of Christ," had accomplished their deliverance. But for this, no message of peace would have come to them from the God against whom they had revolted. But for this, they would have received no revelation of His glory, and would have been left to perish in their heathenism. But for this, the darkness which had descended on the heathen world as the penalty of sin would have become perpetually deeper as the result of persistence in sin. But for this, the force of their old and evil life would never have been broken. But for this, the power of the Holy Ghost would never have come upon them. They had been delivered from their old heathen life because Christ had atoned for their old heathen sins.

The passage is very remarkable. St. Peter is speaking of a great subjective change through which these Christian people had passed, a change in their faith, a change in their morality; but he omits to recognise both the human agencies and the supernatural spiritual forces which had prevailed upon them to renounce heathenism and to become Christians, and he ascribes their emancipation from their former sins and superstitions to the sacrifice which has created new relations between man and God. [55] It is sometimes charged against evangelical theologians, that even if the idea of Atonement is true, they have given it a supremacy which it has no right to claim. We can shelter ourselves under the authority and example of the Apostle. It would be difficult to produce from the writings of any of the modern representatives of evangelical theology a passage like this.

We can understand now why it was that St. Peter thought of Christian believers as an elect race separated from the rest of mankind by the "sprinkling of the blood of Christ;" [56] why it was that when he spoke of the prophets inquiring and searching diligently "who prophesied of the grace that should come" to men in the last days, he added, "searching what or what manner of time the Spirit of Christ which was in them did signify when it testified beforehand the *sufferings* of Christ;" [57] and why he describes himself as "a witness" of those sufferings. [58] To him the death of Christ was the sacrifice for the sins of the world.

The frequent recurrence of this conception of our Lord's Death in the epistle is remarkable, because it seems to have been no part of the Apostle's immediate purpose to strengthen the faith of his readers in the Divine mercy for the remission of sins. From the beginning of the epistle to the end, his constant endeavour is to confirm their hope of immortal glory, to console them in their temporal sufferings, and to stimulate them to the imitation of Christ's example. That he believed that the Death of Christ is rich in motives to Christian holiness, is obvious from passage after passage in which it is made the ground of his practical exhortations. That he also believed that the ultimate design of the Death of Christ is to secure our perfect sanctification, is equally obvious. But how is it that when he appeals to the sufferings of Christ as an argument for Christian virtue, he says that Christ suffered for our sins? How is it that he could not bring himself to say that Christ suffered for our righteousness? The expression would not have been an unnatural one. We speak of men suffering for the freedom of their country, and St. Peter might have spoken of Christ suffering for the righteousness of the Church. But this would have been foreign to his habitual conception of our Lord's Death. Christ suffered for our righteousness by suffering for our sins. Our sins were the immediate cause of His Death, our sanctification was to be one of its ultimate effects.

That St. Peter had a larger knowledge of the transcendent significance of the Death of Christ when he wrote his epistle than when he delivered the discourses contained in the .early chapters of the Acts of the Apostles, can hardly be doubted. Whatever measure of supernatural light came to him on the day of Pentecost, it cannot be imagined that he at once appropriated the whole contents of the Christian revelation; and that neither the sorrows, the sins, the joys and the triumphs of his personal life, during subsequent years, nor his apostolic activity, nor the light of God which is the permanent home of all that are in Christ, did nothing to enrich and strengthen his original idea of the Christian redemption. But he knew from the first that the blood of Christ was shed for the remission of sins, and although he was silent about this great truth in the discourses recorded by St. Luke, he uniformly insisted on that kind of faith in Christ of which this truth is the complete vindication.

The theology of the epistle explains the practical exhortations of the discourses. In Jerusalem, a few weeks after the crucifixion, he had said that the Messiah had been given over "by the determinate counsel and fore-knowledge of God" to the "wicked hands" of men, to be "crucified and slain." [59] They "slew [Him] and hanged [Him] on a tree." [60] In the epistle, he explains why God surrendered the Christ to the power of His enemies; "He bare our sins in His own body on the tree:" [61] and this was the reason of another fact which he had also declared to the Jewish Council — that having been exalted to the right hand of God, Christ had power "to give... remission of sins." [62] To the Jewish rulers St. Peter declared that "there is none other name under heaven given among men, whereby we must be saved," than the name of Jesus Christ of Nazareth, whom they had crucified; [63] — yes, the Jewish rulers themselves could receive salvation only through Him who had been the Victim of their violence and wickedness. The reason is given in the epistle: Christ had "suffered for sins, the Just for the unjust, that He might bring" — them, as well as the rest of mankind — "to God." [64] "To Him," said Peter, addressing Cornelius, "give all the prophets witness, that through His name, whosoever believeth in Him shall receive remission of sins." [65] And according to the epistle, when the prophets predicted the salvation which had at last come to men through Christ, "the Spirit of Christ which was in them" bore testimony to "the sufferings of Christ," as well as to "the glory that should follow." [66]

It is clear that to the very last St. Peter, though a Christian Apostle, was still a Jew. He had soon learnt that the Gentiles were to be admitted to the kingdom of heaven without being required to submit to circumcision and to keep the Mosaic law, but his imagination was always filled with the ancient glories of his race. The wonderful deliverances which God had wrought for them, the sanctity and majesty of the Temple, the sacred functions of the priesthood, the mystery of sacrifice — all these had entered into the very substance of his moral and religious life. He could not escape from their spell. He did not try to escape. They were all transfigured and glorified by the energy of his Christian faith, and they supplied the intellectual forms under which he conceived, and the language in which he expressed, the blessings and prerogatives which are the inheritance of the Church.

He was a Jew for another reason. He was still under the power of the characteristic spirit of his race. By a history of unprecedented glory and of unprecedented suffering — a history which fulfilled and yet defeated the expectations created by those great promises which were their richest inheritance, they had been disciplined to an invincible confidence in their national future. The Paradise described in the earliest pages of their sacred books never seems to have touched the imagination of their poets: throughout their whole literature there is nothing like pathetic regret for its vanished innocence and peace. For Jewish poets, the golden age was in the Future. It was to come with the Christ whose power and righteousness and gentleness were to redress all wrongs, relieve all sorrows, and bring to those over whom He reigned perpetual security, honour, and blessedness. Theirs was a religion of hope.

And St. Peter is the Apostle of Hope, as St. Paul is the Apostle of Faith, and St. John the Apostle of Charity. He is eager for "the inheritance incorruptible and undefiled, and that fadeth not away;" for "the salvation ready to be revealed in the last time;" for "the appearing of Jesus Christ." Like all his race, His eye is on the Future, not on the Past; and to him the gospel seems rather a promise than a history. But with all this, the sufferings of Christ are never forgotten. The sins which exiled us from God, Christ "bare in His own body on the tree, that we being dead to sins should live unto righteousness;" and the glory which will fulfil the new hope which has come to us through Christ's resurrection is inseparably and eternally associated with His Death on the cross.

Throughout the history of the Church no other theory of the Death of Christ than that which represents it as an expiation for the sins of the world has ever given it the same supreme place in the religious thought and life of Christian men. It is among those, and only among those, who have accepted this theory, that we find the apostolic feeling about the Death of Christ. It is reasonable to infer that, substantially, they inherit the apostolic faith.

[1] *Studies of Christianity,* pp. 186-188.

[2] *Studies of Christianity,* pp. 188.

[3] Luke xxiv. 47.

[4] Acts ii. 22; x. 38.

[5] Ibid. ii. 30-36; iii. 13, 22-26; iv. 10; v. 31; x. 43.

[6] Ibid. ii. 23; iii. 14, 15; iv. 10; v. 30; x. 39.

[7] Ibid. ii. 24, 32; iii 15; iv. 10; v. 31; x 40.

[8] Acts ii. 33; iii. 21; v. 31; x. 42.

[9] Ibid. ii. 38; iii. 19, 23; v. 11, 12; x. 42, 43.

[10] Ibid. ii. 38; iii. 19; v. 31, 32; x. 42, 43.

[11] Ibid. ii. 38; iv. 12; x. 43.

[12] *The Life and Light of Men,* pp. 349-351.

[13] Acts ii. 23.

[14] *The Life and Light of Men,* p. 43.

[15] Ibid, p. 156.

[16] Acts ii. 38.

[17] Ibid. iv. 12.

[18] Ibid. x. 43.

[19] Ibid. x. 43.

[20] Ibid. v. 31.

[21] Pet. i. 11.

[22] Ibid. v. 1.

[23] Ibid. i. 2.

[24] Ibid. i. 19.

[25] Ibid. ii. 21-24.

[26] Ibid. iii. 17.

[27] Ibid. iv. 1.

[28] Ibid. iv. 12.

[29] I Pet. i. 4.

[30] Ibid. ii. 9.

[31] Ibid. ii. 4.

[32] Ibid. ii. 5.

[33] Ibid. i. 2.

[34] I Pet. ii. 18. The word which St. Peter uses (ὀικέται) does not necessarily denote that the persons addressed were slaves. It is a milder term than that which is usually employed for that purpose; but the context shows that their position was really that of slavery.

[35] I Pet. ii. 20-24.

[36] Note H.
[37] Lev. xxiv. 16.
[38] Num. ix. 13.
[39] Ibid. xiv. 32, 34.
[40] Ezek. xviii. 19, 20.
[41] Bushnell: *Vicarious Sacrifice*, p. 9.
[42] See *British Quarterly Review*, October, 1866. Pp. 430-435.
[43] "Vix uno verbo ἔμφασις vocis ἀναφέρειν exprimi potest. Nota *ferre* et *offerre*. Primo dicere voluit Petrus, Christum portasse peccata nostra, in quantum ilia ipsi erant imposita. Secundo, ita tulisse peccata nostra, ut ea secum obtulerit in altari. Respicit ad auimantes, quibus peccata primo imponebantur, quique deinceps peccatis onusti offerebantur. Sed in quam aram? ξύλον ait Petrus, lignum, h.e. crucem."— Vitringa: quoted by Alford in loc.
[44] I Pet. iii. 18.
[45] Ibid. iii. 10-13.
[46] I Pet. iii. 14-17.
[47] Note I.
[48] Bushnell: *Vicarious Sacrifice*, p. 442. The words quoted are a comment on Gal. iii. 13, Christ is "made a curse for us."
[49] We are said to suffer with Christ, to be crucified with Him; but Christ is never said to suffer with us.
[50] Ephes. ii. 18.
[51] Rom. v. 2.
[52] Phil. ii. 6-8.
[53] I Pet. i. 18, 19.
[54] If, as some maintain, they were Jews, and if the "vain conversation" from which they had been "redeemed" consisted in Jewish formalism and a reliance on their faithful observance of the external precepts of the ancient faith, and on their loyalty to the traditions of their fathers, the force of the argument in the text is not diminished.
[55] Note J.
[56] I Pet. i. 2.
[57] Ibid. i. 11. More accurately, "the sufferings *destined* or *appointed* to Christ."
[58] I Pet. v. 1.
[59] Acts ii. 23.
[60] Ibid v. 30.
[61] 1 Pet. ii. 24.
[62] Acts v. 30, 31.
[63] Ibid. iv. 12.
[64] 1 Pet. iv. 18.
[65] Acts x. 45.
[66] 1 Pet. i. 11.

# Lecture Five - The Fact of the Atonement: The Testimony of St. John and St. James

In St. Paul's account of his memorable conference with the Apostles at Jerusalem, after the close of his first great missionary journey, he appears to divide the work of evangelising the world between St. Peter and himself. He and St. Peter are, at least, the acknowledged leaders and representatives of the whole movement. [1] For St. John, "the disciple whom Jesus loved," who, in the energy of his moral nature and in the depth of his devotion to his Lord, equalled, if he did not surpass, all his brethren, there seems to be left only a subordinate place.

But if St. Peter was the Apostle of the circumcision, and St. Paul the Apostle of the Gentiles, St. John may, perhaps, be justly called the Apostle of the Christian Church. Apart from the very uncertain tradition that he preached the gospel among the Parthians, there is no reason to suppose that any considerable part of his life was devoted to the conversion either of Gentiles or of Jews. The contrast between the Fourth Gospel and the first three suggests

73

the true character of his work. The Gospels of St. Matthew, St. Mark, and St. Luke appear to preserve those discourses and parables of our Lord, and those passages of His history, which were perpetually repeated by the early Christian preachers when addressing persons who had not yet acknowledged His authority, or who, having submitted to baptism and entered the Church, required further instruction in the elementary facts and principles of the Christian faith. It is quite clear that the Gospel of St. John was written for those who had long been Christians. His catholic epistle has the same character. The readers for whom it was written must either have been born of Christian parents, or if they were heathens or Jews by birth, must have lived so long in the atmosphere of the Church, as to have lost almost all traces of their earlier habits of life and thought. It was not necessary to confirm them in their renunciation of Judaism, or to warn them against continuing in the practice of those coarse vices into which converts from heathenism were in constant danger of relapsing.

Nor was the strength of St. John given, like St. Paul's, to the vindication of Christian truth against heresies which were possible only in the earliest days of the Church, and which were soon to become obsolete. Here and there we may detect the expression of St. John's antagonism to speculations — vague and chaotic in his time — which, in the next century, were developed into Gnosticism; but commonly his mind moves in calm and lofty regions of truth, remote from the agitation of transient controversies. To a thoughtful person living at the close of the first century, St. John, of all the Apostles, would have seemed to be the one whose teaching was likely most powerfully to control the movement of Christian speculation, and to determine both the form and the substance of the theology of the Church.

But M. Reuss hardly exaggerates the truth when he says that St. John has been neglected by those who have organised the dogmatic thought of Christendom; that his characteristic theology, happily for itself, has never been embodied in the systems and creeds of ecclesiastical orthodoxy. "It has retained its virgin purity untouched by the scholasticism of the schools, and has thus escaped the unhappy *mésalliance* which has done such deep injury to the theology of St. Paul." [2] The fortunes of St. John might have been different had not the theological development of the Eastern Church been prematurely arrested. In the West, for reasons which it is not difficult to discover, the supremacy of St. Paul has been almost unbroken from the days of Augustine to our own.

Among many of those who reject the idea of the Atonement, there is a strong desire to assert for St. John his rightful position. It seems to them that he is the representative of a nobler and more spiritual type of the Christian Faith than that which appears in the writings of the Apostle of the Gentiles. Those who contend that "the true Christian knows no covenant or mediation with God, but only the old, eternal, and unchangeable relation, that in Him we live and move and have our being," are in the habit of thinking that their faith

74

is the faith of St. John. [3] That God is life and light and love; that in Christ humanity achieved its ideal unity with the life of God; and that the Christian redemption consists in the final restoration of mankind to union with God in Christ — these it is alleged are the ideas which constitute the substance of Christianity as conceived by "the disciple whom Jesus loved," and they ought to displace the theories of Divine justice, and of expiation, and of an unreal and technical forgiveness of sins, which the Church has built up on the teaching of St. Paul.

It is true no doubt, and should be cordially acknowledged, that Mysticism, which in every age of the Church, and especially in times of general corruption, has had so strong an attraction for the purest and most saintly souls, can place its devotional books — if the perfect and unearthly beauty of very many of them needs any apostolic sanction — under the shelter of the great name of St. John. Even Pantheism, so long as it affirms the reality of sin and the eternal obligation of the Moral Law — if any philosophy which fulfils these conditions can be called Pantheistic — may vindicate its right to recognition as a form of speculation not altogether alien from the Christian faith by an appeal to the same authority. With still greater reason may those theologians claim to be the representatives and guardians of one of the principal elements of St. John's teaching, to whom the Incarnation is the fulfilment of the Divine idea of human nature, and the assurance and the prophecy to those who are in Christ of their eternal fellowship with the life of God.

For all Christian mystics, therefore, and for all who maintain that the Incarnation is the fundamental truth of the Christian revelation, but who on moral and spiritual grounds are hostile to the idea of Atonement, the appeal to the authority of St. John is critical. It must, I think, be admitted that when he wrote his Gospel and his Epistle he had passed altogether out of the atmosphere of Judaism. [4] His thought had taken new forms, and he had learnt to speak a new language. If in both his language and his thought we think we can discern the influence of contemporaneous speculation, there is no reason to suppose that this influence was friendly to the idea of an objective Atonement. It is infinitely improbable that this idea can receive any sanction from the writings of St. John's maturer years, if it is really alien to the Christian faith, inconsistent with the deeper and more spiritual elements of our Lord's teaching, the creation of a formal and legal theory of God's relations to the moral universe, or the result of a determination to preserve in Christianity the rudimentary conceptions and language of Judaism.

It is confessed by those who oppose the doctrine of the Atonement, that St. John is the representative of the highest and most spiritual form of Christian thought. Those conceptions of God which are alleged to be irreconcilable with any theory affirming the necessity or possibility of any other reason for the exercise of the Divine mercy in the forgiveness of sin than the repentance of the sinner himself; those conceptions of the Lord Jesus Christ and of His eternal relations to mankind which are alleged to be obscured and even contradicted by the doctrine of an objective Atonement, whatever form the doctrine may assume; those conceptions of the true nature of the Christian Redemption which it is alleged can never find any adequate expression in a theology which rests on the idea that the Death of Christ was intended to meet any necessities of the Divine nature or government, instead of being intended to act as a great spiritual force on the spiritual nature of man — all these are the very substance and life of St. John's theology. But, like St. Peter, he insists on the exceptional and supreme significance of our Lord's Death. It is "the blood of Jesus Christ" which "cleanseth us from all sin." [5] We come to know the real nature of love in the Death of Christ, for "He laid down His life for us." [6]

If it is urged that by the cleansing from sin in the first of these passages is meant our moral purification only, and that the removal of our guilt is not included, except as the result of deliverance from sin, it is at least remarkable that St. John should have attributed the sanctifying power of Christ exclusively to His Death — not to His teaching, not to the manifestation of the Eternal Life through the whole of His earthly ministry, not to the direct action of the Holy Spirit on the hearts of those who believe. How are we to explain this reference to "the blood of Jesus Christ"?

The line of thought in which it occurs greatly augments its significance. St. John has been speaking of the fellowship of Christian people with the Father and the Son. "God is light, and in Him is no darkness at all. If we say that we have fellowship with Him, and walk in darkness, we lie, and do not the truth. But if we walk in the light, as He is in the light, we have fellowship one with another, and" — what? Does he add that the light in which God dwells, and in which we dwell with Him, so fills and penetrates and transfigures our whole nature, that we sin no more? or that through our fellowship with God His life becomes ours, and that therefore we are delivered from all sin? This was what might have been expected, and the sudden transition from the high transcendental conception of the believer's present relation to God to "the blood of Christ," is startling even to those who habitually think of His Death as the great crisis in the history of the human race. But if St. John wished to speak, not merely of the sanctification of those who "walk in the light," but also of the remission of the sins into which they may be still betrayed, the transition is explained. Even for those who have "fellowship" with God the expiatory power of the Death of Christ continues necessary, for they are not yet beyond the reach of temptation or the possibility of sin. [7]

There are two other passages which are inconsistent with the theory that we receive the remission of sins through Christ only indirectly, and because He delivers us from the power of sin. "I write unto you, little children, because your sins are forgiven you for His name's sake." [8] This clearly implies that there is some objective ground in Christ for the forgiveness of sin. The Divine forgiveness is not the simple and immediate response of Infinite Mercy to human penitence, nor is the sole function of Christ so to reveal God as to awaken faith in the Divine love, sorrow for sin, and a desire for restoration to holiness and to the blessedness of the Divine presence. When these moral and spiritual effects have been produced by Christ's appeal to the conscience and the heart, when sin is confessed, and the troubled soul clings to the mercy of God for salvation, its "sins are forgiven...for *His name's sake.*"

The same idea of a direct relation between the Lord Jesus Christ and the forgiveness of sin is contained in an earlier passage in the same chapter: "My little children, these things write I unto you that ye sin not. And if any man sin, we have an Advocate (παράκλητον) with the Father, Jesus Christ, the righteous" [9] An Advocate with the Father! One whom we may call to our help, who will come forward as our Representative and Patron, to plead our cause! [10] These are not the words of a morbid and gloomy fanatic, to whom the infinitely merciful Father seems a revengeful assertor of personal rights, a stern and unrelenting and terrible Divinity, whose pity and compassion are inaccessible to the tears and prayers of those who have offended Him, and whose blind wrath must be placated first by the blood and then by the intercession of a Mediator. Nor are they the words of a mechanical and unimaginative theologian, to whom the rigid forms under which human tribunals administer an imperfect justice are an adequate representation of the order of the Divine government, and who therefore could conceive of no relaxation or remission of the sentence pronounced on an offender, apart from a legal argument addressed to the Judge, demonstrating that the honour of the Law had been sufficiently vindicated, and the claims of Justice satisfied. They are the words of the most Christian of the Christian Apostles, of the one Apostle who had most completely escaped from the spirit of Judaism, which, it is alleged, had represented God as agitated by the most violent and turbulent of human passions. Nor in escaping from Judaism had he become a Roman, with hard and severe conceptions of law, which he transferred to his theology. Whatever new elements or forms of thought are found in his epistle, beyond those which bear witness to the exceptional intimacy of his communion with his Master, have some kinship to speculations in which the most imaginative philosophy of Asia was blended with the loftiest and most spiritual philosophy of Greece. It is St. John, — the very Apostle of Love, it is St. John who in one brief sentence — "God is love" — has translated into human language all that human language can express of what the Eternal Word revealed of God in a life of transcendent beauty and beneficence; it is St. John who, in the presence of Infinite Love, gives courage and hope to the penitent by saying, "We have an Advocate with the Father." Let these words mean what they will, they are plainly intended to train the soul to a faith in Christ of precisely that kind which the theory of expiation vindicates, but which the "moral theory" of the Atonement excludes. Christ, in some sense, appeals to God for us, and not merely to us for God. He is the life of our holiness, but there is also some power or virtue in Him which, if it is to be known and described by its effects, must be spoken of as a reason or ground on which God forgives us our sins.

What this power or virtue is, St. John describes in the next sentence: "He is the Propitiation for our sins, and not for ours only, but also for the sins of the whole world." [11]

It has been contended that while the pagan meaning of this word is undoubted, and that while it was constantly used by pagan writers to mark the supposed effect of sacrifices, in propitiating the gods to whom they were offered, the Jewish translators of the Hebrew Scriptures into Greek used the word in a widely different sense, and that while the New Testament writers used the accepted sacrificial word they did not use it in the accepted meaning.

"That meaning," says Dr. Young, "as accepted by the pagan world, was throughout an utter falsity. They were no gods to whom the pagan sacrifices were offered; the anger which it was sought to appease by means of these sacrifices was all unreal, and the appeasing effect was mere delusion. But the Apostles of Christianity had something real and true and great to announce in the room of the falsities and fancies of paganism. There was a real God, a real hatred of sin, but at the same time a real and infinite love of the human soul. There was also a real 'propitiation' but immeasurably far away from that which the bewildered pagan mind had pictured. [12]

"A real Propitiation, but immeasurably far away from that which the bewildered pagan mind had pictured." Granted. In what then did it consist?

"Instead of the fiction of an incensed Jupiter or Pluto, there was seen on earth the image of the brightness of the God of love. Christ came not to appease anger, for it was owing solely to the unprompted and unbounded mercy of the Father that He ever lived, and that at last He died on a cross, but to be the wondrous medium of reconciling and restoring human hearts to Him from whom they had revolted. Incarnate love — bleeding, dying love — is the power whereby God is recovering the world to Himself." [13]

This is as true as it is forcible and eloquent; but is this a description of a "real Propitiation"? The idea of Propitiation, whether among Pagans or Jews, is precisely inverted. Neither Pagans nor Jews ever spoke of a "Propitiation for sins" when they intended to speak of that which changed the disposition of the sinner. The pagan sense of the term is admitted: "to offer a propitiation," was to appease by sacrifice or prayer the anger of imaginary gods. The Jewish sense of the term is equally definite. Not a solitary instance can be alleged in which to propitiate, or any of its derivatives, when used in relation to the restoration of kindly relations between man and man, denotes that by which a change is produced in the disposition of a person who has committed an offence; it always refers to that which changes the disposition of the person who has been offended; and when used in relation to offences against the Divine law, it always describes the means by which the sin was supposed to be covered in order that the Divine forgiveness might be secured. [14] To suggest that St. John could have used the word in order to describe the glorious power of Christ over the heart of a sinner, is to invert the fundamental idea which the word uniformly conveyed, and to violate the most obvious principles by which language should be interpreted.

It is true that "Propitiation" was one thing to a Pagan, another thing to a devout Jew, and another thing to a Christian Apostle. It is equally true that "sin" was one thing to a Pagan, another thing to a devout Jew, and another thing to a Christian Apostle; but are we at liberty to argue from this that the word which had been used by Pagan and Jew to denote sin may, perhaps, be used by an Apostle to denote righteousness? Apart from the most decisive evidence of a change of use, would it be legitimate to suppose that the original meaning of the word had been absolutely reversed? It is equally illegitimate to suppose that the word which had been used both by Pagan and Jew to denote the means of appeasing Divine anger, or averting a Divine penalty, is used by an Apostle to denote the means by which God reconciles and restores human hearts to Himself. To establish such a change of meaning, the strongest evidence must be demanded, and no such evidence has been produced.

It is necessary, no doubt, to avoid that "hard-favoured narrow literalism that lives on proof-texts made by paying no regard to the poetic genius of religious language, and by seizing on single clauses that, in figure, seem to favour a certain point, paying no regard to other clauses in other figures, that require to be accepted as qualifiers and correctives;" and it is true that "we have no literal language for religious ideas." [15] But it is also true, and many of those who find it so difficult to recognise any expiatory character in the Death of Christ are the last to deny it, that man was made in the image of God, and that there are deep analogies between the relations of men to each other and their relations to Him. Hence the language which conveys our own moral ideas is not a vehicle altogether unsuitable for the higher service of conveying the thoughts of God; and the terms by which our own moral acts are described may serve to describe the acts of God. The language we use is not "literal" when we speak of God as drawing near to man, stretching out His hand to help us, listening to our prayers; but the expressions are not only sufficiently vivid for the imagination, and sufficiently accurate for the logical understanding, but sufficiently true for the higher reason which alone is directly conversant with religious ideas. They are the creation of that "poetic genius" which has created the language of the affections as well as of religion, of philosophy as well as of faith, — touching and etherealising words of mean, material, and sensuous origin, so as to fit them for the regal uses of the intellect and the heart, translating them from their native home among things seen and temporal, and making them citizens of the kingdom of heaven. But there is nothing capricious in the process by which these transformations are accomplished. The words are sown in corruption, and raised in incorruption; sown in dishonour, raised in glory; sown in weakness, raised in power; but through all changes the outlines of their original form remain, and their identity is preserved.

The "poetic genius of religious language" could not be pleaded as a reason for suggesting that perhaps we mean the same thing when we say that God forgives and when we say that God punishes; when we speak of God being moved to mercy, and when we speak of the soul being moved to penitence. Nor can it be pleaded as a reason for alleging that when Christ is described as a Propitiation for our sins, it may mean that He inclines us to forsake them, and so effects our reconciliation to God. As a Propitiation, His face is turned towards God, not towards man. Propitiation is the immediate antecedent — I will not say the indispensable condition — -of the Divine forgiveness. It is directly related to the function of the Lord Jesus Christ as our "Advocate with the Father," whatever other relation it may have to His function as the Living Word in whom the authority and love of God plead with the heart and conscience of mankind.

Are we then to infer that because St. John uses this word "Propitiation," he believed that there was resentment in the heart of God, like that which the heathen attributed to their divinities, and which they endeavoured to allay by prayers and sacrifices? Must we not take off what Dr. Bushnell describes as "the pagan colour of the word," before it is capable of Christian uses? "Take off the pagan colour?" — Yes; but leave some trace of its original form and power. The "pagan colour" had, in fact, been taken off by the almost uniform use of the word in the Greek translation of the Old Testament. It was contrary to the Jewish habit of thought to speak of "propitiating God," either by prayers or sacrifices, as Jacob propitiated or "appeased" Esau with the present of camels and goats, and sheep and cattle. [16] The heathen "propitiated" their gods, for their gods were capricious and revengeful; but with all the anthropomorphism of Judaism, something restrained the Jews from describing any religious acts as being intended to propitiate Jehovah. Propitiation is spoken of in page after page of the Old Testament; it is expressly represented as having a relation to God, and its purpose is to turn away the wrath of God; and yet God is never, except in one passage, [17] the direct object of the act. When any of the external and ceremonial precepts of the law had been broken, it is not said that the priest is to celebrate an expiatory rite in order to "propitiate God," but in order to make propitiation for the offence or for the offender. These are the uniform expressions. And when sins were committed for which the law provided no expiation, and the anger of the Lord "waxed hot" against the whole people, the same expression reoccurs. "Ye have sinned a great sin," said Moses to the people after they had worshipped the golden calf, "and now I will go up unto the Lord; peradventure I shall make an atonement [or propitiation] for your sin." [18] Though the terrible words were still in his ears, "Let Me alone, that My wrath may wax hot against them, and that I may consume them," [19] he does not say, "Peradventure I shall propitiate God," but, "Peradventure I shall make propitiation for your sin."

The Jews never attributed to Jehovah the unreasoning and unreasonable passion which was ascribed to heathen deities. In Him there is never any causeless anger to propitiate; and, therefore, it was their habit when they spoke of Propitiation to describe it as Propitiation for sin; the justice of the Divine displeasure was always and explicitly acknowledged. The "pagan colour" of the word had already disappeared. If any stain was left, it was completely removed by St. John himself. Christ is indeed our "Advocate with the Father" and "the Propitiation for our sins;" but this is not because the Father is reluctant to forgive and to save us. The Advocate is of the Father's own appointment; the Propitiation is the Father's own provision. "Herein is love, not that we loved God, but that He loved us, and sent His Son" — at the impulse of His own infinite mercy — "to be the Propitiation for our sins." [20]

The argument of this Lecture might be strengthened by adducing those passages from St. John's Gospel in which our Lord speaks of the relation between His Death and human salvation, — passages which are as numerous in the Fourth Gospel as in the first three, and which while of supreme importance as evidence of our Lord's own teaching, are available as illustrations of the theology of the Evangelist himself. But this would be to go over ground which we have gone over already. There is, however, one remarkable passage in which St. John speaks in his own name.

The resurrection of Lazarus had made the claims of Christ more formidable than ever to those who had resolved to reject Him. It was a great and startling miracle. It was wrought in the immediate neighbourhood of Jerusalem, and within a few weeks Jerusalem would be filled with a vast and ungovernable multitude from all parts of the land and from remote countries. This last miracle of the Nazarene teacher would be certain to create universal excitement. It would be talked about in the streets of the city, and in the courts of the temple, and on the house-tops, and in every chamber where the Passover would be celebrated. Innumerable friends of Jesus from the towns and villages of Galilee, and large numbers of foreign Jews, would be certain to cross Olivet to Bethany, to see Lazarus. Jesus Himself, who at former feasts had spoken openly and without fear to great crowds in the Temple, would probably appear there again, and He would have larger crowds than ever to listen to Him. The man whom He had raised from the dead might be with Him. It was impossible to tell what might happen.

And so the chief priests and Pharisees gathered a council, and said, "What do we? for this man doeth many miracles. If we let Him thus alone, all men will believe on Him; and the Romans will come and take away our place and nation. And one of them, named Caiaphas, being the high priest that same year, said unto them. Ye know nothing at all, nor consider that it is expedient for us that one man should die for the people, and that the whole nation perish not." [21] In these words the Evangelist recognized a prophecy declaring the true significance and purpose of the Death of Christ.

If any one cares to suggest that to find a prophecy in the words of such a man as Caiaphas, and at the very moment that he was counselling a selfish and atrocious crime, is evidence of an unspiritual and mechanical conception of Divine inspiration, and proves that St. John must have been under the control of a very unintelligent and superstitious reverence for the chief priest of his race, it is unnecessary for the purposes of this argument to offer any reply. What we are immediately concerned with is St. John's conception of the Death of Christ, and of this the passage is conclusive evidence. Nor would any lingering superstition about the sanctity of the High Priest, or about the Divine significance of words uttered by men invested with sacerdotal authority, invalidate his testimony to the teaching of his Master. The "beloved disciple" might not be emancipated from all the traditions of his country and his age, and he would yet be a trustworthy witness to what Christ had taught on so great a subject as the purpose of His sufferings and Death.

But he requires no apology. From the time the law was given on Sinai, that system of ceremonial worship of which the High Priest was the centre had been the divinely appointed organ and discipline of the religious life of the Jewish people. The High Priest was at once the representative of the nation in the presence of God, and the representative of God to the nation. He, and he alone, had access to that mysterious sanctuary which was made awful by the visible symbol of the Divine Glory. Through him, in periods of national perplexity and peril, Divine oracles had spoken. Around him gathered, in these last and evil times, all the sacred and historic glories of the elect race. Moses had gone, and left no successor. The kings had gone. The prophets had gone. The High Priest remained, the heir of sixteen centuries of wonder and hope, and mystery and glory.

Not yet had he ceased to be "the Lord's anointed;" not yet had the temple in which he ministered, and its altars and sacrifices and festivals, lost the sanctity they derived from their original institution.

But the hour was approaching when his dignity and power were to pass away for ever. The sacred and venerable system over which he ruled, established by the authority of God, was on the eve of dissolution; soon the incense and the sacrifices would cease to be acceptable offerings, and the priests would be dismissed from their service as the consecrated ministers of the Most High. In a few hours the veil of the temple was to be rent by an invisible hand, and Jerusalem would no longer be "the place where men ought to worship." And when the catastrophe was near, in the very hour when the deed was plotted which made it irrevocable, Caiaphas, the representative of all the sacred traditions of Judaism, was compelled — so at least it seemed to St. John — to bear a final testimony to that great truth for the disclosure of which Judaism had been a protracted discipline and preparation. He did not mean it, but he was still High Priest, and there came upon him, in the very crisis of his guilt, the power which had rested on his predecessors in happier days, and the words in which he counselled the most awful of crimes became a prophecy — the last of the prophecies which came through the lips of a descendant of Aaron — the last and also the greatest. He "spake not of himself, but being high priest that year, he prophesied that Jesus should die for that nation: and not for that nation only, but that also He should gather together in one the children of God that were scattered abroad." [22] The ancient light and glory, long obscured, gleamed forth for a moment in the deepening darkness, and then it was extinguished for ever.

"The kingdom of heaven" came at last. The Prince, whose greatness and majesty had been seen afar off by prophets and psalmists, was enthroned at the right hand of God; He received the heathen as His inheritance, and the uttermost parts of the earth as His possession. The wider realms over which He had come to reign were to be governed by nobler laws than those which had regulated the life of the Jewish people, and God was now nearer to man than when He had commanded Moses to erect the Tabernacle in the desert, and when He had filled the Temple of Solomon with His glory.

But it was not at once that even those who believed in the Messiahship of the Lord Jesus discovered that the old order had vanished and given place to a new. The sun had gone down, but the light still lingered on the sacred hills which had been for so many generations the centre of the faith and hope and joy of saints; and long after the authority of the ancient institutions had passed away, Jewish Christians continued to venerate and to practise the customs of their fathers. As might have been expected, it was in the Church at Jerusalem that the traditions of Judaism had the greatest power. Twenty years after the Ascension, a strong party in that Church insisted on the necessity of requiring even Gentile converts to submit to circumcision. [23] Eight or nine years later there were "many thousands" of those who believed who were still "zealous of the law." [24]

Of the Church at Jerusalem, St. James, "the Lord's brother," was the recognized ruler. To what extent he continued to conform to the law of Moses, is uncertain; but it is extremely improbable that there was anything in his life to offend even the strictest and most rigid of the Pharisees who had confessed that Jesus was the Christ. The Gentiles he was willing to release from the obligations of the ancient law; but it seems clear that in his judgment it was, at least, expedient that Jews who had become believers should not abandon the customs of their race. Neither St. Peter, nor even Barnabas, St. Paul's own friend and companion in labour, was resolute enough to resist his influence. At Antioch, "before that certain came from James [Peter], did eat with the Gentiles; but when they were come, he withdrew and separated himself, fearing them which were of the circumcision; and the other Jews dissembled likewise with him, insomuch that Barnabas also was carried away with their dissimulation." [25]

The general impression produced by the references to St. James in the New Testament is confirmed by ecclesiastical tradition. The testimony of Josephus, as quoted by Eusebius, — that the calamities of the siege of Jerusalem "avenged James the Just, who was the brother of Him that is called Christ, and whom the Jews had slain, notwithstanding His preeminent justice [26] — if genuine, proves how completely St. James must have preserved the habits and customs and spirit of his people, and how perfectly he fulfilled the Jewish ideal of sanctity. If spurious, the passage is hardly less significant, for it is quoted not only by Eusebius, but by Origen, and shows that traditions which existed in the Church early in the third century implied that there had never been any violent breach between St. James and those of his countrymen who continued to venerate the ancient law.

The very curious extract from Hegesippus, which is also given by Eusebius, though the details are partly unintelligible and partly incredible, must have had some foundation. St. James is represented as a Nazarite from his birth, drinking neither wine nor strong drink, and abstaining from animal food. No razor ever came upon his head; he never anointed with oil; and he never used a bath. He spent the greater part of his time in the Temple, praying for the people, so that his knees became hard like the knees of a camel. The story of his martyrdom— if through the impossible accessories of fable any substantial fact is accessible — seems to indicate that the Jewish rulers were dreading an outburst of violence among the disciples of Jesus of Nazareth at a Feast of the Passover, and that knowing the authority of St. James over the adherents of his sect, and having confidence in his good sense, moderation, and freedom from fanaticism, they appealed to him to maintain order and quietness; but that from some cause or another this appeal resulted in a public and impressive declaration on the part of St. James to our Lord's Messiahship. [27] Whether or not this is the root of the singular story told by Hegesippus, and quoted without any apparent consciousness of its improbability by Eusebius, the story itself is an evidence of the kind of impression which the early Church had preserved of St. James's character, and of his relations to the Jews who did not believe. No such legend could have sprung up in those early times in connection with the names of any other of the Apostles. Origen could not have given as genuine a passage of Josephus, declaring that in the opinion of many of the Jews their miseries were a Divine judgment for their treatment of St. Paul. Nor is it probable that Hegesippus, writing in the middle of the second century, would have thought it credible that the ecclesiastical rulers of Jerusalem lived on such terms with St. John or even with St. Peter as to enable them to seek apostolic influence to prevent tumults among Jewish Christians excited by the conviction that our Lord's second Advent was at hand. But St. James was a Jew to the last. The other Apostles were scattered over the world, and new scenes and new conditions of life assisted to emancipate them from the habits and thoughts of their youth. St. James never left Jerusalem, and never forsook the Temple. A new Faith had come to him, and a new Hope; but he never passed into the large freedom which was achieved by his apostolic brethren.

If, therefore, the expiatory forms under which the other New Testament writers represent the Death of our Lord Jesus Christ were the result of their Jewish training; if they speak of His blood in connection with the remission of sins and cleansing from sin, only because their religious thought found its most natural expression in language derived from the altars, the sacrifices, the priesthood, and the temple of their early religious associations, in the Epistle of St. James we might expect the constant recurrence of sacrificial metaphors. Here, surely, we shall have the eternal truths of the new revelation clothed in the perishable robes of the ancient ceremonialism. How else can such a man give shape and colour and substance to spiritual ideas?

It is, to say the least, extremely curious that from the beginning of the Epistle to the end he never speaks of the Blood of Christ, or of the Sacrifice of Christ, or of the Propitiation offered by Christ for the sins of the world, or of the Redemption of men through the Death of Christ, or of any of those priestly functions of Christ which are illustrated at such length in the Epistle to the Hebrews. He, the most Jewish of the Apostles, never illustrates the work of Christ from the institutions of Judaism. He is so much of a Jew that he describes the assembly of the Church or its meeting-place as a "synagogue," [28] and yet we search his epistle in vain for a single passage to justify us in describing the Death of Christ as a Sacrifice for sin. The epistle, it is true, is not a long one. Had he written more, it is possible that we should have found in it the same language about the Death of Christ that we find in the writings of the other Apostles. But to those who think that the representations of our Lord's Death in the epistles of St, Paul and St. John are to be accounted for and set aside as being only interesting illustrations of the enduring power of Jewish institutions over their religious thought, the absence of any such representations in the Epistle of St. James must be remarkable. It is clear that the Apostle whose whole life was passed in the atmosphere of Judaism, and who was probably in the courts of the temple every day, was not absolutely obliged to use Jewish metaphors when he explained Christian doctrine or enforced Christian duty. Why then should sacrificial language, when used by St. Paul or St. John to describe the Death of Christ, be peremptorily dismissed as being the accidental result of their Jewish training?

Perhaps, however, it was just because the Levitical ritual was constantly before him that he did not exalt it to Christian uses. Distance may have been necessary to give it enchantment; it was too near in its base and material reality to be transfigured. This explanation is hardly admissible. He was a Jew still, and yet he had an eye to which some of the characteristic elements of Judaism shone with altogether a new light. He could speak of the law of the Christian life as a "law of liberty." Even the visible and formal worship of the temple suggested to him a noble conception of the manner in which Christian men are to serve God. "Pure religion [θρησκεία] and undefiled before God and the Father is this: to visit the fatherless and widows in their affliction, and to keep himself unspotted from the world." "Morality itself" — to quote

85

the comment of Coleridge — "is the service and ceremonial (*cultus externus.* θρησκεία) of the Christian religion. The scheme of grace and truth... has Might for its *garment;*' its very *robe* is righteousness." [29]

Whatever force there may be in these considerations as illustrating the untenableness of the theory that the Apostles spoke of the Death of Christ as a Propitiation for sin, and of His Blood as the condition or means of securing the remission of sins, merely because they were Jews, and could not prevent their religious thought from running in the old channels, the epistle throws the strongest light on the position of St. James and the early Church in relation to the question underlying the whole of the Atonement controversy.

The ultimate question at issue is whether the sole purpose of the life and Death of Christ was to effect a change in the moral and spiritual character of men, and so to restore them to God, or whether there is a direct relation between His Death and the remission of sins. It is clear from this Epistle that though St. James and the early Church may have held the second of these theories, which is the theory maintained in these Lectures, it is impossible that they could have held the first.

The most important doctrinal passage in the epistle is that which occupies the second half of the second chapter, the passage which has occasioned so much perplexity to Protestant theologians on account of its superficial and formal inconsistency with St. Paul's doctrine on Justification. It appears that when St. James wrote there were persons bearing the Christian name who supposed that they were certain of salvation although they lived a very unchristian life. Their case was much worse than that of the converts from heathenism in such Churches as those at Thessalonica and Ephesus, to whom St. Paul had to write grave warnings against coarse and flagrant vices. Converts from heathenism sinned through carelessness, through defective moral discernment, through the strength of old habit, and the influence of the corrupt heathen society with which they were still in necessary contact. St. James was writing to Jews who had been trained in the law of Moses. When they sinned they knew it. But they had come to think that their sin exposed them to no danger, that because they had "faith" they were safe, although faith was not perfected in righteousness. This was the heresy with which St. James had to deal so sharply, a practical heresy of the worst and most fatal kind.

But such a heresy could never have arisen if the Church had been taught to believe that the sole purpose for which Christ came into the world was to redeem us from eternal ruin by making us better men, — creating in us reverence for God's authority, and trust in His love, penitence for sin, and thirst for righteousness. This conception of the work of Christ has many great defects, but it has one great merit; it is a conception in which the Antinomian heresy can never take root. The weeds as well as the healthy crops show the quality and nature of the soil, and if any theory of the work of Christ renders impossible a heresy which actually arose in the Churches which Apostles founded, this is decisive evidence that the theory is not apostolic.

Had the early Church been taught that the Christian salvation is only a salvation from sin, or that whatever else it may be is the result of salvation from sin, it is inconceivable that any persons bearing the Christian name could have supposed that they might be saved by faith without works. The solitary function of Christ would then have been to discipline men to righteousness. Salvation and the recovery of holiness would have been not only inseparable, but identical blessings. For men to speak of being justified, while their temper and character remained unchanged, would have been as impossible as for men to speak of being free while the fetters are on their limbs and the prison doors bolted, or to speak of being in health while suffering the tortures of a painful disease. Some great objective blessing, a blessing altogether distinct from their personal sanctification, and conferred in direct response to faith, must have filled their thoughts, to have made it possible for them to suppose that they could be justified by faith without obedience. Salvation must have been represented to them as something else than a change in their personal life and character effected by the revelation of God in Christ, and something else than the natural and necessary result of such a change.

I may be reminded that the error of these Christian Jews was precisely analogous to that which was committed by Jews who had not acknowledged the authority of Christ. Judaism, it may be alleged, was in its very essence a law requiring righteousness, yet there were some who regarded the bare possession of a law, which they did not keep, as the guarantee of the Divine favour; and so Christianity, as taught by the Apostles, might have made the whole value of the mission of Christ consist in His power to renew and transform the life and character, and yet their doctrine might have been so perverted as to invest a barren and unspiritual faith with the prerogative of justifying. No illustration could add greater strength to the argument on which I am insisting. For it was not the law in itself that gave occasion to the practical heresy of the Jews. There was a Divine promise given to Abraham, and "the law, which was four hundred and thirty years after," could not "disannul" it, so as to "make the promise of none effect." The promise was theirs antecedently to any obedience which they could render to the Divine commandments. The commandments were given, because the promise had been given before; but they forgot that by disobedience they might disqualify themselves for receiving the fulfilment of the promise. The Christians whom St. James rebukes committed a precisely similar mistake. There were great hopes assured to faith, free gifts conferred by God on all who believed in Christ; but they forgot that without personal righteousness they might be incapable of continuing in the Divine love and inheriting eternal glory. The practical heresy bears witness to the truth. The heresy would have been impossible had the Church been taught that the sole purpose of the mission of Christ was to inspire men with the disposition and the power to keep God's commandments.

The manner in which St. James deals with the heresy is equally instructive. He does not deny that it is faith which justifies; he only insists that faith without works is dead; in other words, is no faith at all. Abraham was justified by works — but why? Because faith wrought with his works, and by works was faith made perfect. Curiously enough, Rahab seems to have been regarded by the Jews of those times as a conspicuous example of faith. The writer of the Epistle to the Hebrews gives her a place in the glorious succession of saints, heroes, and martyrs, who "through faith subdued kingdoms, wrought righteousness, obtained promises," and endured with unshaken fortitude all that the hatred and power of wicked men could inflict upon them. St. James also appeals to Rahab, and there is no real conflict between his account of her and what is said of her in the Epistle to the Hebrews. The anonymous writer says: "By faith the harlot Rahab perished not with them that believed not, when she had received the spies with peace." [30] St. James says: "Was not Rahab the harlot justified by works when she had received the messengers, and had sent them out another way?" [31] Which was it that justified her — faith or works? St. James, had he been asked, would have replied — Both. "Faith wrought with [her] works, and by works was faith made perfect."

Had St. James believed that there are no great objective blessings promised to faith, and that Christ saves us only because He accomplishes a subjective change in those who receive Him, the whole argument would have taken a different form. The "moral theory" of the Atonement would have placed in his hands weapons for the destruction of Antinomianism very different from those which he actually employs. He would have insisted that Christ came for no other purpose than to incline and to enable us to fulfil "the perfect law of liberty;" that this was the only end of His Life, His Death, and His Resurrection; that whatever may be the blessedness and whatever the glory to which Christian men are destined, these are the results of the personal holiness which Christ came to produce by revealing the perfect righteousness and infinite love of God, and by conferring the gift of the Holy Ghost. In illustrating the necessity of good works, he would not have limited himself to instances in which the "works" were such immediate effects of faith as to be hardly distinguishable from it — to "works" which were plainly its necessary expression. He would have insisted that sin of every kind is itself the very evil from which Christ came to redeem us, and that restoration to God is identical with restoration to holiness. Instead of satisfying himself with maintaining that faith is dead where works are absent, he would have argued that the power of Christ is unrevealed — the power of His example, the power of His love, the power of His sufferings, the power of His resurrection — where evil habits are not dissolved and evil passions not destroyed.

Ask any theologian who believes in the "moral theory" of the Atonement to refute the heresy that holy living is unnecessary to present justification and to future happiness; tell him to steep his mind in Old Testament thought, and to write as the most Jewish of the Apostles would have written to Jewish Christians; and his argument will bear no resemblance to that of St. James. The existence of the heresy is a proof that the early Church did not believe that the whole value of the work of Christ consists in the power which He had gained by His Incarnation and Death over the human heart; and the proof is completed by the manner in which St. James combats the heresy.

That in the heat of the great conflict for the doctrine of Justification by Faith, Luther should have regarded this epistle with distrust, and even with antagonism, is not wonderful; but there is no epistle in the New Testament which should be read more constantly by evangelical theologians and by all evangelical Christians.

Between St. Paul and St. James there is no real want of harmony. We understand neither of them aright, if we shrink from taking the words of both in their broad and obvious meaning, and if we attempt to "reconcile" them by ingenious and subtle and recondite processes of interpretation. St. Paul speaks as a theologian, and contends that by faith, and by faith alone, are men to be justified; and in this contention he is but affirming the truth to which the Christian revelation in all its parts bears testimony. We are saved by God's infinite grace. We love Him because He first loved us. In God's presence we can urge no claim to deliverance from sin and eternal perdition, except the mercy He has revealed through Christ. The prerogatives and hopes of the least in the kingdom of heaven transcend the merits of the greatest of saints. Saintliness itself is the effect of the sanctifying power of the Holy Ghost. The holiest of men, instead of having most to claim by way of reward, have already received most as the result of grace. To God we can give nothing: we must receive everything from Him. We are justified by faith, for faith is the recognition and acceptance of our true relation to God, which is a relation of dependence from first to last.

St. James speaks, not as a theologian, but as one who has to deal with the concrete Christian life. He maintains that works are as necessary to justification as faith; and in the sphere in which his thought is moving this is true, let theologians say what they will. He speaks the language of common life and of common men. He is not dealing with ideas but with facts. It is quite true that a man is justified as soon as he believes in Christ — justified by faith before he has any chance of doing good works; it is quite true that faith is the solitary condition of remission of sins and entrance into the kingdom of God, but wherever there is faith there will be works; and since a man cannot be justified without faith, he cannot as a matter of fact be justified without works, which always go with it.

So long as the question is kept within the limits of theological science, we must maintain that a man is justified by faith, and by faith alone, without good works: as soon as it passes into the province of the practical Christian life, we must maintain with equal earnestness that apart from good works justification is impossible. Evangelical preachers have never hesitated to maintain the absolute necessity of repentance as an antecedent of faith; they should not hesitate to maintain the absolute necessity of good works as a consequent of faith.

No doubt St. James puts the case very strongly. The works which were present to his mind, and by which he illustrates his argument, were of a kind to enable him to travel to the utmost limit of permissible language; they were, as I have already said, works so immediately resulting from faith as to be hardly distinguishable from it. He makes no distinction between the inward principle and the act which was its necessary effect and expression. "By works a man is justified, and not by faith only." This is something more than saying that where there are no good works there can be no justification; but practically, and in all such cases as those to which he appeals, the one statement is as true as the other, for the works were literally works of faith.

The remembrance of great controversies which have shaken Christendom to its foundations may restrain us even in our strongest and most popular speech within limits which St. James, in the intensity of his hatred and scorn for unrighteousness which sheltered itself under the immunities of faith, was impelled to pass. But his example should remind us that when we are speaking to the hearts and consciences of men we may sometimes have to forget the definitions of the schools. We must sometimes sacrifice the scientific accuracy of our language in order to make truth intelligible to men who are not scientific theologians, or who have made their scientific theology a defence against the reproaches of their own consciences and the Divine denunciations of sin. When spiritual truth has to appear on the common paths of human life, it has to become incarnate, and must accept the infirmities of the human medium through which alone it can reveal itself to mankind.

Especially we should learn from St. James that one of our chief duties is to insist that obedience to the law of God is inseparable from real faith in His love. In our own times, indeed, and in this country, the practical heresies which, from the days of the Apostles, have always arisen wherever the apostolic theology has been vigorously and earnestly preached, have no considerable strength. They may be found in obscure places, but they shun the light. They often, I fear, exist in a vague form in the minds of persons who have received, without much active reflection, the traditional evangelical creed, but they are rarely expressed. Wherever they exist, and in however indefinite a shape, they poison the air, they corrupt Christian morality, they enfeeble the fibre and muscle of the Christian life. They must receive no toleration, but must be driven away and smitten down with a relentless hand.

It may be that some Christian people are only giving an unfortunate and unscriptural expression to a very noble truth when they speak of being "clothed in the imputed righteousness of Christ;" but if "imputed righteousness" is made a cloak for actual sin, they must be made to feel that they are the modern successors of those of whom St. Paul said that their "damnation is just." If the doctrine of the Atonement is so perverted as to lead to the conclusion that because a man believes in Christ as the Propitiation for the sins of the world, he will not have to be made manifest before the judgment seat of Christ, that he "may receive the things done in his body, according to that he hath done, whether it be good or bad," [32] the awful reality of judgment to come must be reasserted with the energy and sternness of apostolic times; and men must be reminded that to St. Paul himself — the great teacher of Justification by Faith — the final judgment was "the terror of the Lord," and was one of the motives which constrained him to fidelity in his apostolic labours.

We should not, however, transform the gospel of the grace of God into a mere system of ethics, because in our times, as in the days of the Apostles, men may turn the very "grace of God into lasciviousness." We should rather recognise in the analogy between the heresies which sometimes claim to be the legitimate results of the evangelical creed, and the heresies which claim to be the legitimate results of apostolic teaching, a fresh testimony and proof that we are the representatives and heirs of "the faith once delivered unto the saints." If there is any form of Christian doctrine which renders it impossible for men to suppose that they can be saved by faith without works — that the Death of Christ secures no objective blessing, and has for its solitary purpose the creation of a new moral and spiritual life — the Epistle of St. James is a conclusive demonstration that this is not the doctrine which was taught by the founders of the Christian Church.

[1] "When they saw that the gospel of the uncircumcision was committed to me, as the gospel of the circumcision was unto Peter." — *Gal.* ii. 7.
[2] Reuss: *Christian Theology in the Apostolic Age.* Translated by Annie Harwood. London: Hodder and Stoughton. Vol. ii.
[3] Fichte: *Characteristics of the Present Age.* Lecture vii. *The Way towards the Blessed Life.* Lecture vi. London: John Chapman.
[4] This is true, although the Fourth Gospel is singularly rich in passages which recognise the Divine authority of Jewish institutions and the Divine presence in Jewish history. St. John has preserved many passages in our Lord's teaching, not contained in the other Evangelists, which show how fully our Lord acknowledged that Judaism *had been* a great revelation of God to man . I do not intend to press the very strong proofs which are supplied by the Book of the Revelation, not because I am doubtful about its Johannine authorship, but because I am anxious to keep the argument from the authority of St. John free from entanglement with the controversies in which that subject is involved.
[5] John i. 7.
[6] Ibid. iii. 16.
[7] "That the forgiveness of sin was present to the Apostle's mind when he spake of the cleansing efficacy of the blood of Christ, is evident from what he goes on to say — that 'if we confess our sins He is faithful and just *to forgive us our sins,* and to cleanse us from all unrighteousness;' as well as from what he adds a few verses thereafter, that 'if any man sin we have an advocate with the Father, Jesus Christ the righteous; and He is the propitiation for our sins,' &c. — Crawford: *The Doctrine of Holy*

*Scripture respecting the Atonement* (first edition), page 50. Cremer *Biblico-Theological Lexicon of New Testament Greek*. Edinburgh, T. & T. Clark. 1872) has a very excellent article on καθαρίζω.

[8] I John ii. 12.

[9] I John ii. I.

[10] "παράκλητος ...he who has been, or may be called to help (Helper;; in Dem. 343, 10, of a legal adviser: ...a pleader, an advocate; one who comes forward in favour of and as the representative of another. Diog... Thus Christ also, in i John ii. I, is termed our Substitute, Intercessor, Advocate."— CREMER; *Biblico-Theological Lexicon*.

[11] I John ii 2.

[12] Dr. Young: *The Life and Light of Men,* pp. 322, 323.

[13] Ibid. pp. 323, 324.

[14] Note K.

[15] BUSHNELL: *Forgiveness and Law,* page 163.

[16] Gen. xxxii. 20.

[17] Zech. vii. 2: and in this case ἐξιλιίσασθαι is not the representative of the Hebrew word for which it usually stands.

[18] Exod. xxxii. 30.

[19] Ibid. xxxii. 10.

[20] 1 John iv. 10. The whole of this argument rests on the use of ἱλάσκομαι in the LXX. It is also true that the Hebrew word which ἱλάσκομαι usually represents never refers *directly* to God, but to the sin which is to be so "covered" as to cause the anger it had produced to cease. This "covering" was an ἱλασμός.

[21] John xi. 47-50.

[22] John xi, 51, 52.

[23] Acts xv. 5.

[24] Ibid. xxi. 20.

[25] Gal. ii. 12, 13.

[26] *Ecc. Hist.* ii. 23.

[27] Eusebius: *Ecc. Hist.* ii. 23.

[28] Jas. ii. 2.

[29] *Aids to Reflection.* Second Edition, page 18.

[30] Heb. xi. 31.

[31] Jas. ii. 25.

[32] Cor. v. 10.

# Lecture Six - The Fact of the Atonement: The Testimony of St. Paul

In examining the testimony of St. Peter, St. John, and St. James, to the fact of the Atonement, it was unnecessary to consider whether they had any supernatural illumination different in kind or degree from that which is common to all who have received the life and light of God. One of them was "the brother of our Lord;" the others were His personal friends, and had lived with Him for two, or perhaps for nearly three, years. After His resurrection He had appeared to them all, again and again, and had spoken to them of "the things pertaining to the kingdom of heaven." [1] St. Peter and St. John He had elected and appointed to tell the story of His life. His sufferings, and His resurrection from the dead, and to preach repentance and remission of sins in His name among all nations." [2] It was impossible that any of the three should have mistaken His mind on a question of such capital importance as that of the ground on which God forgives sin. To establish their authority on other questions relating to the new faith, it may be necessary to show that they received special inspiration; but, apart from special inspiration, their authority on this question is decisive.

The authority of St. Paul rests on other grounds. He had not known Christ during Christ's earthly ministry, but he had seen — so he said — a "heavenly vision;" Christ had appeared to him in a glory brighter than that of the sun which shines on Damascus at midday; he had heard the voice of Christ, and had received from Him a commission to be "a minister and witness" of supernatural revelations. He was sent especially to the Gentiles, "to open their eyes, and to turn them from darkness to light, and from the power of Satan unto God," that they might "receive forgiveness of sins and inheritance among them that are sanctified by faith" in Christ. [3] That the miraculous vision was not the creation of a fevered brain was proved to the men of his own time by his miraculous works; and the truth of what he taught was confirmed by the Divine power which wrought on the hearts of those to whom he preached.

He must have been acquainted with the general outlines of our Lord's earthly history long before he became an Apostle. He must have known that Jesus of Nazareth had been crucified, and that His disciples alleged that He had risen from the dead, and had ascended to heaven. Within six or seven years after these things happened, we have evidence that St. Paul was in Jerusalem, and Jerusalem was ringing with the controversy between the disciples of the Nazarene Messiah and their unbelieving countrymen. The new sect was rapidly gaining adherents; "a great company of the priests were obedient to the faith." [4] He consented to the death of Stephen, and the false witnesses that charged the first Christian martyr with blasphemy "laid down their clothes" at his feet. [5] It was impossible that he should be ignorant of the story which the friends of the Lord Jesus were perpetually repeating. After his conversion he stayed for a short time with the disciples at Damascus, and must have been present at their meetings for worship, must have heard their preaching, and must have talked with them in private about the miracles of Christ, which some of them had probably witnessed, and the discourses of Christ, to which some of them had probably listened.

But he declared that he had not received from man the gospel which he preached, neither was he taught it but "by the revelation of Jesus Christ." I suppose he meant that the full significance of our Lord's earthly history, the nature and laws of His eternal kingdom, were not made known to him by human teachers, but by the immediate illumination of the Holy Ghost. These lofty claims, as I have said, were sustained by miracles. To a Church which he had not visited he wrote of the "mighty signs and wonders" wrought by the Spirit of God in connection with his apostolic labours. [6] To a Church which he had founded, but which was disturbed by factious men who questioned his right to rank himself with "the brethren of the Lord" and with St. Peter, he declared that "in nothing" was he inferior to "the very chiefest apostles," and he appealed with confidence to "the signs of an apostle" which had been wrought among them "in signs and wonders and mighty deeds." [7]

Admitting on such evidence as this the reality of St. Paul's supernatural commission, we need not, for our immediate purpose, discuss the limits of his inspiration. Whether the arguments with which he sustains Christian doctrine are always logical, whether his use of the Old Testament is always legitimate, whether in illustrating the work of Christ he ever mistakes Jewish myths or legends for facts — these are questions to which different replies may be given by those who are agreed in acknowledging that the Lord Jesus Christ really appeared to him on the road to Damascus, and called him to the apostleship of the Gentiles. But that the Gentiles might "receive the forgiveness of sins" was one of the special ends of his apostolic ministry. [8] Whatever other parts of his religious teaching may be erroneous, when he declares the conditions and grounds on which sin is forgiven, his teaching is stamped with the authority of heaven. [9]

There is another line of proof by which this position may be established. St. Paul's claims were violently and persistently opposed. A faction in the Church, and a very powerful faction, resented his refusal to impose the Jewish law on converts from heathenism.

In the Church at Antioch, which was largely composed of Gentiles, the permanent and universal obligation of circumcision was debated with great vehemence; and as the Judaising party refused to acknowledge the authority of St. Paul and his friends, it was resolved to refer the question to the original Apostles who were still in Jerusalem, and to the elders of the Jerusalem Church. With the exception of one brief visit five years before, [10] at a time when the Church was disturbed by persecution, and when the Apostles had probably fled for their lives, he had not been in the sacred city for at least twelve years. At his earlier visit he had seen St. Peter and St. James, "the Lord's brother," but since then, he seems never to have met any of the Apostles. It is clear that he anticipated the results of this appeal to their judgment, with anxiety. Before the Church was called together he had private conferences with its leaders. He explained to them the gospel that he had been preaching during the previous ten or eleven years to the Gentile Churches which he had founded. A schism, a misunderstanding, would be infinitely mischievous. When at last the Church met, the contention seems to have been as sharp as it had been at Antioch. If there had been any divergence between St. Paul's teaching and that of the original twelve on such a subject as the relation of the Death of Christ to the forgiveness of sins, it is certain that this divergence would have been alleged to embitter and aggravate the controversy. But there is no trace that any doctrinal innovations, either on this point or on any other, were charged against him. His solitary offence consisted in his firm and immovable determination that the Christian Church should not be bound and fettered by the rites of Judaism. When the discussion was over, St. James, St. Peter, and St. John gave St. Paul the right hand of fellowship, recognised in him the same mighty power that wrought in themselves, and acknowledged that he was divinely commissioned to preach the gospel to the Gentiles. His faith, therefore, was theirs. The original Apostles declared that the gospel of St. Paul was a true representation of the doctrine of Christ.

A complete investigation of St. Paul's testimony to the Atonement is not possible within the narrow limits of these Lectures. I propose to consider, very briefly, the accounts of St. Paul's preaching, given by himself and by St. Luke, and shall then endeavour to determine his conception of the intention and effect of the Death of Christ, by considering the relation of that conception to the most important lines of thought in three or four of his epistles.
Although he was the Apostle of the Gentiles, he began his apostolic work among the Jews. According to Jewish custom, it was not only the official ministers who were permitted to speak in the synagogue: liberty to address the congregation was allowed to every one who had anything to say; and to the very last, notwithstanding the hostility with which the Jews regarded him, it was St. Paul's habit to avail himself of this liberty. In the synagogues of Damascus, immediately after his conversion, he discussed the claims of Jesus of Nazareth to be received as the Son of God, and the Messiah of Jewish prophecy. [11] Whether in those early times he was accustomed to speak of the relation of our Lord's Death to human redemption, does not appear; St. Luke gives us no report of the substance of his teaching. And of all the discourses which he delivered subsequently in the synagogues of Asia Minor and of Greece, St. Luke has recorded only one." [12] This was delivered at Antioch in Pisidia, and it may be regarded as illustrating the kind of argument which he used with his fellow-countrymen, in vindicating the claims of Christ to their obedience and faith. He begins by recognizing God's election of the Jewish race; he recalls the manifestations of God's goodness to them in the earlier periods of their history, and especially in the establishment of the Jewish monarchy, which was the symbol and prophecy of a diviner kingdom. He reminds them of God's promise to David, and then declares that "of this man's seed hath God...raised unto Israel a Saviour." He quotes John the Baptist's testimony to our Lord. He tells them of the rejection of the Lord Jesus by the rulers and people of Jerusalem, and of His Death and burial. He quotes ancient prophecies, which he maintains were fulfilled in the resurrection of Christ from the dead. And then his very first words are these: "Be it known unto you, therefore, men and brethren, that through this Man is preached unto you forgiveness of sins; and by Him all that believe are justified from all things, from which ye could not be justified by the law of Moses." [13] Nothing is said about the relation of our Lord's Death to the forgiveness of sins and justification; but it seems to be St Paul's intention to declare that perfect release from the guilt of all offences against the Divine law is the immediate result of believing in Christ. Christ is the Saviour whom God had promised to their fathers — the King for whose advent they had been waiting and longing — and "by Him all that believe are justified from all things," from which the

law of Moses provided no means of justification. It looks as if the salvation of which St. Paul speaks were purely objective, and as if it were immediate: there is nothing to imply that it is to be the natural result of a subjective change.

Of his discourses to the Gentiles, passing over his protest against the attempt of the people at Lystra to offer to himself and Barnabas divine honours, the only one recorded is the address on Mars' Hill, which is principally an argument against idolatry, though it closes with the startling declaration that the day has been appointed when God "will judge the world in righteousness," by Jesus Christ; and that of this God has "given assurance to all men" in raising Him from the dead. [14] Repentance is commanded, but nothing is said about forgiveness. Christ is represented only as a Judge. This discourse was probably very unlike those which St. Paul ordinarily delivered to Gentile audiences. All the circumstances were exceptional, and these determined both its substance and its form.

The other discourses of St. Paul contained in the Acts of the Apostles are also of an exceptional character. Three of them are narratives of his conversion: the first, delivered on the stairs of the fortress of Antonia, [15] to the enraged and tumultuous crowd by which a few minutes before he had been nearly killed; the second delivered before Felix at Caesarea, in reply to Tertullus; and the third before Agrippa and Festus. There is also his address to the elders of the Ephesian Church, who met him at Miletus: this is a charge exhorting them to fidelity to the flock over which the Holy Ghost had made them overseers, and he gives awful solemnity to his appeal by reminding them that the Church to which they were called to minister, "the Lord...had purchased — made His own — with His own blood." [16] it is from himself that we must learn the general character of his preaching.

Writing to the Corinthians, St. Paul says: "Christ sent me not to baptise, but to preach the gospel;" and what he meant by preaching the gospel is implied in the words which immediately follow: "not with wisdom of words, lest the cross of Christ should be made of none effect." [17] The principal subject of his preaching was the crucifixion of Christ, and it was his duty not to divert the thoughts of men from that great and mysterious event by learned speculation or glittering eloquence. In the next sentence he describes his preaching as "the preaching of the cross," [18] which is to them that perish foolishness." A few sentences farther on he repeats the description: "The Jews require a sign, and the Greeks seek after wisdom; but we preach Christ crucified, unto the Jews a stumbling block, and unto the Greeks foolishness; but unto them which are called, both Jews and Greeks, Christ the power of God and the wisdom of God." [19] In the next chapter he reminds the Corinthians of the time when He was with them, and when through his ministry they abandoned their heathenism and became Christians. "I brethren, when I came to you, came not with excellency of speech or of wisdom, declaring unto you the testimony of God. For I determined not to know anything among you, save Jesus

Christ and Him crucified." [20] How are we to account for the prominence which is given to the cross?

The Apostle of the Gentiles knew mankind. He was as far as possible from being an irrational fanatic. On some conspicuous occasions he showed that he could practise the most courteous and dexterous conciliation — complimenting Agrippa on his knowledge of Jewish customs and controversies; quoting a Greek poet, to sustain his own doctrine, when addressing Greeks at Athens; appealing to the very party spirit of the Pharisees when he was standing before the Sanhedrim, protesting that he was "a Pharisee and the son of a Pharisee," and that it was concerning "the hope and resurrection of the dead" that he was "called in question." [21] How was it that he deliberately and persistently spoke of the crucifixion, which, according to Dean Stanley, "was and is a scandal to the Jewish nation, as a dishonour to the Messiah," and which was regarded "by the educated classes of Greek and Roman society as a degradation of the [Christian] religion itself." [22] St. Paul wanted both Jews and Gentiles to acknowledge the Lord Jesus Christ as the Son of God and Saviour of mankind: why did he dwell on precisely those facts which provoked the disgust both of Gentiles and of Jews, and confirmed them in their unbelief?

That the Jews of Jerusalem had rejected the claims of Jesus of Nazareth and put Him to death was no reason why Jews in other parts of the world should acknowledge Him as the Messiah. His rejection at Jerusalem, where He was known. His condemnation by the highest authorities of the nation, was *primâ facie* evidence that He was an impostor. His Death must surely have had some very intimate and peculiar relation to His mission, for St. Paul to have insisted on it so strenuously.

Nor could His Death have been represented by St. Paul as having the same character as the death of any other great teacher or reformer who had been destroyed by the jealousy of governments or by popular fury. Plato's philosophy was not "foolishness" to "the educated classes of Greek and Roman society" because he told them how Socrates had been put to death by the Athenians; and the preaching of St. Paul would not have been "foolishness" to the same classes had he spoken of Christ's Death simply as a martyrdom. In that case their hatred and contempt of the Jews would have made them regard the crucifixion of Jesus, notwithstanding the intolerable humiliation of that particular form of death, as creating some slight argument in His favour.

Why then, I ask again, did St. Paul give the cross such prominence in his preaching? Dean Stanley, in his brief essay on the "Cross of Christ," from which I have already quoted, says: "Its outward form was familiar [to the Greeks] wherever the Roman law had been carried out against the slaves and insurgents of the East. It was for them now to discover its application to themselves." [23] "To discover its application to themselves!" If we had had nothing more than these brief references to the supreme place which the cross of Christ held in St. Paul's preaching, it would no doubt have been necessary for us in this age to "discover" for ourselves "its application" to human necessities and human redemption. But even if St. Paul had been disposed to announce the bare fact of the crucifixion, without saying anything about its "application," it is inconceivable that his hearers would have permitted him to leave it unexplained.

For a year and six months he was "teaching the word of God" in Corinth, [24] and the people whom he addressed were very unlike the decorous and silent congregations addressed every Sunday by Christian preachers in our own times. He was interrupted by questions; there was free debate; he was challenged by opponents; he had to solve the difficulties of friends. This crucifixion of the Son of God, which was a stumbling-block to Jews and foolishness to Greeks, would be certain to provoke discussion. He might say that it was a mystery, but he would be pressed again and again to explain why it was permitted to happen, and why he said so little about the teaching and miracles of Christ, and so much about His Death. It was impossible that he should be silent, and leave his hearers "to discover its application to themselves."

We have no reason to suppose that he was unwilling to speak. In the early part of his Epistle to the Corinthians he describes his preaching as "the preaching of the cross." and tells them that when he came to them, his whole preaching was about "Jesus Christ and Him crucified." Towards the end of the epistle he recalls to their memory the gospel they had heard from him, and which they had received; and, reciting the chief points on which he had spoken to them, he says: "I delivered unto you, first of all (ἐν πρώτοις), that which I also received, how that Christ *died for our sins* according to the scriptures." [25] This was among the elementary truths that he preached. He began with this.

The words are remarkable, but they are very intelligible. Similar expressions occur often enough in literature, and in ordinary conversation, and their meaning is too plain to be misunderstood. We speak of men being fined for drunkenness, transported for felony, burnt for heresy, hung for murder, and no one complains that our language is ambiguous. Sometimes men have suffered for offences which they did not commit, have been condemned on false evidence, and punished by mistake. One man committed the theft, and another man has been imprisoned for it; one man was guilty of the murder, and another man has been hung for it. From the prison and the scaffold there have come protestations of innocence. But in the case of Christ there was no mistake, nor was there any protest. He died voluntarily; "died," not because He had committed any crimes for which He deserved death, but "for our sins." We may wonder how it should be possible for Him to have died for our sins; we may contend that it was unjust; but that St. Paul declared that this was one of the fundamental truths which he had "received" from heaven, to make known to mankind, is incontestable.

As he believed that Christ "died for our sins," we cannot be astonished that this was one of the first truths that he made known to men who were unacquainted with the gospel; nor can we be astonished that he should have re-curred to it so frequently that his preaching might be described as "the preaching of the cross." That Christ died for the sins of men, establishes a personal relationship between every man and Christ of the most intimate character, a relationship absolutely unique, and affecting in a very vital and fundamental manner the whole range of human hopes and fears and the history and destiny of the race. It was so strange and so startling a fact, it was a fact of such infinite practical interest, that it was inevitable that St. Paul should give it a foremost place in his preaching.

There was another reason why he made it so prominent. It was one of the great ends of his apostolic commission that the Gentiles should "receive for-giveness of sins;" and if "Christ died for our sins," His Death must have been intimately connected with our forgiveness, and to "preach Christ crucified" was therefore one of his chief apostolic duties.

It appears, therefore, that St. Paul did not simply announce the fact of the crucifixion, and leave men "to discover its inward application to themselves." His explanation of the fact was likely to provoke greater antagonism and re-pugnance than the fact itself. The Jews resented religious teaching which de-nied that their descent from Abraham was sufficient to avert the righteous judgment of God. St. Paul maintained that they were sinners, and that Christ died for the sins of Jews as well as for the sins of Gentiles, and that circumci-sion was no sure guarantee of the Divine favour. This was his great crime, and this was the principal reason why to them "Christ crucified" was "a stumbling-block:" for he asks, "If I yet preach circumcision, why do I yet suf-fer persecution? then is the offence of the cross ceased." [26]

"The educated classes of Greek and Roman society," of whom Dean Stanley speaks, resented his teaching — not merely because the crucifixion was felt to be a "degradation" of the new religion, encumbering it "with associations so low, and addressed, as they would say, to classes so contemptible as the beggars and slaves of the Roman empire," [27] — but also because St. Paul's explanation of the crucifixion degraded themselves, ascribed to them a guilt of which they were unconscious, offered them a forgiveness of which they felt no need, and on terms which must have seemed intolerable. That a Jew-ish religious teacher — a young Galilean peasant — whatever His wisdom and whatever His virtues, whose claims had been rejected by His own coun-trymen, and who had suffered the most ignominious death, had really died for their sins, and that they were to receive forgiveness of sins through Him, must have seemed to "the educated classes of Greek and Roman society" the most preposterous and insane propositions that Eastern fanatics had ever proclaimed as messages from heaven. "Christ crucified" was "unto the Jews a stumbling-block, and unto the Greeks foolishness."

In St. Paul's preaching, then, he maintained that "Christ died for our sins." This was not a phrase which he used now and then, accidentally, and without any very definite meaning. It describes a truth which gave complexion and character to all his teaching. Can we find the same truth in his epistles? Was this conception of the Death of Christ merely elementary, necessary in order to convey to uncultivated and ignorant minds some rude idea of the new faith, but inadequate as a representation of the inner truth of the gospel? or does it reappear in letters addressed to those who were already in the Church, and who had received the illumination of the Spirit of God? Do the epistles of St. Paul assert or imply that there is a great objective element in the work of Christ? Do they connect this with His Death? Do they confirm the impression that the Death of Christ is directly related to the forgiveness of sins? These are the questions which I now propose to investigate.

By general consent, the First Epistle to the Thessalonians is the earliest epistle that St. Paul wrote, or rather the earliest that the Church has preserved. It was written not many months after he had left the newly-converted Christians at Thessalonica to themselves, and may have been suggested by what he heard from Timothy about the moral perils which threatened their Christian integrity, and the speculative questions which disturbed their Christian faith. The enthusiasm with which they had abandoned heathenism, and "turned to God from idols to serve the living and true God," appears to have been so remarkable, that the report of their conversion travelled through the whole of the country, and the first excitement had not yet passed away. But their conscience was uninstructed, and the sobriety and regularity which ought to characterise the Christian life were endangered by the uncontrolled fervour of their religious emotion. Most of them had been heathens, and St. Paul had to warn them against continuing to practise the sensual vices of "the Gentiles that know not God." [28] He had also to tell them that while they were waiting for the glorious coming of Christ they were not to live an idle, turbulent, and fanatical life, but were to live quietly and rationally, attending to their secular business and working at their ordinary trades. [29]

We can imagine the kind of letter which would have been written to such a Church by any one who believed that the redemptive work of Christ is purely subjective. These excited enthusiasts, whose faith was strong and whose charity was fervent, [30] but whose morality was very defective, [31] would have been told that they were altogether mistaken as to the nature of the Christian salvation. They would have been sharply rebuked for permitting their imaginations to be filled with the second advent of Christ, as though redemption were in any sense a future and external blessing. Very much would have been said about sin as being the only evil from which men need deliverance, and it would have been shown that glory, honour, and immortality, are simply the natural and necessary fruit of personal holiness.

But this is not the line that St. Paul follows. He speaks of "the wrath that is coming," [32] "the sudden destruction" [33] which is to overtake impenitent and unbelieving men. From this, the Lord Jesus Christ delivers all who receive the gospel. [34] He enforces the exhortation that Christian people should live as "the children of the light and the children of the day," by adding, "For God hath not appointed us to wrath, but to obtain salvation by our Lord Jesus Christ, who died for us, that whether we wake or sleep we should live together with Him." [35] There are three conclusions to be drawn from this epistle.

I. It is clear that St. Paul's own mind was filled with the conception of the final revelation of the "wrath" of God against human sin, and that he had said very much about it to the Thessalonians when he was with them.

2. It is also clear that he and they were relying on Christ for deliverance from that "wrath;" and however true it may be that those who are to be delivered from the coming wrath are first delivered from present sin, he does not conceive of the future deliverance as being nothing more than the necessary result of a present moral and spiritual change. As yet, the Thessalonian Christians were very far from having obtained perfect sanctification; but since they were in Christ, they were no longer in peril of that "sudden destruction," which might come any day on those that knew not God, and obeyed not the gospel of our Lord Jesus Christ. Because they were in Christ, it might be certain that they would be delivered from sin as well as from wrath, but the two deliverances are conceived of as being co-ordinate. There is an objective salvation as well as a salvation from moral corruption.

3. This objective salvation is connected by St. Paul with the Death of Christ. "God hath not appointed us to wrath, but to obtain salvation by our Lord Jesus Christ, who *died for us,* that whether we wake or sleep we should live together with Him." [36] Because Christ died for us, our destiny is separated from the destiny of those who will be swept away by the wrath of God, and whether we die before "the day of the Lord" comes, or whether it finds us still alive, we are to live together with Christ.

But why should Christ's Death render it possible for those who believe in Him to escape eternal destruction, and to share His own eternal life and blessedness? What relation exists between these two truths, (1) that Christ died, and (2) that we are to be saved from wrath by Him? Some third truth is necessary to mediate between them. It was too familiar to the Thessaionians to require explicit statement. To them St. Paul had preached the same gospel that he was preaching at Corinth when he wrote this epistle: he had "delivered [to them] first of all that which [he] also received, how that Christ died for our sins." This, therefore, is what he meant, and what the Thessalonians would know that he meant when he wrote that Christ "died for us." It is because He died for our sins, that at His coming, whether we are living or dead, He will deliver us from the wrath of God, and exalt us into eternal fellowship with His own blessedness and glory.

The characteristic of the First Epistle to the Thessalonians is the prominence which it assigns to "the day of the Lord," when the supreme penalty is to be inflicted upon the impenitent, and when those who believe are to receive complete and eternal blessedness. Their deliverance from the penalty, and their inheritance of the blessedness, are associated by St. Paul with the Death of Christ.

The Death of Christ is not mentioned accidentally, or in relation to some subordinate and incidental line of thought. It stands in immediate connection with the chief topic of the epistle, and in such a connection with it, as to show that by dying for us Christ delivered us from a great objective danger.

The Epistle to the Galatians, which I propose to examine next, is generally regarded as belonging to a group of epistles, which also includes the two Epistles to the Corinthians and the Epistle to the Romans. All four were probably written about the same time, and they have certain common characteristics. "They exhibit," says Professor Lightfoot, "an unwonted tension of feeling, a fiery energy of expression, which we do not find in anything like the same degree in either the earlier or the later epistles. They are marked by a vast profusion of quotations from the Old Testament, by, a frequent use of interrogation, by great variety and abruptness of expression, by words and images not found elsewhere, or found very rarely in St. Paul. They have also their own doctrinal features,...due for the most part to the phase which the antagonism to the gospel assumed at this time. [37]

Professor Lightfoot accurately describes the Epistle to the Galatians as "the typical epistle of the group." [38] Indeed, it contains in so intense a form all the agonistic elements which appear in the other three, that it stands almost alone. The conflict between St. Paul and the Judaizers had now become a struggle for life or death. The attempt at conciliation which had been made at the Council of Jerusalem' had not succeeded. The compromise, if it had been accepted for a time, and if it still satisfied the more moderate of those who reverenced the ancient customs of the Jewish race, was now utterly rejected by extreme men. Wherever St. Paul went these men followed him. They had acknowledged Jesus as the Christ; they claimed to be the representatives of the faith and practice of the Church at Jerusalem, and to speak with the authority of the original Apostles; and they insisted that it was the duty of Christian Gentiles to submit to circumcision and to keep the law of Moses. It was the old heresy which had troubled the Church at Antioch many years before, and which had occasioned the appeal to the Apostles and Elders at Jerusalem. "Except ye be circumcised after the manner of Moses, ye cannot be saved." [39]

Among the Celtic tribes, which after overrunning the greater part of Asia Minor had been confined at last to a strip of high table-land in the centre of the peninsula, St. Paul had preached the gospel with great success. The excitable, impetuous people abandoned their idolatry, confessed Christ, and received the Apostle '*as an angel of God." Into these Churches just rescued from heathenism, the Judaizers flung the fire of controversy, insisting that so long as men remained uncircumcised they could have no part in the kingdom of God. They also impugned the apostolic authority of St. Paul, and succeeded in persuading very many that the man to whose preaching they owed all their knowledge of Christ was a person of very secondary importance, and had no claims to be regarded as an authoritative teacher of the new faith. [40]

Where St. Paul was when the news reached him that the Judaizers were breaking up the peace of the Churches of Galatia, and corrupting the simplicity of their earlier faith, is doubtful. He could hardly have been still at Antioch; [41] he may have been at Ephesus; [42] or perhaps he was on his way through Macedonia to Achaia; [43] he may even have been at Corinth. [44] Wherever he was, the news greatly astonished him, and provoked his indignation and scorn. It was a mean and dastardly act to take advantage of the ignorance and impressibility of these recent converts from heathenism, [45] and to endeavour to make them parties to a controversy concerning the real character and issues of which they had no means of ascertaining the truth. Why could not these zealous Judaizers fight out the question at Jerusalem or at Antioch? Why did they not meet St. Paul face to face? What manliness, what generosity - to say nothing of Christian charity - was there in traducing his character [46] and denying his authority behind his back, and among the very people who had learnt through him to forsake the temples of heathenism and to serve the true God? St. Paul's whole nature was ablaze. Nor did he wait till the fire went down. At once he dictated a letter to the Galatian Churches, hot with indignation against his opponents, and after eighteen centuries the heat has not gone out of it: it burns still. He speaks of the Galatians themselves with mingled feelings; there is the old affection for them; there is pity, passing at times almost into contempt, for their weakness and inconstancy.

The first two chapters are occupied with the vindication of the independence and authority of his apostolic commission. At the beginning of the third he suddenly opens the great controversy as to the permanent obligation of the Jewish law, by a rapid succession of vehement questions. What malignant spells had been cast upon them that they should have been perverted from the truth — *they* of whom it might be said that they had seen the crucified Christ with their own eyes, [47] so vividly had He been set before them? The full and clear teaching which they had received on the Death of Christ ought to have rendered it impossible for them to have been misled by the Judaizers. Did they receive the Holy Ghost through keeping the law of Moses? or through believing in the Lord Jesus Christ? Were they so utterly senseless as to suppose that, having begun by receiving the Spirit of God, they were to pass on to a higher perfection through observing mere outward rites? All that they had suffered when they had broken with their heathen fellow-countrymen — the mockery, the contempt, the annoyance, the positive persecution which they endured when they first confessed Christ — were these all in vain? would they have been endured for nothing had they not received these new apostles and submitted to circumcision? [48] The present manifestations of the Spirit of God among them — were these associated with the mere legal observances which their new teachers maintained were essential to their salvation, or with that faith in Christ on which St. Paul himself had insisted with such earnestness and emphasis?

These questions alone might have been sufficient to show the Galatians the folly of their new position. But the Apostle was bent on the utter destruction of the heresy of the Judaizers. He knew the strength of their case, knew it better than they knew it themselves, and could have defended it with keener logic and ampler learning than theirs. It was not for nothing that he had been debating for years in Jewish synagogues, nor had he forgotten his own intellectual conflicts when he first submitted to the authority of Christ. With the keen instinct of a practised controversialist he perceived that the theory of his opponents must be exploded from within, and he therefore meets them on their own ground, and appeals to the history and principles of Judaism.

He does not deny — he asserts — the Divine authority of the law. About that, there is no dispute between himself and his enemies. But he maintains that the great distinctions and prerogatives of the Jewish race, of which the Judaizers had made so much, and which they represented as indissolubly associated with circumcision and obedience to the law of Moses, were not conferred upon the Jews because they circumcised themselves and kept the law. Four hundred and thirty years before the law was given, Abraham had received the great promise that in him all nations should be blessed. That promise was the real foundation of all the glory of the Jewish people. The promise could not be disannulled by any subsequent revelations, nor could any new terms be imposed as the condition of its fulfilment. It had been given to Abraham once for all. It had been given to him, not because he kept the Jewish law, for in his days there was no Jewish law to keep. He "believed God, and it was accounted to him for righteousness." Those who have Abraham's faith — not those who put the Divine law in the place of the Divine promise, and who insist that faith such as Abraham had is of no avail apart from obedience to external precepts which Abraham never obeyed — those who have Abraham's faith are Abraham's true descendants, [49] and they will be blessed with him.

The blessing was conferred by promise before the law, and the Apostle instances several respects in which the law was inferior to the promise. But his great point is that the very purpose for which the law was given made it the very extreme of folly to look to the law for justification. It was added to the promise "for the sake of transgressions" (τῶν παραβάσεων χάριν προσετέθη, ver. 19), or as Meyer puts it: "The emergence of sins — namely, in the penal, wrath-deserving, [50] moral form of *transgressions* — which the law brought about, was *designed* by God (who must indeed have foreseen this effect) when He gave the law.... The result which the law, according to experience has on the whole effected,... could not be otherwise than the *aim* of God." [51] Abraham had been justified by faith; the law came, not to justify, but to make it clear to men that they were far more sinful than they had supposed before the law was given. [52]

This is the very crisis of the Apostle's argument. He has brought it to an issue which forces the question — "Is the law then in opposition to the promises of God?" The two seem in irreconcilable antagonism. The promise had given the assurance that in Abraham all nations should be blessed: the law had subjected the very descendants of Abraham to a curse, "For it is written, Cursed is every one that continueth not in all things that are written in the book of the law to do them." [53] Precisely at this point St. Paul appeals to the Death of Christ, and in a manner which renders it impossible to mistake his conception of its character and purpose. The promise is to stand. And why? Why? Because the "curse" — the objective curse which comes on men for breaking the law — is cancelled by Christ. Christ redeemed us Jews who were in so evil a case in consequence of the very law to which the Judaizers wish to bring you into bondage. He "redeemed us from the curse of the law, being made a curse for us; for it is written. Cursed is every one that hangeth on a tree." [54] For you Gentiles, therefore, to be trying to obtain justification by our law, is utterly irrational. The law, while it lasted, subjected us Jews to a curse from which we were not redeemed till Christ "became a curse for us;" and till then, the law was as much a hindrance to your salvation as to ours, for *you* could not inherit the blessing of Abraham while we, his descendants, were under the curse, and the Death of Christ, by which we were redeemed, rendered it possible for "the blessing of Abraham [to] come on the Gentiles through Jesus Christ; that we" — Jews and Gentiles alike — "might receive the promise of the Spirit through faith." [55]

Try, if you can, to remove from that passage the idea that Christ endured the penalty of the law — the curse — in order that those who had transgressed the law might be redeemed from the curse and inherit the promise. Make the Death of Christ an appeal to the hearts and consciences of men, and let there be nothing in it which can be described as a vicarious endurance of penalty, and what becomes of the whole structure of the Apostle's argument? He is discussing with Jews, or with Judaizers, and the idea of Christ's work is translated into terms derived from the Jewish law; but unless the idea is not only lost, but absolutely misrepresented in the translation, the Death of Christ is the ground on which sins are remitted, and it effected an objective Atonement for sin. [56]

The success of the Judaizers in perverting the faith of his Galatian converts revealed to St. Paul the magnitude of the peril which menaced his apostolic work. That Christians who were Jews by birth should still believe in the sacredness of the customs of their fathers, was not wonderful. Reverence for the institutions of Moses ran in their blood; it had been confirmed and deepened by the personal habits to which they had been trained from their childhood; it was more like a natural instinct than an acquired conviction or sentiment, and could hardly be uprooted. It was strengthened by their familiarity with their wonderful history. To a Jew, the abandonment of Jewish customs must have seemed a dissolution of the external and visible ties which

united him to prophets and saints, and a renunciation of the sacred prerogatives which had been the noblest inheritance and chief glory of the Jewish
people in the most prosperous periods of their history, and now constituted
their solitary title to national distinction. It was hard for a Jew to believe that
the advent of the Jewish Messiah had stripped the Jewish race of its ancient
supremacy.

But the Galatian Churches consisted almost exclusively of converts from
heathenism, and even they had been half persuaded that unless they submitted to circumcision, and kept the law of Moses, they still belonged to the profane and evil world from which Christ had come to deliver them, [57] and
were excluded from the kingdom of God.

St. Paul's indignation passed into grave anxiety. None of the Churches he
had founded were safe. Everywhere his apostolic authority was certain to be
challenged; and if it could be challenged successfully in the Churches of Galatia, it was impossible to rely on the constancy of any of his converts. He saw
that his opponents were equally zealous and unscrupulous, and that their
hatred of him was bitter and unrelenting. Their energy was almost equal to
his own. They were numerous, and they had allies in every synagogue all
over the world. They had tracked his steps through Asia Minor: they had followed him to Greece. He was intending to visit Rome, but they might be there
before him. He resolved, therefore, to prepare a comprehensive and complete statement of those great truths which he believed had been specially
committed to his trust, and to send it forward to Rome at once. He had many
friends there; most of them, probably, Jews who had been driven from Rome
some years before by a decree of Claudius Caesar, which had now been repealed or forgotten. He had met them at Corinth, when he was there a few
years before, and at Ephesus, and at other cities in which he had preached
the gospel, and many of them, perhaps, were his own converts. To them he
resolved to give a full exposition of the great truths concerning Justification,
which formed the substance of his characteristic gospel, and also to explain
the true relations between the Jewish race and the Christian Church.

The Epistle to the Romans is not, as some critics have supposed, a treatise
on Justification, with a kind of supplement on the future destiny of the Jewish
people; nor is it, as others have contended, a defence of St. Paul's mission to
the Gentiles, with an introduction intended to illustrate his general conception of Christian doctrine. It is equally a misapprehension to regard the epistle as a defence of his teaching and a vindication of his apostolic work. The
Epistle to the Romans was suggested by the success of the Judaizers in Galatia. St. Paul knew that he stood almost alone, that his life was uncertain, and
that the knowledge of the Churches he had founded was very immature: he
therefore determined to state, once for all, the truths on which the security,
freedom, and future extension of the Christian Church depended. He stated
them — not polemically, nor in the way of self-defence, for there is no reason
to suppose that the controversy had as yet commenced in Rome — but as

systematically as it was possible to state them in the form of a letter. There are some indications that while the epistle as it stands was intended to be sent to Rome, the body of it was intended to be copied and sent to Churches in other cities. I shall attempt to ascertain the precise place which St. Paul assigns to the Death of Christ in the development of doctrine contained in the first half of the epistle.

The thesis of the whole epistle is contained in the words, "I am not ashamed of the gospel of Christ; for it is the power of God unto salvation to every one that believeth, to the Jew first and also to the Greek. For therein is the righteousness of God revealed from faith to faith, as it is written, The just shall live by faith." [58] The precise meaning of these words has been obscured by controversy, and they had better be left as they stand, to receive their explanation from St. Paul's own exposition of them.

There is another revelation, he says, besides the revelation of "the righteousness of God." "The *wrath* of God is revealed from heaven against all ungodliness and unrighteousness of men who hold the truth in unrighteousness." [59] He means, that to those who have eyes to see, it is clear that God is not at peace with sin, and can never be at peace with it. The world would not be what it is if God were at peace with it. A few sentences later, he speaks of the condition of heathen nations as proving the reality and severity of the Divine hostility. As St. Paul travelled from city to city, and from country to country, it seemed to him that he was living in a world which God had forsaken. Men had "changed the glory of the uncorruptible God into an image made like to corruptible man, and to birds, and four-footed beasts, and creeping things;" they had "changed the truth of God into a lie, and worshipped and served the creature more than the Creator, who is blessed for ever;" [60] and therefore God in His anger had left them to drift from sin to sin, from shame to shame, from misery to misery, from darkness to deeper darkness still. They had made their choice, and He let them run their course. He "gave them up to uncleanness, ...to vile affections,...to a reprobate mind." [61] Even the restraints of natural instinct were relaxed, and men committed abominations which cannot be uttered. There was universal disorder; all laws were violated; the most sacred relations were dissolved. Men did not keep faith with each other; they were disobedient to parents; they were envious, insolent, heartless, malignant, cruel, implacable; they were liars, slanderers, murderers. They knew the righteous judgment of God, that they who commit such things are worthy of death, and yet they not only committed them, but were so utterly depraved that they encouraged each other in sin, and provoked each other to the worst immoralities. [62]

But there were some who condemned the gross vices of which the vast masses of the heathen were guilty. St. Paul lays hold of this very condemnation, and uses it with terrible force to establish his position. He turns suddenly round upon all who agreed with what he had said about the corruption of heathen society, and charges them with participation in the general guilt. He

attempts no proof of the. charge, but appeals directly to their consciences —
"Thou art inexcusable, O man, whosoever thou art that judgest: for wherein
thou judgest another, thou condemnest thyself, for thou that judgest doest
the same things." [63] Not by condemning the crimes of others are men to
escape the judgment of God. Those who commit the very crimes which they
condemn, pronounce against themselves a sentence which cannot be challenged; they are treasuring up unto themselves wrath against the day of
wrath, and revelation of the righteous judgment of God, "who will render to
every man according to his deeds;" — yes, "to every man," whether he be Jew
or Gentile, "for there is no respect of persons with God." [64] For the Jew to
suppose that because he had received the Divine law he was certain to escape the Divine wrath, was presumption and folly. Men are not justified by
listening to the law, but by keeping it. But if thou art a Jew, and proud of the
name, and reliest on the law as the sign and guarantee of the Divine favour,
[65] and art glorying in God as the God of thy race, and knowest whose will it
is that men should obey, [66] and approvest those things that are morally
excellent, being instructed out of the law, and hast faith in thyself as being
the teacher and the guide of the rest of mankind, the very light of a world in
darkness — well — hast thou nothing to do with the law except to teach it?
Thou that preachest against stealing, is preaching enough? dost *thou* steal?
Thou that sayest a man must not commit adultery, dost thou commit adultery? Thou that abhorrest idols, dost thou plunder their temples? Thou that
gloriest in the law, through breaking the law, dost thou dishonour the God
who gave it? [67]

As for circumcision, it is the honourable sign of belonging to a race which
stands in a very near relation to God, and which, because it stands in that
relation to Him, has received the law; but if the law is not kept, circumcision
is of no avail. If a Gentile keeps the law, he is justified; if a Jew breaks it, he is
condemned. [68]

But what advantage, then, is there in being a Jew, if a man who is not a Jew
may be justified by keeping the law, and if a Jew cannot be justified without
keeping it? Advantage? The advantage is great, and great on many accounts.
First of all, because to the Jews were committed the oracles of God. For what
if some were unfaithful to the covenant; shall their unfaithfulness destroy the
fidelity of God to His promises? God forbid. Let every man be false, but God's
truth must stand fast, and the very unfaithfulness of men does but illustrate
more gloriously the faithfulness of God. Shall the Jews, then, venture to say
that because the sins of their race had completed the demonstration of the
Divine righteousness, it would be unjust in God to punish them? That would
render it impossible for God to judge the world, for His final judgment of
human sin will also illustrate His own righteousness, and it would even be a
reason for saying, "Let us do evil, that good may come;" but whoever says
that, his damnation is just. [69] Jews and Gentiles are alike sinners. The Jewish Scriptures themselves condemned the sins of which Jews were guilty. For

"there is none righteous, no, not one; ...they are all gone out of the way;... there is none that doeth good, no, not one;... their throat is an open sepulchre;... their feet are swift to shed blood;... there is no fear of God before their eyes." [70] It was of Jews that these terrible words were written. It is not enough, therefore, for a man to be a Jew in order to escape condemnation as a sinner. Every mouth is stopped — the mouth of the Jew as well as the mouth of the Gentile — and the whole world must stand guilty before God. The Jews are in no better case than the Gentiles; they have been surrounded by the restraints of the Divine law, but the law itself condemns them; "for by the law is the knowledge of sin." [71]

This is the line of thought by which St. Paul approaches the statement which immediately follows, of the Divine method of redemption through our Lord Jesus Christ, and it determines, by anticipation, the Apostle's conception of the character of that redemption. The point from which he started was very definite: "The wrath of God is revealed from heaven against all ungodliness and unrighteousness," and he has been establishing the reality and the justice of that wrath through the whole course of his argument. His clear intention is to confirm the necessity of some means of escape from the peril by which "every soul of man that doeth evil" is menaced.

Yes, it may be replied, and all that he has said about the crimes of the heathen, and the powerlessness of the Jewish law to inspire men with the disposition and the ability to keep it, is a demonstration of the necessity of a great moral and spiritual change in human nature. St. Paul believed that this change is effected by the visible presentation to the enfeebled conscience and the corrupt heart, of the possible purity and grace and nobleness of humanity in the faultless perfection of the character of Christ, and by the irresistible manifestation of the Divine love in His sufferings and Death. By this transformation of character we are to be delivered from the Divine displeasure, and from whatever that displeasure involves.

That St. Paul believed in the necessity of a new revelation of God, to produce a moral and spiritual change in man, is of course admitted. That the facts on which he insists in the first three chapters of this epistle prove the necessity of such a revelation, is also beyond dispute. But that he was intending to prove this necessity, is an untenable hypothesis. Had this been his purpose, though he might have used the same materials, the whole structure of his argument would have been different. Review the movement of his thought, and you will discover that at point after point such a purpose would have given it another direction. He would not merely have contended with such earnestness that "the invisible things of [God], from the time of the creation of the world, are clearly seen, being understood by the things that are made, even His eternal power and Godhead, so that [idolaters] are without excuse;" but while alleging that enough had been revealed of the living and eternal God to render idolatry inexcusable, he would have emphasised, not the guilt, but the moral helplessness of the heathen. He would not have been satisfied with showing that the law, on which the Jews relied as a proof of the favour with which God regarded their race, revealed and condemned their sins; he would have spoken of those ineffectual struggles of men to keep the law which he describes so vividly and so pathetically later in the epistle, and would thus have demonstrated the necessity of a new revelation, containing new motives and new powers, to enable men to break with sin, and to live a holy life.

No; St. Paul's intention was to demonstrate that the whole world is exposed to the Divine wrath, and that if men are to be saved, that wrath must be somehow averted. That this was his intention, becomes clearer the more rigorous the examination to which the whole argument is subjected.

This may be granted, and it may still be alleged that the Divine anger is provoked by sin, and that to escape it, a subjective redemption is necessary. Let men cease to sin, and all the evils and perils in which sin involves them will cease too; and the Apostle's argument may culminate in the declaration that men are to be delivered from perdition — not by any objective atonement — but by being transformed into the image of God through the power and grace of the Lord Jesus Christ.

Is it true that the argument culminates in any such declaration? If this is St. Paul's theory of the Christian redemption, he has reached the precise point at which he is required to state it. He ought now to speak of those new spiritual forces which will recover from idolatry and vice those who had failed to recognize the majesty and greatness of God in the shining heavens, and in the grandeur and loveliness of earth and sea; and who, as the result of their idolatry, have descended into dark depths of shameful and abominable sin. The time has come for him to speak of the power over the human heart of the righteousness and love of God as revealed through Christ — a power equal to the achievement of the moral and spiritual regeneration which the law and the prophets had failed to accomplish.

But in those passages of the epistle which immediately follow the declaration of the universal guilt of mankind, is there anything to suggest that the Apostle's mind was occupied with the spiritual influences which now act on the heart and conscience of the race — anything to suggest that Christ delivers men from the Divine wrath solely because He changes their disposition and character; and that by the normal action of "spiritual laws" men gradually escape from the consequences of sin, as through Christ they are gradually attracted and disciplined to holiness? The first few sentences may seem ambiguous. When St. Paul speaks of "the righteousness of God which is by faith in Jesus Christ," [72] it is possible to suppose that he is thinking of that subjective change which is the result of faith in Christ — a change by which man recovers the image of the Divine holiness. The ambiguity may not disappear when he speaks of our "being justified freely by His grace through the redemption that is in Christ Jesus;" [73] but the words which immediately follow, and the contents of the next few pages of the epistle, are an irresistible proof that as yet St. Paul had no thought of the moral and spiritual regeneration which Christ effects in those who believe in Him. He closes his statement of the method by which we are to escape the Divine condemnation before he illustrates either the necessity of ceasing to sin, or the spiritual powers by which our escape from sin is effected.

At present he is wholly absorbed in the question. How are we to be delivered — not from sin — but from guilt, and from the wrath of God, to which our guilt exposes us?

His reply to these questions is very explicit. We are "justified freely by His grace through the redemption that is in Christ Jesus;" [74] and the justification of which the Apostle is speaking is the precise antithesis of condemnation. As condemnation is not the cause, but the effect of sin, so justification is not the cause, but the effect of righteousness. [75] The attempt to include in the conception of justification any other element, and to make it cover the Divine work by which the disposition, character, and conduct of men are changed from sin to holiness, dislocates the whole organization of the Apostle's thought in this part of the epistle. What he meant by our being "justified freely by His grace" appears in the next chapter. Abraham's justification was not the effect produced by Abraham's faith on Abraham's character, but the Divine response to Abraham's faith. [76] "David also describeth the blessedness of the man" whom God justifies, "the man unto whom God imputeth righteousness without works, saying, Blessed are they whose *iniquities are forgiven* and whose *sins are covered.*" [77] And as Abraham's faith justified him — not because it made him a better man, but — because "it was imputed to him for righteousness," [78] our faith in Christ justifies us in the same way. To us also faith "shall be imputed" for righteousness, "if we believe on Him that raised up Jesus our Lord from the dead." [79]

It is an objective justification that St. Paul is describing, a justification by virtue of which we are no longer "guilty before God," and in peril of His wrath. [80]

But how is this transition from guilt to justification accomplished? We are "justified freely through the redemption that is in Christ Jesus." [81] The redemption may include much else, but for the moment the Apostle is representing it as having for its direct result the justification in which we are delivered from guilt and wrath. If we further ask — How is it that this objective redemption is rendered possible by Christ? the answer is given in the words which immediately follow — "Whom God hath openly set forth, for Himself, as a propitiatory offering (through faith) in His blood." [82] It is from the Divine condemnation and the Divine wrath that men need to be delivered. Neither Jew nor Gentile can urge any ground why the condemnation should be revoked and the wrath turned aside, for "every mouth [is] stopped, and the whole world [is] guilty before God." From this just condemnation, from this righteous wrath, there is redemption in Christ; for Christ, "in His blood" — not in His personal holiness merely — has been placed by God before the eye and. heart of all mankind as a propitiatory sacrifice. Sacrifices are not offered to men, but to God, and the direct intention of this Sacrifice is to avert that supreme peril which, according to the preceding argument, menaces the whole race. The Death of Christ is represented— not as the method by which God touches the human heart — but as the ground on which God cancels human guilt, and delivers the guilty from "the wrath" which threatened them.

St. Paul's statement is not yet exhausted. "Propitiation" suggests the idea of an appeal to the infinite mercy of God to lay aside His wrath; but the Apostle proceeds to say that the Sacrifice of Christ is also a revelation of the righteousness of God; and the form in which this statement is made precludes all misapprehension. "God hath openly set forth Christ, for Himself, as a propitiatory sacrifice,...in His blood,...for the sake of manifesting His righteousness on account of the pretermission or [*overlooking*] in the forbearance of God of sins which had passed." [83]

In the times which preceded the coming of Christ, God, in His longsuffering, had not revealed His righteousness in the adequate punishment of sin. But this manifestation was made in the Death of Christ as a Sacrifice for the sins of men.

Christ did not die, therefore, merely to save men of future ages from sinning; His Death was something more than an appeal to the human heart and the human conscience; it had been rendered necessary by the pretermission of sin in ages gone by. He revealed "the righteousness of God," which had been obscured by God's forbearance.

But the revelation of righteousness was related to the future as well as to the past; for Christ was openly set forth as a Propitiatory Sacrifice "for the revelation of [God's] righteousness in the present time, in order that He may be just, and the justifier of him that believeth in Jesus." [84] The righteousness of God, which might otherwise have been revealed in His punishment of the sins of former ages, sins which in His forbearance He had passed over, and which would also have been revealed in His punishment of sinful men whom He now justifies and saves, is revealed in the Sacrifice of Christ.

It would be difficult to find words in which the objective character of the Death of Christ could be more explicitly asserted. It is from "wrath" that we need to be saved, and Christ has been openly set forth as a Propitiation. The wrath is the antagonism of God's Righteousness to sin - sin which, in His forbearance, He had passed over in the times preceding the advent of Christ - sin which He is now ready to remit in the case of every man that believes in Christ; the Righteousness which in both cases is withheld from its direct expression is yet revealed, and it is for the sake of revealing it that Christ dies.

The fourth chapter is a parenthetical vindication of the doctrine of Justification by Faith against the possible objection that the doctrine is inconsistent with the revelation of God to the Jewish race. Inconsistent with that revelation! St. Paul appeals to Abraham, from whom the Jews inherited all their prerogatives. He believed in God, and it was "counted unto him for righteousness;" and descending the line of Jewish history more than a thousand years, he invokes the authority of David to sustain the position that "God imputeth righteousness without works."

In the fifth chapter he resumes the main line of his thought, and develops the results of this Justification. Even now he says nothing of any subjective results. He is still absorbed in those objective blessings which the Death of Christ, and the Justification which is effected through it, secure for those who believe.

"Being justified by faith we have peace with God." [85] To suppose that the Apostle means that our own hostility to God's authority and righteous law is subdued, or that the conflict and confusion of our own inner life pass into harmony, is to import into his words ideas which, however true, are foreign to the province of truth over which his thought has been travelling, and to destroy the organic relation of this chapter to all that has preceded it. God is hostile to sin; as sinful men, we were in danger of being swept away by His wrath; but the danger has passed by; He is at peace with us through the Lord Jesus Christ.

Through Christ, too, "we have had access by faith into this grace wherein we stand." [86] That which prevented us from approaching God, and made us exiles from the light and honour of the Divine presence, has been removed. God's wrath against sin repelled us, but Christ is our Propitiation. God's righteousness, which would have been suppressed had He invested with privilege and prerogative those who deserved punishment, has been revealed in Christ's Death: we have therefore "access into this grace" through Him. St. Paul does not intend to say that we are inclined to approach God, but that what hindered our approaching Him has disappeared, through Christ. Nor is this all. "We rejoice in hope of the glory of God:" [87] we who were looking forward with dread to "the revelation of the righteous judgment of God," are now exulting in the confident expectation of receiving from God eternal glory.

And "we glory in [our present] tribulations also," for these do but make the hope stronger and firmer; and "the hope maketh not ashamed." [88] Why? Does he say, "Because the power of the Death of Christ is already delivering us from sin, and, therefore, we are sure that we must at last emerge from all the evils incident to sin, so that ultimately consummate moral perfection will necessarily be crowned with consummate blessedness "? No. "The hope maketh not ashamed; because the love of God" — His love for us — "is shed abroad in our hearts by the Holy Ghost which is given to us." [89] We have no reason to fear that the fire and hail of God's anger will descend upon us; the storm has moved away, or we have risen above it; and as the light and heat of the sun are shed abroad through the heavens at noonday, so the love of God for us is already shed abroad in our hearts. This manifestation of the love of God, which makes the hope of escaping His wrath so confident, is accomplished by the power of the Holy Ghost, who illuminates for us the transcendent expression of Divine mercy in the Death of Christ.

"For when we were yet without strength, in due time Christ died for the ungodly." [90] This is the first recognition that the epistle contains of the moral weakness of men, although that moral weakness ought to have been the dominant theme of the whole argument had St. Paul believed that the solitary object of the revelation of God in Christ was to give new energy to our moral and spiritual life, and to redeem us from the penalties of sin by restoring us to holiness. While he is intent upon establishing his original thesis that through sin men are exposed to the Divine wrath, and that by sin they incur the hostility of the Divine righteousness, while he is moving towards the great statement of the gospel contained towards the close of the third chapter, that the Death of Christ is at once the propitiation for the sins of man, and the revelation of the righteousness of God, he emphasises human guilt, and appears oblivious of human weakness. As soon as he speaks of the Death of Christ as a demonstration of the Divine love, he represents the moral condition of the race under a new aspect. "When we were yet without strength, Christ died: "our weakness appealed to God's pity, though our sin provoked His anger. The change, however, is only momentary; the primary reason that Christ died was not that we were "weak," but that we were guilty, and the Apostle recurs at once to his old position — "Christ died for the ungodly" The mention of the Divine love suggested our helplessness: as soon as he speaks of the Death of Christ the idea of our guilt returns, and the idea of helplessness disappears.

Further, the Death of Christ is a complete and final proof of God's love for us. Men will hardly die for the just — to say nothing of the unjust — though, perhaps, for a good man some would even dare to die; but, "while we were yet sinners, Christ died for us." [91] In what sense Christ died for us he has already defined: we were sinners, and therefore exposed to the Divine wrath, and in danger of suffering whatever evils the righteousness of God might inflict upon us. Christ's Death was a propitiation for our sins and a revelation of God's righteousness. "Much more then, being now justified by His blood, we shall be saved." From what? From sin? No; even now St. Paul has not escaped from the thought of that tremendous doom which threatened us — the doom which is to descend at the last day upon the unsaved. "We shall be saved from [the] wrath through Him." [92] He repeats the thought in another form — "For if, when we were enemies, we were reconciled to God by the Death of His Son, much more, being reconciled, we shall be saved by His life." [93] This incessant reappearance of one unvarying conception of the effect of the Death of Christ is profoundly significant. "We were enemies" — God was hostile to us, and He ceased to be hostile because Christ died as a Propitiation for our sins. Now that reconciliation has been effected by the Death of Christ, the living Christ will not leave us at last unsheltered from the wrath which He died to avert. This account of what Christ has accomplished for us, and accomplished for us by His Death, is closed with a triumphant sentence, in which it is declared that now "we joy in God" — in the very God whose laws we had broken and whose anger we had provoked. But the Apostle cannot even now repress another reference to that supreme event, on the ground of which God has ceased to be a terror to us — "we joy in God through our Lord Jesus Christ, by whom we have now received the reconciliation." [94]

Is the proof complete? — the proof that St. Paul represented the Death of Christ as being in such a sense a revelation of the Divine righteousness and a Propitiation for human sin, that all who believe in Him are liberated from those dreadful judgments which, had Christ not died, the righteousness of God would have inflicted on them as the expression and effect of its eternal hostility to sin, and from that "wrath of God" which, had Christ not died, would have consumed them?

It is not easy to imagine how the proof can be strengthened; but all lingering doubt of St. Paul's true intention must disappear after reading the next chapter of the epistle.

The fifth chapter closes with a parallel or contrast between Adam and the Lord Jesus Christ, and with a brief reference to the true function of the Mosaic law, which came in, side by side, with sin, "that the offence might abound;" but St. Paul alleges that the clearer discovery of the greatness of human sin has only illustrated the transcendent greatness of the Divine grace. This suggests the form of the question with which the sixth chapter opens — a question which might take the place of volumes of controversial theology on the Pauline doctrine of justification, and is a decisive proof that the Pauline conception of the relation between the Death of Christ and the remission of sins is irreconcilable with the "Moral Theory" of the Atonement, whatever form that theory may assume.

"What shall we say, then?" asks the Apostle. "Shall we continue in sin?" — we who are "justified by faith," we who "have peace with God," we who once were "enemies," but who are now "reconciled to God by the death of His Son" — "shall we continue in sin, that grace may abound?" [95] Such a question would have been irrelevant and impossible if St. Paul had believed that Justification is a change of character, and that the reconciliation effected by the Death of Christ is primarily a removal of man's antagonism to God and righteousness.

Theologians who maintain that the only purpose for which Christ died was to appeal to the moral and spiritual nature of man, and to inspire the human heart with sorrow for sin and the love of God, do not find it necessary, after elaborating their theory of Justification, to discuss any such question as this. For them, the direct and only intention of the Death of Christ is to rescue men from sin and to restore them to holiness. Even their most bitter and unscrupulous opponents can never object that the gospel, as they preach it, may perhaps encourage evil men to continue in their evil practices; nor can their most ignorant and unintelligent adherents so misapprehend their meaning

115

as to imagine that they may be "saved from wrath" through Christ, and yet continue in sin.

But the theory of St. Paul was open to this objection, and he thought it necessary to avert this misapprehension. He was represented as releasing men from all obligations to righteousness, as preaching a salvation which permitted, and even provoked, men to multiply their crimes, in order that the grace of God might be glorified: "We be slanderously reported, and...some affirm that we say. Let us do evil, that good may come." [96] The report was a slander, but had he represented the Death of Christ as saving us from future destruction only because of its moral effect in saving us from present sin, the slander would have been impossible. The misrepresentations of a theory have always some relation to its characteristic spirit and principles. If a theologian, whose writings are lost, is denounced by hostile controversialists for obscuring the grace and sovereignty of God, and ascribing to man all the merit of his own salvation, we may be certain that he did not insist very strongly on the Divine decrees; if he is denounced for teaching fatalism, we may be certain that he did not emphasise human responsibility, and make the freedom of the human will the centre of his theological system. It was "slanderously reported" that St. Paul preached a gospel which did not require men to cease to sin. The slander throws an intense light on his teaching. He could not have taught the "Moral Theory" of the Atonement.

When he first refers to this slander, he does not stay to discuss it: he repels it with a vehement disclaimer: If men say, "Let us do evil, that good may come," their "damnation is just." [97] But after closing his statement of the doctrine of Justification, he returns to the perverse inference which his enemies had drawn from his preaching, and he returns to it for the sake of removing all mistake from the minds of his friends. The manner in which he deals with it is extremely instructive.

"Shall we continue in sin, that grace may abound?" It is impossible, as I have said already, that any such question could be raised, either in the course of developing the "Moral Theory" of the Atonement, or after the doctrine of Justification associated with that theory had been defined and illustrated. But if it were raised, nothing is easier than to imagine the kind of reply that the question would receive. It would be said that the righteousness which comes to us through Christ is real, and not fictitious; that for men to be justified through Christ, means that through Him they are actually made just; that if in any sense He died to avert the Divine wrath and the penalties of sin, He averts them by redeeming us from sin itself, and in no other way; that the peace with God into which we enter through faith in Christ is the result of the cessation of our hostility to God's authority and the disappearance of our distrust of His love; that the reconciliation which Christ has effected does not remove any antagonism on God's part towards us, but resolves our will into harmony with the Divine will; that the hypothesis of continuing in sin after

Justification involves a contradiction in terms, since Justification means nothing else than deliverance from sin, or the result of that deliverance.

This, however, is not the reply which is given by St. Paul. It is not a reply which it was possible for him to give. He could not have given it without breaking up his previous argument and reconstructing it on a new basis. Instead of showing that his idea of Justification involves the idea of actual holiness in the person who is justified, or that Christ justifies us in no other way than by making us holy — which would have been the most obvious, most direct, and most conclusive answer to the question, "Shall we continue in sin, that grace may abound?" — he moves into a region of truth altogether new. What he has said about Justification he leaves exactly as it stands, without any explanation, and his thought takes a new departure. "Continue in sin, that grace may abound? God forbid!" [98] By the faith in response to which for Christ's sake we are justified, we are also brought into a mysterious and transcendental union with Christ. We were baptized into His death; we were buried with Him; with Him we rise to a new life in God. Henceforth we are in a new world, because our life is new. The evil self, the root of all our sin, was crucified with Christ: for us to continue in sin is therefore impossible. [99] The argument extends through the whole of the sixth and seventh chapters, and I need not summarise it.

The point to be noticed is this: St. Paul does not return upon his previous line of thought, and show that Justification is in itself inconsistent with the idea of personal sinfulness: he places redemption from sin side by side with Justification, as another result of the Death of Christ, a second element of the redemption which Christ has accomplished for us. In the first five chapters of his epistle he has shown how through Christ we are delivered from "the wrath of God [which] is revealed from heaven against all ungodliness and unrighteousness of men;" and how we are able, through Christ, to look forward without terror to "the day of wrath and revelation of the righteous judgment of God." The infinite evils to which we were exposed have passed away because the Death of Christ is an adequate revelation of the righteousness of God, and an adequate Propitiation for the sins of men. But of our restoration to holiness he has said nothing. The effect of the Death of Christ in atoning for human sin is so immediate, so independent of any change in human character, that he has now to enter on a new line of argument, in order to show that those who are justified cannot continue in sin.

Reject the idea of an objective Atonement and of an objective Justification founded upon it, and you must not only strain to unnatural and impossible meanings, words, phrases, and whole sentences in which these ideas are conspicuously present; you must do violence to the plan and structure of nearly the whole of the first half of the epistle. The statement in the first two chapters of the grounds on which the intervention of Christ was necessary is inappropriate; the critical declaration in the third chapter, that Christ has been set forth as "a Propitiation... in His blood," is misleading; the conclusion of the argument in the early verses of the fifth chapter, that "being justified by faith we have peace with God," is premature; the necessity for discussing the question at the opening of the sixth chapter, "Shall we continue in sin, that grace may abound?" is unintelligible; and the discussion which extends through the sixth and seventh chapters lies far remote from the most direct and decisive reply with which the question might have been met. These seven chapters, if every other passage in his epistles were doubtful, would constitute a sufficient and impregnable demonstration that St. Paul believed in an objective Atonement.

But the Epistles to the Galatians and the Romans were suggested by the transient exigencies of a sharp and bitter controversy. Is it not possible that the conception of the Death of Christ which these epistles contain was a merely transient phase of the Apostle's thought? The suggestion is, on many grounds, extremely improbable; but let us test it by an appeal to the epistles of the imprisonment.

Three or four years passed by, and the Apostle was in Rome, a prisoner — charged by his countrymen with exciting the Jews in every part of the empire to sedition, and with the crime of profaning the temple. He had appealed from the tribunal of a provincial governor to the Emperor, and, after a long imprisonment at Caesarea, had been sent to Rome, to be acquitted or condemned. The ardent, restless nature of St. Paul must have chafed at first under the restraints of his imprisonment, but perhaps it was well for him, and well for us, that the exciting and exhausting labours of his apostolic ministry should have been interrupted by enforced seclusion and rest.

When he reached Rome, more than two years passed before his case was heard, and these were among the happiest and most fruitful years of his life. He had considerable freedom. Some of the friends to whom he had sent kindly messages in his Epistle to the Romans were still in the city. He had a house of his own, and appears to have been visited by large numbers of persons who were curious to learn the faith of the new sect from one of its most eminent teachers. His fierce controversies with the Judaizers were practically over. There were some indeed, even in Rome, who preached Christ of "envy and strife," and "of contention, not sincerely," thinking to add affliction to his bonds; [100] but he does not seem to have been greatly agitated by their opposition to him.

His mind was occupied with new thoughts. In the Churches of Phrygia there began to appear premonitions of a fresh danger to the simplicity of the Christian faith. A singular blending of the great facts of the gospel with Jewish asceticism and the wildest Oriental speculations on the origin and order of the universe, fascinated the imagination of the Christian Churches which had been founded in that part of Asia, and excited in the mind of St. Paul grave apprehensions. In the Epistle to the Colossians he opposed the true Christian *Gnosis* to the false philosophy which was usurping its place; and the idea of the Death of Christ as a sacrifice for sin emerges precisely at those points where, on our theory, we should expect it to emerge, and the epistle contains some very important contributions to that conception of the relation of Christ to the universe which appears indispensable to a true theory of expiation.

Both in the Epistle to the Colossians, and in the epistle written at the same time and despatched by the same messengers, and known to us as the Epistle to the Ephesians, St. Paul passes into a sphere of thought which he hardly touches in any of his earlier writings. He was in Rome, the centre and heart of an empire whose boundaries seemed destined to include the human race. Already the authority of the imperial city extended westwards over Spain and Gaul to the Atlantic; northwards to the mountains of Caledonia, to the Rhine, and the Danube; eastwards to the Euphrates; southwards to the borders of the African desert. The various nations inhabiting these vast territories — nations differing in their origin, their language, their laws, and their customs, separated by mountains and by seas — had been gradually subdued by the power of Rome, and were now included in one mighty and majestic political organization. If for sixty years the empire had received no considerable accessions of territory, the influence of Roman manners and of Roman law had been silently effacing national distinctions and assimilating heterogeneous and hostile races; the subject provinces had been gradually losing the spirit and traditions of independence, and had been learning to identify their own honour and prosperity with the renown of the Roman name. Policy, not the consciousness of weakness, had arrested the extension of the empire; and it must have appeared to St. Paul and his contemporaries, that if occasion arose for attempting new conquests, the turbulent barbarians that inhabited the forests of northern Europe and the shores of the Euxine, and even the shadowy monarchies of the remote East, must yield to the irresistible shock of the legions of Rome.

Is it a mere fancy to suppose that it was the impression produced on the imagination of the Apostle by the vastness and grandeur of the Roman power, the symbols of which were perpetually before his eyes, as well as the boldness of the speculations which were corrupting the faith of the Church at Colosse, and, perhaps, of the Church at Ephesus, that led his thoughts into glorious regions of truth, which he had before seen afar off, but which now became completely his own?

God has "made known to us the mystery of His will," it being His eternal purpose, a purpose He resolved to accomplish "in the dispensation of the fulness of times, to gather together in one all things in Christ, both which are in heaven, and which are on earth; even in Him" [101] — in Him who is seated at the right hand of God, "far above all principality, and power, and might, and dominion, and every name that is named, not only in this world, but also in that which is to come." [102]

This restoration of the whole universe to perfect unity in Christ — where was it so likely to take possession of the mind of St. Paul as in the city of

Rome, which through eight hundred years had been gradually subduing nation after nation, giving them laws, giving them peace, and organising them into one great political system, until now it seemed to have within its grasp the government of the human race? May we not imagine that to the Apostle, the empire appeared a rude and earthly but not ignoble symbol of the final comprehension of heaven and earth in one august and blessed and glorious kingdom under the authority of the Lord Jesus Christ?

In that Divine and eternal polity all who believe in Christ — Jews, who belonged to a race which for ages had been hoping for His coming, Gentiles, who heard of Him for the first time when the gospel was preached to them — are alike comprehended; and St. Paul prays that the Christians at Ephesus may receive the illumination of the Holy Ghost, that they may know the future glory of the kingdom into which they have been received. This glory he associates with the "exceeding greatness" of the Divine power, which raised Christ from the weakness and shame and humiliation of death to the throne of God, and which is already working in all that believe, and accomplishing for them a similar glorification. A great civilising state changes the face of every country it annexes; drains the marshes, clears the forests, works the mines, opens new roads, establishes new forms of industry, builds stately cities; provinces which were worthless when it conquered them, it covers with fertility and wealth. So, according to St. Paul, God, who has made us His possession and inheritance, will make us worth having. What His power wrought in the resurrection of Christ, and the enthronement of Christ at His own right hand, is the illustration and prophecy of what His power will ultimately accomplish in us; and only the Spirit of God can reveal to us what will be "the riches of the glory of [God's] inheritance in the saints." [103]

But there was a time when both Christian Jews and Christian Gentiles, who are now looking forward to this great future, and who already share the life and sonship of the Lord Jesus Christ, were "children of wrath even as others." [104] The case of the Gentiles seemed, indeed, more desperate than that of the Jews. For the Jews had been separated from the rest of mankind by a symbolic rite, which constituted them, in some sense, an elect nation. They had received their national polity from God; their national existence rested on Divine promises of immeasurable meaning, promises which it was difficult to believe had been wholly lost, even by the sins which had provoked the Divine anger. They were "the children of wrath," and yet they were "nigh" unto God; for through all the shameful crimes of their national history God had never recalled the promises which He had given to the head and founder of their race; and even in the worst times their inspired prophets and psalmists had consoled them in their sufferings, and rebuked their sins, by appealing to the future glory of the Christ who was to be the heir of the throne of David, and in whom the hopes of the descendants of Abraham were to be fulfilled. But the Gentiles were "without Christ." No sure vision of the Divine Deliverer and King had been the solace and strength of any Gentile nation;

they were "aliens" from that "commonwealth" in which the kingdom of God on earth had already taken a rudimentary form; they were "strangers" to those "covenants of promise" in which the Jews found assurance of a Divine interference for their redemption; the great "hope" was not theirs; their golden age was in the past, not in the future; and while they had vague traditions of days when heaven was near to earth and the gods dwelt with men, they were not anticipating a time when the old glory would return; and they were "without God" in the world. [105]

How had they been recovered from this utter desolation? "Children of wrath," and excluded even from that earthly polity which was the transient shadow of the Divine kingdom, — how had they been restored to God? The Apostle replies that by assuming that nature which is common to Jew and Gentile, and by bringing to an end the temporary and separate privileges of the Jewish people, Christ slew the "enmity" by which Jew and Gentile were divided; they stood apart no longer; and He reconciled both unto God "in one body by the cross." [106] But was not this a moral redemption? Was it not accomplished by changing the spirit and character of men; by revealing to the Gentiles the true and living God, whom they had forsaken to worship idols; and by revealing to the Jews a wealth of Divine love which broke their hearts with penitence for sin, and constrained them to confess that the law which "came by Moses" was infinitely surpassed by the "grace and truth" which came by Jesus Christ?

Read the development of the Apostle's thought, and you will discover that this is not the form under which he presents the Christian redemption. The "peace" which Christ brought about between Jew and Gentile was the result of the removal of the objective cause of separation, the breaking down of "the middle wall of partition" between them. The "peace" between man and God which Christ secured, the reconciliation of Jew and Gentile to God by the cross, was — not the removal of human antagonism to God — but of Divine antagonism to man. We were "children of wrath," and Christ came and "preached the glad tidings of peace [107] to you who were afar off and to them that were nigh." [108] He proclaimed peace to those who were in peril of the Divine anger, made known the good news that God was no longer hostile to them. The image present to the Apostle's mind is that of an imperial power sending messengers to provinces with which it had been at war — messengers whose first business was to make known that the war was over. And this reconciliation between God and the human race had been accomplished "by the blood" and "by the cross" of the Lord Jesus Christ. Through Him, and as the result of this, reconciliation, both Jew and Gentile have access by one Spirit to the Father. The restoration of the universe to an eternal unity in Christ has begun; the old division between the descendants of Abraham and the heathen world has disappeared; in their religious life, all Christians of all nations, whatever their temporary and external distinctions, are already one in Christ; and in Him they are already parts of that great temple of which Christ is the corner-stone, and in which God will dwell. [109]

What is remarkable in this epistle is that not only before he enters into these large and wide disclosures of the eternal purpose of God in relation to the universe, does St. Paul speak of our having "redemption through the blood of Christ, the forgiveness of sins, according to the riches of His grace;" [110] that not only after he has ended them, and passed into practical exhortations to Christian morality, does he charge the Ephesian Christians to "walk in love, as Christ also loved us, and gave Himself for us;" [111] but that in the very heart of the lofty and fervent statement of his conception of the Divine thought in relation to the universe, he recognises the unique and supreme function of the Death of Christ. For him, the cross of Christ is the very centre of that Divine movement which extends as far as his vision can reach, and to the remotest limits of the created universe, including alike the obscurest of the sons of men and the regal powers of the heavenly world. God had resolved to "gather together in one all things in Christ," and for the fulfilment of this vast purpose Christ proclaims that God is at peace with those who had once been "children of wrath," and the peace is the result of His own Death on the cross.

We began the investigation of St. Paul's teaching on the Death of Christ by examining the account he gives of his own preaching: the investigation may be closed by an examination of a very remarkable passage in which he gives an account of some of the motives and forces by which he was sustained in the sufferings and labours of his apostleship. It would be easy to construct from his epistles a very complete representation of the complex and varied elements of his personal life. Blended with his most strenuous argument, with his sharpest rebukes, and with all his ethical teaching, there are constantly-recurring disclosures of his inward spiritual history. His epistles are veritable "confessions."

These disclosures cover several successive pages of his second epistle to the Church at Corinth. He speaks of the troubles, perplexities, persecutions, which came upon him in Christ's service, but describes his great and constant sufferings as "this light affliction," lasting but for a moment," and as working out for him "a far more exceeding and eternal weight of glory;" [112] he acknowledges that he earnestly longed for the perfect blessedness of the life to come; and that instead of fearing death he was willing, and more than willing, to die, that he might be at home with Christ. [113] And yet when he anticipated the second advent of the Lord, which will perfect the glory of the Church, he was conscious of a certain awe and fear. He so laboured in his apostolic ministry that at last he might be accepted of Christ. For he says, "We must all" — we whose sins God has forgiven for Christ's sake, as well as the rest of mankind — we apostles, who have preached the unsearchable riches of God's grace, as well as those who have listened to our preaching and rejected it — "we must all be made manifest before the judgment seat of

Christ, that every one may receive the things done in his body according to that he hath done, whether it be good or bad." [114] That he would have to give an account of the manner in which he had discharged his trust, that he would receive reward or suffer loss according to the measure of his zeal, industry, and courage, was a motive to fidelity. But it was not only of the judgment-seat of Christ that he thought.

"The love of Christ constraineth us." [115] The word he uses (συνέχει) is singularly expressive. Christ's love left him no choice as to what he should live for, brought him under the control of an irresistible yet most gracious necessity, hedged him in on the right hand and on the left, controlled him with a constancy like that with which the great forces of the universe rule the planets and determine the orbit in which every one of them must move. And it is impossible to read his epistles without discovering that Christ's love had been so revealed to him that it had taken possession of his thought and of every active energy of his nature, and stirred the profoundest depths of his emotion. Sometimes in a long passage the name of Christ occurs in almost every alternate line; sometimes he breaks away from an argument at the bare mention of Christ's name, unable to govern the vehement impulse to dwell upon Christ's glory and grace; at other times, just as a ship is gradually swept out of her direct course by a strong and silent current in the sea, St. Paul is gradually carried away from the point for which he seemed to be making, by the habitual drift of all his deepest affections towards Christ.

And how had the love of Christ been manifested? In His incarnation? In His parables, so bright with hope to those who have been guilty of the darkest sin? In His gracious promises? In His miracles of kindness? In His merciful words to harlots and publicans? In the tears He shed when He thought of the calamities which were coming on the city of Jerusalem? All these St. Paul passes over. "The love of Christ constraineth us, for we thus judged that if One died for all then all died." [116]

According to St. Paul, therefore, the Death of Christ was something more than the ultimate proof of the sincerity of His claims and an example of invincible fidelity to God; it was something more than an appeal to the heart and conscience of men. It was a representative death. He so "died for all" that the race died in Him. His Death was the true crisis in the history of every man. And in His resurrection — for He both "died.... and rose again" for us— the race entered into a new world. This was the Divine idea. Those who live through Christ have not merely been brought under the power of new motives to live a righteous life, they have ascended into a new creation; old things have vanished away, behold all things have become new. New heavens stretch over them; they walk on a new earth; they "know.... no man after the flesh;" yea, even if they once knew Christ after the flesh, if they were His personal friends during His life in the old world, if they were among His kindred, those transient ties are dissolved; they have entered into other relations with

123

Him, determined by the conditions of life in that new creation into which both He and they have now entered. [117]

Further, this new creation is "of God," "who reconciled us to Himself by Jesus Christ, and gave to us the ministry of reconciliation," and the substance of that ministry was this: "God in Christ reconciled the world unto Himself." If we ask in what sense He effected this reconciliation, the reply is contained in the words which follow — *Not imputing their trespasses unto them..."* [118] If we further ask what relation there is between Christ and the non-imputation to mankind of those trespasses by which God's righteous condemnation had been merited, the reply to this further question is given in the boldest representation of Christ's redemptive work to be found in the New Testament: God "made Him to be Sin for us who knew no sin, that we might be made the righteousness of God in Him." [119] This was the ultimate foundation of the Apostle's ministry, and the ground on which in Christ's stead, and as Christ's ambassador, he could entreat men to be reconciled to God. God reconciles us to Himself, according to St. Paul, not in the first instance by delivering us from sin, but by not imputing our sins to us: the reconciliation is primarily, not the removal of our hostility to God, but the cessation of God's hostility to us. The ground of this reconciliation lies in the fact that God made Christ to be Sin for us, and its ultimate result is that we are made the righteousness of God in Him. [120]

I ask again is the proof complete? St. Paul was a great preacher, and whatever wealth and variety of spiritual knowledge appeared in his preaching, the cross of Christ was the centre of it all, and he taught that "Christ died for our sins." [121] He had to maintain an incessant controversy for many years with those who were endeavouring to cramp the freedom of the new and larger faith by imposing on Christian Gentiles the obligations of the Jewish law; and he maintained that the law could never give eternal life, but could only bring a curse upon all who were under its authority, but that Christ has redeemed us from the curse of the law by being made a curse for us. He was the most illustrious of missionaries, and that he was "the apostle of the Gentiles" was his proudest distinction next to that of being the servant, the slave, of the Lord Jesus Christ; and to the heathen he declared that God was at peace with them, because Christ had died. He warned men of the wrath to come, and told them that they were to obtain salvation by "our Lord Jesus Christ, who died for us,... that we should live together with Him." The peril to which the world is exposed is created by its guilt, and for release from guilt he maintained that there is no hope except in Him whose Death is at once the revelation of the righteousness of God and the Propitiation for the sins of men. He saw that it was the Divine purpose to gather the whole universe into one great spiritual polity, and this purpose he affirmed was to be accomplished by Christ, through whose Death God in His infinite mercy had made peace between Himself and the human race. Already those who believed in Christ had been translated into a Divine kingdom, a new creation, and this great deliverance was effected by Christ, in whose Death all died to this present evil world, and in whose resurrection all that believe in Him rose to a life in God — He being made Sin for us, that we might be made the righteousness of God in Him.

The Death of Christ, as the objective ground of the Divine forgiveness of human sin, was the substance of St. Paul's preaching; it was the central idea of his theology; it was the spring of the mightiest motives by which he was animated in his apostolic work.

[1] Acts i. 3.

[2] Luke xxiv. 46-48.

[3] Acts xxvi. 13-18.

[4] Acts vi. 8.

[5] Ibid. vii. 58.

[6] Rom. xv. 19.

[7] 2 Cor. xii. 12.

[8] Acts xxvi. 18.

[9] Note L.

[10] The visit recorded in Acts xi. and xii. I follow the chronology of Conybeare and Howson.

[11] Acts ix. 20, 22.

[12] Ibid, xiii 14-41.

[13] Acts xiii. 38, 39.

[14] Acts xvii. 22-31.

[15] Or of the barracks within the fortress. Conybeare and Howson: *St. Paul*, vol. ii. 262.

[16] Acts xx. 28. In the Atonement controversy, it is of no practical importance whether the received reading, τοῦ Θεοῦ, is adopted, or the more probable reading, τοῦ κυρίου, which has the support of nearly all the modern editors of the text.

[17] 1 Cor. i. 17.

[18] Ver. 18.

[19] Ver. 22-24.

[20] 1 Cor. ii. 1-3.

[21] Acts xxiii. 6.

[22] *The Epistles of St. Paul to the Corinthians*. A. P. Stanley. Second Edition, page 51.

[23] *The Epistles of St. Paul to the Corinthians*. A. P. Stanley. Second Edition, page 50.

[24] Acts xviii. 11.

[25] I Cor. xv. 3.

[26] Gal. v. 11.

[27] *The Epistles of St. Paul to the Corinthians*. A. P. Stanley. Second Edition, page 51.

[28] 1 Thess. ii. 3-8.

[29] Ibid. iv. 11.

[30] 1 Thess. iii. 6, 9, 10.

[31] Ibid. iv. 3-7.

[32] Ibid. i. 10.

[33] Ibid. v. 3.

[34] Ibid. i. 10. "Jesus which delivered us [our Deliverer, τὺ ῥυόμενον] from the wrath to come." — See Ellicott, *in loc.*

[35] 1 Thess. v. 9, 10.

[36] 1 Thess. v. 9, 10.

[37] *St. Paul's Epistle to the Galatians.* J. B. Lightfoot, D.D. Second Edition, page 43.

[38] Ibid.

[39] Acts xv. i.

[40] "Ces Galates étaient gens faciles à séduire; le dernier qui venait leur parler au nom de Jésus était presque sûr d'avoir raison." — E. Renan: *St. Paul*, 311.

[41] This, however, is M. Kenan's theory. *St. Paul*, p. 313, note.

[42] This is the common hypothesis.

[43] For which Professor Lightfoot argues.

[44] The theory of Conybeare and Howson.

[45] "L'espèce de lâcheté qu'il y avait à s'attaquer á des gens faibles, dociles, sans défense, et qui ne vivaient que de confiance en leur màitre, le révolta."— E. Renan: *St. Paul*, 314.

[46] "And I, brethren, if I yet preach circumcision, why do I yet suffer persecution?" (Chap. v. 11.) "At this point the malicious charge of his enemies rises up before the Apostle: 'Why, you do the same thing yourself; you caused Timothy to be circumcised.' To this he replies: 'What do I, who have incurred the deadly hatred of the Judaizers, who am exposed to continual persecution from them, do I preach circum-

cision?'" — Lightfoot, *in loc.*

[47] Professor Jowett paraphrases chap. iii. 1: "O senseless Galatians! who hath bewitched you who had such lively experience of the truth which now with such levity ye throw, aside? Of whom it might be said that ye saw Christ with your own eyes." *The Epistles of St. Paul to the Thessalonians, Galatians, &c.* Second Edition, *in loc.* It is curious that though ἐσταυρωμένος occupies the emphatic position in the sentence, Professor Jowett omits all recognition of it in his paraphrase.

[48] I have given in the text what I suppose is generally regarded as St. Paul's meaning in chap. iii. 4, but it almost seems as though he meant that they might have escaped all the sufferings incident to their change of religious faith had they at the very first submitted to circumcision. In that case their heathen fellow-countrymen would have regarded them simply as Jewish proselytes, and the Jews were so numerous in that part of Asia Minor, and had received such special favour from the Roman Government, that for them to have become Jews would have brought them into little or no trouble.

[49] οὗτοι υἱοί εἰσιν Ἀβραάμ. iii. 7. The οὗτοι is emphatic.

[50] Rom. iv. 15.

[51] Meyer: *Critical and Exegetical Handbook to the Epistle to the Galatians. In loc.*

[52] "To give men that consciousness of sin which makes sin to be what it is."— Jowett, *in loc.*

[53] Gal. iii. 10-12.

[54] Ibid. 13.

[55] Note M.

[56] Gal. iii. 15.

[57] "Who gave Himself for our sins, that He might deliver us from this present evil world." — *Gal.* i. 4.

[58] Rom. i. 16, 17.

[59] "*Who keep down the truth through immorality,* do not let it develop itself into power and influence on their religious knowledge and moral condition." — Meyer, *in loc.*

[60] Rom. i. 23.

[61] Rom. i. 24-28.

[62] Ibid. i. 29-32.

[63] Rom. ii. 1.

[64] Ibid. ii. 5-11.

[65] "In the law the Jew saw the Magna Charta of his assurance of salvation." — Meyer, in loc.

[66] τὸ θέλημα — κατ' ἐξοχήν. "Whose will it was that was to be obeyed on the part of man, was obvious of itself." — Meyer, in loc.

[67] Rom. ii. 2-24.

[68] Ibid. ii. 25-29.

[69] Rom. iii. 1-8.

[70] Ibid. iii. 9-18.

[71] Ibid. iii. 19, 20.

[72] Rom. iii. 22.

[73] Ibid. iii. 24.

[74] Ibid. iii. 24.

[75] Condemnation may, no doubt, confirm the moral and spiritual condition of a man, and render him more desperate in sin than ever; and the justification of a sinful man may constitute the turning-point in his history, giving him hope instead of despair, and restoring to him those spiritual influences and that access to God which render it possible for him to overcome sin. But, formally and strictly, condemnation and justification are related to each other in the manner described in the text.

[76] Rom. iv. 1-5.

[77] Ibid. iv. 6, 7.

[78] Ibid. iv. 22.

[79] Ibid. iv. 24.

[80] Note N.

[81] Ibid. iii. 24.

[82] Ibid. iii. 25. Meyer's exposition of Rom. iii. 20-25 is singularly valuable.

[83] Rom. iii. 25.

[84] Rom. iii. 26.

[85] Rom. v. 1.

[86] Ibid. v. 2.

[87] Rom. v. 2.

[88] Ibid. iii. 2.

[89] Ibid. v. 5.

[90] Rom. v. 6.
[91] Rom. v. 7, 8.
[92] Ibid. v. 9.
[93] Ibid. v. 10.
[94] Rom. v. 11.
[95] Rom. vi. 1.
[96] Rom. iii. 8.
[97] Rom. iii. 8.
[98] Rom. vi. 2.
[99] Rom. vi. 3-7.
[100] Phil. i. 15, 16.
[101] Eph. i. 9, 10.
[102] Ibid. i. 20, 21.
[103] Eph. i. 18.
[104] Eph. ii. 3.
[105] Eph. ii. 12.
[106] Ibid. iii. 16.
[107] ἐλθὼν εὑηγγελίσατο εἰρήνην.
[108] Eph. ii. 1 7.
[109] Eph. ii. 19, 22.
[110] Ibid. i. 7.
[111] Ibid. v. 2.
[112] 2 Cor. iv. 17.
[113] Ibid. v. 1-3.
[114] 2 Cor. v. 10.
[115] Ibid. v. 14.
[116] 2 Cor. v. 14.
[117] 2 Cor. v. 15, 17.
[118] Note O.
[119] 2 Cor. v. 18-21. Note P.
[120] Titus ii. 1 1-14.
[121] I Tim. ii. 5, 6.

# Lecture Seven - General Considerations Confirmatory of the Preceding Argument

In the preceding Lectures I have endeavoured to prove that to the Apostles the Death of our Lord Jesus Christ was the objective ground of the remission of sins; that this conception of His Death is contained in the teaching of our Lord Jesus Christ Himself; and that the mysterious sufferings of His last hours, and the dread with which He anticipated them, are inexplicable unless we believe that "He bare our sins in His own body on the cross," and died as a Sacrifice and "Propitiation for the sins of the world."

Assuming that the argument is conclusive, we who confess that the Lord Jesus Christ is God manifest in the flesh, and who receive the Apostles as trustworthy representatives of His teaching, must accept the fact that by His Death He atoned for the sins of men, although we may be unable to construct a theory of the Atonement. There are, however, some general considerations by which, perhaps, the impression of the argument may be strengthened.

There are very many persons who believe that the idea of an objective Atonement was invented in order to satisfy the exigencies of rigid theories concerning the Divine justice. In these days the great theologians of the Church have an evil name. It is imagined that in their speculations on the character of God, and on His relations to mankind, they forgot that He has revealed Himself as our Father, and that Love is the life and glory of all His moral perfections. Theology — this seems to be a common opinion — was merciless in its judgment of human nature, exaggerated the evil of sin, and refused to recognize its palliations. It ascribed to God its own gloomy and uncompassionate spirit, and conceived of Him as filled with fierce anger against the human race. Then it became necessary to discover some means of allaying His wrath, and therefore the Death of Christ was represented as the ground on which the sins of the world are forgiven. Or, the formalities and harsh severities of human law were attributed to the Divine government of the universe, and the transfer of the sins of the world to Christ was a clumsy invention, in order to make it appear that the penalties of the law are inflicted, although the sins of the guilty are remitted. Arguments in support of the idea of an objective Atonement, drawn from the teaching of Christ and of His Apostles, are regarded as mere special pleading, intended to sustain a dogma which has been constructed to satisfy the artificial necessities of cumbrous and unspiritual theological systems.

All this is precisely the reverse of the truth. Theologians did not invent the Idea of an objective Atonement in order to complete the symmetry of their theological theories. They have invented theory after theory, in order to find a place for the Idea. That the Death of Christ is the ground on which sin is remitted has been one of their chief difficulties. To explain it, they have been driven to the most monstrous and incredible speculations. Had they been able to deny it, their work would have been infinitely simplified.

The Idea is not the creation of dogmatic theology, nor does it depend upon dogmatic theology for its hold on the heart and faith of the Church.

In the age immediately succeeding that of the Apostles, the Christian Church appears to have felt no curiosity about the manner in which the Death of Christ accomplishes human redemption; or, rather, the forms in which the great truth had been represented by the Apostles themselves were still sufficiently fresh and unworn to satisfy the practical necessities of the Christian life.

Converts from heathenism as well as converts from Judaism were familiar with the ceremonial of sacrifice, and it was sufficient for them to know that the Death of Christ was a sacrifice for their sins. Slaves were constantly bought and sold and ransomed; and when they were told that Christ gave His life a ransom for them, they had a very vivid apprehension of the greatness of the deliverance they owed to Him. The Fact that Christ died for us, and died for our sins, was an article of faith, but they had no Theory about it.

Clement exhorts the Corinthians to "reverence the Lord Jesus Christ, whose blood was given for us;" [1] he reminds them that —

"On account of the love He bore us, Jesus Christ our Lord gave His blood for us by the will of God; His flesh for our flesh, and His soul for our souls." [2]

Rahab, who for some inexplicable reason is selected, both by the writer of the Epistle to the Hebrews and by St. James, as an illustrious example of faith, reappears, and the scarlet cord which she was to hang in her window is made the symbol and prophecy of our deliverance from destruction by the blood of Christ:—

"Thus they made it manifest that redemption should flow through the blood of the Lord, to all them that believe and hope in God." [3]

That Rahab's scarlet cord should have been used as a type of the blood of Christ, is a very striking proof of the powerful hold which the idea of redemption through Christ's Death must have had upon the mind of Clement; if indeed this fanciful and even grotesque allusion originated with him, and was not one of the "commonplaces" of Christian thought in his time.

Polycarp greatly rejoiced that the faith of the Philippians was still strong, and was bringing forth fruit to "our Lord Jesus Christ, who for our sins suffered even unto death." [4] He reminds them that their "hope" and "the earnest of [their] righteousness" is "Jesus Christ,—

"Who bore our sins in His own body on the tree, who did not sin, neither was guile found in His mouth, but endured all things for us, that we might live in Him." [5]

He charges them also to imitate the fidelity and patience of Ignatius, and Zosimus, and Rufus, and of others among themselves who had been martyred for the faith; and of St. Paul, and of the rest of the Apostles, for they "have not run in vain;" and they

"Are [now] in their due place in the presence of the Lord, with whom also they suffered. For they loved not this present world, but Him who died for us, and for our sakes was raised again by God from the dead." [6]

In the epistle ascribed to Barnabas, but which could hardly have been written by him, there is language of the same kind. Once, indeed, he advances a step in the speculative direction, for he says: —

"If therefore the Son of God, who is Lord [of all things], and who will judge the living and the dead, suffered, that His stroke might give us life, let us believe that the Son of God *could not* have suffered except for our sakes." [7]

What life and force remained in the apostolic conception of the Death of Christ, after the Apostles had passed away but before the age of speculation began, may be seen in the noble passage often quoted from the Epistle to Diognetus: —

"When our wickedness had reached its height, and it had been clearly shown that its reward, punishment and death, was impending over us; and when the time had come which God had before appointed for manifesting His own kindness and love — how the one love of God, through exceeding regard for men, did not regard us with hatred, nor thrust us away, nor remember our iniquity against us, but showed great long-suffering, and bore with us— He himself took on Him the burden of our iniquities, He gave His own Son as a ransom for us, the Holy One for transgressors, the Blameless One for the wicked, the Righteous One for the unrighteous, the Incorruptible One for the corruptible, the Immortal One for them that are mortal. For what other thing was capable of covering our sins than His righteousness? By what other One was it possible that we, the wicked and the ungodly, could be justified, than by the only Son of God? O sweet exchange! O unsearchable operation! O benefits surpassing all expectation! that the wickedness of many should be hid in a single Righteous One, and that the righteousness of One should justify many transgressors." [8]

But it was impossible for the simplicity of the apostolic tradition to continue unaffected much longer by the rising intellectual activity of the Church. At the close of the second century, and the beginning of the third, the attempt was made by Irenaeus in the West, and by Origen in the East, to give some reply to the questions which were necessarily raised by the language in which the Church had been taught to speak of the Death of Christ, and by the faith which that language expressed. It is no part of my intention to sketch, even in outline, the wayward and perplexed movements of speculative thought which then began, and which, at the end of sixteen hundred years, have not yet arrived at any satisfactory conclusion. What I am anxious to illustrate is the fact which is often forgotten, but which is equally certain and obvious, that the Church did not come to believe in the objective value of the Death of Christ because the doctrine had been developed in theological systems, but that theological systems were constructed in order to explain and justify the doctrine which the Church already believed.

The theologians soon discovered that the task which they had undertaken was one of extraordinary difficulty, and that some of the explanations which first occurred to them involved conclusions which it was impossible to accept. Gregory Nazianzen, who was born a few years after the victory of orthodoxy at the Council of Nicaea, and who died towards the close of the fourth century, states, in a well-known passage, with considerable force and vivacity, the perplexities into which the mind of the Church had been plunged, and proposes his own solution of them.

"To whom," he asks, "and on what account, was the blood which was shed on our behalf poured out, that precious and illustrious blood of Him who was God, and both High Priest and Sacrifice? We were held fast by the devil since we were sold as slaves under sin, and had purchased pleasure by vice. If, now, the price of redemption is given only to him who has possession of the captives, then I ask, To whom was this ransom given, and on what ground? To the evil one? Oh, what a monstrous outrage! Then the robber received not merely a ransom from God, but received God Himself as the price of our redemption! Magnificent wages for his tyranny, on the payment of which justice required him to spare us! If, however, the ransom was paid to the Father, how, in the first place, can this be? for it was not God who had possession of us. And, in the second place, for what reason should the blood of His only begotten Son give any satisfaction to the Father, who did not even accept Isaac when his father [Abraham] offered him, but changed the sacrifice of a rational being into that of a ram? Is it not clear that the Father received the sacrifice, not because He Himself demanded or needed it, but for the sake of the Divine government of the universe (δί οἰκονομίαν), and because man must be sanctified through the incarnation of the Son of God." [9]

John of Damascus, in the eighth century, expressed himself with equal vehemence against the theory that the "ransom" for the deliverance of the human race had been paid to the devil.

"He who assumed death for us, died and offered Himself to the Father; for we had committed wrong towards Him, and it was necessary for Him to receive our ransom, and we thus be delivered from condemnation. For God forbid that the blood of the Lord should be offered to the tyrant." [10]

But notwithstanding protests of this kind, it is clear that this extraordinary hypothesis exerted a powerful influence over the thought of the Church down to the eleventh century, and even later. In the East, Gregory of Nyssa, early in the fourth century, had stated the theory in a form which implies that we were saved by a Divine fraud. He argued that through sin the human race had come under the dominion of the devil; that Jesus offered Himself to the devil as a ransom for us; that the devil, although ignorant of the real greatness of Christ, cared more for Him than for all mankind besides, and accepted the offer. The human race was therefore released, but the devil discovered that he had been outwitted, for he could not retain Christ in his power. Gregory maintains that this was a perfectly fair proceeding on God's part; for since the devil had deceived men for the purpose of seducing them, God had a right to deceive the devil for the purpose of redeeming them. [11] In the Western Church, a century later, Augustine states the theory in a less dramatic and less offensive way.

"What then," he asks, "is the righteousness by which the devil was conquered? What, except the righteousness of Jesus Christ? And how was he conquered? Because when he found in Him nothing worthy of death, yet he slew Him. And certainly it is just that we whom he held as debtors should be dismissed free by believing in Him, whom He slew without any debt. In this way it is that we are said to be justified in the blood of Christ." [12]

A very curious piece of logic! Had the devil never done a wrong thing before, never committed any other great act of injustice, on the ground of which we might have been released from his power, if his crime in killing Christ was really the moral reason for our redemption?

It is clear that when this theory of the Atonement prevailed, it was not because the Church felt that the justice of God required Christ to die that the Church believed that the Death of Christ delivered us from the penal consequences of sin. Perhaps, indeed, there was some obscure idea of justice underlying even this strange conception of a transaction with the devil; but the broad fact is that the Church believed that the Death of Christ was somehow the reason why we are delivered from hell, and, for want of a better explanation, supposed that He gave His life to the Evil One as a ransom for us.

That the theory was still powerful even in the twelfth century, appears from one of St. Bernard's vehement attacks on Abelard. Abelard is represented as saying that all the teachers of the Church since the Apostles agreed (omnes doctores nostri post apostolos conveniunt) in the opinion that the Death of Christ had redeemed us from the power of the devil. [13] St. Bernard does not condemn Abelard's statement as untrue, but he is confounded by the presumption which permitted him to say: "All the doctors of the Church are of this judgment — I think differently." "Which," he demands, "is the more intolerable, the blasphemy or the arrogance of these words? Which more damnable, the audacity or the impiety?" St. Bernard himself, with great rhetorical fire, maintains the traditional view.

"The Lord said, 'I will save thee and deliver thee; fear not.' Thou askest, 'From what power?' Thou art not willing that the devil should have or should have had power over man — nor I, I confess; but neither thy will nor mine can hinder it. If thou wilt not confess nor say it, those who have been redeemed by the Lord, those whom He has redeemed from the hand of the enemy, know it and say it.

*Thou* wouldst not deny it, if thou wert not still in the enemy's hand; thou canst not render thanks with the redeemed, - thou who art not redeemed." [14]

St. Bernard afterwards states the theory a little more calmly. It amounts to this: — The devil had a certain authority over man, not acquired lawfully, but criminally usurped, and yet justly permitted. Man was, therefore, justly held in captivity — the justice being neither in man nor the devil, but in God. The devil, though He had no claim on Christ, laid his hand upon Him, and so we, who were justly in the devil's hands, are liberated. [15]

This rude and coarse hypothesis maintained its place in the Church for nearly a thousand years. Early in the third century it had been sanctioned by the great authority of Origen; in the twelfth century, when St. Bernard wrote, it must still have been the popular theory. Is the hypothesis intolerable, monstrous, and profane? Granted. But the more intolerable, the more monstrous, the more profane it is, the more conclusively it proves the depth and strength of the faith of the Church in the reality of the objective element in the Atonement. In the earliest ages Christian men were quite sure that Christ died to deliver them from some great objective evil, and that deliverance from this evil was the immediate effect of His Death. They were willing to accept even this preposterous explanation of the manner in which His Death delivered us, if no better could be found. But nothing can be more certain than that the idea of an objective Atonement was not invented to satisfy such a theory as this: the theory was a most irreligious method of illustrating the idea.

It also deserves notice that the idea was so plainly and incontestably a fundamental part of the Christian faith, that those who rejected the theory of a transaction with the devil did not exclude from their conception of the Death of Christ the objective aspect which that theory was intended to represent. Gregory Nazianzen, as we have seen, suggested his own solution of the mystery. Athanasius speaks of Christ as *paying the debt in our stead* which we had incurred by sin. [16] And throughout the whole period during which the theory that the Death of Christ ransomed us from the power of the devil retained its ascendency, a far nobler conception of the nature and effect of His sufferings was continually appearing in the devotional and practical writings of the Church. [17]

Towards the end of the eleventh century the appearance of Anselm's *Cur Deus Homo* indicated, if it did not create, a complete change in the movement of theological speculation. The theory is developed in a discussion between Anselm himself and one who professes to hold so firmly the faith of our redemption, that even if he were unable to comprehend by any reasoning what he believes, his faith would not be torn from him. He wishes to learn, however, what necessity or reason there was that God, since He is omnipotent, should have taken upon Him the lowliness and infirmity of human nature in order to its restoration. [18] Anselm showed considerable controversial art in throwing his treatise into the conversational form. It relieved him from the necessity of urging, in his own name, the objections which appeared to him to be fatal to the traditional theory that Christ died to redeem us from the power of Satan. These objections, naturally enough, are alleged by Boso, who plays the part of the inquirer. Boso tells Anselm why it is that "the reason we are accustomed to give" for the Incarnation and Death of Christ failed to satisfy him. He says that both man and the devil belonged to God; the devil had persuaded man to forsake their common Master and go over to him; the devil, as a traitor, had received the runaway; as a thief, the devil had received his fellow-thief, together with what he had stolen from his Lord. Instead of being under any kind of obligation to give Satan a ransom as the price of man's deliverance, God had nothing to do but to punish Satan for getting man into his power, "for each of them was a thief, since the one at the other's persuasion had stolen himself from the Lord."

"If," he says, "God, the Judge of all, were to take man, who is, as we see. His own possession, out of the power of one who so unjustly takes possession of him, whether for the purpose of punishing him in some other way than by the instrumentality of the devil, or for the purpose of sparing him, what injustice would there be in this? since although it be just for man to be tormented by the devil, yet the devil would be unjust in tormenting him? Man, indeed, deserved to be punished, and by none more fitly than by him at whose persuasion he had consented to sin. But the devil never merited any right to punish him." [19]

Boso pursues the argument through two chapters, without any remonstrance from Anselm. His objections are left unanswered, and it is clear that Anselm thought them unanswerable.

The foundation of Anselm's own theory of the Atonement lies in his conception of the nature of sin.

He argues that —

"*Sin is nothing else than not to render to God His due...*The entire will of a rational creature ought to be subject to the will of God.... He who does not render to God this honour which is due to Him, robs God of what is His own, and dishonours God; and this is what it is to sin...Every one who sins [is] bound to pay back the honour of which he has robbed God; and this is the satisfaction which every sinner is bound to pay to God." [20]

Further: —

"Nothing is less tolerable in the order of things than that a creature should rob his Creator of the honour due to Him and not repay Him that of which He robs Him.... If nothing be more great or good than God, nothing can be more just than that which preserves His honour in the disposing of events, even the Supreme Justice, which is nothing else than God Himself." [21] "That God should lose His own honour is impossible; for either the sinner of his own will pays what he owes, or God takes it from him against his will. For either man of his own free will exhibits that subjection to God which is due from him, whether by not sinning, or by making amends for his sin, or else God subjects him to Himself by tormenting him against his will, and by this means shows Himself to be his Lord, which the same refuses of his own will to acknowledge." [22]

Anselm shows afterwards that, from the nature of the case, it was not in man's power to make amends for his sin. If, he argues, it were necessary either that the whole world, and whatever is not God, should perish and be reduced to nothing, or that a creature should do the very smallest action contrary to the Divine will, the creature would have no right to sin, even for the preservation of the whole creation. The satisfaction, therefore, which is necessary for the slightest sin, must outweigh in value the whole universe.

No one, however, *ought* to make satisfaction for the sin of man except man; and no one *can* make this satisfaction except God Himself. [23] He who makes satisfaction for human sin must therefore be God-man.

The conditions under which Christ, the Son of God and the Son of man, by whom Anselm has thus argued that the work of Atonement must be accomplished, can make the necessary satisfaction for the sins of the race, are thus defined: —

"Reason has taught us that it is necessary for Him to have something greater than all things short of God, which He may willingly and not of debt give to God But this cannot be found either beneath Him or outside Him It must be found, then, in Himself..... He is to give, therefore, either Himself or something out of Himself. [24] But He himself and all that he has belongs to God. This gift then must be understood thus: that He shall in some way devote to the honour of God, either Himself, or something coming from Himself, in a way in which He is not in debt bound to do If we were to say that He shall give Himself to obey God, so as, by perseveringly keeping His righteousness, to submit Himself to His will, to give this would not be to give what God did not require from Him as a debt; for every rational creature owes this to God He must, therefore, give Himself or something out of Himself to God in some other way. .... But to give His life, or to lay down His life, or to deliver Himself to death for the honour of God is what — "as a debt — God would not require of Him; for since there will be no sin in Him, He will be under no obligation of dying, as we said before."

Anselm then explains why the Mediator should render honour to God by dying, and the reason he gives is consistent with his whole theory, and wholly different from that which rests the necessity of the Atonement on the necessity of recognizing and maintaining the justice of the penalty which is due to sin. He asks: —

"If man sinned by pleasure, is it not consistent that he should make satisfaction by pain? And if he were so overcome by the devil as to dishonour God by sinning with such ease as that he could not have been more easily overcorne, is it not just that man, in making satisfaction to God for sin, should overcome the devil with such difficulty as that greater there could not he? Is it not meet that whereas he so stole himself from God by sinning, that he could not have stolen himself more completely than he did, in making satisfaction he should so give himself to God as that he could not possibly give himself more completely?"

Boso acknowledges that nothing can be more reasonable. Anselm continues:-

"Now, then, man can suffer nothing more painful or with greater difficulty for the honour of God, willingly and not of debt, than death; and in no way can more completely give himself to God than when he delivers himself to death for His honour. [25] But when Christ bore with calm patience the injuries and insults and the death of the cross, with the thieves, brought on Him on account of His righteousness which he obediently kept, He gave an example to men that they should swerve from the righteousness which they owe to God for no inconveniences which they may experience.... No man besides Him ever gave to God by dying what he would not at some time be compelled to lose, or ever paid what he did not owe. But He of His own accord offered to the Father what He would not have been compelled to lose, and He paid for sinners what He did not owe for Himself."

For this transcendent act of homage to the Father, Christ must not go without a recompense.

"He who recompenses any one, either gives what that one has not got, or forgives what may be required of him. Now before that the Son did so great an action, all things which the Father had were His; neither did He ever owe what might be forgiven Him."

To recompense Christ was therefore impossible. But if the Son wished to give what is due to Him to another, the Father could not justly prevent Him.

"It is both lawful for the Son to give what is His own, and the Father cannot pay what He owes *Him* except to some one else. On whom," then asks Anselm, concluding the argument, "should He more consistently bestow the fruit and recompense of His own death than on those for the sake of saving whom...He became Man, and to whom (as we have said) by dying He set an example of dying for righteousness' sake; for in vain will they be followers of Him if they are not partakers of His merits? Or whom may He more justly make inheritors of what is due to Him (of which He is not in want Himself), and of the superabundance of His fulness, than His own.... brethren, whom He sees encumbered with so many and such heavy debts, pining away with want in the depth of misery; so that what they owe for their sins may be forgiven them, and that of which (by reason of their sins) they stand in need may be given them." [26]

This long account of Anselm's theory in Anselm's own words was necessary in order to give a sufficiently clear and strong impression of the idea on which the theory rests. His mind was filled with the august greatness of God. "Sin is nothing else than not to render to God His due." It is an affront to His Infinite Majesty. It is not regarded as a crime — a revolt against those moral laws which God is morally bound to maintain — it is of the nature of a personal offence against Himself. The Atonement is therefore an act of homage to God in which His supremacy is recognized— an act of homage having such transcendent value that it outweighs the sins of mankind, and creates an adequate reason for remitting them.

The great schoolmen who followed him did not simply accept and vindicate the theory of Anselm: they modified it, developed it, and even introduced into it some foreign elements. Abelard, indeed, went very far towards the absolute exclusion of all objective significance from the work of Christ, and maintained that by His blood

"We are justified and reconciled to God, because by the singular grace which God has manifested to us in giving us His Son, who assumed our nature, and, having become man, persevered even unto death in instructing us by His teaching and example, God has more closely attached us to Himself by the bonds of love, and because true charity, fired by such a gift of God's grace, cannot shrink from any suffering for His sake." [27]

Abelard, however, exerted only a transient and disturbing influence on the development of the theory of the Atonement in the Middle Ages, and he did nothing to affect the fundamental principle on which all Anselm's speculations are built. Throughout the period of Scholasticism, the Atonement continued to be regarded as a satisfaction offered to God for the personal wrong committed against Him by our sin.

In Anselm and in some of his successors the theory was redeemed from its offensive character by the practical identification of the eternal law of righteousness with the Divine will. With God, according to Anselm, "there is no freedom but to do what is expedient or what is fitting.... In that it is said that what He wills is just, and what He wills not is not just, this is not to be understood as though if God were to will anything inconsistent [si Deus vult quodlibet inconveniens], it would be just because He willed it. For if God were to will to lie, it does not follow that it is just to lie, but rather that he who so wills is not God." [28]

But the prevalent tendency to conceive of God as the supreme Personality, on whose will all things depend carried some later writers to most pernicious conclusions. Duns Scotus, in harmony with the fundamental position of his philosophy, that the will is superior to the reason, both in God and man, makes the moral law the expression of God's arbitrary will. [29] All existing moral distinctions are purely contingent: they might, if God so pleased, be absolutely reversed. [30] This conception of God's relation to the moral law necessarily involved the degradation of the idea of the Atonement.

With the intenser religious earnestness, and especially the deeper sense of sin which originated the Reformation of the sixteenth century, came a third great movement in theological speculation on the real nature and purpose of the Death of Christ. Ritschl, to whom "the scientifically rounded doctrine of Duns Scotus" appears a truer expression of the attitude assumed by Catholic Christendom in the Middle Ages towards this problem than the doctrine of Thomas Aquinas, [31] has defined very sharply the distinction between the doctrine of the schoolmen and the doctrine of the reformers. He says that "the satisfaction of Christ was regarded by the schoolmen as a necessity arising from the arbitrary will of a mighty possessor of private rights, while the reformers sought its explanation in the public law of the law-ordered community in which God and man are constituent parts: in the one case it is regarded as the arbitrary compensation for a personal injury, and in the other as the necessary punishment of a violation of law." [32] It is doubtful, I think, whether the perfect historical truth of this sharp contrast can be maintained.

To Anselm, at least, God was something more than "a mighty possessor of private rights;" nor did Anselm believe that the Atonement was "a compensation for personal injury" exacted by God's "arbitrary will." Anselm himself would have contended that the only principle and guarantee of the moral order of the universe are found in that personal supremacy of God which sin refuses to acknowledge, and to which the Death of Christ has rendered awful homage. But Ritschl appears to have described with singular accuracy the real spirit and tendency of the mediaeval speculations on this great mystery. His account of the theories of the reformers is equally felicitous. At first, indeed, they were not distinctly conscious that their conception of the Atonement differed from that which had been generally accepted by the Church, and even some modern writers on the history of doctrine have represented the Protestant doctrine as being substantially identical with that of Anselm. The reformers were immediately occupied with the question of the conditions on which the benefits of Christ's Death become ours, rather than with the question of the real nature and grounds of the Atonement which Christ's Death had effected. But the one question was soon seen to involve the other, and Protestant theologians gradually came to use language about the Death of Christ and its relations to the forgiveness of sins, which, if it was not perfectly new, had rarely been heard before, and had never been uttered with the same energy and vehemence. The rudiments of their theory may be found in earlier writers, and there had been a special preparation for it, both in the deeper moral life which began to appear in some parts of Christendom in the fifteenth century, and the fresh theological thought which that life awakened. [33]

But it is scarcely possible to imagine anything more startling, even to those who had retained the principles of the *Cur Deus Homo* in their integrity, than such a passage as that which occurs in Luther's commentary on Gal. iii. 13: *Christ hath redeemed us from the curse of the law, being made a curse for us,*

"The doctrine of the gospel (which of all others is most sweet and full of singular consolation) speaketh nothing of our works or of the works of the law, but of the inestimable mercy and love of God towards most wretched and miserable sinners: to wit, that our most merciful Father, seeing us to be oppressed and overwhelmed by the curse of the law, and so to be holden under the same, that we could never be delivered from it by our own power, sent His only Son into the world, and laid upon Him the sins of all men, saying, 'Be Thou Peter, that denier; Paul, that persecutor, blasphemer, and cruel oppressor; David, that adulterer; that sinner which did eat the apple in Paradise; that thief which hanged upon the cross; and, briefly, be Thou the person which hath committed the sins of all men. See therefore that Thou pay and satisfy for them.' Here now cometh the law, and saith, I find Him a sinner, and that such a one as hath taken upon Him the sins of all men, and I see no sins else but in Him, therefore let Him die upon the cross; and so he setteth upon Him, and killeth Him. By this means the whole world is purged and cleansed from all sins, and so delivered from death and all evils."

No doubt this is popular rhetoric, and popular rhetoric of a very intense and fervent kind. But Luther's rhetoric is only Luther's creed set on fire by imagination and passion. To take words like these as though they were a literal and scientific statement of what Luther believed about the Death of Christ, would be to violate the most ordinary principles which must govern the interpretation of language. But he meant what he said, and the substance of the passage is this — Christ so assumed the penal responsibilities of mankind, that all who believe in Him are delivered from the penalties of sin. The law has inflicted on Him the sufferings which but for His mercy would have been inflicted on us.

The conception of the Atonement which suggested this description of it is the precise antithesis of the conception in the *Cur Deus Homo*. Anselm — though not with unvarying consistency — represents the voluntary submission of Christ to death as a transcendent act of righteousness and of devotion to the honour of God, and maintains that God rewarded Christ by forgiving the sins of men. Luther represents the Death of Christ as the endurance of the suffering due to the sins of our race. On Anselm's theory, Christ has secured our salvation because in His Death He clothed Himself with the glory of a unique righteousness, for which God rewards Him. On Luther's theory, Christ has secured our salvation because in His Death He clothed Himself with the sins of the human race, so that God inflicted on Him the sufferings which the sins of the race had deserved. The theological distance between the two theories can hardly be measured. They are alike only in this, that they both affirm that the Death of Christ is the ground on which our sins are forgiven. [34]

The six chapters of Calvin's *Institutes,* in which he discusses the doctrine of Redemption, [35] deserve very careful consideration. They show the extent to which, in the early days of the Reformation, the Protestant leaders included in their conception of the Atonement very much that has been imperfectly recognized or altogether suppressed in the popular theology of Protestantism; and they also show that Calvin, as well as Luther, held that forensic idea of the Death of Christ which is expressed with such fervour in Luther's commentary on the Galatians.

But the truth of Ritschl's representation of the essential principle of the Protestant theory is best illustrated by the manner in which the subject is treated by those theologians who represent the complete and systematic development of the characteristic theology of the Reformation. Of these, Francis Turretin is perhaps the most distinguished. In his *Institutio Theologiae Elencticae* he has a chapter in which he discusses the question — *Whether it was necessary that Christ should satisfy the Divine justice for us?* [36] The reasons which he alleges, in maintaining the affirmative against the Socinians, indicate the completeness of the change which had passed over theological thought since the time of Anselm. He urges: —

1. That the retributive justice of God is one of His natural and essential perfections; that God cannot divest Himself of it; and that He cannot refrain from exercising it.

2, That sin is moral evil, and differs intrinsically and necessarily from holiness; and that there is a necessary and natural connection between moral evil and physical evil: that the wisdom, the goodness, and the justice of God all require that sin should be punished.

3. That death is the sanction of the law, and that what the law threatens must be executed, if the truth of God is to be maintained.

4. That the gospel declares, as a matter of fact, that Christ endured a bloody and terrible death for us.

5. That to deny that it was necessary that Christ should die in order to satisfy the Divine justice, appears to diminish the greatness of God's love for us in not sparing His own Son, but freely giving Him up for us all. If, indeed, justice had created no obstacle to the free forgiveness of our sin, the grace of God in freely forgiving us would have been very great; but it is seen to be far greater, now that we know that although justice inexorably demanded that our sin should be punished, God's desire for our salvation resulted in the wonderful reconciliation of justice and mercy which has been illustrated in the Death of Christ.

Turretin then replies to the old objection that to maintain the necessity of a satisfaction for sin is to deny the absolute power of God, to limit His freedom, and to dishonour the infinitude of His mercy. He closes the argument by contending that while God has the right to remit sin, the exercise of that right is necessarily limited by justice; and that if He remitted sin without a satisfaction, the majesty of the law would be violated. The relation in which God stands to the sinner is not a mere private relation, like that of a creditor to a debtor, or a master to a slave; it is not an arbitrary relation arising out of positive institutions; it is not a relation originating in private utility; it involves public morality; it is the relation of a Ruler and a Judge; it is founded in the nature of things. Private rights may be waived at the will and pleasure of the individual in whom they are vested, but public rights can be waived only on public grounds.

Mastricht, another of the great Protestant theologians of the seventeenth century, maintains the necessity of a satisfaction for sin on similar grounds. It was required (1) by the unchangeable purpose and decree of God that He will not remit sin without inflicting its just penalty; (2) by His veracity, which has pledged Him to punish sin with death; (3) by His original and necessary holiness and justice, which render it impossible for Him not to hate sin; and in Holy Scripture the hatred of God for sin does not denote the mere sentiment of hatred, but its effect — the determination to punish it. The necessity of a satisfaction for sin arises also (4) from the intrinsic demerit of sin; those who sin deserve death, and the Judge of all the earth must be just; (5) from the nature of law, which is mere advice unless sustained by penalties, and these penalties must be not only threatened, but executed. Again, (6) the wisdom of God as Moral Ruler would not allow Him to permit the interests of the universe to be injured by suffering the law to be violated with impunity. Finally, (7) the fact that God has permitted His only-begotten and well-beloved Son to endure the penalties of sin for us, is a conclusive proof that, apart from the Death of Christ as a satisfaction for sin, our salvation was impossible. [37]

In the same sense in which the true character of the scholastic theory of the Atonement may be said to be most perfectly expressed in the exaggerated and degraded form which it received from Duns Scotus, the true character of the Reformation theory may be said to be most perfectly expressed in the exaggerated and degraded form which it received from Grotius.

The Atonement, as all Protestants acknowledged, was not a mere vindication of God's personal claims, a compensation offered to Him for personal wrongs: it was demanded by Justice, by the majesty of public law, which must be maintained by God's authority, and which sin has transgressed. Grotius grasped with firmness and tenacity precisely that element in the theory of the reformers by which it was most sharply distinguished from the theory of the schoolmen. He was a jurist, an ambassador, and a statesman; and to him the Divine administration of the universe was but a higher form of that political life with which he was so well acquainted. His theory is developed with great clearness and fulness in his *Defence of the Catholic Faith concerning the Satisfaction of Christ,* [38] written in reply to Socinus. The ultimate principles on which the Grotian doctrine rests are laid down in chaps, ii. and iii., in which the old Socinian conception of punishment is discussed with great acuteness, and completely destroyed: unfortunately, the theory by which it is replaced is almost equally untenable. He argues (chap, ii.) that God is not to be considered as being the mere Judge of the moral universe: if He were nothing more than a Judge, He would have simply to administer the law, and would have no power to remit the punishment of the guilty, even if the punishment were borne by the innocent. Nor, in inflicting punishment, is God to be regarded as the party that has been injured by sin; He is not even to be regarded as the mere representative of the moral universe, which may be supposed to have been injured by sin. For, in the first place, the right to punish does not belong to the party that has received injury from an offence. No man is a proper judge in his own cause. [39] Nor, secondly, has an injured person — as such — a right to insist on *punishment;* all that he can claim is *compensation.* Grotius might have said that the law gives him his remedy in a civil action for damages, not in a criminal prosecution. Nor, again, when God punishes sin, is He to be considered as though He were acting merely as the absolute Owner of the universe, whose claims on the love and service of His creatures have not been satisfied. If this were His only relation to us, these claims might be freely remitted. All punishment has for its end the common good. [40]

But Grotius argues (chap, iii.) that the penal law maybe relaxed. While there are some laws which are eternal and unchangeable, as that God cannot lie, or deny Himself, or perform evil actions, positive laws nave not this inflexible character. To the objection that, in the very nature of things, it is just that the guilty should be punished according to their deserts, he replies, that while from the relation of the sinner to God as the supreme Ruler, his sin naturally and necessarily makes him liable to punishment, it is not absolutely and universally necessary that the adequate punishment should be inflicted. It belongs to the very nature of things that every sinner deserves punishment, but not that every sinner should be actually punished. [41]

There was nothing in the nature of God to prevent Him from forgiving sin without exacting any atonement for it. But He had to consider the moral effect which such an exercise of His prerogatives would have produced on the universe.

The sufferings which are threatened against those who transgress the Divine commandments are a terrible warning against sin: if these sufferings are not inflicted, the moral interests of the universe require that the authority of the law should be maintained in some other way. Grotius contended that this end is secured by making forgiveness conditional on the sufferings of Christ. He gave up, as Ritschl has said, "the idea of penal satisfaction for past sins," and substituted for it the idea of a "penal example for the prevention of future sins." [42] The Grotian theory of the Atonement has had great influence on the modern theology of English Nonconformity.

From this brief review of the history of the doctrine, it appears that for nearly a thousand years many of the most eminent teachers of the Church were accustomed to represent the Death of Christ as a ransom by which we are delivered from captivity to the devil; that for nearly five centuries the most eminent teachers of the Church were accustomed to represent the Death of Christ as an act of homage to the personal greatness and majesty of God; that during the last three centuries the great Protestant Churches have represented the Death of Christ as having a relation neither to the devil nor to the personal claims of God, but to the moral order of the universe. While the fundamental conception of the Atonement has been passing through these remarkable changes, the doctrine has been involved in other controversies of hardly inferior magnitude. There have been controversies as to whether Christ died for all men, or whether He died for the elect only; or whether, as was suggested as early as the third century by Origen, the effects of His Death extend to the whole universe. There have been controversies as to whether the Death of Christ was in itself an adequate Atonement for human sin, or whether its adequacy depends upon God's acceptance of it as adequate. When the Death of Christ was regarded as a kind of concession to the devil, there were controversies as to whether the concession was necessary in the nature of things, in order to effect our redemption; the same controversy was renewed under other forms when the Death of Christ was regarded as an act of homage to the Divine Majesty; and it has reappeared among Protestants, to whom the Atonement is neither a concession to the claims of Satan, nor even an acknowledgment of the personal claims of God. Whether, if men were to be saved, the Atonement of Christ was necessary or not; whether its effects extend to all mankind or only to the elect; whether it consisted in His righteousness, which was tested by His sufferings, or whether the sufferings themselves constituted its very essence; whether it was intended to redeem us from the power of Satan, or to propitiate the injured majesty of God, or to assert the eternal principles of the Divine government — all these questions have divided the Church. The Fathers attempted to explain why it is that through the Death of Christ we escape from the penalties of sin, and their explanations were rejected by the schoolmen. The schoolmen attempted to explain it, and their explanations were rejected or modified by the reformers. The reformers attempted to explain it, and within a century after the Reformation, Grotius and his successors were attempting to explain it again. But the faith of the great body of the Church in the fact that Christ's sufferings came upon Him because of our sin, and that on the ground of His sufferings we are delivered from the penalties of sin, has survived the theories which were intended to illustrate it.

The Idea of an objective Atonement invented by theologians to satisfy the exigencies of theological systems! It would be almost as reasonable to maintain that the apparent motion of the sun was invented by astronomers in order to satisfy the exigencies created by astronomical theories. The Idea has perplexed, and troubled, and broken up successive systems of theology. It was precisely because they failed to account for it that theological systems which were once famous and powerful, and from which their authors hoped for an immortal name, have perished. If it had been possible to expel the Idea from the faith of Christendom, the task of theology would have been made wonderfully easier. *The history of the doctrine is a proof that the idea of an objective Atonement was not invented by theologians.*

But perhaps this Idea was forced upon theologians by the superstitious dread with which, in all ages, vast masses of men have regarded the awful powers of the invisible world. The Jews had their sacrifices, the heathen had theirs. Is it not possible that the Death of Christ came to be regarded as having expiatory power because the Church itself was slow in apprehending the infinite love of God, and therefore insisted that only by suffering could the Divine wrath be propitiated?

It is true, and the truth has great significance, that the craving for a sacrifice for sin is one of the deepest instincts of the religious life of the race. It is also true that this craving is satisfied by the Christian Atonement. But that, apart from the clearest and most emphatic declarations of Christ Himself and His Apostles, the Church should ever have supposed that His Death could be the ground on which God forgives the sins of mankind, is incredible.

How could such an extraordinary supposition have originated?

From the very first, the general outlines of the history of our Lord Jesus Christ were made known to all who received the Christian faith; His life and His Death constituted the very substance of the gospel, the foundation on which the Apostles rested all their teaching. The Church knew that the crucifixion was a great crime. The considerations which might be urged to alleviate the guilt of a barbarous people in putting to death the teacher of a pure religious faith, which was hostile to all their habits and all their traditions, cannot be pleaded in palliation of this supreme offence. It is true that Jesus of Nazareth was not the kind of Messiah that the Jewish nation was expecting and longing for. There was nothing in His teaching to gratify their hopes of secular glory, or their passionate desire to avenge the wrongs and sufferings of many centuries upon their heathen oppressors.

But He acknowledged the authority of Moses and the prophets; He worshipped in the temple; He kept the national festivals; and if sometimes He disregarded the obligations which were imposed upon the Jewish people by their rabbinical teachers, He vindicated His violation of the rules of an artificial and technical sanctity by appealing to the fundamental principles of the Divine law. His discourses were rooted in the national faith, and enriched with illustrations from the national literature. Those parts of His teaching by which the people were most offended and perplexed were placed under the sanction of institutions and events which were most sacred to the heart of every Jew. It was precisely when He was asserting what was most incredible and most irritating to His hearers that He showed Himself to be in most perfect sympathy with them in relation to their national history. He spoke to Nicodemus, for instance, of the redemptive power of His Death, but He sheltered the truth under an allusion to one of the greatest miracles in the wilderness. "As Moses lifted up the serpent in the wilderness, even so must the Son of man be lifted up: that whosoever believeth in Him should not perish, but have everlasting life." He made the manna which kept the nation alive for forty years the symbol of Himself, when He taught the people of Galilee that they could have eternal life only in Him. It was at the Feast of Tabernacles, which commemorated the history of the wanderings of their fathers in the desert, that He cried, "If any man thirst, let him come unto Me and drink," in obvious allusion to the water which God gave to the people from the rock when they were ready to perish. It was at the same feast that He made the lofty claim to be "the Light of the world," declaring that whoever followed Him should not walk in darkness, but should have "the light of life;" recalling to the crowds that listened to Him the pillar of fire which shone on the camp of the Israelites during the night. [43] From first to last our Lord tried to make it clear to the Jewish nation that He had not come to rob them of their ancient glories, or to ask them to renounce the faith or the hopes of their fathers — that His mission was not to destroy the law or the prophets, but to fulfil.

His whole policy — if we may venture to use in connection with Him a word which has an evil stain, from its application to the indirect and selfish courses of ambitious men — was a policy of conciliation until conciliation became useless. He endeavoured to make it easy for the religious authorities of the nation to receive Him as the Christ. Before He created any enthusiasm among the people, or provoked among them any distrust of their ecclesiastical rulers, He appealed to the ecclesiastical rulers themselves, and His appeal was made in a form to which it ought not to have been difficult for them to respond. When He drove out the sheep and the oxen and the traders from the courts of the temple, He appeared in the character of a Jewish reformer, and was moving on lines marked out for Him by the common faith and common sentiments of the Jewish people. The act implied no revolution in religious belief or religious ceremonial: it was a vindication of the sanctity of the temple, and a protest against those who, in violation of their own avowed convictions, and for the sake of their own advantage, consented to its profanation. Any "ruler of the Jews" with an honest reverence for what he professed to regard as the very Home of God, would have recognized in this bold act of the young Galilean peasant the expression of a devout zeal, would have accepted with humility the just rebuke which it implied, and would have sympathized with the courage and piety which prompted it.

Our Lord gave ample time to the ecclesiastical authorities to consider in what spirit they would respond to this appeal. For nearly a year he seems to have remained in the neighbourhood of Jerusalem. He did nothing to make it hard for the "rulers" to recognize His claims. He avoided as much as possible everything that was likely to create popular excitement. He does not appear to have spoken often to great crowds of people until the leaders of the religious life of the nation had fully resolved to oppose Him. When their antagonism had been clearly manifested, He did not irritate and intensify it by attempting to create a hostile "party" for Himself among the people living in Jerusalem, but went to a remote district, as if He wished to give the ecclesiastical authorities a fair opportunity for reconsidering their antagonistic position and retreating from it. But He came up to the great festivals, and His presence there was a proof that He had no desire to create a religious or national schism.

Nor did He wound the hereditary pride and prejudice of the rulers of the Jewish people by an immediate appeal to the Gentiles against their jealousy and injustice. We hear of Him once in the neighborhood of Tyre and Sidon, and once in the neighbourhood of Banias, but He made no attempt to secure Gentile adherents. It is very curious and significant that although a great part of His time was spent in the towns and villages on the banks of the Lake of Galilee, the Gospels never speak of Him as entering the city of Tiberias, which was chiefly inhabited by pagans. He told the Syrophenician woman, who entreated Him to have mercy on her daughter, that He was "not sent but unto the lost sheep of the house of Israel; [44] and He restricted the mission of the twelve Apostles to their own countrymen: "Go not into the way of the Gentiles, and into any city of the Samaritans enter ye not: but go rather unto the lost sheep of the house of Israel." [45]

He was equally careful to avoid giving any just alarm to the civil power. He did not attempt to excite popular passion; He never seems to have spoken of the political greatness and splendour of the nation in former times, nor of the achievements of the patriotic heroes of the Jewish race. He never denounced the Roman rule. When on one occasion the people were in the mood to "take Him by force and make Him King, He departed again into a mountain Himself alone." [46]

He did not merely avoid giving unnecessary offence either to the people, the priests, or the civil rulers; His whole life was an appeal to every lofty and generous and kindly principle of human nature — an appeal which only base selfishness, intense religious conceit, and a deep hostility to moral goodness, could have altogether resisted.

The history of the development of the hostility against Him in Jerusalem is remarkable. The first great outbreak was the immediate effect of His alleged violation of the Sabbath, in healing the man at the Pool of Bethesda on the Sabbath day. The next was provoked by a similar transgression - if it was a transgression - of the Sabbatic law, the healing on the Sabbath of a blind beggar who seems to have been well known in the city. On each of these occasions the original offence was aggravated by the personal claims which He advanced when challenged to defend it; but as the supernatural character of the beneficent works which He had wrought does not seem to have been disputed, it is astonishing that, instead of considering these claims seriously and earnestly, the very people who confessed the reality of His miracles were eager to kill Him. The final determination of the rulers to put Him to death, was the result of their fear that a great popular reaction in His favour might be produced by the resurrection of Lazarus. He did good and suffered for it. Every one of the more violent movements against Him originated in a miracle. [47]

Mr. John Stuart Mill, in discussing the two great historical instances of judicial iniquity, the condemnation of Socrates, and what he describes as "the event which took place on Calvary rather more than eighteen hundred years ago," expresses the opinion that "the feelings with which mankind now regard these lamentable transactions, especially the later of the two, render them extremely unjust in their judgment of the unhappy actors." "These," he says, "were to all appearance, not bad men, not worse than men commonly are, but rather the contrary; men who possessed in a full, or somewhat more than a full measure, the religious, moral, and patriotic feelings of their time and people; the very kind of men who, in all times, our own included, have every chance of passing through life blameless and respected." [48]

The apology cannot be admitted. They did not know the awful magnitude of their crime, and this ignorance was alleged by the Divine Sufferer Himself when He invoked the mercy of God upon His murderers: "Father, forgive them, for they know not what they do!" But if they did not know that their

145

offence was the greatest of which mankind could be guilty, and that all sub-sequent ages would look back upon it with fear and dismay, as transcending in horror all other atrocities, they knew that the crime was a great one. The Apostles and friends of Christ were not in the habit of using hard words even of those who murdered their Master; but the accounts which they have given us of the deeds of those whom Mr. Mill calls "the unhappy actors" in this "lamentable transaction," condemn them to eternal infamy. The Death of Christ was brought about by a deliberate conspiracy, in which the conspira-tors were the official leaders of the religious life of the nation. They pur-chased the treachery of one of the most intimate friends of our Lord; they produced false witnesses against Him on His trial; they paid other false wit-nesses to declare that the story of His resurrection was a lie, and that His dis-ciples had taken away His body while the soldiers slept. Desiring nothing more themselves than to drive the Romans from the country, they charged Him before Pilate with treasonable designs against Caesar, and they knew the charge was false. Pilate, with all the power of Rome at his back, while he acknowledged that he could find no fault in the prisoner, gave Him up to the fear and jealousy of the priesthood and the fury of the people.

These are the men who, in Mr. Mill's judgment, were "to all appearance, not bad men, not worse than men commonly are, but rather the contrary!"

Whatever they were — good men or bad men — men of more than average virtue and moral respectability, according to the judgment of Mr. Mill — or men actuated by base, malignant, and cruel passions, according to the com-mon judgment of mankind — the history told by His friends, and received by the Church in every part of the world, attributes to those who compassed the Death of Christ a succession of atrocious crimes, — crimes atrocious in themselves, apart from the awful greatness of the Victim. And yet, through eighteen centuries, with almost unbroken unanimity, the Christian Church has maintained that the Death of Christ is the ground on which God grants to mankind the forgiveness of sin.

Again I ask, How could such an extraordinary idea have originated?

We are so familiar with the phrases in which this idea is expressed, that the strangeness of the idea itself is hardly apprehended by us. Suppose that, after the children of Israel had been in the wilderness for several years, a conspiracy had been formed against Moses, and that he had been deliberate-ly and treacherously tortured and slain, because he refused to renounce his great claims as the divinely-commissioned lawgiver and chief of the nation. Can we imagine that within a few years after his death the Jewish people could have come to imagine that on the ground of the death of Moses God was willing to forgive all the sins they had committed since leaving Egypt? Can we imagine that a long succession of religious teachers, extending from the time that the descendants of Abraham entered into the Land of Promise to the final catastrophe in which their national institutions perished, would have told them that whenever they repented of idolatry, or of any other vio-

146

lation of the Divine law, the death of Moses would be the Divine reason for pardoning their offences? Instead of this, would there not have been an annual fast, at which, through generation after generation, the crime would have been confessed and the Divine mercy implored? And whenever a prophet threatened the men of his own times with the Divine vengeance for their sins, would he not have told them that they were the true descendants of those who had hardened their heart against God in the wilderness, and whose offences — this being the very chief — had provoked God to swear in His wrath that they should not enter into His rest?

Had Moses perished at the hands of his inconstant and ungrateful and rebellious fellow-countrymen, I can imagine prophet after prophet insisting on his sufferings and death, in order to inspire the people with a fidelity to God like that which had been illustrated in the martyrdom of their great leader; and the Church might have made a similar use of the crucifixion of Christ. It has made a similar use of His crucifixion. But what we have to account for is the universal prevalence of the idea that, while those who put Christ to death committed the greatest of human crimes, His Death was the Propitiation for the sins of the world. I can account for the prevalence of that idea in one way, and only in one way. It was a great and essential element in the original gospel which the Apostles were charged to preach to all nations. The Church received it from the Apostles. The Apostles received it from Christ.

[1] I *Epistle*, c. xxi.

[2] Ibid. c. xlix.

[3] Ibid. c. xii.

[4] *Epistle to Philippians*, c. i.

[5] *Epistle to Philippians*, c. viii.

[6] Ibid. c. ix.

[7] *Epistle of Barnabas*, c. vii.

[8] *Epistle to Diognetus*, chap. ix. The translation of this passage, and of the preceding passages from the Apostolic Fathers, is that given in vol. i. of the *Ante-Nicene Library*, published by Messrs. Clark, of Edinburgh, and edited by Dr. Alexander Roberts and Dr. James Donaldson.

[9] Gregorius Nazian.: Opera. Cologne, 1680. Vol. i. pp. 691, 692.

[10] Shedd's *History of Christian Doctrine*, vol. ii. 252.

[11] Gregorius Nyss.: Opera. Paris, 1615. Vol. i. 516.

[12] *On the Trinity*, p. 330. Works of Augustine. Edited by Marcus Dods. Edinburgh: Messrs. Clark. Vol. vii.

[13] M. Remusat (*Abelard*, vol. ii. p. 435) says that he has discovered no passage in Abelard's writings in which he makes so sweeping an assertion as this; but that there are, on the other hand, passages in which he refers to the theory of our being redeemed from the power of the devil as an opinion of not much importance. He thinks it possible that St. Bernard had found the statement in a part of the introduction to Abelard's "Book of Sentences," which has been lost. It is not, however, Abelard's alleged statement which is so important, as the manner in which St. Bernard deals with it.

[14] S. Bernard: *De Erroribus Abaelardi*, cap. v. Opera. Lugduni, Parissiis, 1845. Vol. ii. p. 57.

[15] S. Bernard: *De Erroribus Abaelardi*, cap. v. Opera. Lugduni, Parissiis, 1845. Vol. ii. p. 57.

[16] See passages in Shedd, vol. ii. p. 243. Athanasius, however, had far larger and deeper con-

ception of the nature of Christ's redemptive work than this metaphor would suggest. Some of the profoundest hints of the true direction in which to look for a theory of the Atonement occur in his Four Discourses against the Arians, especially in chapter xxi. He has been most inadequately represented by the few writers on the history of dogma with whose works I happen to be acquainted; and the common impression of him in England among those who are not adherents of the "Catholic" party — Roman or Anglican — is extremely unjust. It is unfortunate for him that his name should have been given to the "Athanasian" Creed.

[17] See, for instance, the closing paragraphs of the Tenth Book of Augustine's *Confessions.*

[18] *Cur Deus Homo,* cap. ii.

[19] Cur Deus Homo, cap. vii. The translation is by "A Clergyman," and was published by Messrs. Parker, in 1858.

[20] Ibid. c. xi.

[21] *Cur Deus Homo,* c. xiii.

[22] Ibid. c. xiv.

[23] Book ii. c. 6.

[24] "Ratio quoque nos docuit, quia oportet eum majus aliquid habere quam quidquid sub Deo est quod sponte det et non ex debito Deo...Hoc autem nec sub illo nec extra ilium inveniri potest...In ipso igitur inveniendum est...Aut igitur seipsum aut aliquid de se dabit." — *Cur Deus Homo.* Schlawitz, Berlin, 1857, pp. 65, 66.

[25] Cur Deus Homo, c. xi.

[26] *Cur Deus Homo,* c. xix.

[27] Abaelard: *Comment, super Epistol. ad Rom.* Opera. Edit J. P. Migne. Paris, 1855. Page 836. Abelard, however, recognized the objective value of Christ's intercession.

[28] *Cur Deus Homo,* lib. i. cap. 12.

[29] See Ueberweg's *History of Philosophy.* Translated by Morris. Hodder & Stoughton. Vol. i. pp. 452-457.

[30] Ideo, potest aliam legem statuere rectam, quas si statueretur a Deo, recta asset quia nulla lex est recta nisi quatenus a Dei voluntate acceptatur." Quoted in Julius Muller, *On the Christian Doctrine of Sin* (Clark's Translation). Vol. i. p. 97. Muller adds that "Scotus recognizes an unconditional necessity in the fundamental law of love towards God, and in all which this logically includes. Divine arbitrariness refers only to the sphere of finite beings and their relations."

[31] *A Critical History of the Christian Doctrine of Justification and Reconciliation.* By Albert Ritschl. Translated by J. S. Black. Edinburgh: Edmonston & Douglas. 1872. P. 60.

[32] *A Critical History of the Christian Doctrine of Justification and Reconciliation.* By Albert Ritschl.

[33] Wycliffe taught that "it is a light word to say that God might of His power forgive this sin [Adam's] without the aseeth [satisfaction] which was made for it, for God might do so if He would; but *His justice would not suffer it,* but requires that each trespass be punished, either on earth or in hell. And God may not accept a person to forgive his sin without satisfaction." (*Tracts and Treatises of Wycliffe,* page 84.) Wessel says, "The Lord Jesus is not only Mediator between God and man, but is rather Mediator for man between the God of justice and the God of mercy; for *it behoves that the whole law of God's justice should be fulfilled,* without failure of one jot or tittle, and as this has been achieved by Jesus," &c. (Ullman's *Reformers before the Reformation,* vol. ii. p. 450. See also Ritschl: Critical History of the Christian *Doctrine of*

Justification, &c. Page 158.)

[34] Note Q.

[35] Book ii. chaps. 12-17.

[36] *Institutio Theologiae Elencticae.* Geneva, 1682. Vol. ii. pp. 453-463.

[37] Peter Van Mastricht: *Theoretico-Practica Theologia,* Amsterdam. Page 616.

[38] *Defensio Fidei Catholicae de Satisfactione Christi.* Hugonis Grotii Opera. Vol. iv. Basle, 1732.

[39] "Est quidem recepta regula neminem esse idoneum in suâ causâ judicem." - Page 306.

[40] "Poena enim omnis propositum habet bonum commune; ordinis nimirum conservationem et exemplum." - Page 308.

[41] "Quod ergo is qui deliquit poenam meretur, eoque punibilis est hoc ex ipsa peccati et peccatoris ad superiorem relatione necessario sequitur, et proprie naturale est. Ut vero puniatur quivis peccator, poena tali quae culpae respondeat, non est necessarium simpliciter et universaliter: neque proprie naturale, sed naturae satis conveniens." —Page 310.

[42] Ritschl, 313.

[43] See *Commentaire sur l'Évangile de S, Jean.* By F. Godet. Vol. ii. 186, 207.

[44] Matt. xv. 24.

[45] Ibid. x. 50.

[46] John vi. 15.

[47] Godet: *Commentaire sur l'Évangile de S. Jean,* vol. ii. p. 309.

[48] *On Liberty.* Second edition, pp. 48, 49.

## Lecture Eight - The Remission of Sins

In the preceding Lectures I have endeavoured to prove that the sins of men were the cause of the Death of Christ in a sense in which they were not the cause of the death of those whose fidelity to truth and to conscience, to the highest welfare of mankind and to the authority of God, has provoked the intolerance and the vengeance of wicked men, and won for them the glories of martyrdom; and that on the ground of His Death the sins of men are forgiven.

The proof has been derived from the history and teaching of our Lord Jesus Christ Himself, and from the testimony of His Apostles, who upon this point, if upon no other, may be supposed to have known His mind.

It being assumed that adequate evidence has been alleged of the existence of a direct relation between the Death of Christ and the Remission of sins, we have now to investigate that relation, and to discover, if we can, the principles and laws which it illustrates. The Fact that Christ died to make Atonement for sin having been established, is it possible to construct a Theory of the Atonement?

The inquiry upon which we are about to enter is different in kind from that which is now closed, and is of inferior importance. It is not the theory of the Death of Christ that constitutes the ground on which sins are forgiven, but the Death itself; and the faith, which is the condition on our side of receiving "redemption through His blood," is trust in Christ Himself as the Son of God and Saviour of men, not the acceptance of any doctrine which explains how it is that salvation comes to us through Him. For this Trust, it is not necessary that men should acknowledge even the Fact that the Death of Christ is the propitiation for the sin of the world; much less is it necessary that they should receive from others or elaborate for themselves a Theory of propitiation. It is enough that the authority and love of Christ have been so revealed to them that they rely on Him for eternal salvation.

But if it be true that there is a direct relation between the Death of Christ and the Remission of sins, the inquiry into the grounds of that relation is an inquiry of transcendent speculative importance, and may possibly issue in discoveries concerning the character and ways of God of transcendent practical interest.

On the very threshold of this investigation, we are met by a grave and startling difficulty: — Is the Remission of sins possible?

The answer to this question has been anticipated. Our Lord Himself declared that "the Son of man hath power on earth to forgive sins." [1] To a man sick of the palsy, whom He miraculously cured, He said, "Son, be of good cheer, thy sins be forgiven thee;" [2] and to a woman of evil character, who, in her sorrow and shame, had crept to His feet and washed them with her tears, He said, "Thy sins are forgiven:... thy faith hath saved thee: go in peace." [3] He told His disciples before He suffered, that His blood was to be "shed for the Remission of sins;" [4] and after His Resurrection, He "opened their understanding, that they might understand the Scriptures, and said unto them. Thus it is written, and thus it behoved Christ to suffer, and to rise from the dead the third day; and that repentance and Remission of sins should be preached in His name." [5] That the Apostles, wherever they went, spoke to both Jews and heathen of the Remission of sins, as one of the chief elements of the salvation to be secured by believing in Christ; that in their letters to Christian Churches they spoke of the Remission of sins as one of the chief elements of the salvation which those who believed in Christ had already received, is a fact too familiar to every reader of the New Testament to require either proof or illustration.

But among those who do not acknowledge that the Death of Christ is a Propitiation for the sins of the world, there is a tendency either to deny that the Remission of sins is possible, or to depreciate its importance; and this tendency has very much to do with the rejection both of the Doctrine and of the Fact of the Atonement. It arises from a theory of the relation of God to the moral universe in which the idea of Atonement can find no place.

To attempt a philosophical demonstration of the possibility of the Remission of sins is not my purpose. But I propose to examine a theory which, if it were true, would require us to believe that in the nature of things sin can never be remitted. In the statement of this theory I shall freely avail myself of the language of one of its most effective advocates. Dr. John Young.

Law is defined to be "the expression of will," and to have "its ground in authority." "Authority, supposing adequate power, ultimately rests on rectitude and wisdom." The laws of the physical as well as of the spiritual universe are the expression of the will of God. "In the physical region no resistance is possible, and law reigns serenely and supremely. But in the spiritual sphere the created will has run counter to the Divine will, and darkness and death have supplanted light and life." "Human sin,...so far as it extends,...aims to defy established authority" — the authority of God and of the laws of God — "and to disown and cast off all subjection." But "in spite of what...seems, but only seems, to trample them down,...spiritual laws are mighty, are almighty. They cannot be violated, cannot even be resisted; that is, with impunity, and without exacting an incipient and immediate satisfaction. The reign of law in all the departments of the material creation is proclaimed with extraordinary confidence by those who have devoted themselves to the study of physics: equal and even greater confidence should be felt in the universality and supremacy of spiritual laws." There is a legitimate presumption that the "invariable sequence" in the phenomena of the physical universe, which has been discovered by observation and experiment, "will indefinitely continue to be;" but "no amount of experience in the past can render a divergence from the hitherto observed order, however improbable, either contradictory or impossible — impossible, that is to say, in the nature of things." "It is far otherwise, it is diametrically the reverse with the great laws of the spiritual universe. They are what they are, of themselves, of necessity. Moral good and moral evil are immutable... 'The laws of the spiritual universe do not depend even on the highest will. The great God did not make them, they are eternal as He is. The great God could not repeal them, they are immutable as He is. In perfect harmony with the Divine will, they are nevertheless independent even of it; and as they were not created, so they cannot be annulled or altered, even by the Almighty."

"Spiritual laws, widely distinguished from material laws, are separated by a still vaster difference from merely human ordinances and arrangements." Human laws "must be more or less unwise and unjust." There is also "an inevitable uncertainty in them, a doubtfulness and a degree of untrustworthiness, which tend to shake confidence, and materially to weaken the foundations of authority." The innocent are punished, the guilty escape. On account of these very elements of imperfection by which the authority of human laws is menaced, it is indispensable that their majesty should be asserted, and that, when broken, they should be vindicated and avenged: if not, the dearest interests of society will be wantonly sacrificed.

"But on no such grounds as these, nor on any other grounds whatever, do spiritual ordinances need or admit of either vindication or protection, or support from human or Divine hands. Defender or avenger they have none, and they need none. *Without aid from any quarter they avenge themselves, and exact, and continue without fail to exact, so long as the evil remains, the amount of penalty - visible and invisible - to the veriest jot and tittle, which the deed of violation deserves.* Essentially and perfectly wise and right, they are irresistible, in the case of the obedient and the rebellious alike. There is no formal trial of the criminal, there is no need for investigating the question and determining the amount of guilt or of innocence. Without inquiry and without effort, each case discovers and exposes itself. No judicial verdict is pronounced, and no officer of justice is appointed to carry out the sentence; but *at once, punishment or reward, visible or invisible, or both, dispenses itself, and in the amount in which either is merited.* Spiritual laws are self-acting; with all their penalties and sanctions they are immediately self-acting, and without the remotest possibility of failure or mistake." [6]

Dr. Young has given definite and systematic expression to thoughts which, in a vaguer form, may be recognized in very much of the religious literature of our times. If this is a true conception of the order of the moral and spiritual universe, the idea of Atonement must be given up, and very much besides that most Christian people would be reluctant to lose.

The idea of Atonement must be given up, for the purpose of Atonement is to create an objective ground on which Remission of sins may be granted to the penitent. But on this theory — if I understand it — the Remission of sins is impossible, unless, indeed, the familiar phrase is to receive some new and alien meaning. [7]

For it is alleged that whenever the eternal Law of Righteousness is violated, the law inflicts "the amount of penalty — visible and invisible — to the veriest jot and tittle, which the deed of violation deserves." It is not from the hand of God that the wicked receive the punishment of their wickedness, nor is it from the hand of God that the righteous receive the reward of their righteousness. — "Punishment or reward, visible or invisible, or both, dispenses itself, and in the amount in which either is merited." God simply looks on. The vast machine of the moral universe is self-acting. In no proper sense is He the Moral Ruler or Judge of men.

The old difficulty of the scribes, — "Why doth this man thus speak blasphemies? who can forgive sins but God only?" — reappears in a new form. If God Himself speaks of forgiving sins, this theory raises the objection that "the justice of the universe...is a tremendous fact, an eternal and necessary fact," which God Himself cannot set aside; [8] and that the Divine authority, whatever its limits, is as powerless to forgive sin as it is to reverse or even to modify the eternal and necessary distinction between good and evil.

The functions of God in relation to the eternal Law of Righteousness and the government of the moral universe are, on this theory, precisely similar to our own. All that He can do for the sinner is to make such appeals to the sluggish conscience and the corrupt heart as shall restore to the one its authority and vigour, and inspire the other with a hatred of sin and a love of goodness. God has resources for this great work which we cannot command; but His work is the same in kind as that which is being done by all who are striving to make men better. He is just as unable as we are to say, "Thy sins be forgiven thee." The penalty "must come down. It lies in the essential nature of things that it must come down. Ever and ever, justice inflicts an inevitable penalty, and exacts the completest satisfaction." [9]

To prevent misapprehension, it may be well to state most explicitly, at the very commencement of this discussion, that I do not regard the Remission of sins as being absolutely identical with escape from the penalties of sin. Sin is sometimes forgiven, although some of the penalties of sin are not recalled. But the Remission of sins must be understood to include the cancelling of at least the severest penalties with which unforgiven sin is justly visited; and the theory of Dr. Young, therefore, which asserts that the penalties of sin, "to the veriest jot and tittle," are uniformly and necessarily inflicted, involves the conclusion that the Remission of sins is impossible. [10]

It is difficult, I think, to reconcile this theory with the actual facts of human life. From the dawn of speculation men have been perplexed by the apparent confusion and irregularity in the affairs of the world which obscure those august moral laws whose authority is declared to be so steadfast, and whose penalties are alleged to descend in the very moment of transgression, and to be uniformly exacted "to the veriest jot and tittle." The penalties of sin, both "visible and invisible," which are alleged to be universally and relentlessly inflicted "to the veriest jot and tittle," are constantly evaded, escaped, or alleviated.

Two men are equally guilty of drunkenness and profligacy. But one of them is a man of robust constitution: he has wealth and leisure. He sins, and sins flagrantly; but he shoots in the autumn, hunts in the winter, and spends the summer in his yacht on the coast of Scotland or of Norway. The other has weak health, and is compelled by his circumstances to live a sedentary life. The one, notwithstanding his vices, lives till he is seventy, and is vigorous to the last; the other is the victim of miserable diseases, and dies an ignominious death long before he is fifty. Where is the equality in the "visible" penalties of sin? The eternal laws appear to receive the bribes of the rich and to trample on the helplessness of poverty.

An Englishman is guilty of vicious excesses, and as soon as the penal suffering comes upon him he receives relief from the affluent and merciful resources of modern medical science, and with care and temperance he may escape from pain, and practically recover all his physical health. An inhabitant of a barbarous island in remote seas is guilty of precisely the same excesses, and the moral blame which attaches to him is less, because of his inferior moral advantages; but his strength is rapidly wasted by disease and suffering, and in a few years, perhaps in a few months, a horrible death avenges his crime. Where is the equality in the "visible" penalties of sin? The eternal laws appear to be strong to punish the ignorant, but in the struggle with science they suffer defeat.

By fraud skilfully contrived, and as skilfully concealed, one man creates a fortune. With wealth, the temptation to dishonesty disappears; he spends his money generously, and wins universal honour and affection for integrity and charity. The penalties "visible and invisible" with which society would justly have visited his offence, — penalties so terrible that to most men the severest physical torture would bring less anguish, — are altogether escaped. Another man is guilty of the same fraud, contrived and concealed with equal skill. But at a critical time the engines of an American steamer break down in the middle of the Atlantic, and his American remittances are a fortnight late; or a clerk on his way to the post-office is knocked down by a cab, and his Australian letters miss the mail; and then comes the fatal discovery. He is ruined for life, ruined in fortune and ruined in reputation. He is the object of universal indignation and scorn. His friends fall away from him. He cannot look his own children in the face. After he has exhausted the sentence which human laws have inflicted upon him, he spends the wretched remainder of his days in some foreign city, where his name and his evil deed are unknown, and sinks at last broken-hearted into an obscure grave. Where is the equality in either the "visible" or the "invisible" penalties of sin? Where is the certainty with which these penalties are exacted? The eternal laws appear to be thwarted and deceived by human cunning, and to be indebted to accident for the vindication of their authority.

Among the outcasts of every great city, and sunk to the very lowest depths of moral degradation, you may find men whose evil fortune and evil character are the natural and almost inevitable result of a solitary sin committed so long ago that it has been forgotten by nearly every one but themselves. They drank too much, or they told a lie, or they used a few pounds belonging to their employer. For that one offence they were punished with the loss of an honourable position and an adequate income, which would have been theirs for life. They lost their character, and though they tried hard to be trusted again, no man would trust them. Their calamities made them desperate. They were betrayed into fresh vices. Gradually all their self-respect perished, and whatever moral energy they possessed disappeared. They had slipped into a dark river whose currents were too strong for them, and they have been swept on to hopeless misery and shame.

And among the most honourable and prosperous people living in pleasant houses by which these wretched outcasts creep in their filth and rags, you may find men who were guilty of precisely the same offences, and who for a time seemed to be descending rapidly to the same ruin. But there was a love which clung to them with an agony of earnestness for their salvation; a love which shrunk from no sacrifice to give them a chance of recovering all that they had lost; a love which, by the tenderness of its compassion and by its patience and constancy, restored to the despairing heart its vanished faith in the love of God. At last the victory was won, and those who seemed destined to wretchedness and disgrace were restored to virtue and honour. Human love fought against their evil fate, and conquered it. Where — I ask again — is the equality in the penalties of sin? Where is the certainty with which they are alleged to be exacted?

In the actual condition of the world, either some men suffer too much for their sin, or some men suffer too little. Nor is there any reason to believe that those who escape from the visible and external penalties of their crimes endure an exceptional agony of self-reproach. The probabilities seem to point to precisely the opposite conclusion. Physical disease, loss of property, public dishonour — when these come upon a man as the result of his vices — often reveal to him for the first time the magnitude of his guilt, and his inward humiliation and self-contempt increase with the increase of his external calamities. Nor, again, do those whose offences are most numerous and most aggravated suffer most keenly from the stings of conscience. Conscience becomes feebler and feebler as men continue in sin, and those who ought to feel the greatest shame for wrong doing, feel the least. With augmented guilt there is almost uniformly diminished sensibility to the moral sufferings with which the consciousness of guilt ought to be followed.

The vengeance of these eternal laws, which is said to be so stern and unrelenting in inflicting the complete penalty of every transgression, appears less certain and less exacting than the retributive justice by which the authority of human laws is vindicated. It is soothed and bought off by wealth. It is averted by science, as the lightning is turned aside by a lightning-rod from the towers of a palace or the spire of a church, and buried peacefully in the earth. It penetrates only by accident through disguises which conceal and protect the basest crimes. It surrenders to the pleadings of compassionate love those who had merited the worst terrors it could inflict. All generous hearts are in a perpetual confederacy — a confederacy extending through all countries, and growing in strength from one generation to another — to rescue the guilty from the evils with which these laws justly menace them, and to alleviate the evils which have come upon the guilty already. And the most terrible sufferings which these laws ever inflict — the sufferings produced by the sharp and vehement reproaches of conscience — are felt least by the greatest offenders. The theory that "sin never for an instant fails to receive its desert," [11] that the full penalty of sin, "visible and invisible, to the veriest jot and tittle," is always exacted, is contrary to the uniform experience of the human race.

It is equally contrary to the uniform teaching both of the Old Testament and the New to represent God as an otiose Spectator of the moral order of the universe, having no other function in relation to moral government than to watch and to approve the perfect manner in which rewards and penalties are distributed by self-acting spiritual laws.

The ancient historical Scriptures are crowded with illustrations of the energy with which He punished the wrong-doing both of individuals and nations. It is impossible to read these books and to suppose that they were meant to teach that "self-acting" spiritual laws brought a flood upon the old world, rained fire upon Sodom and Gomorrah, destroyed the first-born of Egypt, excluded from the Land of Promise Aaron and Moses, and nearly the whole generation that crossed the Red Sea. The idea throughout — whatever value may be attached to the history — is too clear to be misapprehended: it was the Jewish faith that God is on the side of righteousness, and that positive punishments are inflicted by His own hand on those that sin. This was the faith of psalmists and prophets. Sometimes they appeal to God's compassion to recall the terrible ministers of His righteous indignation. Sometimes they acknowledge the forbearance which delayed the execution of punishment, that the sinful people might have time to repent. Sometimes they warn their own countrymen and heathen nations that, at last, the anger of God will only be the more terrible, and the calamities it will inflict the more appalling, if His long-suffering does not constrain them to forsake their sin and to keep God's commandments. It is a Living Person, according to these ancient books, who punishes the sins and rewards the righteousness of men.

The New Testament produces the same impression as the Old. The theory that sin is always punished, adequately punished, and instantly punished, by "self-acting" spiritual laws, is in violent antagonism to the teaching of our Lord Jesus Christ and of His Apostles. Christ Himself said, "The Father judgeth no man" — He did not give as the reason of this that "self-acting" spiritual laws render the judgment of God unnecessary; He claims the authority and responsibilities of judgment for Himself — "but hath committed all judgment unto the Son." [12] Instead of telling men that rewards and punishments are sufficiently dispensed by "self-acting" spiritual laws, He speaks of a time when "the Son of man shall come in the glory of His Father, with His angels; and then He shall reward every man according to his works." [13] St. Peter placed the future judgment of the world by Christ among the most elementary truths which the Apostles had been appointed to proclaim: "He commanded us to preach unto the people, and to testify that it is He who was ordained of God to be the Judge of quick and dead." [14] St. Paul warned the Athenians that God "hath appointed a day in which He will judge the world in righteousness by that Man whom He hath ordained;" [15] and he reasoned with Felix— not about "self-acting" spiritual laws — but about "judgment to come." [16] In the epistles, the future judgment is appealed to as adding fresh solemnity to many Christian duties: "Why dost thou judge thy brother?... we shall all stand before the judgment-seat of Christ:" [17] this was the way in which St. Paul enforced the duty of mutual forbearance and toleration among Christian brethren. "We must all stand before the judgment-seat of Christ; that every one may receive the things done in his body, according to that he hath done, whether it be good or bad:" [18] the anticipation of that supreme hour was one of the motives which sustained St. Paul himself in the faithful and zealous discharge of his apostolic ministry. When he charged Timothy to "preach the word," to "be instant in season, out of season;" to "reprove, rebuke, exhort with all longsuffering and doctrine," St. Paul reminded him that he would have to give account to Christ of his ministerial fidelity: "I charge thee before God, and the Lord Jesus Christ, who shall judge the quick and the dead at His appearing and His kingdom." [19]

We are told by the advocates of this theory that "God has no unsettled accounts, no outstanding claims." [20] What, then, is meant by "the riches of His goodness, and forbearance, and longsuffering"? [21] What is meant by *treasuring* up "wrath against the day of wrath, and revelation of the righteous judgment of God"? [22] What is meant by the "indignation and wrath, tribulation and anguish," which are to come at last "upon every soul of man that doeth evil"? [23] What is the terror of that manifestation of Christ when He "shall be revealed from heaven... in flaming fire, taking vengeance on them that know not God, and obey not the gospel of our Lord Jesus Christ"? [24] If "self-acting" spiritual laws have already inflicted or are already inflicting the complete penalty of sin, what place is there for the awful solemnities of the judgment, and for the fresh woes inflicted on the impenitent by the terrible sentence, "Depart from Me, ye cursed, into everlasting fire, prepared for the devil and his angels"? [25]

This plausible theory, which is held vaguely by very many who have never elaborated it into a definite philosophical form, and which is exerting a wide and most mischievous influence on modern theological thought, rests on the ambiguity of the word "Law."

There are ethical laws, and there are laws of nature: laws which ask for the free and loyal obedience of the will, and laws which are illustrated by the unvarying sequence of antecedents and consequents in spheres from which freedom is excluded.

What may be described as the structural laws of the moral and spiritual life of man are of the second kind. The alternative of obedience and transgression is never submitted to our choice. Sin is invariably followed by a deterioration of our moral and spiritual nature. By repeated acts of transgression evil habits are invariably strengthened. Evil passions acquire constant accessions of energy if they are not controlled. By wrongdoing we become less able to discriminate between good and evil, and those forces of our nature which refuse to listen to the voice of duty are strengthened in their revolt; the sensibility of conscience is diminished, and the authority of conscience is impaired. In other words, the more we sin, the harder it becomes to forsake sin. These laws are in a very true sense "self-acting." They are precisely analogous to the laws of our physical organisation, and to the laws of the material universe, and to the laws which belong to the province of political economy and of sociology. "Defender or avenger they have none, and they need none."

The laws of hydrostatics are never violated. If the walls of a great reservoir are built of sufficient strength to resist the pressure of several hundred thousand tons of water, those laws ensure the safety of the houses which lie near. If the walls are not strong enough to resist the pressure, the reservoir bursts, and the houses are destroyed. In the second case, it is not the laws of hydrostatics that are violated by the engineer whose mistake is the occasion of the calamity; it is not his business either to obey or to transgress them; from him they can ask nothing, and can receive nothing. The laws which he has violated are laws of a very different kind — laws which are in no sense "self-acting." He ought to have carefully calculated the pressure of the water; he ought to have estimated the comparative strength of sloping and of perpendicular walls in bearing the pressure; he ought to have determined whether

157

the strength of the reservoir was proportioned to its depth; he ought to have taken care that the material of which the walls were constructed was of a kind to resist the action of water and frost. These laws are not "self-acting." He was at liberty to violate them, and his violation of them caused all the destruction of life and property which came from the catastrophe he might have averted. To confound the laws which the engineer ought to obey, but which he sometimes transgresses, with the laws of nature, which are absolutely uniform in their operation, is an error precisely similar to that into which Dr. Young has been betrayed, and which is the foundation of his theory. The laws of hydrostatics "execute themselves, without the formalities of an inquiry — without the intervention of a judge." But those other laws which the engineer violated require vindication. The penalty which he deserves, if he has been guilty of culpable negligence, does not descend upon him at once: sometimes it does not appear to descend upon him at all. The physical results of his carelessness or ignorance come upon innocent victims. He may be in another country, beyond the reach of public indignation. He may be dead. If the causes of the accident are investigated, the verdict may be false, or human laws may have no power to punish him.

Obvious and simple as is the distinction which I am trying to make clear, some additional illustration may be necessary. If a studious man works too long at his books, or a statesman at his desk, and takes no exercise, it is not the laws of nature which are violated. Those laws retain an undisturbed authority and power. In due time his heart becomes feeble and his brain sluggish. His appetite fails, and he is unable to sleep. The laws which make these consequences of his way of living absolutely certain are "self-acting;" they are laws which he can neither obey nor transgress. The laws which are violated are of another kind. He desires to be in health, he ought to play as well as work; he ought to take sufficient sleep, and take it regularly; he ought to walk, run, jump, or ride. These laws are not "self-acting:" if they were, no student or statesman would die of brain disease or heart disease through violating them. A man may obey them or not as he pleases. There are times when it is a clear duty not to obey them, — when the exigencies of the public service, or the interests of science, or the claims of children, create an obligation to protracted and excessive labour, even at the cost of incurring painful disease and at the risk of sinking into a premature grave.

In the same way, the laws of political economy are "self-acting." If a government imposes protective duties it fetters the development of industry and makes the nation poorer. Whether the nation likes it or not, this is the inevitable result. There may be reasons which justify a government in saying that higher ends than national wealth require these duties to be maintained. But the law which requires the government to repeal these duties when they are imposed simply in the interest of a powerful class is not "self-acting:" it needs very vigorous defenders. It may be resisted until there is danger of revolution.

The sociological law that in states where political power is vested in the great masses of the people, popular ignorance is a perpetual menace to public security, and will certainly entail great public evils, is another law which is "self-acting;" but the law which requires the government to institute an effective and universal system of popular education is a law of another kind. It needs the voluntary concurrence of those who ought to obey it; its authority may be defied until the opportunity of saving the nation is lost for ever; the results of disobedience may descend on the innocent instead of the guilty.

Dr. Young's theory ignores the difference between the laws which ought to guide, but which often fail to guide the conduct of persons, and the laws which determine the sequence of phenomena; between ethical laws and those laws which in every sphere of man's individual and social life, from the lowest to the highest, are the same in kind as the laws of the physical universe. These latter laws — laws of nature they may be called — require no "defender;" for they cannot be attacked; no "avenger," for they can never be insulted; no "vindication," for they uniformly assert their authority without the concurrence of the will. But ethical laws are simply imperative, and they may be defied and disobeyed. It is a law that men should be truthful, just, kindly, and devout; but large numbers of men are untruthful, unjust, cruel, and profane.

If it be said that ethical laws are "self-acting" because disobedience is always followed by an adequate penalty, this is no reason for classifying them with natural laws, disobedience to which is impossible. Nor can the penalty — supposing it to be invariably exacted — which follows the transgression of an ethical law be alleged as a proof that the law is "self-acting." The law requires a man to tell the truth: it cannot be said that this law is obeyed because if a man lies he suffers for it. In the very act of suffering, his revolt against the authority of the law may become more violent.

The *precepts* of ethical law are not "self-acting;" they require the free concurrence of the human will, and the human will may determine to resist them. Nor has it been proved that the *penalties* of ethical law are "self-acting;" they may require the free concurrence of the Divine will: and it seems possible at least that the Divine will may determine to remit them.

It is admitted that when ethical laws are violated the violation should be avenged by adequate penalties. These penalties, as I have already endeavoured to show, are not instantaneous. Nor in this life do they appear to be either certain or sufficient. There are indications of a vast confederacy of most varied forces on the side of righteousness. But either the organisation of these friendly powers is incomplete, or their resources are inadequate, or their action is restrained by the control of a supreme authority; or else it was never meant that they should invariably exact the complete penalty due to the violation of ethical laws. Whatever the explanation may be, the complete penalty "to the veriest jot and tittle" is not immediately inflicted. The theory which affirms that it is, breaks down. Some more coherent argument is necessary before we surrender the hope to which the hearts of men have clung in all ages, that it is possible to escape from the penalties of wrong-doing. Nothing that this theory contains can cause us to hesitate in receiving the declaration of Christ's infinite love, that He came into the world and died on the cross in order that the Remission of sins might be actually conferred upon us.

The exigencies of what is called the "moral theory" of the Atonement have led some of its advocates to impose upon the phrase "the Remission of sins" a sense foreign to all the usages of language. The true idea of Remission, though not suppressed, is relegated to a position of insignificance, and the Remission of sins is made to include as its chief element another blessing of a different order. Forgiveness may include something more than the cancelling of guilt, if guilt is defined to be "liability to punishment on account of sin," [26] and orthodox theologians may have given an incomplete and unsatisfactory account of this wonderful and transcendent blessing; but when Dr. Bushnell says that "in discussing the great question how it is that God forgives," we are discussing how it is that He "accomplishes the restoration of fallen character," and when he says that these two questions are the "same," [27] he confounds two inquiries which have been always recognized as distinct, not only by theologians, but by the indestructible instincts of human nature; and he imposes on the language of Christ and His Apostles concerning the Remission of sins a sense which the language was never intended to convey.

That the Remission of sins, if it stood alone, would leave us unsaved, is one of the commonplaces of Christian theology; but it does not follow that the Remission of sins includes the blessings which are necessary to complete our salvation, or is to be confounded with them. So long as the human heart is conscious of a twofold misery — the misery of being under the Divine condemnation, and the misery of being under the tyranny of evil habits which it cannot throw off, and of evil passions which it cannot subdue — it will passionately cry for a twofold deliverance. It is one thing to receive the Divine pardon, it is another to recover the Divine image. The first is the initial grace granted to the penitent sinner, the second is the glory of the perfected saint. That in the Divine order the forgiveness of sin, when sin is first confessed and forsaken, is always associated with the new birth in which the life of God is given to man, the ,life which is ultimately revealed in the consummate energy and beauty of moral and spiritual character, is not only true; it is so true that their inseparable association as the two great elements of the Christian redemption has been asserted, in varying forms indeed, but with unbroken unanimity and with strenuous earnestness, by the theologians and preachers of every Church, of every country, and of every age. They always *go together;* but they go together, and they are not the same.

Dr. Bushnell identifies or confounds them because he regards the Remission of sins, in the strict sense, as a blessing of no considerable value. Remission, he says, "both in Greek and English, is a popular word, which signifies in common speech a *letting go;* that is, a letting go of blame, a consenting to raise no impeachment farther, and to have all wounded feeling dismissed...It is only a kind of formality, or verbal discharge, that carries practically no discharge at all. It says 'go,' but leaves the prison doors shut." [28] It is true that when a man has a vivid apprehension of what sin really is, he desires the Divine forgiveness, not only for its own sake, but because until he receives it the power of the Divine life cannot be revealed in him and he cannot be redeemed from moral and spiritual evil. It is not true, however, that the whole misery of a sinful man's condition lies within the sphere of his own moral and spiritual nature, and that the Remission of sins in the proper sense of the words is "only a kind of formality." Only "a kind of formality!" It is no wonder that the awful reality of the propitiation for the sins of the world is denied, when the Remission of sins is declared to be nothing more than this. For a mere "formality" it would not have been worth while for Christ to die.

The Remission of sins is regarded as "a kind of formality" only because it is believed that in no sense is God hostile to those whose sins are unforgiven, and because the Divine "wrath" is supposed to be a mere figure of speech. Perhaps the principal origin of the modern tendency to reject the idea of an objective Atonement is to be found in that temper of mind which indisposes us to believe that there is any anger against sinful men in the heart of God to be allayed, and in that conception of His character which excludes the possibility of His being hostile even to those who are guilty of the worst offences. It is partly because sin does not provoke our own wrath that we do not believe that sin provokes the wrath of God. It appears to be one of the results of modern civilisation that men are very rarely kindled to fiery passion of any kind. This is perhaps especially true of modern Englishmen. Neither in love nor in hatred, neither in admiration nor in anger, are we so intense and vehement as some other races. We take fire slowly, and though we are capable, in time and under favourable circumstances, of great heat, the heat is mostly without much flame. The coldness which perhaps belongs to our blood is increased by our education and by national sentiment. To our great injury all strong emotion is discouraged. We are rather ashamed to let it be seen that we feel strongly about anything. One of the great things to be desired for ourselves as a nation — one of the great things to be desired just now for all the nations of Christendom — is that we should love more fervently all that is lovable, hate with an intenser hatred all that deserves to be hated, admire with a franker and less critical admiration whatever is admirable, and despise and scorn more heartily what is mean, despicable, and base."

But apart from the general sluggishness of our passions, there are other and deeper reasons why we are not often indignant at sin. Sin does not seem to us a very evil thing. We have become accustomed to it. We have learnt to tolerate it. When our personal interests or the interests of those we love are injured, when our pride and vanity are wounded, we occasionally become hot; but we are rarely filled with wrath against men simply because they have done wrong. Unless we are in some way made to suffer by their sin, or unless there is something flagrant and tragic in its circumstances, our pulses are not stirred.

We cannot help remembering our own sinfulness, and this checks our indignation. Who are we, that we should be angry with our brother because he has broken God's law? In condemning him, we condemn ourselves.

Perhaps, too, the man who has sinned struggled long against temptation, and was at last surprised into wrong-doing when he was weary of struggling, and when his watchfulness was relaxed. Already he may be suffering shame and remorse, and the good that is in him, and which was suppressed for a moment, may be recovering its ascendency. It is not for us to let our anger burn against him, but to strengthen him with our sympathy and love. [29]

Such thoughts as these almost always come to us when we meet with particular cases of wrong-doing. They form us to the habit of regarding those who are guilty of sin with a feeling very different from indignation. We think of whatever palliates the crime and lessens the responsibility of the criminal. We hope that in the worst man the love of goodness has not altogether perished, and we instinctively take sides with his better nature against all that is evil and hateful in him.

But sometimes this habit of hopefulness and charity gives way. The fire breaks out, and is not to be quenched. When a man who knows better, lies to our face, lies deliberately, and lies persistently; when a man in a position of great trust, and who ought never even to have felt a temptation to dishonesty, is proved to have been guilty of elaborate fraud, of fraud extending through many years, during which he was affecting to be chivalrously honourable; when cruel suffering is inflicted in our presence on the weak and the defenceless— then the fury long suppressed blazes out. No words are fierce enough to express our passionate indignation, and for a moment, or for an hour, we know something of what it is for wrath to be kindled against sin. The feeling is a right one. We are angry, and sin not. We should sin if we were not angry. We sin because we are not angry in this way oftener.

Anger provoked by moral evil is a just and noble emotion. It is the attribute of the strongest and most generous natures. Both in the Old Testament and the New it is very frequently ascribed to God, and the revelation of God in Christ would have been incomplete if the indignation of Christ had never been provoked by the sins of men. He came, indeed, to reveal the Divine love and compassion for our race; but on one occasion the malignant spirit of the Scribes and Pharisees provoked His anger, though the Evangelist who tells the story adds immediately that He was "grieved for the hardness of their hearts;" [30] and after He had wept over Jerusalem, as He looked upon it across the valley of the Kedron from the Mount of Olives, He went into the city, and in vehement words denounced its crimes and predicted its destruction. Grief and anger, tears and indignant threatenings — we must include them all in a complete conception of what Christ revealed concerning God's thoughts of human sin. That God is incapable of the groundless irritation and unreasonable passion of which we are sometimes guilty, needs no proof. He is equally incapable of looking upon sin without displeasure; and sin unrepented of and unforsaken provokes not mere displeasure, but wrath — wrath which will some day be revealed in all its terrible and fiery energy. From this wrath Christ came to save us. We are exposed to it no longer when we receive Remission of sins. To speak of the Remission of sins as "a kind of formality" is to disparage "the exceeding riches" of that grace through which those who are "children of wrath" escape their doom, and become the heirs of immortal blessedness and glory.

Although the temper of our times makes it difficult for us to believe that the anger of God against sin, and against those that are guilty of sin, can ever become "a consuming fire," it is perhaps easier for us to believe that He is angry with the sinful and the impenitent than to believe that, in any real sense, He is hostile to them. Anger within certain limits is not inconsistent with love. Indeed, the measure of our love for others is often the measure of our anger against them when they do wrong. A comparative stranger may tell us a lie, and we may feel nothing but contempt and disgust; but if our own child, or a friend for whom we have strong affection, tells us a lie, there is often intense anger as well as intense grief. That God should be angry with us though He loves us, is perfectly intelligible; and we may even find it possible to believe that His anger may at last become so great, that if it were revealed, the revelation would utterly consume and destroy us. That He should be hostile to men on account of sin, is not so easy to believe; but unless we believe it we must suppress and reject a large part of the teaching of the New Testament. God has a great love for mankind. This is the central truth which has given light and glory to the long succession of His supernatural revelations to our race. It has received its highest proof and illustration in the Life, Death, and Resurrection of our Lord Jesus Christ, and in the blessings which God has conferred upon mankind in Him. . For eighteen centuries the Church has proclaimed this truth, with unequal earnestness, but with a firm and invincible faith. The gloomiest theological systems have never been able altogether to obscure its brightness. In the coldest ages it has kindled the most fervent passion in the hearts of saints; in ages of general intellectual depression it has given inspiration to poets, and has lighted up the fires of a glorious eloquence. But to deny that He can be hostile to men on account of sin, is to emasculate and degrade our conception of Him. He is not a mere "good-natured" God. His righteousness as well as His love is infinite.

Take a case: — You have a child who is the light and joy of your home; her voice is sweeter to you than any music, and her face is fairer and brighter than a summer's morning. Her thoughts are as pure as mountain air; her life is as stainless as mountain snow. She is on the threshold of womanhood, and the very flower and perfection of her loveliness and beauty have come. And a wretch, whose crime human language has no terms black enough to describe,

163

and human laws no punishment terrible enough to avenge — deliberately, by hypocrisy, by lying, by a deep laid scheme, worked out with elaborate cruelty — betrays her trust, ruins her virtue, and then flings her from him on to the streets of a strange city. He has no compunction for his crime. If the opportunity comes to him again he will repeat it. Tell me now — What ought to be God's relation to such a man as that? Ought God to be at peace with him? God forbid! If He were, there would be no justice in the universe. My hope and strength and consolation in the presence of such a crime as this, come from the certainty that wherever that man goes, under whatever disguises he may live, whatever his wealth may be, whatever his rank, he is pursued by One who is the relentless enemy of his sin — and who will be his relentless enemy if he will not renounce his sin — an enemy from whose grasp he cannot escape, whose strength he cannot resist, and whose justice and wrath, if he does not repent, will inflict upon him an awful penalty. Even to the worst of men indeed God manifests patience and longsuffering. The Divine mercy clings to them while there is any hope, and endeavours to redeem them. It is better, infinitely better, that they should repent than that they should suffer. But the Divine hostility becomes more intense as the Divine grace is resisted, and if they refuse to repent they are treasuring up unto themselves "wrath against the day of wrath, and revelation of the righteous judgment of God."

An extreme case does but illustrate the real nature of the sin that is in all of us, and of God's antagonism to it. The sin may not be developed in a gross form; it may not be of a kind to startle our own conscience; it may not bring upon us the strong condemnation of other men; but God cannot endure sin in any form. In the vast and awful conflict between righteousness and sin, which gives tragic interest to the history of the universe, God is irrevocably on the side of righteousness, and on the side of those who are striving to be righteous. But for the transcendent work of mercy consummated by Christ on Calvary, God would be not only hostile to sin, but hostile to those who take sides with sin, from the first moment of their revolt against the eternal law of righteousness. For sin is a personal act; it has no existence apart from the sinner.

But it was one of the chief elements of the apostolic gospel that in and through Christ God is ready to be at peace with us. In a very true sense He is at peace with us already. His hostility to our sins has received adequate expression in the Death of Christ, and now He is ready to confer on us the Remission of sins for Christ's sake. The Remission of sins is something more than "a kind of formality." It brings to the man who has received it a sure and permanent escape from the hostility and the wrath of God.

To reassert the austere truths on which I have felt it my duty to insist in this Lecture, and in speaking of which I have, perhaps, lost the calmness of the lecturer in the vehemence of the preacher, is one of the most urgent duties of these times. Until they are restored to their original place in the thought and faith of the Church, the Death of Christ, as an Atonement for the sins of the world, will never awaken in our hearts the wonder and awe and passionate gratitude with which it filled the hearts of saints in former centuries; our theory of the Atonement will be impoverished, and what remains of it will rest on no sure and firm foundation. While these truths are relegated to obscurity and silence, even if they are not consciously and avowedly rejected, we shall not be likely to have much success in preaching the gospel.

It is of no avail for us to plead that we have an invincible reluctance to speak of them, and that they are too awful for contemplation, even in our silent and solitary thought. We are under the most solemn obligation to receive ourselves, and to make known to others, whatever God has revealed concerning the condition and destiny of our race. To refuse to consider the terrible penalties which menace those who have not received the remission of sins, will lessen the urgency of our solicitude for their eternal redemption; and if we fail to warn them that while they persist in their impenitence and unbelief they are exposed to "indignation and wrath, tribulation and anguish," we cannot clear ourselves of responsibility for their eternal perdition.

Nor is it of any avail to plead that to tell men they have provoked the Divine hostility and the Divine wrath, is likely to repel them from Christ, rather than to attract them to Him. We are bound to tell them the real facts - concealing nothing, alleviating nothing. Christ Himself is responsible for the revelation He has made to our race. To improve upon it, to suppress what we think is likely to provoke resentment; to insist incessantly on what we think is likely to conciliate, is no part of our duty. It is for us to "use great plainness of speech," "not walking in craftiness, nor handling the word of God deceitfully."

I, too, believe that the great function of the Church is to make known the infinite love of God as revealed through Christ, and the greatness and glory of the Christian salvation. But Christ did not come to tell men that they had incurred no guilt by their revolt against God's authority, or that their guilt exposed them to no penal sufferings in the world to come, or that in this world God regarded them with no anger. If the guilt had not been great, the Remission of sins which He died to obtain for us would have been an inconsiderable blessing; if the penalties which He professed to avert were unreal, there would be no reason for being grateful to Him for deliverance from them; if there had been no righteous anger in the heart of God, the propitiation which He made for the sins of the world would have had no significance or value. One of the chief reasons why men do not trust in Christ to save them, is that they do not believe that there is anything from which they need to be saved.

Nor is it of any avail to plead that if men can be made conscious of sin, and of their need of redemption from sin, it is unnecessary to provoke their antagonism by speaking of the terrors which threaten the impenitent. Antagonism! Is it true that impenitence justly deserves God's anger and hostility, and will be justly punished with the pains of the second death? If it is, then this antagonism involves guilt; it arises from an inadequate apprehension of the evil of sin; so long as it continues there is revolt against the eternal Law of Righteousness; latent revolt — if through suppression of the truth concerning the Divine hostility and wrath, and the future penalties of sin, the antagonism is not provoked; active revolt — if the truth produces resentment, and is rejected as inconsistent with the character of God.

If it is true that a sinful man needs the Remission of sins, as well as strength to sin no more, and if the Remission of sins is no mere "formality," but a wonderful manifestation of the Divine mercy, to be received with devout joy and immeasurable gratitude; then, while guilt is implicitly denied, though moral and spiritual weakness is acknowledged, there is an unsettled controversy between man and God, and until this controversy is terminated, there can be no real reconciliation.

Perhaps we have not sufficiently considered that it is possible for men to "hunger and thirst after righteousness," and yet to ignore the authority of God; possible for them to confess that He is supreme, and yet never to identify Him with that ideal Law which they know they have violated, and which they now want to fulfil. They desire moral and spiritual excellence very much as they might desire physical vigour and beauty, or large and varied intellectual accomplishments. They do not recognize the Divine authority, they care only for the perfection of their own nature. If they appeal to God, they do not think of Him as One who has a right to require them to do His will; they only rely upon His mighty and merciful aid to enable them to be loyal to their own conscience, and to achieve the ideal sanctity which haunts their imagination and has won their hearts. They think of Him as having a fulness of moral and spiritual life from which they may receive inspiration and strength, but they do no homage to His awful sovereignty. It is not His law they have transgressed; it is not His law they want to obey. It is His only as it is theirs — His, only because He acknowledges, as they acknowledge, that it is holy, just, and good. His most august prerogative — the characteristic prerogative of Deity — has never been revealed to them. The awe with which they would regard Him, if they had discovered that to violate the eternal Law of Righteousness is to sin against Him, and that therefore it belongs to God, as it can belong to none besides, to grant Remission of sins, they have never felt. They yield Him reverence, but they withhold worship. There is a homage due to God, different in kind as well as in degree from that which can be given to any of His creatures. It is the homage, transferred to a living Person, which the conscience offers to the authority of the eternal Law of Righteousness. The refusal to offer it is often the last expression of man's revolt against God; it is encouraged and confirmed by a theology which maintains that salvation consists exclusively in deliverance from sinfulness, and which fails to assert with equal earnestness and energy the necessity of the Remission of sins.

Will it be urged that to excite the fears of men by dwelling on the wrath of God and on the terrors of perdition, is to condescend to appeal to their coarser passions, and to do dishonour to the spiritual dignity of the Christian faith? I am conscious of no "condescension" when I appeal to the same elements of human nature to which Christ appealed when He warned men of "the worm that dieth not and the fire that is not quenched;" and when He said that "the Son of man shall send forth His angels, and they shall gather out of His kingdom all things that offend and them which do iniquity, and shall cast them in a furnace of fire: there shall be wailing and gnashing of teeth." I am conscious of doing no dishonour to the spiritual dignity of the Christian faith when, with St. Paul, I give God thanks for the grace of the Lord Jesus Christ, who delivers us from the wrath to come.

To proclaim the Remission of sins, as well as to make known the power and grace by which sinful men may recover the image of God, was one of the chief duties of the Apostles, and it is one of the chief duties of the Church in every age. To deny the possibility of Remission, to depreciate its value, is to "pervert the gospel of Christ."

In the remaining Lectures I have to attempt to illustrate the relation between the Death of Christ and this great act of the Divine mercy. Whether the attempt fails or succeeds, I trust that the argument of the preceding Lectures may enable some to repeat with a more earnest faith the article of the ancient creed, "I believe in...the forgiveness of sins," and to look back with more devout wonder and more fervent gratitude upon that mysterious Sacrifice by which the forgiveness of sins was secured for us.

[1] Matt. ix. 6.
[2] Matt. ix. 2.
[3] Luke vii. 48-50.
[4] Matt. xxvi. 28.
[5] Luke xxiv. 45-47.
[6] John Young, LL.D.: *The Life and Light of Men*, pp. 87, 88. The preceding pages of the text are a summary — Dr. Young's own words being freely used — of pp. 79-87 of the same work.
[7] It is only fair to Dr. Young to say that in other parts of this volume he speaks of God as forgiving sin, without any attempt to impose any unusual sense on the words. It is no part of the design of these Lectures, however, to criticise Dr. Young's able treatise; and I have quoted the passages which appear in the preceding pages, only because they express very clearly a tendency of modern religious thought which is very hostile to the doctrine I have to illustrate. On Dr. Young's argument and apparent inconsistencies, see Note R.
[8] *The Life and Light of Men*, page 115.
[9] Ibid, page 119.
[10] The theory that the penal consequences of sin are justly and necessarily remitted when sin is followed by adequate repentance, is not touched in this Lecture. It rests upon a conception of punishment to which a reply is attempted in Lecture ix.
[11] *The Life and Light of Men*, page 96.
[12] John v. 22.
[13] Matt. xvi. 27.
[14] Acts x. 42.
[15] Ibid. xvii. 31.
[16] Ibid. xxiv. 25.
[17] Rom. xiv. 10.
[18] 2 Cor. v. 10.
[19] 2 Tim. iv. I.
[20] *The Life and Light of Men*, page 96.
[21] Rom. ii. 4.
[22] Ibid. ii. 5.
[23] Ibid. ii. 8, 9.
[24] 2 Thess. i. 7, 8.
[25] Matt. xxv. 41.
[26] "Obligatio ad poenam ex peccato." — Turretin: *Institutio Theologiae Elencticae*, vol. i. 654, note.
[27] *The Vicarious Sacrifice*. First (London) edition, page 245.

[28] *The Vicarious Sacri-* | [29] See Paley's charm- | tives of Anger. *Moral Phi-*
*fice*, pp. 359, 360. | ing passage on the Seda- | *losophy*, book iii. chap. 6.
| | [30] Mark iii. 5.

## Lecture Nine - The Theory of the Atonement: Illustrated by the Relation of Our Lord Jesus Christ to the Eternal Law of Righteousness

We are now free to resume the investigation which was arrested by the theory discussed in the last Lecture. The Remission of sins is possible. Can we discover why it is that the Remission of sins is granted to men on the ground of the Death of Christ?

It may be thought that a simple and direct reply to this question is given by the representations of the Death of Christ contained in the New Testament. Christ gave His life as a "ransom" for us; and therefore we are emancipated from all the evils which we had incurred by sin. Christ "bare our sins," "died for our sins," "died for us," as an innocent man, if this were possible, might take upon himself the guilt of a criminal, and die in his place; and, therefore, the penalties of our sin are remitted. Christ is the "Propitiation for our sins;" and, therefore. He has allayed the Divine anger, so that God, for His sake, is willing to forgive us.

But these representations of the Death of Christ as a Ransom, as a Vicarious Death, as a Propitiation, though they illustrate the cause of His sufferings and their effect, and contain all that is necessary for faith do not constitute a theory. As they stand, they are not consistent with each other. For a good citizen to bear the punishment of a convicted criminal, is one thing; for a generous philanthropist to pay the ransom of a slave, is a different thing; for a friend or a relative of a man who has done wrong to propitiate the anger of a powerful superior, is a different thing again. In the first case the intervention is intended to meet the claims of criminal law; in the second, to purchase what can be estimated at a definite money value; in the third, to soothe wounded feeling. The fundamental principles on which we should have to construct our whole theory of the value and efficacy of the Death of Christ would vary, as we adopted the first or the second or the third of these illustrations as containing adequate account of the Atonement.

Nor is it possible by any rough process of combination to work these heterogeneous illustrations of the great fact into a coherent conception of it. A slaveholder who receives a ransom as the condition of liberating his slave is not propitiated; he may have no resentment that needs propitiation; he is paid the commercial value of his property. When there is righteous anger against a base and ungrateful action, it cannot be soothed by anything that has the nature of the money payment which purchases the freedom of a

168

slave; nor could righteous anger be propitiated by the infliction of pain on the innocent instead of the wrong-doer.

There are difficulties of another kind in trying to construct a theory on the lines of any of these illustrations. If the Death of Christ is supposed to receive its full interpretation when described as a Ransom, to whom was the Ransom paid? Was it paid, as some of the Fathers supposed, to the devil? That hypothesis is revolting. Was it paid to God Himself? That hypothesis is incoherent; God Himself provided the Ransom, He could not pay it to Himself; and when we are redeemed, we do not cease to be under the power of God, for we become His in a deeper sense than we were before. Was it paid by Christ to rescue us from the power of the Father? That hypothesis is intolerable; there is no schism in the Godhead; "God, commendeth His love toward us, in that while we were yet sinners Christ died for us." Was the Ransom paid by the Divine mercy to the Divine justice? That hypothesis is mere rhetoric. Was it paid by God to the ideal Law of Righteousness which we had offended? Criminal law knows nothing of ransoms, and a ransom cannot be paid to an idea.

If, again, the nature of the Death of Christ is supposed to be completely expressed when it is represented as a Propitiation, new difficulties emerge, and some of the same difficulties reappear in a new form. How can the incidents of propitiation, as known among ourselves, assist us to understand a propitiation which originates with the injured person? Or are we to conceive of God as working down His resentment by suffering for us, and so propitiating Himself? [1] Or are we to think of Christ as being filled with compassion, and subduing the wrath of the Father by the perfection of His obedience and the urgency of His intercession?

If we adopt the remaining illustration, and attempt to construct a theory of the Death of Christ on the hypothesis that it corresponded to what would occur in the administration of human justice if some illustrious man, as conspicuous for his virtue and public services as for his rank, died as a substitute for a number of obscure persons who had been guilty of treason, we are confronted at once by an objection which admits of no reply. Such a substitution could not be admitted. It would be contrary to the principle of justice, and in the highest degree injurious to the state.

These illustrations of the nature and effect of the Death of Christ are illustrations, and nothing more. They are analogous to the transcendent fact only at single points. The fact is absolutely unique. The problem before us is to form some conception of the Death of Christ which shall naturally account for all these various representations of it; and no solution of the problem is to be found by attempting to translate these representations, derived from transient human institutions and from the mutual relations of men, into the Divine and eternal sphere to which this great Mystery belongs. The administration of human justice is at the best imperfect, and can never closely correspond to the Divine government of the moral universe; and the mutual relations of men can never be accepted as adequately illustrating the relations between God and ourselves.

The descriptions of the Death of Christ in the New Testament, as a Sacrifice, a Propitiation, a Ransom, are of infinite practical value; but we misapprehend the true principles and methods and aims of theological science if we make these descriptions the basis of a theory of the Atonement. They constitute the authoritative tests of the accuracy of a theory. A theory is false if it does not account for and explain these descriptions. But to construct a theory we must put these descriptions aside, and consider the Death of Christ itself, in its real relations to God and to man. A theory — worth calling a theory — must rest immediately on the foundation of fact. For the facts we may have to rely, partly or altogether, on testimony. Even the most distinguished scientific inquirers are constantly obliged to build their theories on observations and experiments which they have not made or verified for themselves, but which they receive on the testimony of others. But though facts may be ascertained by testimony, the relation between facts and theories must be direct. We must endeavour to arrive at our theory of the Atonement by an investigation of the Death by which it is alleged that Atonement has been effected. If our theory contains a true account of the Death of Christ, all the forms under which it is represented in the New Testament will be illustrated and explained.

Our Lord Jesus Christ Himself declared that His blood was to be "shed for the remission of sins." Can we discover anything in His Death which promises to throw light on its expiatory power?

There are three considerations which invest the Death of Christ with unique and tragic interest.

1. It was the Death of the Son of God, of God manifest in the flesh.

2. It was a voluntary Death. He came into the world to die. He declared that He laid down His life by His own free will, and that no man could take it from Him.

3. Immediately before His Death He was forsaken of God. When we remember the original glory in which He dwelt with the Father, His faultless perfection, and His unbroken communion with the Father during His life on earth, this is a great and awful mystery. That sinful men, even though they have been transformed into saints, should sometimes lose the sense of the Divine presence and the Divine love, is explicable; but how was it that He, the Son of God, was forsaken by the Father in the very crisis of His sufferings? He Himself had anticipated this desertion with a fear which sometimes became terror. It seems not only possible, but probable, and even more than probable, that the intense and immeasurable suffering which wrung from him the cry, "My God, My God, why hast Thou forsaken Me?" was the immediate cause of His Death. On any hypothesis it accelerated His Death.

In investigating the connection between this mysterious Death and the remission of the sins of men, I propose to inquire: —

170

1. *Whether this connection can be explained by the existence of any original relation existing between the Lord Jesus Christ and the penalties of sin, or — to state the question more generally — between the Lord Jesus Christ and the eternal Law of Righteousness, of which sin is the transgression?*

2. *Whether this connection can be explained by any original relation existing between the Lord Jesus Christ and the race whose sins needed remission?*

The first inquiry will occupy the present Lecture, the second inquiry will occupy the next.

What, then, is the relation between the Lord Jesus Christ and the penalties of sin? What is the relation between the Lord Jesus Christ and the eternal law of righteousness, of which sin is the transgression?

To these questions we have authoritative replies, both from Himself and His Apostles. In several of His discourses He declares that it belongs to Him to "reward every man according to his works." [2] He will "send forth His angels, and they shall gather out of His kingdom all things that offend, and them which do iniquity; and shall cast them into a furnace of fire: there shall be wailing and gnashing of teeth." [3] His lips are to pronounce the sentence by which the final and irrevocable destiny of every man will be determined. He will say to the righteous, "Come, ye blessed of My Father, inherit the kingdom prepared for you from the foundation of the world;" [4] and to the wicked, "Depart from Me, ye cursed, into everlasting fire, prepared for the devil and his angels." [5] "The Father judgeth no man, but hath committed all judgment unto the Son." [6] The Apostles, in various forms, reassert this truth. St. Peter told Cornelius that Christ "was ordained of God to be the Judge of quick and dead." [7] St. Paul warned the Athenians that God had "appointed a day in the which He will judge the world in righteousness by that Man whom He hath ordained;" [8] and the great Apostle looked forward himself to the solemn hour when "we must all be manifested before the judgment-seat of Christ; that every one may receive the things done in his body according to that he hath done, whether it be good or bad." [9] *The penalties of sin are to be inflicted by Christ.*

The final judgment of the world is, however, only part of a larger function. After our Lord's resurrection He said to His disciples, "All power (ἐξουσία) is given unto Me in heaven and in earth;" [10] and on this claim he rested the apostolic commission to "disciple all nations, baptizing them into the name of the Father, and of the Son, and of the Holy Ghost;" teaching them to observe all things that He had commanded them. St. Peter declared that Jesus had been exalted to be *"Prince"* as well as "Saviour;" [11] and that He is "both Lord and Christ." [12] St. Paul describes Him as "the Lord both of the dead and the living;" [13] says that He has received "a name which is above every name: that at the name of Jesus every knee should bow, of things in heaven, and things in earth, and things under the earth;" [14] and that "He must reign till He hath put all enemies under His feet." [15] *The Lord Jesus Christ is the Moral Ruler of the human race; moral responsibility is responsibility to Him.*

In the argument for the Divinity of Christ these claims have a great place. It is inconceivable that God should invest a creature with his function of judging the world, and that He should transfer to a creature the moral allegiance due to Himself. The "kingdom" was received by Christ from the Father, because Christ had voluntarily laid aside His Divine glory, and had become man. He was capable of receiving it, because in His humiliation He had not ceased to be Divine.

But we may approach the whole subject in another way. In these Lectures it is assumed that Christ was the Eternal Word, who "was in the beginning with God," and that "all things were made by Him, and without Him nothing was made that was made." [16] The question we have to determine is the relation between God Himself and the eternal Law of Righteousness.

All Christians, all theists, acknowledge that God is the Moral Ruler of mankind and of the whole moral universe. What does this acknowledgment imply?

Does it imply that the will of God — using the word will in the same sense in which we use it when speaking of the will of man — is the origin of the antithesis between right and wrong, and the ultimate ground of moral obligation — that goodness is good only because God commands it, and evil evil only because God forbids it? There are many reasons which make this hypothesis incredible and intolerable.

If it were true, it would be difficult to account for the recognition of moral obligation where the existence of God is denied or doubted. A man who is uncertain whether there is a God or not, may know that he ought to tell the truth, to act justly, to be kindly and temperate; and he may recognize the moral evil of falsehood, injustice, cruelty, and intemperance. It is not necessary to convince him that there is a God, and that God has commanded men to be virtuous, before he can see the distinction between virtue and vice, or before he can recognize the moral obligation that rests upon him to be virtuous.

Dean Mansel argues that —

"The fiction of an absolute law, binding on all rational beings, has only an apparent universality; because we can only conceive other rational beings by identifying their constitution with our own, and making human reason the measure and representative of reason in general." [17]

If the "absolute law binding on all rational beings" is a "fiction," and if it has only an "apparent universality," because we can only conceive other rational beings by identifying their constitution with our own, and making human reason the measure and representative of reason in general," then even in mathematics there are no truths which we can affirm to be absolutely and universally true. On this hypothesis there may be some rational beings whose "constitution" is so different from ours, and the laws of whose "reason" are so unlike the laws by which "human reason" is governed, that they may legitimately believe that the three angles of a triangle are equal to three right angles, though we are compelled to believe that they are equal to two.

172

This sceptical philosophy rests on a radical disbelief in the trustworthiness of the human faculties, a disbelief which, if its consequences were clearly apprehended and frankly accepted, would make every exercise of the human intellect an irrational waste of time, and all endeavours after righteousness an irrational waste of strength. We can trust none of our intellectual faculties unless we can trust those which enable us to apprehend the truths of pure mathematics as universal and necessary, and which affirm the distinction between truths of this order and those which are merely contingent. Nor can we trust any of our faculties — not even those by which we come to believe in the Divine existence — unless we can trust those by which we apprehend the universal and necessary obligation of justice and truth, and which affirm the eternal distinction between good and evil. In impeaching the authority of our moral intuitions, Dean Mansel undermines the foundations of religious faith.

In answer to Dean Mansel's question, "Why...has one part of our constitution, merely as such, an imperative authority over the remainder? What right has one portion of the human consciousness to represent itself as *duty*, and another merely as *inclination*?" [18] I reply in the noble words of Butler: —

"There is a superior principle of reflection or conscience in every man, which distinguishes between the internal principles of the heart as well as his external actions; which passes judgment upon himself and them; pronounces determinately some actions to be in themselves just, right, good; others to be in themselves evil, wrong, unjust: which, without being consulted, without being advised with, magisterially exerts itself, and approves or condemns him the doer of them accordingly." [19]

Butler adds that if "not forcibly stopped," this judicial and imperial faculty "naturally and always of course goes on to anticipate a higher and more effectual sentence which shall hereafter second and affirm its own." Perhaps so; but in the case of vast numbers of men there is no real recognition of the authority of God, although there is a very real recognition of the authority of conscience and of the necessary and immutable distinction between right and wrong. To very many who confess that He exists, God is little more than an hypothesis to account for the origin of the universe, and their moral life is altogether removed from His control. If what they suppose to be their faith in God were to disappear, their intuition of the eternal antagonism between good and evil would not be at all obscured; their abhorrence of vice would not be less vigorous; their love of virtue would not be less fervent. But it is unnecessary to pursue this discussion. Butler's account of the manner in which conscience exercises its functions, before there is any anticipation of the corroborative sentence of God, is a complete answer to Dean Mansel's inquiry as to the right "of one portion of the human consciousness to represent itself as duty," while another is to be regarded as "merely an inclination."

Dean Mansel might as well have asked what right has one sense to claim authority to reveal to us the phenomena of vision, while another can reveal only the phenomena of sound? There is no schism among the senses. Every one of them performs its own functions. The authority of the eye to reveal to us the phenomena of vision is indisputable; it actually reveals those phenomena; it alone reveals them. This ends the controversy. And conscience alone lays claim to be the representative and minister of the law of duty. Inclination endeavours to control the will by force: it is unable to speak, as conscience actually speaks, in the name of the eternal Law of Righteousness. The supremacy of conscience is, as Butler says in another passage, "a constituent part of the idea, that is, of the faculty itself; and to preside and govern, from the very economy and constitution of man, belongs to it. Had it strength as it had right, had it power as it had manifest authority, it would absolutely govern the world." [20]

Butler's argument is a vindication of the authority of conscience; it is also a vindication of the eternal and necessary distinction between right and wrong. For conscience does not invoke the authority of God before it condemns vice and approves virtue, or before it affirms that man is bound to obey the Law of Righteousness. We know that falsehood, cruelty, and injustice are evil things in themselves, and that they would be evil though no Divine authority had forbidden them; and we know that the opposite virtues are good in themselves, and that they would be good though no Divine authority had commanded them. Righteousness gains an infinite support when it is known that God requires us to be righteous; but even in the absence of that knowledge, conscience confesses that the Law of Righteousness has an eternal and necessary authority.

If the will of God is the original fountain of all moral distinctions; if righteousness is right only because He commands it, and if sin is evil only because He forbids it; if, therefore, had He so willed, all the virtues would have merited our moral condemnation, and all the vices our moral approval; how is it possible for us to love and reverence God because of His moral excellence? When we do homage to Him because of His justice, goodness, and truth, we imply that if He were not just and good and true, He would have no claim to our homage. But there can be no reason for celebrating the glory of His justice if, had He so pleased, injustice would have been equally glorious; and if goodness and truth are not in themselves more beautiful and noble and right than cruelty and falsehood, we do Him no honour by confessing that "His compassions fail not," and that "His truth endureth for ever." God can have no moral perfections if the distinction between good and evil is the creation of the Divine will.

There is another and insuperable objection to this theory. Righteousness is the fulfilment of moral obligations; but moral obligations can never be originated by mere will, even if that will be the will of God. A mere command can never create a duty unless there is an antecedent obligation to obey the authority from which the command proceeds. All the virtues are enforced by the authority of God; but unless before God has commanded anything all His creatures are bound to obey Him, His commandments can create no obligation to be virtuous. His power may make it our interest to obey Him, but our interest is not our duty. "Why am I bound to obey? Am I bound to do God's will because God has been infinitely kind to me? That involves the concession of an eternal moral obligation to be obedient to One who has shown me infinite kindness. Because if I am disobedient, I shall incur punishment? That involves the concession of an eternal obligation to avoid suffering. Because, as a creature, I am naturally subject to God? That involves the concession of an eternal obligation resting on the creature to obey the Creator. Duty is inconceivable if moral obligation does not exist antecedently to the Divine commands. [21]

The objections which have been urged against the theory that derives all moral distinctions from the will of God, may be urged in another form against the theory that finds the origin of these distinctions in the nature of God. Conscience does not rest the moral obligation of justice on the fact that God is just, but affirms that justice is of universal and necessary obligation. We do not reverence righteousness merely because by righteousness men become like God: we reverence God Himself because He is righteous, thus affirming that righteousness in itself, and not simply because it is a Divine attribute, is deserving of reverence.

What then is the relation between God and the eternal Law of Righteousness? Are we to conceive of that Law as independent and supreme, claiming allegiance from the Creator as well as from His creatures? Is God Himself subject to its authority, even as we are? Is there a throne, even an ideal throne, loftier and more august than His? a sceptre, even an ideal sceptre, by which even He is governed, and which from eternity to eternity He obeys?

This hypothesis is as untenable as either of those which have been already discussed. We instinctively reject it: even in idea nothing can be higher than God. There appears to be a conflict for supremacy between God and the eternal Law of Righteousness. But such a conflict is impossible. The solution of the difficulty may perhaps be found in a statement of the actual history of our ideas of Righteousness and of God.

Conscience in the earliest and most rudimentary stages of its development recognizes in particular actions the distinction between good and evil, and affirms that the idea of goodness involves the obligation to be good. As conscience acquires clearness and strength of vision, it discovers what was implicitly contained in its earliest judgments, that the distinction between good and evil is not arbitrary, contingent, and mutable, but is the expression of an eternal and necessary law.

The possession of the moral faculty, however, is not the only regal prerogative of human nature. We are capable of knowing God, and when God is revealed we discover in a living Person the same august and supreme authority which conscience confessed in the eternal Law of Righteousness. It is the recognition of this which appears to be the very root and essential principle of worship, and which creates the distinction, in kind and not merely in degree, between the homage we offer to God, and the love, the reverence, the trust with which we may regard created perfection. The wonder with which we witness the manifestations of wisdom and power greater than our own, does not gradually approach worship, as the wisdom and the power are manifested in grander and grander forms. Nor does the love inspired by moral purity and goodness gradually approach worship, as the purity and goodness rise nearer and nearer to our loftiest ideal of moral excellence.

Wonder, however profound, and love, however fervent, never become worship until they are blended with another element — with a homage to the authority — not merely the perfections — of God, corresponding to the homage which conscience offers to the authority of the moral law. The supremacy of the law is absolute and irreversible. But when God is truly known, conscience, without revoking or qualifying the acknowledgment of this supremacy, confesses that the authority which it had recognized in an ideal law is the awful and glorious prerogative of a living Person.

The relation between God and the eternal Law of Righteousness is, therefore, unique. He is not, as we are, bound by its authority; in Him its authority is actively asserted. To describe Him as doing homage to it — although a phrase which it may sometimes be almost necessary to employ — is by implication to strip Him of His moral sovereignty: the homage which is due to the law is due to Him. The law does not claim Him as the most illustrious and glorious of its subjects; it is supreme in His supremacy. His relation to the law is not a relation of subjection but of identity. Hence "He cannot be tempted of evil." In God the law is *alive;* it reigns on His throne, sways His sceptre, is crowned with His glory.

It is possible to conceive of the authority of the eternal Law of Righteousness apart from God. An Atheist knows the meaning of the word ought, and may confess that the obligations of duty are absolute. But apart from the authority of the eternal Law of Righteousness as expressed in the Divine will, it is not possible to conceive of God. My conception of God is not only incomplete, but fatally defective, while I acknowledge nothing more than that He created all things; that He sustains all things; that His power is almighty, and His knowledge without limit; that He is perfectly just and infinitely good; that He is "glorious in holiness, fearful in praises, doing wonders." If I am to worship Him and to obey Him, — if, in other words, He is to be my God, — I must recognize His absolute sovereignty over my moral and spiritual life; and God, as a living Person, must have the same authority over my will that conscience acknowledges in the eternal Law of Righteousness.

We may now consider the relation between God and the penalties of sin. To discover this relation, we have to investigate the idea of punishment, and to determine what is meant by saying that sin is justly punished.

Is punishment to be regarded as a reformatory process, a process intended to promote the moral benefit of the sufferer? If it were that and nothing more, and if the justice of punishment consisted in its fitness to produce a favourable moral impression on the sinner, God would be free to inflict or to remit the penalties of the Law without regard to any other consideration than the moral disposition of the person by whom the precepts of the Law had been violated. The severity of punishment would have to be measured, not by the magnitude of the sin for which it is inflicted, but by the difficulty of inducing the sinner to amend. If even the greatest sin were immediately succeeded by hearty repentance, there would be no mercy in withholding punishment; for since, on this theory, the justice of punishment consists in its reformatory power, it could not be justly inflicted where reformation had been already produced by other and gentler influences. It also follows that if there are cases - and such cases are easily conceivable - in which repentance is less likely to be awakened by inflicting pain and disgrace than by conferring new joy and honour, in these cases the lightest penalty would be unjust, and justice would require that the life of the sinner should be made brighter and happier on account of his sin. By a very slight exercise of ingenuity it might be shown that the theory which rests the justice of punishment on its reformatory power, involves the most grotesque consequences, and consequences which are repugnant to our most elementary moral convictions.

And yet the influence of this conception of punishment may be very distinctly recognized in some modern speculations on the Atonement. The conception may be traced far back in the history of theological thought, but it was made popular by those wise and generous reformers of our criminal code to whom we owe the abandonment of the brutal and brutalising punishments by which, till very recent times, all European states endeavoured to secure the protection of life and property.

In avenging a solitary crime which might never have been repeated, the law created a hardened and desperate criminal. A change of system was demanded not only by the merciful instincts of humane hearts, but by the principles of social expediency; for the criminal law was increasing the number of criminals, and making criminal offences more formidable. But the popular theory which was alleged in justification of the change was both false and pernicious. From the principle that in punishing crime it is both the duty and the interest of the State to attempt to reform the criminal, it was inferred that the object of punishment is the criminal's reformation. This inference, although no man was irrational enough to carry it out to its ultimate results, seriously affected the spirit and temper with which a considerable number of persons regarded the administration of criminal law. It made the gaol a philanthropic institution, and the treadmill an instrument of national education, invented for the benefit of an exceptionally unfortunate and backward class of scholars.

The theory was utterly rotten. Society has no right to send a man to gaol, to feed him on bread and water, and to make him pick hemp or work the treadmill, merely because society thinks that a discipline of this kind would do him good. He must deserve to be punished, or the law has no right to punish him. If in punishing him the law can make him a better man, well and good; but it is the fact that the criminal deserves to suffer which constitutes the ultimate foundation of criminal law, and apart from this the infliction of suffering is a monstrous tyranny and injustice.

Between human legislation and Divine, between the imperfect processes by which the State punishes the violation of its imperfect laws and the processes of eternal justice, the analogy is very incomplete. But when we consider sin as a transgression of the eternal Law of Righteousness, this principle that the transgression deserves punishment reappears. The conscience affirms it vehemently. The fear of punishment is often the earliest form in which a sinful man acknowledges the authority of the Law which he has broken. Nor is the punishment regarded either by the conscience or by the terror-stricken heart as a painful process to effect future reformation; it is the suffering which has been deserved by past sin. To make it anything else than this, is to destroy its essential character.

Another conception of punishment represents it as an expedient for strengthening the authority of the Law by creating a new motive to obedience. The distinction between this second conception and the first is very simple and obvious. According to the first conception, punishment is a painful discipline, intended to bring a man who has broken the Law to a better state of mind and heart. It rests upon the principle that the criminal must be reformed. According to the second conception, it is an appeal to the fears of those who have not yet broken the Law, and is intended to prevent them from breaking it. Punishment may, perhaps, make the bad man worse than he was before, but his sufferings are meant to deter other men from doing wrong. The pain suffered by the criminal is inflicted for the sake of confirming the virtue of those who are as yet free from crime. The theory originated with jurists and statesmen. When transferred to the sphere of the Divine government, it requires us to regard the penalties of sin, not as the righteous retribution of past offences, but as a severe expedient for preventing future offences. If, therefore, any more merciful and equally effective method can be devised for maintaining the authority of the eternal Law of Righteousness, punishment may be dispensed with.

But even in relation to human law this theory is fatally defective. "The suffering of a criminal," it has been well said, "benefits the public because it is deserved; it is not deserved because it benefits the public." That human governments are bound to consider whether the specific penalties attached to specific violations of the law are likely to diminish crime, is no doubt true; but the question whether the penalties are just, is a preliminary question, which cannot be righteously or safely ignored. The suffering may be actually inflicted for the sake of protecting the State, but the State commits a crime unless the criminal has deserved to suffer; and if to the conscience of the nation the severity of the suffering appears to exceed the magnitude of the crime, the authority of the law is enfeebled rather than strengthened. On the other hand, if, when a great crime has been committed, the criminal is acquitted through some technical defect in the evidence, or receives a light and inadequate sentence, public indignation is provoked; not because the opportunity has been lost of giving to citizens who are tempted to crime an impressive and edifying moral lesson which would be likely to restrain them from similar offences, but because justice has been baffled, and the criminal has not received his deserts.

The idea of retribution, which underlies ordinary criminal justice, cannot be excluded from our conception of the penalties which God inflicts upon those who have sinned. It belongs to the very essence of that conception. He does not punish some of His creatures merely because their sufferings will do good to the rest, but because they deserve to suffer. The penalties which He inflicts are not affected by the same limitations which affect the penalties inflicted by human governments. To punish all moral offences, and in exact proportion to their varying magnitude, requires other resources than human legislators possess, and other powers than human tribunals can command. These resources and powers belong to God.' Nor is it the function of human governments to assert throughout every province of human life all the obligations of the eternal Law of Righteousness, and to vindicate the justice of all its penalties. But this function is involved in the very idea of God. When we are considering the relation of God to the penalties of sin, and investigating the question whether, and on what conditions, they can be remitted, it is unsafe to regard these penalties as nothing more than an expedient for preventing sin — an expedient which may, therefore, be immediately exchanged for any other method which would secure the same moral result. It is necessary to remember that the penalties of sin are primarily an expression of the principle that the sinner deserves to suffer, and if the penalties are remitted, we have to inquire whether it is possible for this principle to be suppressed, or whether it must be asserted in some other form.

A third conception of punishment represents it as an effect of God's personal resentment against those who have offered an insult to His personal dignity, or as the assertion of His personal claims against those who have withheld from Him His personal rights. If a servant who has been treated considerately and generously is guilty of an habitual and contemptuous disregard of his master's authority, and malignantly slanders his master's character, he cannot wonder if his master is offended and indignant, nor can he complain at being dismissed from his master's service, though the dismissal may involve him in ruin. If a man refuses to pay his just debts, the creditor may vindicate his claim by whatever processes of law are open to him, even at the cost of the utter destruction of the debtor's property.

And it is alleged that sin is of the nature of a personal offence against the majesty of God, and that punishment is the expression of God's just resentment. Or the absolute obedience which God's creatures owe to Him is alleged to be of the nature of a personal debt, and when their obedience is withheld,

179

punishment is a vindication of His personal claims against them. But the master whose anger has been provoked by the carelessness or the insolence of a servant may magnanimously overlook the offence and retain the offender in his service. The creditor may cancel the debt. Resentment against those by whom we have been personally wronged may be just, but there are innumerable cases in which generosity and compassion are stronger than resentment, and incline us to forgive. Personal claims — if they are exclusively personal— may be waived. If this theory of sin and its punishment were complete, God would be free to inflict or to remit punishment at His own good pleasure.

But even in such cases as those which I have selected to illustrate the theory, it sometimes happens that the inclination to be magnanimous and generous has to be restrained. A master who has been treated very badly by his servant may sometimes be morally obliged to express his resentment in the severest form. He is the accidental representative of that social authority, the assertion and maintenance of which are essential to the strength and tranquillity of the organisation of society. As an individual, he might be merciful. As a master, he cannot. A creditor whose claims are dishonestly resisted may be morally obliged to insist on the payment of his debt. As an individual, he might be ready and even anxious to remit the payment; but he is the accidental representative of justice, and though by prosecuting the debtor he may incur a great loss both of time and money, he cannot decline the duty which has accidentally fallen to him. There are other cases in which the obligation to make an offender suffer for his offence is still more obvious and stringent. An officer in the army who never inflicted punishment for disobedience to his orders, a sovereign who never inflicted punishment for conspiracy and treason against his authority, would add a second crime to the crime whose penalties he remitted. It is part of their very function and duty to punish these offences.

This theory of punishment rests upon a false theory of the moral authority of God. In a sense it is true that God has "personal claims" on our reverence and obedience, but the phrase is an ambiguous one. A father has personal claims on the love, respect, and obedience of all his children; he has also personal claims on those of his children to whom he may have lent money when they commenced business. These two sets of claims, however, are not the same in kind. He can release them from the obligation to repay the money debt; he cannot release them from the obligations of filial respect and obedience. Nor can God release His creatures from the obligation to reverence and obey Him. If He were only the accidental Representative of the idea of moral authority, or the official Defender and Minister of the eternal Law of Righteousness, He would have claims upon us which He could not waive. But we have seen that He is very much more than this. The ideal supremacy of the eternal Law of Righteousness — as Law — and with all its immutable authority — is revealed to us under a concrete and personal form, in His personal sovereignty over all His moral creatures.

If, therefore, the punishment of sin is to be defined as a vindication and assertion of the personal rights and claims of God against those who have sinned, it must be remembered that the Divine claims which sin resists, and the Divine rights which sin refuses to acknowledge, are essentially different from the claims and rights which are in such a sense personal that they can be remitted at pleasure. They are claims and rights which it is morally necessary that God should maintain. The penalties in which these claims and rights are vindicated may, perhaps, have something of the same necessary character; and it may be just as impossible for God to decline the assertion of the principle that those who sin against Him deserve to be punished, as it is for Him to decline the assertion of the principle that all His moral creatures are bound to worship Him and to keep His commandments. The penalties of sin may be, in a very true sense, a vindication of the personal claims and rights of God; but whether these penalties must be relentlessly inflicted, or whether, and on what conditions, they may be remitted, are questions involving principles which do not at all affect the vindication of personal claims and rights of a different order.

The easy solution of all difficulties about the Remission of sins, suggested by the obligation resting on ourselves to forgive those who have sinned against us, ignores the fundamental distinction between the relations of individual men to each other and their common relation to God. As individuals, we have no right to punish other men for their sins against us, because we have no authority over them. The right to punish is inseparable from the obligations of authority, and the obligations inseparable from authority may sometimes make the infliction of punishment a duty.

We conclude, therefore, that the only conception of punishment which satisfies our strongest and most definite moral convictions, and which corresponds to the place it occupies both in the organisation of society and in the moral order of the universe, is that which represents it as pain and loss inflicted for the violation of a law. If the law is a righteous law, if the severity of the penalty is not out of proportion to the magnitude of the offence, the punishment is just; the offender has deserved whatever he suffers. Suffering inflicted upon a man to make him better in the future is not punishment, but discipline: to be punishment, it must be inflicted for evil deeds done in the past. Suffering endured for the sake of benefiting society is not punishment: if accepted voluntarily, it is the heroism of self-sacrifice; if inflicted by arbitrary authority, it is injustice on the one side and martyrdom on the other. What a man suffers from the resentment of another is not punishment, but mere persecution and annoyance, unless the suffering is the effect of moral indignation provoked by real or imaginary wrongs committed against the person by whom the suffering is inflicted: according as the wrongs are imaginary or real, the punishment is unjust or just.

181

That the suffering inflicted is deserved is a necessary element in the conception of punishment. We have now to determine God's relation to the ill-desert of a man who has transgressed the eternal Law of Righteousness, and to the suffering which may justly come upon him for his transgression. God cannot be separated, even in idea, from the Law which has been violated, and which affirms the principle that sin deserves to be punished. Is it necessary, or is it not, that this principle should be asserted, and asserted by God Himself?

If it is not asserted, if it is ignored and suppressed, then the eternal Law of Righteousness can be no longer perfectly identified with the will of God; and if the Law is separated from the will of God, conscience will vehemently maintain that the Law is supreme; and in the case supposed will protest that while on the one hand the creature has dishonoured the Law by sin, the Creator has completed the dishonour by refusing to acknowledge the ill-desert of sin. Such a separation, however, between the ideal Law and the Divine Will is impossible. God would cease to be God if His Will were not a complete expression of all the contents of the eternal Law of Righteousness.

Is it then inevitable that God should inflict the penalties which sin has deserved? Has he no choice? Is it impossible that He should be merciful? Does He act as a blind, unconscious force? Is the moral government of the universe a vast and awful mechanism, dispensing rewards and punishments from eternity to eternity in exact proportion to righteousness and sin? Is there no difference between being under the iron rule of a Law and being under the rule, gracious as well as just, of a living God? To these questions the Christian revelation and the irrepressible instincts of our moral and spiritual nature give the same replies.

It is necessary to look a little more closely into the nature of punishment if we are to discover the solution of the difficulty in which questions like these originate. In common, popular speech, we say that "the sinner *ought* to suffer;" but this is a very loose expression, loose even to inaccuracy. When so used, the word "ought" has a very different force from that which belongs to it when we say that "a man *ought* to be honest and to tell the truth." By being honest and truthful, a man fulfils a duty. But a man who has committed a sin fulfils no duty by merely suffering for his sin. His mere suffering is not obedience: while he suffers, his whole nature may be in fiercer revolt than ever against the Law which he has transgressed, and the penalty of which he is enduring. There may be no more righteousness in him when his suffering is keenest than there was before his suffering commenced: his mere suffering has no virtue in it.

When we use the phrase that a man who has committed a crime "ought to suffer for it," we generally mean nothing more than that he deserves to suffer; or if anything more than this is meant, we mean that some one who has the authority and power is under a moral obligation to make him suffer.

Punishment gives to the sufferer occasion for manifesting humility, patience, and a spirit of penitent submission to the pain which he has deserved by his offences; and if he does not manifest these virtues he incurs fresh guilt. But the duty of manifesting them arises from the fact that by some external force or authority he is being made to suffer the just consequences of his past offences. *Whatever moral element there is in punishment itself — as punishment — is derived from the person or power that inflicts it.*

What is meant by the law being more honoured when a man of high rank suffers imprisonment or death for his crimes, than when one of the common people suffers precisely the same penalty? Something, perhaps, is to be ascribed to the impression produced by the contrast between his splendid position and his miserable fate, and something to the fact that his rank awakens universal interest both in his offence and in its punishment. But what is specially significant in his suffering is this — that justice is felt to overbear all the common influences by which men are swayed. If the judicial authority or the executive power had been accessible to fear or to corruption, his illustrious name, his social influence, his wealth, would have perverted the course of law, and secured his immunity. When, therefore, such a man is put on his trial, the fidelity and courage of the public ministers of justice are tested; and if they do not swerve from the line of judicial duty, the law receives unusual homage — homage derived not from the rank of the criminal who suffers — but from the steadfast and resolute integrity which does not permit his rank to shelter him. That in exceptional cases like this it is the moral effort necessary to inflict the penalties of violated law which constitutes the highest moral element of punishment, is acknowledged by the common instincts of mankind and, in all cases, punishment receives its moral significance from the fact that the infliction of it is the active assertion of the principle — either by a person or a law — that those who have violated a law deserve to suffer.

Whatever moral significance might attach to the punishment of sin if punishment were inflicted by "self-acting" spiritual laws, its moral significance is immeasurably heightened if, in every case, it is the immediate or remote effect of a Divine volition. According to the Christian theory of the universe, all the forces which are in league with the eternal Law of Righteousness have received their commission and their power from God Himself.

It is by the Will of God that man has been so constituted that his physical health and vigour are promoted by industry, temperance, and the exercise of firm restraint on all the violent passions. The same Will is revealed in the laws which, under every form of social organisation, and in the rudest as well as in the most complex conditions of human society, are more or less obviously on the side of justice, truthfulness, purity, and an unselfish devotion to the public interests. And if, on the whole, the relations of physical nature to mankind are friendly to virtue; if the very severities and uncertainties of man's external condition train him to fortitude, to courage, to the mastery of his inferior appetites, and to a prudence which is akin to morality; if even after the long ages of preparation which preceded what we have been accustomed to call the creation of man, and which if it is called by any other name will retain all its former mystery — if, I say, even then there remained very much to be done before many parts of the world could be a safe or pleasant home for our race; if pestilential marshes had still to be drained; if there were still savage beasts in the forests and venomous creatures in the grass; if it was an imperative necessity that in order to "replenish the earth" man must also "subdue it," so that when God "rested" from His work man's work began; and if in this struggle with the evil and malignant elements of his position some of the best elements of man's moral nature were to receive their most vigorous discipline; — in all these provisions for the development of our moral life we recognize the manifestations of the wisdom, the goodness, and the righteousness of God. Even the miseries which are inflicted by causes in the presence of which human skill and industry and courage are power-less — the irresistible calamities which come upon men from protracted drought, from hurricanes, from volcanic eruptions, from earthquakes — test and invigorate many heroic virtues, and give occasion for the exercise of those forms of compassion which are called forth by misfortunes and suffer-ings in which there is no trace of guilt. These terrible destructive forces have also a place in that Divine order which has for its highest end, not the materi-al comfort, but the moral perfection of mankind.

The infinitely various evils which by the very constitution of human nature and the irreversible laws of human society avenge wrong-doing, are also the effect of the Divine Will. Gross vices are grossly punished. Those who are guilty of secret and undiscovered sins are tormented even in this world, and their strength consumed by a "worm that dieth not" and "a fire" that cannot be "quenched." Falsehood and treachery bring upon men shame and con-tempt. The sins of parents are sharply punished by the sins of their children. The wealth and glory of the proudest states are destroyed by the private vic-es of the people and the public crimes of their rulers. And if, on this side of death, innumerable offences against the eternal Law of Righteousness ap-pear to escape detection and penalty, that revelation which has brought "life and immortality" to light, is dark with threatenings of the "indignation and wrath, tribulation and anguish," which will confront the impenitent in the world to come. From the final judgment of God there can be no escape, and upon those who have resisted His authority and rejected His grace He will inflict the just penalties of their sins.

The sufferings which punish sin in this world, and the sufferings which will punish it in the next, are the expression of the irreconcilable antagonism of God to sin, and to those who persist in sinning. They are an assertion by God Himself of the principle that those who sin deserve to suffer. It is this which gives them their transcendent significance.

There are times when the calamities with which sin is punished even in this world seem to us so severe that we are driven to exclaim, "Hath God for-gotten to be gracious?" The punishments which menace it beyond death are so appalling, that though we see them dimly and afar off, they paralyse us with terror. Yet the Divine compassion is infinitely more tender than our own. If God were indifferent to the sufferings of His creatures, if it cost Him nothing to inflict upon them now the temporal miseries which are the penalties of transgression, and to expel them at last, by an irrevocable sentence, from the light and blessedness of His presence, the profoundest moral element of His acts of retributive justice would disappear. The Divine compassion immeasurably augments the significance of the punishments which by the Divine volition are inflicted on sin.

But if the punishment of sin is a Divine act — an act in which the identity between the Will of God and the eternal Law of Righteousness is asserted and expressed — it would appear that, if in any case the penalties of sin are remitted, some other Divine act of at least equal intensity, and in which the ill desert of sin is expressed with at least equal energy, must take its place. [22]

The heart of the whole problem lies here. The eternal Law of Righteousness declares that sin deserves to be punished. The Will of God is identified both by the conscience and the religious intuitions of man with the eternal Law of Righteousness. To separate the ideal law — or any part of it — from the Living and Divine Person, is to bring darkness and chaos on the moral and spiritual universe. The whole Law — the authority of its precepts, the justice of its penalties — must be asserted in the Divine acts, or else the Divine Will cannot be perfectly identified with the eternal Law of Righteousness. If God does not assert the principle that sin deserves punishment by punishing it, He must assert that principle in some other way. Some Divine act is required which shall have all the moral worth and significance of the act by which the penalties of sin would have been inflicted on the sinner.

The Christian Atonement is the fulfilment of that necessity. The principle that suffering — suffering of the most terrible kind — is the just desert of sin is not suppressed. It would have been adequately asserted had God inflicted on man the penalties of transgression. It is asserted in a still grander form, and by a Divine act, which in its awful sublimity and unique glory infinitely transcends the mere infliction of suffering on those who have sinned. The penalties are not simply held back by the strong hand of infinite love. He on whom the sins of men had brought the dread necessity of asserting the principle that they deserved to suffer, and who, as it seems to us, could not decline to assert it — He through whose lips the sentence of the eternal Law of Righteousness must have come, condemning those who had sinned to exile from the light and life of God — He by whose power the sentence must have been executed — He Himself, the Lord Jesus Christ, laid aside His eternal glory, assumed our nature, was forsaken of God, died on the cross, that the sins of men might be remitted. It belonged to Him to assert, by His own act, that suffering is the just result of sin. He asserts it, not by inflicting suffering on the sinner, but by enduring suffering Himself.

Nor is this all. To affirm that, on the cross, the Moral Ruler of our race endured what He might have inflicted, is an inadequate representation of the truth. If God's love for His creatures invests the Divine act which punishes them with its highest moral value, the love of the Eternal Father for the Son invests with infinite moral sublimity the Divine act which surrendered Him to desertion and to death, that the justice of the penalties of sin might be affirmed before the penalties were remitted. The mysterious unity of the Father and the Son rendered it possible for God at once to endure and to inflict penal suffering, and to do both under conditions which constitute the infliction and the endurance the grandest moment in the moral history of God.

The question of the grounds on which the Moral Ruler of mankind could so identify Himself with our race as to assume our nature, and endure suffering instead of inflicting it on us, is the question to be discussed in the next Lecture: for the present I must assume that in this endurance of suffering the Lord Jesus Christ was acting in harmony with His original and Ideal relations to mankind. The point we have reached is this: the moral significance of the suffering by which sin is punished is derived from the fact that the suffering is inflicted by the Will of God. In the Death of Christ, He to whom it belongs to inflict suffering endures suffering instead of inflicting it. In stating the problem which arises on the hypothesis that God has resolved to remit the penalties of sin, I said that "if God does not assert the principle that sin deserves punishment, by punishing it, He must assert that principle in some other way. Some Divine act is required which shall have all the moral worth and significance of the act by which the penalties of sin would have been inflicted on the sinner;" and I repeat that "the Christian Atonement is the fulfilment of that necessity." It was a greater act to submit to such suffering as Christ endured than to inflict it.

As yet our theory is incomplete. But when the heart is shaken by fears of future judgment and "the wrath to come," a vivid apprehension of the Death of Christ, as the voluntary death of the Moral Ruler and Judge of the human race, will at once inspire perfect peace. Without further explanation, the conscience will grasp the assurance that since He has suffered, to whom it belonged to inflict suffering, it must be possible for Him to grant Remission of sins.

This conception of the Atonement contains a complete reply to the question which Mr. Martineau says has never been answered. He asks —

"How is the alleged immorality of letting off the sinner mended by the added crime of penally crushing the sinless? Of what man — of what angel — could such a thing be reported, without raising a cry of indignant shame from the universal human heart? What should we think of a judge who should discharge the felons from the prisons of a city because some noble and generous citizen offered himself to the executioner instead?" [23]

Mr. Martineau must accept all our facts before he has a right to bring a moral charge against our doctrine. He must not discuss the Evangelical theory of the Atonement on the Unitarian theory of the Person of Christ. But his analogy is doubly false; false to his own conception of God, false to our conception of Christ. On *his* theory, God can pardon the sins of men without an atonement, but a judge can only acquit or condemn — the prerogative of pardon does not belong to him. On *our* theory, Christ is infinitely more than the most "noble and generous of citizens" who could offer himself to the executioner instead of the guilty. He is Himself the representative - and more than the representative - of the law which has been violated. The question which Mr. Martineau has asked is irrelevant. The true question is — Whether the act of Christ, in enduring the suffering which He must otherwise have inflicted, is an "immorality," "a crime," which should raise "a cry of indignant shame from the universal human heart"?

For an answer to that question I can trust "the universal human heart" to which Mr. Martineau appeals. Wherever the real facts have been known, instead of "a cry of indignant shame," there has been a cry of thanksgiving and of worship. Had God insisted that before He would forgive sinful men, some illustrious saint or some holy angel should endure the agonies of Gethsemane and the awful sorrow of the cross; had He refused to listen to the prayer of the penitent until His anger had been allayed, or His retributive justice received what would have been an unreal satisfaction, through the sufferings of one of His creatures who had kept all His commandments, then Mr. Martineau's question could have received no answer. However voluntary, however eager might have been the sacrifice on the part of saint or angel, God could not have accepted it without perplexing and confounding all our conceptions of His moral character. But is there any "immorality," any "crime," anything to provoke "a cry of indignant shame," in the resolve of God Himself, in the person of Christ, to endure suffering instead of inflicting it? Will any man who confesses that Jesus Christ is God manifest in the flesh cry "shame" when He, the Moral Ruler of men, to avoid the terrible necessity of condemning us to eternal death, assumes our nature, is tempted in the wilderness, endures the ingratitude, malignity, and scorn of those whom He has come to save, submits to be charged with blasphemy, spat upon, scourged, nailed to the cross, passes into that "outer darkness," into which He must otherwise have driven the human race for its crimes, and dies of a broken heart through the greatness of His sorrow? "Immorality!" It is the most wonderful proof of the infinite love of God. "Crime!" It is the supreme manifestation of God's moral perfection. But for this, we might have thought that self-sacrifice, which is the flower and crown of all human-excellence, was impossible to God. We see now that every form of heroic love and mercy by which our hearts are thrilled in the story of the noblest of men, is but the shadow of the transcendent and eternal perfection of the Most High. "An indignant cry of shame!" It is this expression of the righteousness and grace of the Moral Ruler of mankind which has kindled the most passionate love that has ever glowed in the hearts of men on earth, and it is this which is celebrated in the most rapturous anthems which are ever heard in heaven.

[1] See Dr. Bushnell: *Forgiveness and Law*, page 41, seq.

[2] Matt. xvi. 27.

[3] Ibid, xiii, 41, 42.

[4] Matt. xxv. 34.

[5] Ibid. xxv. 41.

[6] John v. 22.

[7] Acts x. 42.

[8] Ibid. xvii. 31.

[9] 2 Cor. v. 10.

[10] Matt, xxviii. 18.

[11] Acts v. 31.

[12] Ibid. ii. 36.

[13] Rom. xiv. 9.

[14] Phil. ii. 9, 10.

[15] 1 Cor. xv. 25.

[16] John i. 2, 3.

[17] *Bampton Lecture.* Third edition, page 111.

[18] *Bampton Lecture,* page 111.

[19] *Sermons on Human Nature,* Sermon 2. Works. Vol. i. page 23.

[20] *Sermons on Human Nature.* Sermon 2. Works, i. 27.

[21] See *British Quarterly Review,* October, 1867. Page 486, and especially

[22] As much as *this* might be concluded *a priori.* The form in which the necessity has actually been met could never have entered into the mind of man, nor could we have determined whether it was possible for the necessity to have been met in any other form.

[23] *Studies of Christianity,* page 188.

the reference in the note to Mr. J. S. Mill.

## Lecture Ten - The Theory of the Atonement: Illustrated by the Relation of Our Lord Jesus Christ to the Human Race

In the preceding Lecture I endeavoured to illustrate the transcendent significance and value which the Death of Christ derives from His original relation to the eternal Law of Righteousness, and especially to the penalties which menace the transgression of its commandments.

But this account of the Sacrifice of Christ, though true as far as it goes, appears to be inadequate. It leaves unexplained some of the most frequent and familiar forms under which the Death of Christ is represented in the New Testament, For although the redemption of mankind is spoken of both by Christ Himself and by His Apostles as originating in the love and righteousness of God, the language of the New Testament seems to imply that in some sense Christ died in the name of the human race. It is not God alone who has part in the great Mystery. Christ was a Sacrifice and Propitiation for us, though not by our own choice and appointment. His Death is described as an appeal to God's infinite mercy coming from the human race itself, or from One who has a right to speak and act and suffer as its Representative. This aspect of the Death of Christ has no place in the partial conception of it which we have reached by considering the relation of Christ to the eternal Law of Righteousness.

Again; this partial conception of it leaves the impression on the mind that the Death of Christ had something of a dramatic character, and that its value lies in its dramatic effect. The theory — if I may so speak —seems to be "in the air." If it can be shown that the original and ideal relation of the Lord Jesus Christ to the human race constitutes a reason why He should become a Sacrifice and Propitiation for our sins, the conception of His Death illustrated in the preceding Lecture will rest on more solid and secure foundations. I have now, therefore, to attempt to illustrate the theory of the Atonement from the original relation of the Lord Jesus Christ to the human race.

I can hardly hope that the attempt will be very successful. For this relation has never yet been clearly apprehended either by the Christian Church as a whole, or by any considerable section of it. The Athanasian conception of the Trinity has been incorporated into the very life of Christendom. The conception has been differently defined in the East and in the West; it has been greatly modified — in Europe at least — by the philosophical systems which have successively controlled the speculation of the Church during the last thirteen or fourteen hundred years; but it was the genuine development and expression of the Christian consciousness of the early centuries, and it has become an essential element of the Faith of the universal Church. That man is justified by Faith alone, has secured the same kind of consent among all the great Protestant communities. The doctrine is not the exclusive property of theologians, nor is it merely a dogma imposed by theologians on the unlearned. It has an intense, and, in the truest meaning of the words, a vital interest, wherever there is genuine religious earnestness. It gives to the religious life of Protestantism its characteristic type. For that conception of the Trinity which the unknown author of the Athanasian Creed has endeavoured to express in terms which had been created for him by the fierce and subtle controversies of many generations, terms which to us may seem cumbrous, and even profane, but every one of which is a significant historical monument, — for that conception of Justification which is common to all the great Protestant confessions, hundreds of thousands of men would be ready to suffer imprisonment and death. As much might be said of any other doctrine, true or false, that has become a real power in the religious life of mankind. Men, women, and children would be hung or burnt in crowds rather than deny that Christ created the world, and that He died for it.

But this cannot be said of any doctrine concerning that relation of Christ to the human race which illustrates the theory of the Atonement. That in some sense Christ is the Head and Representative of mankind is a truth "which has not been derived from philosophy, but has lived eternally in the faith of Christendom." [1] This conception of Him is wrought into the very structure of apostolic doctrine. It has been insisted upon with great energy in recent years by Mr. Maurice and his disciples in this country. In Germany it has held a great place in theological speculation from the time of Schelling. That Christ is the Head and Representative of, at least, the elect and regenerate portion of mankind, is what is meant by orthodox theologians when they say that Christ is the Second Adam; and this is the truth which underlies the doctrine of "imputed righteousness." Christian Mysticism has always earnestly maintained that Christ is the very life of regenerate souls, and that complete union

189

with Him is the condition of consummate holiness and blessedness. This truth has been made the ultimate ground of theories which assert the mysterious and supernatural efficacy of the sacraments.

But no clear and articulate conception of that relation of Christ to mankind which renders it possible for Him to sustain a representative character, appears to have rooted itself in the popular theology, or in the moral and spiritual life of Christendom. The sense in which Christ in His redemptive sufferings and work is the representative of the race, has been illustrated or obscured by an appeal to imperfect human analogies. It seems to have been forgotten that His representative character is absolutely unique. The general and growing dissatisfaction with the theory of expiation has probably arisen partly from this cause, and it will be impossible for that theory to retain its place in the theological thought of the Church, unless it can be shown that the Death of Christ as a Propitiation and Sacrifice for the sins of men is the highest expression of an eternal relation between Christ and the human race, — a relation which, though it might never have been discovered in the absence of specific revelation, has nothing in it to offend the higher reason or to provoke moral antagonism, and is capable of verification by the Christian consciousness.

The relation of Christ to mankind is, however, only part of a larger question — the relation of Christ to the created universe.

The Church has been content to acknowledge that Christ created all things, and that in some sense He upholds all things. It has never felt any keen and practical interest in the nature of His permanent relation to the universe. In its dread of Pantheism, and in its eagerness to maintain the freedom and personality of the living God, it has rather shrunk from conceiving any other kind of relation between the Creator and the creation than that which exists between the builder of a house and the house he has built. But there are many passages in the New Testament which are inconsistent with such a conception as this. In the first chapter of the Fourth Gospel — which contains the Christian idea of creation, as the first chapter of the book of Genesis contains the Jewish idea — Christ is identified with the Word, who was in the beginning with God, and was God, and through whom all things came into existence. In the opening verses of the anonymous epistle to the Hebrews, Christ is represented as the Son of God and heir of all things, the brightness of God's glory, in whom the eternal splendours of the Divine nature are revealed, the express image of God's person, by whom God made the worlds, and the word of whose power is their perpetual support. St. Paul, in the Epistle to the Colossians, [2] describes our Lord Jesus Christ as "the image of the invisible God" — "the first-born of every creature." [3] The antithesis seems to suggest that Christ is allied — if not in the same way, yet by relations equally vital — at once with God and the created universe. In Him "the image of the invisible God," the actual perfections of God, are revealed to the

190

thought of the universe, and in Him "the first-born of all creation," the ideal perfections of the universe, are present to the thought of God.

This conception of Christ's relation to the universe the Apostle proceeds to develop. "For in Him were all things created that are in heaven, and that are in earth, visible or invisible, whether they be thrones, or dominions, or principalities, or powers: all things were created by [or *through*] Him and for [or *unto*] Him. And He is before all things, and in Him all things consist."

This remarkable passage contains St. Paul's theory of the relations between Christ and the universe, (1) Christ, "the First-born," was — if I may venture to say it — the eternal prophecy of creation. In Him the perfection and glory dwelt from eternity which in the creation have been manifested in time. What the creation, in its ideal perfection, was to be to the Father, had from eternity found a transcendent expression in Christ. [4] (2) When, at last, the universe was created, Christ was the very ground and root of its existence; it was the revelation of His thought; its life was "in Him." (3) Nor was the creative act the immediate act of the Father; the Divine power — if we may use words which only remotely suggest the truth — travelled through Christ: all things were created "through Him." (4) Nor, again, was the universe created for itself: its final cause, its ultimate end, and its consummate perfection, are to be found in Christ: all things were created "for Him" or "unto Him." (5) And, apart from Him, the universe, as a universe, could not continue in existence; it would fall into disorder and sink back into chaos; for "in Him all things consist."

It is probable that the Apostles were led up to this conception of the relation between Christ and the universe by their consciousness of the relation between Christ and themselves, in which they believed that the ideal relation between Christ and the human race was receiving its fulfilment. From the relation between Christ and the human race, the transition to the relation between Christ and the universe was not difficult. The whole conception had an ethical and spiritual — not a merely metaphysical — origin. They reached it, not by *a priori* speculation, but by an orderly development of spiritual thought, controlled and directed by the Holy Ghost. Their thought took its departure from what they knew for themselves about their own relation to Christ, and was enriched at point after point by the constant remembrance of the great fact that Christ was God manifest in the flesh. To attempt to illustrate this conception' of Christ's relation to the universe, would lead us too far away from the subject of this Lecture. It will be sufficient for our immediate purpose if we consider the specific relation of Christ to the human race.

As I have already suggested, the original and ideal relation of Christ to all men was probably revealed to the Apostles through His relation to themselves and the Church; and in illustrating the apostolic conception of the original and ideal relation between Christ and the human race, as that conception was determined by the actual relation between Christ and all who believe in Him, it may be well to follow the order of St. Paul's thought in his account of the relation between Christ and the whole creation.

Christ was "the First-born" among many brethren. His eternal holiness and wisdom and power and joy were the ideal forms of that perfection which all who are born of God are destined to inherit through Him. Into His "image" all who had been received into His kingdom were being transformed. And, according to God's idea of the human race, all men were to participate in His glory. In a true and deep sense, Christ is "the First-born of all creation;" all ranks and orders of created beings, and even the material works of the Divine power — through whatever is fair and noble in them — have a relationship to Christ more or less intimate or remote. Between man and Christ, according to God's thought, the relationship was meant to be near and vital.

As the Apostles knew that their Christian life and all its prerogatives and hopes had come to them through Christ, and were not the immediate effect of the Father's power and love, so they believed that all men were created "through Him."

Further, the Apostles knew that Christ was the very end of their existence. This was their joy and their glory. They called themselves His slaves, and said that He had "bought" them— "bought" them, not to make them free, but to make Himself their Master; and the only freedom they knew, or desired to know, was the freedom which they found in His service. "None of us," they exclaimed, "liveth to himself, and no man dieth to himself. For whether we live, we live unto the Lord; and whether we die, we die unto the Lord: whether we live therefore, or die, we are the Lord's. For to this end Christ both died, and rose, and revived, that He might be the Lord both of the dead and the living." [5] The Apostles laboured that they might "be accepted of Him." [6] They exhorted their fellow-Christians to live a good and upright life, that they might "adorn the doctrine of God our Saviour in all things." [7] They were "delivered unto death for Jesus' sake." [8] And neither in their evangelistic activity, nor in their personal righteousness, nor in their sufferings, did they suppose that they were proving the vigour of their own virtue and winning credit for themselves. Only their weakness, their folly, and their sins were their own: their strength came from Christ, and to Him belonged all the glory of their fidelity, their courage, their holiness, and their zeal.

That they might in this sense become Christ's, it had been necessary that He should "purchase" them "with His own blood," and "give His life" a ransom for them. They appeal to the Death of Christ, as investing His claims upon them with an infinite and most pathetic urgency. But had the race never sinned the race would have been His. By His Death He did but recover what He had lost. The kingdom over which He reigns had revolted from Him; but it was originally His own. Not the Church merely, but the human race was created "for Him."

But the most important element in their conception of the original and ideal relation of mankind to Christ — or at least the most important in connection with the theory of the Atonement — is that which probably constituted the root of the declaration that "in Him were all things created," especially when taken in connection with the declaration that "in Him all things consist." The passages in the apostolic epistles which describe Christians as being "in Christ" are almost innumerable. The truth which these passages affirm had been taught by Christ Himself; it was verified by the consciousness of the Church.

The forms in which this truth is expressed are extremely varied. It is said that we were "created in Christ Jesus unto good works;" [9] that God "chose us in Him before the foundation of the world;" [10] that we were "circumcised" in Christ; [11] that "if One died for all, then all died" — died in Him; [12] that we are "buried with Him;" [13] that we are "risen with Him;" [14] that God "raised us up together [with Christ] and made us sit together in heavenly places in Christ Jesus," [15] and "blessed us with all spiritual blessings in heavenly places" in Him. [16] Conduct that becomes Christians is described as "good conversation in Christ." [17] Children are charged to obey their parents "in the Lord." [18] Christian people who have been estranged from each other are exhorted to "be of the same mind in the Lord." [19] Christian Churches are told that their "labour is not in vain in the Lord." [20] The grace that is given to us is "given us in Christ Jesus." [21] St. Paul longs after his converts at Philippi "in the bowels of Jesus Christ;" [22] and he says to the Galatians, "I have been crucified with Christ: nevertheless I live; yet not I, but Christ liveth in me." [23] Christians who have died are described as "the dead in Christ." [24] The whole Church is "the body of Christ," and "as we have many members in one body, and all members have not the same office, so we, being many, are one body in Christ." [25] The Church is "the fulness of Him that filleth all in all." [26]

Passages like these, and they might be indefinitely multiplied, are too numerous and too varied, and they belong too obviously to the very substance of apostolic thought, to be dismissed as merely metaphorical. No doubt they are metaphorical, but metaphors stand for something; and metaphors like these affirm the existence of a very wonderful relation between all the regenerate and Christ.

The existence of that relation is reaffirmed by the consciousness of the Christian Church. The extravagances of Mysticism are but the exaggeration of a truth which is known more or less perfectly to all in whom the power and grace of the Lord Jesus Christ have been revealed. Christian holiness is nothing else than a revelation of the inexhaustible energy of the holiness of Christ. Self-culture, the great law of natural ethics, is unknown in the supernatural life; or, if known, the law assumes altogether a different form. The Christian man does not simply develop and perfect his own life; he is constantly receiving and appropriating the life and power of the Son of God. Christ does not merely exhort us to repent, and reveal new motives by which we should be constrained to repent: He gives repentance, [27] — inspiring us with His own sense of the evil of sin. His own sorrow for it, and His own desire that we should sin no more. We escape from evil habits and evil passions, — not by the force of any moral struggles which can be called our own: sometimes the habits fall away from us at the touch of Christ, as the chains fell away from Peter at the touch of the angel; sometimes the passions are expelled by the power of Christ, as evil spirits were driven out of men by His word; and if we struggle for freedom, we are conscious that we are "strong" only "in the grace that is in Christ Jesus." [28] Even in the presence of violent temptation there are some Christian people to whom it seems that the victory is given them by Christ rather than achieved by themselves through Christ's help, and who say that they do but "stand still, and see the salvation of the Lord." And though to others, and perhaps to most, there is real and prolonged conflict, their own part in it disappears when they look back on their triumphs; and they declare, in no false humility, but in their desire to express the exact truth, that if they have rescued their moral nature from the power of sin, "they got not the land in possession by their own sword, neither did their own arm save them; but [God's] right hand and [God's] arm, and the light of [God's] countenance, because [God had] a favour unto them."

In the development of the virtues and perfections of the Christian life, as distinguished from conquest over sin, it is, if possible, still more obvious that the life and power of Christ are revealed in us. We lose our selfishness and hardness through receiving, direct from Him, the spirit of compassion which moved Him to relieve every form of human infirmity and suffering. His fervour kindles our zeal. The spirit "of power and of love" [29] is an inspiration received from Christ. In none of our "works" can we boast; for "we are God's workmanship, created in Christ Jesus unto good works, which God before ordained [or prepared] that we should walk in them." [30] Hence the possibilities of the Christian life are not to be measured by our native resources, but by the infinite perfection of Christ Himself. We dwell in Him; He dwells in us; and He is the living prophecy of the height and glory of our holiness — a prophecy never to be fulfilled on earth or in heaven, but perpetually moving towards fulfilment, through struggle and sorrow and frequent defeat in this world, and through endless ages of joy and triumph in the world to come. This, I suppose, is the ultimate secret of Christian sanctification — an "open secret," a secret of infinite simplicity, and yet hard to learn. As we never find rest in the mercy of God until we discover that neither our penitence, nor our amendment of life, nor our faith, can create any claim to the Remission of sins, and are willing to receive it as God's free gift "for Christ's sake;" so we can never receive perfect deliverance from sin until we become so anxious for holiness itself as to care nothing for winning any personal credit by becoming holy, — until, renouncing the hope of achieving victory over sin for ourselves, renouncing even the desire to achieve it for ourselves, we are willing to accept victory and freedom as part of that large inheritance which God has given us in Christ.

Our relation to Christ is absolutely unique. And yet, perhaps, some imperfect symbol of it may be found in our relation to the material universe. Man is a free personality, encompassed by a system of forces which transcend all the measures of his science. To these forces, which we now learn are perhaps but various forms of one great Force which remains constant from age to age, man is mysteriously related, and from moment to moment he is dependent on them. In every thought, however light and wayward, that passes through his intellect; in every emotion, however transient, which ripples across the surface of his moral life; in every volition; there is some expenditure of that part of this universal energy which has been accumulated in the nerves and tissues of his physical organisation. Whatever power belongs to man comes to him from the appropriation of force from without. In the earlier ages of human history the savage made some of that force his own by taking food, in which the force had been accumulated; by breathing free air; by drinking the water which ran in streams at his feet or which he procured by painful labour from the rock. All the vigour of muscle and all the keenness of sense which he possessed became his because he had received into his physical nature, and had laid up there, some fractional part of the force which surrounded him. When he struck down his prey at night, he expended in the blow some of the energy which he had made part of himself in the morning. When he began to dig the ground, he was using the energy which had been given to him by the wild fruits and the wild creatures on which he had previously lived. His work was, in a very true sense, not his own; it was the revelation of the universal Force, which, in ways of which he never dreamt, had become the servant of his will.

The history of the material progress of the race is the history of the growing power of man, arising from the gradual extension of his alliances with the forces which surround him. His proudest achievements are their work rather than his. He arms himself with the strength of the winds and the tides. He liberates the latent energy which has been condensed and treasured up in coal, transforms it into heat, generates steam, and sweeps across a continent without weariness, and with the swiftness of a bird. He makes the electric fluid his messenger, and it carries his words under the ocean to remote shores. Moving freely among the stupendous energies by which he is encompassed, he is strong in their strength, and they give to his volitions — powerless apart from them — a large and effective expression.

The history of man's triumphs in the province of his higher and spiritual life is also the history of the gradual extension of his alliance with a Force which is not his own. There is no proportion between the native strength of his will and the perfection which he achieves through Christ. Every good work is a manifestation of the Divine power, in which alone we can be strong. Every form of Christian perfection — "love, joy, peace, longsuffering, gentleness, goodness, faith, meekness, temperance," — is a "fruit of the Spirit," an expression in our personal life of the perfection of the life of Christ. In the spiritual, as in the material sphere, man is a free personality surrounded by a vast and immeasurable Power which is not his own, but through which his history may become bright with the glory of the noblest achievements. In Christ we are "made partakers of the divine nature." [31]

The parallel is extremely imperfect. At one point it breaks down altogether, for material forces are unconscious, and we make their energy ours without their voluntary concurrence, while the spiritual Power which becomes our own is the Power of a free Personal Life. But though the parallel is imperfect, it may assist us to grasp one of the fundamental truths of the Christian faith, and it may suggest the perilous error into which we may be betrayed by our very zeal in advocating that truth. Scientific men, having their imagination filled with the vastness of that universal and indestructible energy which they say assumes varied forms in all material phenomena, have gone on to affirm that the human will is but one of its Protean manifestations. Devout mystics, overpowered with awe and wonder by the energy of the life of God, in which, and in which alone, they were conscious that they were living, have gone on to affirm that the will of God is the only active force in the universe. In ancient and in modern times materialism has suppressed the personality and the will of man in the presence of the awful forces of the physical universe. In ancient and in modern times mysticism has suppressed the personality and the will of man in the presence of the living God. The Christian philosophy of human nature might perhaps be roughly defined as a form of Pantheism in which the moral freedom of man and the moral freedom of God are resolutely and consistently vindicated.

Our Lord Jesus Christ has illustrated in the simplest and most perfect manner the nature of the relation between ourselves and Him. "Abide in Me, and I in you. As the branch cannot bear fruit of itself, except it abide in the vine; no more can ye, except ye abide in Me. I am the vine, ye are the branches: he that abideth in Me, and I in him, the same bringeth forth much fruit: for apart from Me ye can do nothing." [32] This is an exhaustive statement of the truth: to this neither saint nor Apostle can add anything. We truly live only as we live in Christ. Our highest life is life derived from Him.

Out of this relation to Christ arises our relation to the Father. There is nothing technical, formal, or artificial in the prerogative of Divine sonship which is conferred on all that are in Christ. They are not merely "*called* the sons of God." The name represents a fact. They share the life of the Son of God, and no other name can express the relation to the Father which the sharing of that life originates.

The Apostles speak of our having "access" to the Father "in Him" and "through Him." Christ Himself said, "I am the Way:... no man cometh to the Father but by Me." [33] This does not mean merely that because of what Christ has done and suffered for the salvation of mankind the sins are remitted which excluded us from the Divine presence. It is not the Atonement of Christ alone, or the revelation which Christ has made to us of the Divine love, through which we come to God. Christ Himself is "the Way:... no man cometh to the Father but by [Him]." That for us sinners Christ might be the "Way" to the Father, it was necessary — as I hope to show presently — that He should die as a Sacrifice for our sins. But He Himself is the "Way." Through our union with Christ, His trust and joy in the Father become ours, and the light of God, in which He dwells, becomes our home. Through Christ's original, eternal, and unique relationship to the Father we are raised into a relationship to God which renders possible a freedom and blessedness of communion with Him which is "unspeakable and full of glory."

To bring this discussion to a close: there are two great laws which are involved in that relation to Christ which He Himself illustrated in the parable of the Vine, and to the reality of which the Christian consciousness bears testimony: —

1. The power and perfection of our moral and spiritual life are a perpetual revelation of the power and perfection of the life of Christ. There is no element of holiness in us that is not derived from Him. As the life of Christ is being perpetually revealed in us in richer and nobler forms, the moral and spiritual glory of Christ is the ultimate ideal to which we are continually approaching, but which we shall never reach.

2. Our own relation to the Father is determined by the relation of Christ to the Father. By no fictitious imputation or technical transfer, but by virtue of a real union between the life of Christ and our own life, His relation to the Father becomes ours. It is ours with the same qualifications with which His life is ours. In Him both the life and the relation exist in a transcendent form.

But these two laws which are involved in the actual relation to Christ, of all to whom He has given eternal life and "power to become the sons of God," were involved in the original and ideal relation of the human race to Himself. This appears to be implied in the prologue of St. John's Gospel. "In Him was life" — the life of the human race — "and the life was the light of men." [34] According to the Divine idea of human nature, man was to live by perpetual fellowship with the life of the eternal Word, and in that life was to inherit all the knowledge, purity, and blessedness of which "light" is the beautiful symbol. As the life of the Eternal Word or Son of God was to be the life of the human race. His relation to the Father was also to be ours. Had we never sinned, our history would have been a perpetual ascent towards His supreme holiness, and even the earliest movements of our moral and spiritual life would have found their ideal expression in Him. His relation to the Father would, therefore, have been ours from the very first.

In the light of this original and ideal relation of the Lord Jesus Christ to our race, can we discover any relation between His Death and the Remission of our sins? I think we can.

I. On any theory of human redemption it is morally necessary that, on the part of those who have sinned, there should be a real and frank consent to the justice of the penalties from which redemption releases them. While there is any resentment on our part against the righteousness of the law by which we are condemned, our antagonism to God, whose will is inseparable from that law, remains. In the endeavour to subdue this resentment, some men have passed through protracted and convulsive struggles, and have confessed at last that the resentment was still unsubdued. It was easy for them to acknowledge that they had sinned, but there was an invincible recoil from yielding a perfect moral consent and submission to the righteousness of the penalties of their sins. We are conscious that this consent and submission ought to be given, and that so long as we shrink from it the controversy between God and us cannot be closed. It is an offence to resent the penalties of the eternal Law of Righteousness, as well as to transgress its precepts. That the penalties should be remitted while we recoil from submitting to the authority of the awful principle which they vindicate, seems morally impossible.

The Lord Jesus Christ, the Moral Ruler of the human race, instead of inflicting the penalties, has submitted to them; He has "died, the Just for the unjust," and has been "made a curse for us." This supreme act becomes ours — not by formal imputation — but through the law which constitutes His life the original spring of our own. His eternal trust in the Father, His eternal joy in the Father, His eternal love for the Father, are the root of the trust and joy and love of which we are conscious in the Divine presence. In the strength of His trust we have faith in God; in the fulness of His joy we rejoice in God; and the fires of our love for God are kindled by the fervour of His love for the Father, And when we are troubled by the bitter remembrance of sin, and are almost crushed by a sense of the magnitude of the just penalties of sin; when we are striving to humble ourselves before the infinite justice of God, and to confess that were these penalties to be inflicted on us, the Judge of all the earth would do right; we find in the Death of Christ the perfect expression and fulfilment of that submission which we know ought to be manifested by ourselves. He did not merely confess our sin; He did not merely acknowledge that we deserved to suffer. He endured the penalties of sin, and so made an actual submission to the authority and righteousness of the principle which those penalties express. What we had no force to do. He has done; and through our union with Him, His submission renders our submission possible. This is but a particular illustration of the universal law that the moral and spiritual perfection of Christ is the ultimate root of our own perfection. The act in which He submitted to the righteousness of the law by which we were condemned, is the very life and vigour of the moral act in which we in our turn make the same submission; and the moral element which constitutes the significance of our own act has already received in His, its highest possible expression. His submission is, therefore, a ground on which our sins may be forgiven.

2. Through His Death, the relation of Christ to the Father is no longer of a kind to render it untrue to our relation to God. Sin had introduced an element into our life which rendered it impossible, except on the hypothesis of

an amazing and incredible fiction, for the original relation of Christ to the Father to continue to be the ideal of the relation of the human race to God. In the presence of God, and in the region to which the spiritual life of man belongs, fictions can have no place. If, therefore, we were still to be related to God through Christ, it would seem to be necessary that there should be included in His actual relation to the Father an expression of the truth of that relation into which we had come through sin. That expression is found in His Death.

He was forsaken of the Father, and He died. His other sufferings were such as the innocent may endure in serving the sinful and the wretched. On the cross He submitted to the actual penalty of sin. I will not say that it was *necessary* that He should submit to the penalty of sin in order that our original and ideal relation to God through Him should be preserved or recovered, for I shrink from confident *a priori* speculations on this great mystery; and if I sometimes speak of the impossibility of redemption apart from the Death of Christ, I only mean that by His Death He has accomplished what we are unable to imagine could have been accomplished in any other way.

Had He simply made a confession of sin in our name — the theory advocated by Dr. Macleod Campbell in his very valuable treatise on the Atonement — He would still have remained at a distance from the actual relation to God in which we were involved by sin. He has done more than this. By submitting to the awful experience which forced from Him the cry, "My God, My God, why hast Thou forsaken Me?" and by the Death which followed. He made our real relation to God His own, while retaining — and, in the very act of submitting to the penalty of sin, revealing in the highest form — the absolute perfection of His moral life and the steadfastness of His eternal union with the Father.

By His Death, therefore, Christ has rendered it possible for us, notwithstanding our sins, to retain or to recover our original and ideal relation to God through Him; and since the loss of that relation was one of the greatest penalties of sin, what Christ suffered in order that our relation to God through Him might be maintained or restored, may be justly described as the ground on which our sins are remitted.

3. There is another way in which the Death of our Lord Jesus Christ is related to our redemption. I approach it with great hesitation, because it is involved in great obscurity.

St. Paul, in his Second Epistle to the Corinthians, has these remarkable words, "We thus judge, that if one died for all, then all died." [35] These words, if they stood alone, might perhaps be fairly regarded as a strong rhetorical statement of the effect which ought to be produced on our hearts by the infinite love of Christ in dying for us. It might be said that since He died for us, the greatness of His love ought to dissolve all our relations to "this present evil world," and bind us in perfect and eternal loyalty to Himself; that we ought to live as though death had already separated us from the common excitements and sorrows and triumphs of mankind; for us old things should have passed away, and all things become new. But in several other of his epistles he speaks of Christ's Death as though it were a real event in our own history. In the Epistle to the Romans [36] he rests two elaborate arguments on what he takes for granted as known to those to whom he is writing — the fact that Christ's Death was in some sense their own death. He argues first, that having died to sin in the Death of Christ, it is impossible that we should continue to live in sin. Christ "died unto sin once," and now He liveth unto God. [37] We also died with Him, and in His resurrection we have risen to a new life. He argues, secondly, that according to a recognized principle of Jewish theology the Law has no power over those who have passed into the life beyond the grave, and that we, having died in Christ, are therefore under the law no longer. [38]

The conception which is the foundation of these arguments, and which he assumes to be a recognized element of Christian faith and consciousness, reappears constantly in St. Paul's writings: it reappears so frequently, and in such forms, that it cannot be treated as being nothing more than a rhetorical representation of the great moral effect which our belief in the Death of Christ ought to have on our spirit and character. It seems to have suggested the exhortation of St. Peter, to which it is difficult to give a very exact interpretation. "Forasmuch then as Christ hath suffered for us in the flesh, arm yourselves likewise with the same mind: for he that hath suffered in the flesh hath ceased from sin; that he no longer should live the rest of his time in the flesh to the lusts of men, but to the will of God." [39]

In his Epistle to the Galatians St. Paul affirms that he himself had thus died in Christ. "I am crucified with Christ: nevertheless I live; yet not I, but Christ liveth in me." [40] And many Christian persons have declared that they are conscious that in the Death of Christ their old and evil life perished.

It is far less difficult to apprehend the fact that we live in the life of Christ, than the fact that we died in His Death; but the teaching of St. Paul seems to be explicit. The destruction of evil within us is the effect and fulfilment in ourselves of the mystery of Christ's Death, as the development of our positive holiness is the manifestation of the power of His life.

This is the Pauline doctrine, and I repeat that it has been verified in the consciousness of large numbers of Christian people. I accept this relation between the Death of Christ and the death of our own evil self as a fact, though I may be unable to offer any explanation of it.

The fact, however inexplicable, is of great significance. The prayer of a devout Mahometan — "Give me first, O Allah! a death in which there is no life, and then a life in which there is no death" — expresses a craving which has been felt by all who have passed through the severer moral and spiritual struggles which sometimes precede the consciousness of restoration to God and victory over sin. How many of us have cried, in the bitterness of our despair, "There is no redemption possible to us. We have waited for God, and He has not come to us." We have meditated on His infinite glory and goodness, and we have been unable to stir the stagnant affections of our spiritual life. We have listened to fervent appeals, to which the hearts of other men yielded, and we remained unmoved. We have read what saints have written of the blessedness of God's service, and have not been constrained to serve Him. We have tried to pray, and our prayers had no devotion in them. We have thought of the agony of Gethsemane and the desolation of the cross, but if we were touched for a moment to penitence, and if for a moment it seemed as though we were about to break away from our sins, and to become the loyal servants of Christ, even the love of Christ soon spent its strength, and we remained as cold and undevout as before. "Would to God," we have exclaimed, "that I could cease to be myself; that this evil nature of mine could be destroyed, and leave nothing of itself behind; that I could die, if only I might have a new life, with better instincts, diviner impulses — that the passion, the sluggishness, the selfishness, the unbelief, which seem to constitute my very self, could be smitten with lightning from heaven, and perish, — perish utterly, and perish for ever." Yes, the prayer of the devout Mahometan expresses what has been the innermost desire of innumerable hearts — "Give me a death in which there is no life, and a life in which there is no death."

The prayer receives its answer in Christ; in His Death our sin dies, and in His life the very life of God is made our own. How the Death of Christ effects the destruction of our sin, we may be unable to tell. Perhaps that great moral act by which Christ consented to lose the consciousness of the Father's presence and love — an act different in kind from any to which holy beings, in their normal relation to God, can be called — rendered it possible for us to sink to that complete renunciation of self which is the condition of the perfect Christian life; for that renunciation is also unique, and has no parallel in the normal development of a moral creature. But it is enough that we know the fact that in God's idea, and according to the law of the kingdom of heaven, we are crucified with Christ. Sometimes through our union with Him sin may seem to perish as by a sudden blow. More frequently it dies slowly — dies as those died who were put to death by crucifixion. The nails are driven through its hands; it is tortured with an unsatisfied thirst; there are convulsive struggles which last long, and which show that vitality has not gone out of it. It seems to perish at last by exhaustion. But it is actually crucified, if only our union with Christ is complete, and though it may still live, its power over us is gone.

No assertion on God's part of the ill desert of sin, no submission on our part to the justice of the penalties of sin, could have made it morally possible for the penalties of sin to be remitted in the absence of a complete security for the disappearance of sin. This moral security has been created by the sufferings of Christ on the cross. The Death of Christ is the death of sin. It is, therefore, a ground on which sin may be forgiven.

The general outlines of that conception of the relation of the Death of Christ to the Remission of sins at which we have arrived may be stated in four propositions. The first three have been illustrated in the present Lecture; the fourth was illustrated in the preceding Lecture.

I. The Death of Christ is the objective ground on which the sins of men are remitted, because it was an act of submission to the righteous authority of the Law by which the human race was condemned — a submission by One from whom on various grounds the act of submission derived transcendent moral significance, and because in consequence of the relation between Him and us — His life being our own — His submission is the expression of ours, and carries ours with it. He was not our Representative in a sense which would imply that because He submitted to the just authority by which the penalties of sin are inflicted we are released from the obligations of submission. The sufferings, indeed, were His, that they might not be ours; He endured them, that we might escape from them. But the moral act of Christ in submitting to those sufferings, while it remains for ever alone in its unique and awful grandeur, involves a similar moral act on the part of all who have "access" to God through Him.

A real submission to the righteousness of God in condemning us was necessary before the penalties of sin could be remitted. This submission was made by Christ; it was made for us, on our behalf, in our name. But we have a part in it. In a real and not merely a technical sense the act is ours. It is ours because through our relation to Him it has made possible to us, though in an inferior form, a similar consent to the righteousness of the penalties which we have deserved. It is ours, for it is the transcendent expression and act of that eternal life in which we live, and which is perpetually revealed in our own character and history.

2. The Death of Christ is the objective ground on which the sins of men are remitted, because it rendered possible the retention or the recovery of our original and ideal relation to God through Christ which sin had dissolved, and the loss of which was the supreme penalty of transgression.

3. The Death of Christ is the objective ground on which the sins of men are remitted, because it involved the actual destruction of sin in all those who through faith recover their union with Him.

4. The Death of Christ is the objective ground on which the sins of men are remitted, because in His submission to the awful penalty of Sin, in order to preserve or to restore our relations to the Father through Him, there was a revelation of the righteousness of God, which must otherwise have been revealed in the infliction of the penalties of sin on the human race. He endured the penalty instead of inflicting it.

That these four propositions include a complete theory of the relation of the Death of Christ to the remission of human sin, I am not so presumptuous as to imagine. But if they can be sustained, they offer some explanation of the great fact that the Death of Christ did not merely manifest the infinite mercy of God, but really effected reconciliation between God and man.

I believe that the conception of the nature of the Atonement which is contained in these propositions, accounts, and accounts naturally, for all the various expressions which are used by our Lord Himself and His Apostles in describing the unique character and the unique effects of His Death. Further, I believe that this conception justifies those representations of the Death of Christ, the substantial truth of which receives strong confirmation from their general acceptance by the Christian Church during eighteen centuries.

The Death of Christ may be described as an Expiation for sin, for it was a Divine act which renders the punishment of sin unnecessary.

It was a Vicarious Death. He died "for us," "for our sins," "in our stead." For the principle that we deserved to suffer was asserted in His sufferings, that it might not have to be asserted in ours. He was forsaken of God, that we might not have to be forsaken. He did not suffer that He might merely share with us the penalties of our sin, but that the penalties of our sin might be remitted.

It was a Representative Death, the Death of One whom the elder theologians were accustomed to describe as the new Federal Head of the human race, or of the Church. The technical language of theologians obscured and even concealed the truth which it was intended to express. The Lord Jesus Christ is in very truth, by the original law of the universe, the Representative of mankind.

It may be described as a Ransom — an act of God by which we are delivered or redeemed from the calamities which threatened us so long as we were exposed to the punishment of sin, and by which we are also delivered or redeemed from those moral and spiritual evils from which there was no escape except through the restoration to us of the life of God.

It was a Satisfaction to the righteousness of God, in whatever sense the punishment of the guilty can be spoken of as a Satisfaction to the righteousness of God.

It was a Sacrifice for sin — an acknowledgment, such as we could never have made for ourselves, of the greatness of our guilt; an actual submission on our behalf to the penalty of guilt, and a confession that our very life had been justly forfeited by our sins.

It was a Propitiation for sin - a Propitiation originated and effected by God Himself, through which we are brought into such relations to God, that all moral reasons for withholding from us the remission of sins disappear. As an act of submission to the righteousness of the Law by which we were condemned, an act done in our name, and ultimately carrying our submission with it, it "has the property" — to quote the formal definition of a Propitiation given by one of our own theologians — "of disposing, inclining, or causing the judicial authority to *admit* the expiation; that is, to assent to it as a valid reason for pardoning the offender." [41]

Or, to state what seems to me to be the complete truth, the Death of Christ was a Propitiation for the sins of men because it was a revelation of the righteousness of God on the ground of which He can remit the penalties of sin; because it was an act of submission to the justice of those penalties on behalf of mankind, an act in which our own submission was really and vitally included; and because it secured the destruction of sin in all who through faith are restored to union with Christ. It is, therefore, the supreme and irresistible argument by which we can now sustain our appeal to God's infinite mercy to grant us forgiveness of sin and deliverance from the wrath to come.

"God is great, and we know Him not." To this confession we must come at last. We may know enough to inspire us with perfect faith in His righteousness and love, and even in this life "the pure in heart" may see His face and find in His presence "fulness of joy;" but when we know most, we can only exclaim, "O the depth of the riches both of the wisdom and knowledge of God! how unsearchable are His judgments, and His ways past finding out!" Even if we think that some mysteries have been partially disclosed to us, we often find that we cannot make clear to others what has become clear to ourselves. In the history of all who consecrate their chief thought and strength to meditation on the ways of God to man, there are times when mist and clouds which have hung for years over fair provinces of truth are suddenly broken and scattered by light from the upper heavens. The vision we have long waited for has come at last, and we think that we shall be able to relieve the doubts and resolve the perplexities of many hearts. But we speak, and what we most wanted to say is unsaid; we write, and are conscious that there is only a precarious relation between our real thought and what we have written. As "the heart knoweth its own bitterness, neither doth a stranger intermeddle with its joy," so it seems that our most vivid apprehensions of truth must remain our own; they can receive no precise and adequate expression.

When we are depressed and discouraged by such thoughts as these — conscious that we ourselves know very little of the great principles and laws which we are sure must be illustrated in the Death of Christ, and that what we know we are unable to make plain to other men, it may be a relief to us to remember that the triumphs of the Christian faith are won — not by the symmetry and perfection of theological theories, but by the great facts of the gospel. If it were otherwise — if we could say nothing to any purpose of the infinite love of Him who for us sinners and for our salvation "was made flesh and dwelt among us," because we cannot resolve the difficulties involved in the Incarnation; nothing of that supernatural change without which no man can "see the kingdom of God," because we cannot penetrate the mysteries of the new birth; nothing of the glory, honour, and immortal blessedness which are the inheritance of all that are in Christ, because there are innumerable questions concerning the life beyond death to which we can give no reply; — we should have to leave undischarged the most sacred duties to which God has called the Church.

The power of the great Sacrifice for the sins of the world lies in itself, and not in our explanations of it. Even when the doctrine of the Church has been most corrupt, the Death of Christ has continued to appeal to the hearts of men with unique and all but irresistible force.

For nearly two centuries the nations of western and southern Europe were inspired with a common enthusiasm and a common purpose. Princes mortgaged their kingdoms, nobles sold their lands, scholars deserted their books, the common people left their homes, to join the armies of the Cross, and to rescue the Holy Land from the infidel. The hearts of little children caught fire, and they gathered in thousands and tried to make their way across unknown countries, through dark forests and over great rivers, to share the sanctity and the glory of the enterprise. And what was the supreme object of that romantic and heroic struggle? It was not to recover the site of the ruined cities in which Christ had revealed His beneficent and supernatural power, healing the sick, giving sight to the blind, hearing to the deaf, and speech to the dumb, — nor the village on the eastern slope of Olivet, in which He had raised Lazarus from the dead, — nor the mountain on which He was transfigured, — nor the little town among the limestone hills of Galilee which was the home of His childhood and His youth. The sepulchre of Christ was dearer and more sacred to the hearts of the crusaders than all the scenes of His living ministry; and while that was in the hands of the unbelievers, it seemed to them that Christendom was faithless to the memory of its Lord. They were guilty of shameful crimes; but the whole movement is a singular proof of the strange and mighty power of the Death of Christ over the imagination and passions of mankind. Nor can I doubt that in those vast armies, whose covetousness, and treachery, and cruelty, and lust made the Christian name infamous throughout the East, there were multitudes of men of pure life and noble temper, whose hearts had been inspired by the Death of Christ with penitence and hope and immeasurable gratitude; and who, because they knew of no other way in which they could consecrate their strength and valour to Christ's service, resolved to rescue His sepulchre from dishonour.

In modern Jerusalem there is no more affecting sight than that which is witnessed at every Easter festival in the chapel erected over the spot on which, according to the tradition both of the Eastern and of the Western Church, the Saviour of mankind was crucified. Across the marble floor, hour after hour, in endless succession, pilgrims of many nations and of many tongues move slowly on their knees, with streaming tears and every manifestation of deep and reverential devotion; and when they reach the sacred rock in which they believe that the cross was fixed, they cover it with passionate kisses. The tradition is untrustworthy, the devotion superstitious; but who can tell what love and faith and worship Christ may recognize in the hearts of those who in this rude way are fulfilling His own words, "I, if I be lifted up, will draw all men unto Me"?

Those prostrations, those tears, those vehement demonstrations of affection and gratitude, are but pathetic symbols of the invisible and nobler effects which the power of the cross has produced in every age and in every land. Its power is still unspent. The cross is the very symbol of the infinite righteousness and of the infinite love of God. It confirms the severest condemnation which our consciences can ever pronounce on our crimes; it reveals a mercy which transcends all our hopes. The awful yet glorious fact that the Son of God, the Creator of the heavens and the earth, the Ruler and Judge of our race, died a cruel death, that we might have the Remission of sins, will for ever thrill the hearts of men with wonder and sorrow, with devout reverence and great joy. The very first disciples that followed Christ on earth, followed Him on the testimony of the Baptist, "Behold the Lamb of God, which taketh away the sin of the world;" and when long afterwards, heaven was revealed to one of the two who received this testimony, the "new song" which he heard from the saints who see the glory of their Lord was this: — "Thou wast slain, and hast redeemed us to God by Thy blood, out of every kindred, and tongue, and people, and nation;" and he tells us that "ten thousand times ten thousand" angels, and "thousands of thousands," prolonged the cry, "Worthy is the Lamb that was slain to receive power, and riches, and wisdom, and strength, and honour, and glory, and blessing;" and still the rapture spread, "and every creature which is in heaven and on earth, and under the earth, and such as are in the sea, and all that are in them," caught up the exulting strain, "saying, Blessing, and honour, and glory, and power be unto Him that sitteth upon the throne, and unto the Lamb for ever and ever." For us, too, we trust that some day heaven will be opened; and we trust that all its glory will be ours — not in transient vision — but as an everlasting inheritance.

Meanwhile, as we listen to the music and the triumph of those lofty songs in which some day we hope to join, let us entreat God so to reveal to us the infinite love of Christ, through whose blood we have redemption, even the forgiveness of sins, that it may kindle in our hearts on earth the same fervent and grateful enthusiasm with which it will inspire us in heaven; and let those of us who are called to the ministry of the gospel resolve that henceforth, with stronger faith and intenser earnestness, we will preach "Christ and Him crucified."

[1] Dr. Dorner: *History of the Development of the Doctrine of the Person of Christ,* Vol. iii. div. 2, p. 232.
[2] Col. i. 15-17.
[3] Or, "of all creation."
[4] Note S.
[5] Rom. xiv. 7-9.
[6] 2 Cor. v. 9.
[7] Titus ii. 10.
[8] 2 Cor. iv. 11.
[9] Eph. ii. 10.
[10] Ibid. i. 4.
[11] Col. ii. 11.
[12] 2 Cor. v. 14.
[13] Rom. vi. 4.
[14] Col. iii. 1.
[15] Eph. ii. 6.
[16] Ibid. i. 4.
[17] I Pet. iii. 16.
[18] Eph. vi. 1.
[19] Phil. iv. 2.
[20] 1 Cor. xv. 58.
[21] 2 Tim. i. 9.
[22] Phil. i. 8.
[23] Gal. ii. 20.

[24] I Thess. iv. 16.
[25] Rom. xii. 4, 5.
[26] Eph. i. 23.
[27] Acts v. 31.
[28] 2 Tim. ii. 1.
[29] 2 Tim. i. 7.

[30] Eph. ii. 10.
[31] 2 Pet. i. 4.
[32] John xv. 4, 5.
[33] John xiv. 6.
[34] John i. 4.
[35] 2 Cor. v. 14.

[36] Rom. vi. vii.
[37] Ibid. vi. 10.
[38] Note T.
[39] 1 Pet. iv. I, 2.
[40] Gal. ii. 20.
[41] Dr. Pye Smith.

# Appendix

## *Note A*

Cum suavissima de satisfactione Christi doctrina, praecipuum sit salutis nostrae caput, fidei anchora, spei azylum, charitatis norma, ut sancte monet Athanasius; atque adeo vera Christianismi basis pretiosissimumque Christianorum κειμήλιον; quâ salvâ et illius structura constat, et istorum consolatio, et quâ rursus vel eversâ vel corruptâ totius religionis compagem luxatam et dissipatam ruere necesse est: nihil antiquius divinae veritatis cultoribus esse debet, quam ut accurato pensiretur examine, et in apertâ luce collocata, ab omnibus agnosci, firmaque ex verbo dei fiducia constanter retineri possit." [1]

## *Note B*

Dr. Crawford, in his admirable volume on *The Doctrine of Holy Scripture Respecting the Atonement* (Blackwood and Sons, Edinburgh and London, 1871), has given a complete account of the Scripture passages in which the various elements of the doctrine of the Death of Christ appear. As I have attempted no such exhaustive presentation of the usual Scripture argument for the Atonement, and indeed have endeavoured to exhibit the argument in altogether another form, it may be of service to many readers to have an outline of Dr. Crawford's classification. I therefore give it, with some slight changes of form, in this note.

**I. Passages which Speak of Christ**

(1) *As dying for sinners.*

"The Son of man came not to be ministered unto, but to minister, and to give His life a ransom for many." [2]

"This is My body which is given for you." [3]

"This cup is the new testament in My blood, which is shed for you." [4]

"The bread that I will give is My flesh, which I will give for the life of the world." [5]

"I am the good shepherd; the good shepherd giveth his life for the sheep...I lay down My life for the sheep...No man taketh it from Me, but I lay it down of Myself. I have power (authority) to lay it down, and I have power to take it again. This commandment have I received of My Father." [6]

"This is My commandment, that ye love one another, as I have loved you. Greater love hath no man than this, that a man lay down his life for his friends." [7]

"When we were yet without strength, in due time Christ died for the ungodly. For scarcely for a righteous man will one die: yet peradventure for a good man some would even dare to die. But God commendeth His love toward us, in that, while we were yet sinners, Christ died for us." [8]

"He that spared not His own Son, but delivered Him up for us all, how shall He not with Him also freely give us all things?" [9]

"If one died for all, then all died; and He died for all, that they which live should not henceforth live unto themselves, but unto Him which died for them, and rose again." [10]

"He hath made Him to be sin for us, who knew no sin; that we might be made the righteousness of God in Him." [11]

"I am crucified with Christ: nevertheless I live; yet not I, but Christ liveth in me: and the life which I now live in the flesh I live by the faith of the Son of God, who loved me, and gave Himself for me." [12]

"Christ hath redeemed us from the curse of the law, being made a curse for us." [13]

"Christ hath loved us, and hath given Himself for us an offering and a sacrifice to God for a sweet smelling savour." "Christ loved the Church, and gave Himself for it." [14]

"God hath not appointed us to wrath, but to obtain salvation by our Lord Jesus Christ, who died for us." [15]

"There is one God, and one mediator between God and men, he man Christ Jesus, who gave Himself a ransom for us." [16]

"Our Saviour Jesus Christ gave Himself for us, that He might redeem us from all iniquity." [17]

"We see Jesus crowned with glory and honour, who was made a little lower than the angels for the suffering of death, that He by the grace of God should taste death for every man." [18]

"Christ also hath once suffered for sins, the just for the unjust, that He might bring us to God." [19]

"Hereby perceive we the love of God, because He laid down His life for us." [20]

(2) *As suffering for sins.*

"He was delivered for our offences." [21]

"God, sending His own Son in the likeness of sinful flesh, and for sin, condemned sin in the flesh." [22]

"I delivered unto you first of all that which I also received, that Christ died for our sins according to the scriptures." [23]

"Who gave Himself for our sins, that He might deliver us from this present evil world." [24]

"This man, after He had offered one sacrifice for sins for ever, sat down on the right hand of God." [25]

"Christ also hath once suffered for sins, the Just for the unjust." [26]

"He was wounded for our transgressions. He was bruised for our iniquities." "For the transgression of My people was He stricken." [27]

(3) *As bearing our sins.*

"Christ was once offered to bear the sins of many." [28]

"Who His own self bare our sins in His own body on the tree." [29]

"The Lord hath laid on Him the iniquity of us all." "By His knowledge shall My righteous servant justify many; for He shall bear their iniquities. He was numbered with the transgressors, and He bare the sin of many." [30]

(4) As *being "made sin" and "made a curse for us."*

"He hath made Him to be sin for us, who knew no sin; that we might be made the righteousness of God in Him," [31]

"Christ hath redeemed us from the curse of the law, being made a curse for us." [32]

## II. Passages which ascribe to the Death of Christ

(1) *The removal and remission of sins, and deliverance from their penal consequences.*

"Behold the Lamb of God, which taketh away the sin of the world." [33]

"Now once in the end of the world hath He appeared to put away sin by the sacrifice of Himself" [34]

"This is My blood of the new testament, which is shed for many for the remission of sins." [35]

"The blood of Jesus Christ His Son cleanseth us from all sin." [36]

"It behoved Christ to suffer, and to rise from the dead the third day: and that repentance and remission of sins should be preached in His name among all nations." [37]

"Through His name whosoever believeth in Him shall receive remission of sins." [38]

"Through this man is preached unto you the forgiveness of sins: and by Him all that believe are justified from all things, from which ye could not be justified by the law of Moses." [39]

"He hath made us accepted in the beloved. In whom we have redemption through His blood, the forgiveness of sins, according to the riches of His grace." [40]

"Who hath delivered us from the power of darkness, and hath translated us into the kingdom of His dear Son: in whom we have redemption through His blood, even the forgiveness of sins." [41]

"Unto him that loved us, and washed us from our sins in His own blood, and hath made us kings and priests unto God and His Father; to Him be glory and dominion for ever and ever." [42]

"As Moses lifted up the serpent in the wilderness, even so must the Son of man be lifted up: that whosoever believeth in Him should not perish, but have eternal life. For God so loved the world, that He gave His only begotten Son, that whosoever believeth in Him should not perish, but have everlasting liie. For God sent not His Son into the world to condemn the world; but that the world through Him might be saved." [43]

"God hath not appointed us to wrath, but to obtain salvation by our Lord Jesus Christ, who died for us." [44]

(2) *Justification.*

"By His knowledge shall My righteous servant justify many; for He shall bear their iniquities." [45]

"God commendeth His love toward us, in that, while we were yet sinners, Christ died for us. Much more, then, being now justified by His blood, we shall be saved from wrath through Him." [46]

"Justified freely by the grace of God through the redemption that is in Christ Jesus: whom God hath set forth to be a propitiation through faith in His blood, to declare His righteousness, ...that He might be just, and the justifier of him who believeth in Jesus." [47]

(3) *Redemption.*

"The Son of man is come, not to be ministered unto, but to minister, and to give His life a ransom for many." [48]

"Feed the Church of God" (or of the Lord), "which He hath purchased with His own blood." [49]

"All have sinned, and come short of the glory of God; being justified freely by His grace through the redemption that is in Christ Jesus: whom God hath set forth to be a propitiation through faith in His blood." [50]

"Ye are not your own, for ye are bought with a price: therefore glorify God in your body, and in your spirit, which are God's." [51]

"God sent forth His Son, made of a woman, made under the law, to redeem them that were under the law." [52]

"In whom we have redemption through His blood, the forgiveness of sins." [53]

"Neither by the blood of goats and calves, but by His own blood He entered in once into the holy place, having obtained eternal redemption for us." [54]

"Ye were not redeemed with corruptible things, as silver and gold, from your vain conversation received by tradition from your fathers; but with the precious blood of Christ, as of a lamb without blemish and without spot." [55]

"Thou wast slain, and hast redeemed us to God by Thy blood out of every kindred, and tongue, and people, and nation." [56]

(4) *Reconciliation to God.*

"If, when we were enemies, we were reconciled to God by the death of His Son, much more, being reconciled, we shall be saved by His life." [57]

"And not only so, but we also joy in God through our Lord Jesus Christ, by whom we have now received the atonement." [58]

"All things are of God, who hath reconciled us to Himself by Jesus Christ, and hath given to us the ministry of reconciliation; to wit, that God was in Christ, reconciling the world unto Himself not imputing their trespasses unto them; and hath committed unto us the word of reconciliation." [59]

"Reconciling both (Jews and Gentiles) unto God in one body by the cross, having slain the enmity thereby." [60]

"And you, that were sometime alienated and enemies in your mind by wicked works, yet now hath He reconciled in the body of His flesh through death, to present you holy and unblamable and unreprovable in His sight." [61]

### III. Passages in which the Lord Jesus Christ is represented

(1) *As a Propitiation for sin.*

"And He is the propitiation for our sins: and not for ours only, but also for the sins of the whole world." [62]

"Herein is love, not that we loved God, but that He loved us, and sent His Son to be the propitiation for our sins." [63]

"A merciful and faithful high priest in things pertaining to God to make reconciliation" (more properly, propitiation or expiation) "for the sins of the people." [64]

"Whom God hath set forth to be a propitiation through faith in His blood, to declare His righteousness for the remission of sins." [65]

(2) *As a Priest.*

"The Lord hath sworn, and will not repent, Thou art a priest for ever after the order of Melchisedec." [66]

"The high priest of our profession, Christ Jesus." [67]

"A merciful and faithful high priest in things pertaining to God." [68]

"A high priest over the house of God." [69]

"A great high priest, that is passed into the heavens, Jesus the Son of God." [70]

"Such an high priest became us, who is holy, harmless, undefiled, separate from sinners, and made higher than the heavens." [71]

(3) *As a Representative.*

"Every high priest taken from among men is ordained for men in things pertaining to God." [72]

"Surety of the better covenant." [73]

"By one man sin entered into the world, and death by sin; and so death passed upon all men, for that all have sinned.... Therefore as by the offence of one judgment came upon all men to condemnation; even so by the right-eousness of one the free gift came upon all men unto justification of life. For as by one man's disobedience many were made sinners, so by the obedience of one shall many be made righteous." [74]

"Now is Christ risen from the dead, and become the first-fruits of them that slept. For since by man came death, by man came also the resurrection of the dead. For as in Adam all die, even so in Christ shall all be made alive...The first man Adam was made a living soul; the last Adam was made a quickening spirit. ...The first man is of the earth, earthy: the second man is the Lord from heaven. As is the earthy, such are they also that are earthy: and as is the heavenly, such are they also that are heavenly. And as we have borne the image of the earthy, we shall also bear the image of the heavenly." [75]

### IV. Passages which Represent the Sufferings of Christ

(1) As *"sacrificial."*

Under this head, "Behold the Lamb of God," &c., should reappear. To these may be added —

"Christ our passover is sacrificed for us." [76]

"Walk in love, as Christ also hath loved us, and hath given Himself for us an offering and a sacrifice to God tor a sweet smelling savour." [77]

"These are they which came out of great tribulation, and have washed their robes, and made them white in the blood of the Lamb. Therefore are they before the throne of God, and serve Him day and night in His temple: and He that sitteth on the throne shall dwell among them." [78]

"Almost all things are by the law purged with blood; and without shedding of blood is no remission. It was therefore necessary that the patterns of things in the heavens should be purified with these; but the heavenly things themselves with better sacrifices than these. For Christ is not entered into the holy places made with hands, which are the figures of the true; but into heaven itself, now to appear in the presence of God for us: nor yet that He should offer Himself often, as the high priest entereth into the holy place every year with blood of others; for then must He often have suffered since the foundation of the world: but now once in the end of the world hath He appeared to put away sin by the sacrifice of Himself. And as it is appointed unto men once to die, but after this the judgment: so Christ was once offered to bear the sins of many; and unto them that look for Him shall He appear the second time without sin unto salvation." [79]

"Every priest standeth daily ministering, and offering oftentimes the same sacrifices, which can never take away sins. But this man, after He had offered one sacrifice for sins, for ever sat down on the right hand of God; from henceforth expecting till His enemies be made His footstool. For by one offering He hath perfected for ever them that are sanctified." [80]

## V. Passages which connect our Lord's Sufferings with His Intercession.

I Tim. ii. 5, 6; i John ii. i, 2; Rev. v. 6; already quoted, reappear, and —

"He humbled Himself, and became obedient unto death, even the death of the cross. Wherefore God also hath highly exalted Him, and given Him a name which is above every name: that in the name of Jesus (not at) every knee should bow." [81]

## VI. Passages which Represent the Mediation of Christ

(1) As *procuring the gracious influence of the Holy Spirit.*

"Jesus spake this of the Spirit, which they that believe on Him should receive: for the Holy Ghost was not yet given; because that Jesus was not yet glorified." [82]

"It is expedient for you that I go away: for if I go not away, the Comforter will not come unto you; but if I depart, I will send Him unto you." [83]

"I will pray the Father, and He shall give you another Comforter, that He may abide with you for ever, even the Spirit of truth." [84]

"The Comforter,... whom I will send unto you from the Father." [85]

"The Holy Ghost, whom the Father will send in My name." [86]

"Therefore being by the right hand of God exalted, and having received of the Father the gift of the Holy Ghost, He hath shed forth this, which ye now see and hear." [87]

"Christ hath redeemed us from the curse of the law, being made a curse for us: (for it is written, Cursed is every one that hangeth on a tree): that the blessing of Abraham might come on the Gentiles through Jesus Christ; that we might receive the promise of the Spirit through faith." [88]

"Not by works of righteousness which we have done, but according to His mercy. He saved us, by the washing of regeneration and renewing of the Holy Ghost; which He shed on us abundantly through Jesus Christ our Saviour." [89]

(2) As *conferring all Christian graces which are fruits of the Spirit.*

"Of His fulness have all we received, and grace for grace." [90]

"Abide in Me, and I in you. As the branch cannot bear fruit of itself, except it abide in the vine; no more can ye, except ye abide in Me. I am the vine, ye are the branches: he that abideth in Me, and I in him, the same bringeth forth much fruit: for without Me ye can do nothing." [91]

"I thank my God always on your behalf, for the grace of God which is given you by Jesus Christ; that in everything ye are enriched by Him, in all utterance, and in all knowledge; even as the testimony of Christ was confirmed in you: so that ye come behind in no gift ." [92]

"Of Him are ye in Christ Jesus, who of God is made unto us wisdom, and righteousness, and sanctification, and redemption." [93]

"Blessed be the God and Father of our Lord Jesus Christ, who hath blessed us with all spiritual blessings in heavenly places in Christ: according as He hath chosen us in Him before the foundation of the world, that we should be holy and without blame before him in love." [94]

"We are His workmanship, created in Christ Jesus unto good works." [95]

"Unto every one of us is given grace according to the measure of the gift of Christ." [96]

"In Him dwelleth all the fulness of the Godhead bodily. And ye are complete in Him." [97]

(3) *As delivering us from the dominion of Satan.*

"For this purpose was the Son of God manifested, that He might destroy the works of the devil." [98]

"Now is the judgment of this world: now shall the prince of this world be cast out. And I, if I be lifted up from the earth, will draw all men unto me." [99]

"He took part of flesh and blood, that through death He might destroy Him that had the power of death, that is, the devil; and deliver them who through fear of death were all their lifetime subject to bondage." [100]

"And having spoiled principalities and powers, He made a show of them openly, triumphing over them in it." [101]

(4) *As obtaining for us eternal life.*

"The Son of man must be lifted up, that whosoever Delieveth in Him should not perish, but have eternal life." [102]

"Verily, verily, I say unto you, He that heareth My word, and believeth on Him that sent Me, hath everlasting life, and shall not come into condemnation; but is passed from death unto life." [103]

"This is the will of Him that sent me, that every one which seeth the Son, and believeth on Him, may have everlasting life: and I will raise him up at the last day." [104]

"Verily, verily, I say unto you, He that believeth on Me hath everlasting life." [105]

"I am the living bread that came down from heaven: if any man eat of this bread, he shall live for ever: and the bread which I shall give is My flesh, which I will give for the life of the world." [106]

"My sheep hear My voice, and I know them, and they follow Me: and I give unto them eternal life; and they shall never perish, neither shall any man pluck them out of My hand." [107]

"In My Father's house are many mansions: if it were not so, I would have told you. I go to prepare a place for you. And if I go and prepare a place for you, I will come again, and receive you unto Myself; that where I am, there ye may be also." [108]

"Father, the hour is come; glorify Thy Son, that Thy Son also may glorify thee: as Thou hast given Him power over all flesh, that He should give eternal life to as many as thou hast given Him." [109]

"Where sin abounded, grace did much more abound: that as sin hath reigned unto death, even so might grace reign through righteousness unto eternal life by Jesus Christ our Lord." [110]

"For the wages of sin is death; but the gift of God is eternal life through Jesus Christ our Lord." [111]

"I endure all things for the elect's sake, that they may also obtain the salvation which is in Christ Jesus with eternal glory." [112]

"Being made perfect. He became the author of eternal salvation unto all them that obey Him." [113]

"He is the mediator of the new testament, that by means of death, for the redemption of the transgressions that were under the old testament, they which are called might receive the promise of eternal inheritance." [114]

"The God of all grace hath called us unto His eternal glory by Christ Jesus." [115]

"This is' the record, that God hath given to us eternal life, and this life is in His Son." [116]

"Keep yourselves in the love of God, looking for the mercy of our Lord Jesus Christ unto eternal life." [117]

**VII. Passages which indicate the state of the Saviour's Mind in the Prospect and in the Endurance of His Sufferings.**

"I lay down My life, that I might take it again. No man taketh it from Me, but I lay it down of Myself. I have power to lay it down, and I have power to take it again." [118]

"I have a baptism to be baptised with; and how am I straitened till it be accomplished." [119]

"Now is my soul troubled; and what shall I say? Father, save Me from this hour: but for this cause came I unto this hour." [120]

"Then Jesus cometh with them unto a place called Gethsemane, and saith unto the disciples. Sit ye here, while I go and pray yonder. And He took with him Peter and the two sons of Zebedee, and began to be sorrowful and very heavy. Then saith He unto them, My soul is exceeding sorrowful, even unto death: tarry ye here, and watch with Me. And He went a little farther, and fell on His face, and prayed, saying, O My Father, if it be possible, let this cup pass from Me: nevertheless, not as I will, but as Thou wilt. And He cometh unto the disciples, and findeth them asleep, and saith unto Peter, What, could ye not watch with Me one hour? Watch and pray, that ye enter not into temptation: the spirit indeed is willing, but the flesh is weak. He went away again the second time, and prayed, saying, O my Father, if this cup may not pass away from Me except I drink it, Thy will be done. And He came and found them asleep again: for their eyes were heavy. And he left them, and went away again, and prayed the third time, saying the same words." [121]

"My God, My God, why hast thou forsaken me.?" [122]

## VIII. Passages which speak of the Mediation of Christ in relation

(1) *To the free calls and offers of the gospel.*

"I am the way, the truth, and the life: no man cometh unto the Father, but by Me." [123]

"Other foundation can no man lay than that is laid, which is Jesus Christ." [124]

"There is one God, and one mediator between God and men, the man Christ Jesus." [125]

"Neither is there salvation in any other: for there is none other name under heaven given among men, whereby we must be saved." [126]

(2) To *the necessity of faith in order to obtain the blessings of the gospel.*

"As many as received Him, to them gave He power to become the sons of God, even to them that believe on His name." [127]

"He that believeth on Him is not condemned: but he that believeth not is condemned already, because he hath not believed in the name of the only begotten Son of God." [128]

"He that believeth on the Son hath everlasting life: and he that believeth not the Son shall not see life; but the wrath of God abideth on him." [129]

"Jesus said unto them, I am the bread of life: he that cometh to Me shall never hunger; and he that believeth on Me shall never thirst." [130]

"Through this man is preached unto you the forgiveness of sins: and by Him all that believe are justified from all things, from which ye could not be justified by the law of Moses." [131]

"Believe on the Lord Jesus Christ, and thou shalt be saved." [132]

"I am not ashamed of the gospel of Christ: for it is the power of God unto salvation to every one that believeth." [133]

"Therefore we conclude that a man is justified by faith without the deeds of the law." [134]

"Being justified by faith, we have peace with God through our Lord Jesus Christ: by whom also we have access by faith into this grace wherein we stand, and rejoice in hope of the glory of God." [135]

"Christ is the end of the law for righteousness to every one that beheveth." [136]

"In Christ Jesus neither circumcision availeth anything, nor uncircumcision; but faith which worketh by love." [137]

"By grace are ye saved through faith; and that not of yourselves: it is the gift of God: not of works, lest any man should boast." [138]

**IX. Passages which speak of the Mediatorial Work and Sufferings of Christ in relation**

(1) To *His covenant with the Father.*

"I came down from heaven, not to do Mine own will, but the will of Him that sent Me. And this is the Father's will that sent Me, that of all which He hath given Me I should lose nothing, but should raise it up again at the last day. And this is the will of Him that sent Me, that every one which seeth the Son, and believeth on Him, may have everlasting life." [139]

"And the bread which I will give is My flesh, which I will give for the life of the world." [140]

(2) To *His union with believers.*

"Abide in Me and I in you." [141]

"If we have been planted together in the likeness of His death, we shall be also in the likeness of His resurrection." [142]

"Always bearing about in the body the dying of the Lord Jesus, that the life also of Jesus might be made manifest in our body." [143]

"I am crucified with Christ: nevertheless I live; yet not I, but Christ liveth in me: and the life which I now live in the flesh I live by the faith of the Son of God, who loved me, and gave Himself for me." [144]

"Quickened together with Christ, and raised to sit together in heavenly places in Christ." [145]

"That I may know Him, and the power of His resurrection, and the fellowship of His sufferings, being made conformable unto His death." [146]

"Buried with Him in baptism, wherein also ye are risen with Him." [147]

"Your life is hid with Christ in God." [148]

**X. Passages which speak of the Death of Christ**

(1) As *a manifestation of the love of God.*

"God so loved the world, that He gave His only begotten Son, that whosoever believeth in Him should not perish, but have everlasting life." [149]

"God commendeth His love toward us, in that, while we were yet sinners, Christ died for us." [150]

"He that spared not His own Son, but delivered Him up for us all, how shall He not with Him also freely give us all things?" [151]

"In this was manifested the love of God toward us, because that God sent His only begotten Son into the world, that we might live through Him. Herein is love, not that we loved God, but that He loved us, and sent His Son to be the propitiation for our sins." [152]

(2) As *furnishing an example of patience and resignation.*

"Let us run with patience the race that is set before us, looking unto Jesus,... who endured the cross, despising the shame.... Consider him that endured such contradiction of sinners against Himself, lest we be wearied and faint in our souls." [153]

"If when ye do well, and suffer for it, ye take it patiently, this is acceptable with God. For even hereunto were ye called: because Christ also suffered for us, leaving us an example, that ye should follow His steps." [154]

"If any man will come after Me, let him deny himself, and take up his cross daily, and follow Me. For whosoever will save his life shall lose it: but whosoever will lose his life for My sake, the same shall save it." [155]

(3) As *designed to promote our sanctification,*

"For their sakes I sanctify myself, that they also might be sanctified through the truth." [156]

"By the which will we are sanctified through the offering of the body of Jesus Christ once for all" [157]

"Jesus, that He might sanctify the people with His own blood, suffered without the gate." [158]

"He died for all, that they which live should not henceforth live unto themselves, but unto Him which died for them, and rose again." [159]

"Who gave Himself for our sins, that He might deliver us from this present evil world." [160]

"Christ loved the church and gave Himself for it; that He might sanctify and cleanse it with the washing of water by the word, that He might present it to Himself a glorious church, not having spot, or wrinkle, or any such thing j but that it should be holy and without blemish." [161]

"He gave Himself for us, that He might redeem us from all iniquity, and purify unto Himself a peculiar people, zealous of good works." [162]

"Who His own self bare our sins in His own body on the tree, that we, being dead to sins, might live unto righteousness." [163]

[1] Francisci Turretini: *De Satisfactione Christi Disputationes.* Geneva, 1667, Opera, vol. iv. p. i.

[2] Matt. xx. 28.
[3] Luke xxii. 19.
[4] Ibid xxii. 19, 20.
[5] John vi. 51.

[6] Ibid x. 11, 15, 18.
[7] Ibid xv. 12, 13.
[8] Rom. v. 6-8.
[9] Ibid, viii, 32.

[10] 2 Cor. v. 14, 15.
[11] Ibid. v. 21.
[12] Gal. ii. 20.
[13] Ibid. iii. 13.
[14] Eph. v. 2, 25.
[15] 1 Thess. v. 9. 10.
[16] 1 Tim. ii. 5, 6.
[17] Titus ii. 13, 14.
[18] Heb. ii. 9.
[19] I Pet. ill. 18.
[20] I John ill. 16.
[21] Rom. iv. 25.
[22] Ibid. viii. 3.
[23] Cor. xv. 3.
[24] Gal. i. 4.
[25] Heb. x. 12.
[26] I Pet. iii. 18.
[27] Isa. liii. 5, 8.
[28] Heb. ix. 28.
[29] I Pet. ii. 24.
[30] Isa. liii. 6, 11, 12.
[31] 2 Cor. v. 21.
[32] Gal. iii. 13.
[33] John i. 29.
[34] Heb, ix. 26.
[35] Matt. xxvi. 28.
[36] 1 John i. 7.
[37] Luke xxiv. 46, 47.
[38] Acts x. 43.
[39] Ibid. xiii. 38, 39.
[40] Eph. i. 6, 7.
[41] Col. i. 13, 14.
[42] Rev. i. 5, 6.
[43] John iii. 14-17.
[44] 1 Thess. v. 9, 10.
[45] Isa. liii. 11.
[46] Rom. v. 8. 9.
[47] Ibid, iii. 24-26.
[48] Matt xx. 28.
[49] Acts xx. 28.
[50] Rom. iii. 23, 24.
[51] 1 Cor. vi. 19.
[52] Eph. i. 7.
[53] Col. i. 14.
[54] Heb. ix. 12.
[55] I Pet. 1. 18, 19.
[56] Rev. v. 9.

[57] Rom. v. 10.
[58] Rom. v. 11.
[59] 2 Cor. v. 18, 19.
[60] Eph. ii. 16.
[61] Col. i. 21, 22.
[62] 1 John ii. 2.
[63] 1 John iv. 10.
[64] Heb. ii. 17.
[65] Rom. iii. 25.
[66] Psa. cx. 4.
[67] Heb. iii. 1.
[68] Ibid. ii. 17.
[69] Ibid. x. 21.
[70] Ibid. iv. 14.
[71] Ibid, vii. 26.
[72] Ibid. v. 1.
[73] Ibid. vii. 22.
[74] Rom. v. 12, 18, 19.
[75] 1 Cor. xv. 20-22, 45-49.
[76] 1 Cor. v. 7.
[77] Eph. v. ii.
[78] Rev. vii. 14, 15.
[79] Heb. ix. 22-28.
[80] Ibid. x. 11-14.
[81] Phil. ii. 8, 9, 10.
[82] John vii. 39.
[83] Ibid. xvi. 7.
[84] Ibid. xiv. 16, 17.
[85] Ibid. xv. 26.
[86] Ibid. xiv. 26.
[87] Acts ii. 33.
[88] Gal. iii. 13. 14.
[89] Titus iii. 5, 6.
[90] John i. 16.
[91] John xv. 4, 5.
[92] 1 Cor. i. 4-7.
[93] Ibid. i. 30.
[94] Eph. i, 3, 4.
[95] Ibid. ii. 10.
[96] Ibid. iv. 7.
[97] Col. ii. 9, 10.
[98] I John iii. 8.
[99] John xii. 31, 32.
[100] Heb. ii. 14, 15.
[101] Col. ii. 15.
[102] John iii. 14, 15.

[103] John v. 24.
[104] Ibid. vi. 40.
[105] Ibid. vi. 47.
[106] Ibid. vi. 51.
[107] Ibid. x. 27, 28.
[108] Ibid. xiv. 2, 3.
[109] Ibid. xvii. i, 2.
[110] Rom. v. 20, 21.
[111] Rom. vi. 23.
[112] 2 Tim. ii. 10.
[113] Heb. v. 9.
[114] Ibid. ix. 15.
[115] 1 Pet. v. 10.
[116] 1 John v. 11.
[117] Jude 21.
[118] John x. 17, 18.
[119] Luke xii. 50.
[120] John xii. 27.
[121] Matt. xxvi. 36-44.
[122] Matt. xxvii. 46.
[123] John xiv. 6.
[124] 1 Cor. iii. 11.
[125] 1 Tim. ii. 5.
[126] Acts iv. 12.
[127] John i. 13.
[128] Ibid. iii. 18.
[129] Ibid. iii. 36.
[130] Ibid. vi. 35.
[131] Acts xiii. 38, 39.
[132] Ibid. xvi. 31.
[133] Rom. i. 16.
[134] Ibid. iii. 28.
[135] Rom v. 12.
[136] Rom. x. 4.
[137] Gal. v. 6.
[138] Eph. ii. 8, 9.
[139] John vi. 38-40.
[140] Ibid. vi. 51.
[141] John xv. 4.
[142] Rom. vi. 5.
[143] 2 Cor. iv. 10.
[144] Gal. ii. 20.
[145] Eph. ii. 5, 6.
[146] Phil. iii. 10.
[147] Col. ii. 12.
[148] Col. iii. 3.
[149] John iii. 16.

[150] Rom. v. 8.
[151] Ibid. viii. 32.
[152] 1 John iv. 9, 10.
[153] Heb. xii. 1-3.
[154] I Pet. ii. 20, 21.

[155] Luke ix. 23, 24.
[156] John xvii. 19.
[157] Heb. x. 10.
[158] Ibid. xiii. 12.
[159] 2 Cor. v. 15.

[160] Gal. i, 4.
[161] Eph. v. 25-27.
[162] Tit. ii. 14.
[163] I Pet. ii. 24.

## *Note C*

The controversy on the testimony of the Baptist, "Behold the Lamb of God that taketh away the sin of the world," turns on two points: — (1) What was the precise force of the testimony? (2) How did John come to regard our Lord as the Lamb of God?

(1) That John described our Lord as the Lamb of God, because of the patience and gentleness with which He would endure the evils which were to come upon Him in fulfilling His mission — an interpretation for which the names of Paulus, Gabler, Kuinol, and Ewald, are alleged — is inconsistent with the critical words, "which taketh away the sin of the world." There must be some relation between the descriptive name which is given to Christ and the work which is ascribed to Him. A lamb might very naturally be selected as a symbol of meekness; but why should Christ because of His meekness be described as "taking away the sin of the world"? So interpreted, the testimony is not homogeneous. John had been accustomed to describe our Lord as "mightier" than himself; had he intended to say that the Christ, by the power of His teaching, or of His character, or of the Spirit with which He would baptise men, would deliver them from sin, there would surely have been a reassertion of our Lord's *power;* but power is not an idea associated with a lamb. Moreover, whenever in other passages the Lord Jesus Christ is described as a lamb by the sacred writers, whenever there is any comparison between Him and a lamb, it is on the ground of His sacrificial death. It seems unreasonable, therefore? to exclude the sacrificial idea from the testimony of the Baptist.

Old Testament usage is altogether against interpreting John as meaning that our Lord — as a "lamb" — was to take away sin by His moral and spiritual influence. In Exod. xxxiv. 7, we have ἀφαιρῶν ἀνομίας applied to God in the sense of removing sin in the way of forgiveness. In 1 Sam. xv. 28, Saul appeals to Samuel and says, "I pray thee pardon my sin" (ἆρον δὴ τὸ ἁμαρτημά μου). In 1 Sam. XXV. 28, Abigail, speaking to David, says, "I pray thee forgive the trespass (ἆρον δὴ τὸ ἁμαρτημά) of thine handmaid." If John the Baptist did not mean that Christ was to lift up from the world the burden of its sin by forgiving it — an inconceivable hypothesis when He is described as "the Lamb of God," — John must have meant that He would lift up the burden of sin by expiating it. The αἴρων represents the נָשָׂא of the Old Testament. Had the Baptist followed the usage of the LXX., which in passages where parts of נָשָׂא denote the *bearing of sin* — *i.e.,* the bearing of its punishment — uses

220

corresponding parts of λαμβάνω or φέρω, he would have failed to convey his precise idea. He was not thinking so much of our Lord's taking our sins upon Himself, as of His taking them from us. We might, however, have used the participle of ἀφάιρω, as the LXX. in Lev. x. 17. The testimony includes the *result* as well as the *act* of expiation.

By the taking away of the sin of the world (ὁ αἴρων τὴν ἁμαρτίαν τοῦ κόσμου) we must not understand that John meant simply that our Lord was to *bear* the sin of the world. What he means is that Christ was to take up the sin of the world to carry it away. The burden that had been weighing on men so heavily, and which they had no strength to bear, Christ was to lift up and remove. The sin was laid upon the Sacrifice, in order to be removed from the sinner.

The sacrificial idea being conceded, there is still some uncertainty as to the Baptist's meaning. It has been maintained by a long succession of authorities that St. John intended to describe our Lord as the true Paschal Lamb. The probability of this interpretation would be greatly strengthened if the suggestion of Bengel could be defended, that a Feast of the Passover was near. It appears, however, that two days after the testimony was given our Lord was on His way to Galilee. [1] On "the third day" — whether after the testimony now given, or after the conversation with Nathanael — He was at Cana: "after that He went down to Capernaum," where He remained for a short time. Then St. John tells us that as "the Jews' Passover was at hand," Jesus went up to Jerusalem, [2] and He seems to have arrived there before the feast actually began. The time He spent in Capernaum is doubtful, but had the Passover been near when the Baptist gave his testimony, it does not seem probable that our Lord would have gone northward to Galilee instead of southward to Jerusalem. Hengstenberg [3] endeavours to make a strong point of the fact that, while John the Baptist speaks of Christ as a sin-offering, lambs were rarely offered as sin-offerings — the great exception, as he contends, being the lamb of the Passover. That the paschal lamb was a vicarious sacrifice, and that the Israelites, in whose houses the paschal lamb had been slain, escaped the doom which would otherwise have come upon them, is obvious; but it is not so clear that the paschal lamb was regarded as being in the ordinary sense of the term an offering for sin, nor do I know that it was so described in the Old Testament. In the ritual of the Passover [4] there is nothing said about the confession of sins and the laying the hands of the offerer upon the head of the victim, in order to express the transfer of his sins to the sacrifice. Had the Baptist spoken of Christ as the Lamb of God slain for the redemption of the world, the allusion to the paschal lamb would have been obvious: as it is, the allusion seems more than doubtful. Those who listened to him could hardly have caught it.

Another interpretation, which is also supported by a strong array of authorities, discovers in the testimony a reference to Isa. liii. But had the Baptist intended to make a direct reference to this great prophecy, it seems probable that he would have described Christ — not as the Lamb of God — but as the *Servant* of God. It is true that in ver. 7 the *Servant* of God is described as being "brought as a lamb to the slaughter;" and it is added that "as a sheep before her shearers is dumb, so He openeth not His mouth;" but these are incidental allusions. The prophet does not conceive of the great Sufferer as a sacrificial lamb, but as "a man of sorrows and acquainted with grief," who is not merely sacrificed, as were the sacrificial victims, with as little pain as possible, but is "stricken,...smitten,...afflicted, ...wounded,...bruised:" "chastisement" is inflicted upon Him, and He has to submit to "stripes."

The most natural theory seems to be that John had somehow come to know that the sufferings of the Messiah predicted in the Old Testament, sufferings to be endured because of our sins, were to be endured by Christ, and were to be endured by Him in order to "take away our sins;" and that, wishing to describe Him as a sacrifice for sin, John felt instinctively that among the sacrificial victims the fittest symbol of the meek and gentle personality of our Lord was the lamb.

2. But how did John come to think of our Lord as a sacrifice for sin? Very much has been written to show that the idea of a suffering Messiah was not altogether foreign to Jewish thought in our Lord's time, and that the idea that the death of saints may constitute an expiation for the sins of the nation, is also to be discovered in uninspired Jewish literature. [5] It seems, however, extremely doubtful whether *before our Lord's baptism* John had any idea that the Christ whose coming he had been commissioned to announce would atone by His Death for the sins of men. In the earlier preaching of the Baptist the Messiah is a Messiah of power and even of terror. He is to baptise with the Holy Ghost; He is to burn up the chaff with unquenchable fire; the Baptist himself is not worthy to unloose the strap of His sandal; the Messiah is mightier than His forerunner. *After the baptism of our Lord* John's testimony included new elements. Among the rest, it included his description of Christ as "the Lamb of God which taketh away the sin of the world." When our Lord came to John to submit to baptism, John shrank from administering it to Him. He had no sins to confess or to forsake - why should He be baptised? Our Lord said, "Suffer it to be so now, for thus it becometh us to fulfil all righteousness." Is it unreasonable to suppose that after the baptism was over, John was anxious to learn what Jesus meant by identifying Himself with the extortionate publicans and the rapacious soldiery? Is it unreasonable to suppose that our Lord - who in submitting to the rite of baptism, must have had what we may almost venture to describe as a new consciousness of the terrible nature of the work He had undertaken - told John that He had come to redeem the world from sin by making the sin of the world, in some sense. His own.

However clear the meaning of such passages in the Old Testament as Isaiah liii. may seem to us; whatever may have been the speculations of Jewish Rabbis about a suffering and atoning Messiah— a Messiah Ben Joseph, whose death was to be the condition of the glorious triumphs of the Messiah Ben David, [6] — or about the atoning sufferings of the Messiah in Paradise before His appearance on earth; [7] or about the atonement which the Messiah was to accomplish on earth while He was unknown, and befoie He asserted His claims to the throne of David; [8] there is nothing in the four Gospels, at least, to suggest that the idea had taken hold of the popular mind; and even our Lord's disciples, who knew of John's testimony, do not seem to have apprehended the prediction it contained of their Master's sufferings. Had the idea of a suffering Christ been a really active element in the Jewish mind, it is difficult to believe that after John had uttered such words as these, the disciples should have failed to receive any deep impression from our Lord's repeated references to His Death.

[1] John i. 43, compared with John i. 35.
[2] Ibid ii. 13.
[3] *Commentary on the Gospel of St. John*, vol. i. 76.
[4] Exod. xii. 21-28; Deut. xvi. 1-8.
[5] See Hengstenberg: *Christology of the Old Testament,* vol. iv. 347-364; Dr. Reynolds: *John the Baptist,* 374, 375.
[6] See Hengstenberg: *Christology,* vol. iv. 357, seq.
[7] Ibid. 362.
[8] Ibid. 362.

## *Note D*

In *A Treatise on the Physical Cause of the Death of Christ,* by William Stroud, M.D., [1] the proof that our Lord's Death was the immediate result of mental agony is elaborated with great skill and learning. His theory is stated in the following paragraphs at the commencement of part 1. chap. 4: —

"In the preceding chapter it is presumed to have been demonstrated that neither the ordinary sufferings of crucifixion, nor the wound inflicted by the soldier's spear, nor an unusual degree of weakness, nor the interposition of supernatural influence, was the immediate cause of the Saviour's Death. The first of these conditions was inadequate, the second followed instead of preceding the effect, and the third and the fourth had no existence. What then, it will be asked, was the real cause?

"In conformity with the inductive principles announced at the commencement of this inquiry, it must have been a known power in nature, possessing the requisite efficacy, agreeing with all the circumstances of the case, and by suitable tests proved to have been present without counteraction. It will be the object of the ensuing observations to show that the power in which these characters perfectly and exclusively concurred was **agony of mind, producing rupture of the heart**. To establish this conclusion numerous details will be adduced, but the argument itself is short and simple. In the Garden of Gethsemane, Christ endured mental agony so intense, that had it not been limited by Divine interposition, it would probably have destroyed His life without the aid of any other sufferings; but having been thus mitigated, its effects were confined to violent palpitation of the heart, accompanied with bloody sweat. On the cross this agony was renewed, in conjunction with the ordinary sufferings incidental to that mode of punishment; and having at this time been allowed to proceed to its utmost extremity without restraint, occasioned sudden death by rupture of the heart, intimated by a discharge of blood and water from His side, when it was afterwards pierced with a spear."

The doubts which have been thrown on the genuineness of Luke xxii. 43, 44 (including the words, "His sweat was as it were great drops of blood falling down to the ground") do not affect the force of the general argument.

Although for many years Dr. Stroud's argument had seemed to me perfectly conclusive, I was glad to have it confirmed by the singularly interesting letters from high medical authorities appended to Dr. Hanna's *Last Day of our Lord's Passion*. [2]  Dr. James Begbie, Fellow and late President of the Royal College of Physicians of Edinburgh, writes: [3] "I cannot help accepting as correct the explanation which Dr. Stroud has offered — and which you have adopted, and so strikingly applied— of the physical cause of the death of Christ, namely, rupture of the heart, and consequent effusion of blood into the pericardium, the investing sheath of that organ."

Dr. J. Y. Simpson, Professor of Medicine and Midwifery in the University of Edinburgh, regards the theory as having the strongest probabilities in its favour. He says: [4] "Ever since reading, some ten or twelve years ago, Dr. Stroud's remarkable treatise *On the Physical Cause of the Death of Christ,* I have been strongly impressed with the belief that the views which he adopted and maintained on this subject are fundamentally correct. Nor has this opinion been in any way altered by a perusal of some later observations published on the same question, both here and on the Continent.

"That the immediate cause of the Death of our blessed Saviour was — speaking medically — laceration or rupture of the heart, is a doctrine in regard to which there can be no absolute certainty; but, assuredly, in favour of it, there is a very high amount of circumstantial probability." He adds: [5] "No medical jurist would, in a court of law, venture to assert, from the mere symptoms preceding death, that a person had certainly died of rupture of the heart. To obtain positive *proof* that rupture of the heart was the cause of death, a *post-mortem* examination of the chest would be necessary. In ancient times such dissections were not practised. But the details left regarding Christ's Death are most strikingly peculiar in this respect, that they offer us the result of a very rude dissection, as it were, by the gash made in His side after death by the thrust of the Roman soldier's spear. The effect of that wounding or piercing of the side was an escape of blood and water, visible to the Apostle John, standing some distance off; and I do not believe that anything could possibly account for this appearance as described by that Apostle, except a collection of blood effused into the distended sac of the pericardium in consequence of rupture of the heart, and afterwards separated, as is usual with *extravasated* blood, into those two parts, viz., (1) crassamentum or red clot, and (2) watery serum. The subsequent puncture from below of the distended pericardial sac would most certainly, under such circumstances, lead to the immediate ejection and escape of its sanguineous contents in the form of red clots of blood and a stream of watery serum, exactly corresponding to that description given in the sacred narrative, 'and forthwith came there out blood and water,' an appearance which no other natural event or mode of death can explain or account for."

The letter of Dr. John Struthers, Lecturer on Anatomy Surgeons' Hall, may be given at length.

"Dear Dr. Hanna, — I do not think that any intelligent medical man will read Dr. Stroud's treatise *On the Physical Cause of the Death of Christ*, without being satisfied with the explanation. No other hypothesis will satisfactorily explain the separate escape of blood and water from a wound in that region, and all the incidents attending the death of Christ are entirely accounted for by the hypothesis of rupture of the heart, and the separation of the watery and the red constituents of the blood within the distended pericardium, on the puncture of which they would escape forcibly. The various cases of rupture of the heart from mental emotion, with similar separation of the watery and the red parts of the blood, collected by Dr. Stroud, and also his cases of bloody sweat, form a body of extremely interesting illustration and proof, and altogether the treatise is a monument of careful research and cautious reasoning.

"To medical men it has a special additional value, as accounting for incidents which force themselves upon the medical mind for explanation. Those of my brethren who have not read Dr. Stroud's book, must be much puzzled, as I was before I had read it, to account for the escape of water after, and distinct from, blood, from a wound in that part of the body — supposing the words 'blood and water' to be accepted literally, which there need be no hesitation now in doing. Of course the rupture of the heart is in every aspect the great point of interest, the escape of the blood and water being of importance only as an incident which, having been seen, requires explanation, and as further bearing on the previous rupture of the heart.

"To all, Dr. Stroud's treatise must be interesting, not as raising or gratifying curiosity, but as an intelligent explanation of the incidents themselves, and, still more, as a new illustration of the awful agony which our Redeemer must have suffered. I was indebted to you for first bringing Dr. Stroud's book under my notice, and I have since repeatedly recommended it to the notice of my medical friends and students. I find lately that the first edition is now exhausted, and hope that it will not be long before a new edition of so valuable a work makes its appearance. — Believe me with much respect, yours very sincerely, "John Struthers."

[1] London: Hamilton and Adams, 1847.

[2] Edinburgh: Edmonston and Douglas, seventeenth edition, 1868.

[3] Page 333.

[4] Pp. 335, 336.

[5] Pp. 337. 338.

# Note E

For an extremely able and learned account of Jewish sacrifices, see *The Typology of Scripture,* [1] by Patrick Fairbairn, D.D.

In *The Jewish Temple and Christian Church* [2] I have given a sketch of the various kinds of Levitical sacrifices that had relation to transgressions of the Jewish law, [3] and have discussed their relation to the Idea of Atonement. In illustration of the statement in the text that no sacrifices secured forgiveness for specific moral offences, I extract two or three passages in which the apparent exceptions to the rule are considered and explained.

"If a man had knowingly failed to bear testimony in a court of law against men whom he knew to be justly accused of a crime, he was required to confess his sin and to bring a lamb or a kid for a sin-offering; or, if he was poor, two turtle-doves or two young pigeons, or a small quantity of fine flour; and then his sin was to be forgiven . The moral element in this case would generally be very slight and insignificant. Desirable as it is that all who know anything that would inculpate a guilty man should bear their testimony at his trial, I suppose that there are many circumstances which most of us would regard as morally releasing us from the obligation to volunteer adverse evidence; and many suppose that it was for the neglect of this that the offering was to make atonement and obtain pardon. But even if the law refers to the case of one who has actually been a witness in court, but has been silent on what would have demonstrated the guilt of the accused, the silence would commonly be occasioned by natural affection, by friendship, by generous compassion for the guilty; and though a sin against the State would, when morally considered, be a very slight offence, the telling half the truth when a man had promised to tell all, equivocation, falsehood, perjury, could not be cancelled by the offering of a lamb, or by any offering at all. The concealment of damaging evidence to which the provision of the law points, was not an act of falsehood, but a want of adequate zeal for the infliction of just penalties on the guilty. If the man's repentance of his omission was sufficient to lead him to confess and to provide the sacrifice, his failure might well be forgiven. This law is an indication of the firmness and resoluteness with which the whole nation was to unite in the administration of criminal justice, rather than of any tendency in the Jewish law to relax moral obligations by promising forgiveness, on the bare ground of a ritual sacrifice, to what we call sin.

"If a man had sworn an oath to do good or to do evil, the force of which he did not at the time perceive, or which he was unable, unwilling, or forbidden by the Divine law to perform, he had to bring the same sin-offering as in the case last mentioned, and was assured of forgiveness. Among ourselves, if a man 'pronounce with his lips' words whose meaning and purpose he does not apprehend, utters a vow in a state of intoxication, for instance, utters it under some transitory delusion, utters it under the influence of deception practised upon him by others, it would not be considered binding at all. His soul is under no obligation; his lips, not his will, have offended. But the Jewish lawgiver, solicitous for the sanctity of holy things, does not permit him to retreat from his oath without acknowledging his involuntary error, and bringing the appointed sacrifice: then he might retreat and be forgiven. This cannot be regarded as a case of a moral offence actually forgiven because a sacrifice has been offered."

Again: "If a man who had received property in trust was guilty of fraud in relation to it; or committed a fraud against his partner in business; or dishonestly kept lost property which he had found; or by an oath unjustly deprived another of property; or, finally, by any deception, or by any high-handed wrong-doing, enriched himself at another's expense, he was to bring a trespass-offering and restore the property, adding to it a fifth of its value, and the sin was to be forgiven. It is rather startling to find that actual pardon was promised for crimes like these upon making compensation and bringing the sacrifice; but a little consideration may perhaps diminish the surprise. It is clear that the law did not apply to those whose crimes had been detected by others, or could be punished by public justice. Severer penalties than these were inflicted by the magistrate. The thief, if brought before the public tribunals, had to restore, according to circumstances, twofold, fourfold, or fivefold what he had taken, or was sold into bondage. Breach of trust, or denying the possession of property that had been found, was punished by requiring the restitution of double its value. But if a man guilty of any of these crimes had not been brought before the magistrate, or, through defective testimony, or judicial feebleness or corruption, had escaped the penalty, this law of the trespass-offering appealed to his conscience to make public confession of his guilt, to implore God's pardon by sacrifice, and to make adequate compensation to him who had been wronged. If conscience responded to this appeal — if he was able to overcome the natural shame which would prevent him from publicly acknowledging his crime, if he restored the property, augmented by a fifth of its value, his repentance might surely be accepted as genuine. He could give no further proof of the reality of his sorrow than this voluntary confession and voluntary restoration. He was therefore assured of forgiveness.

"But this is not an instance of a crime being pardoned simply on the ground of a sacrifice being offered. The consequences of the crime were voluntarily and completely repaired; a heavy pecuniary penalty was voluntarily borne, and public shame was voluntarily endured, in obedience to the Divine law. Nothing is said in the rubric of the trespass-offering concerning the necessity of repentance to make the sacrifice effectual; the reality of the repentance is naturally and justly taken for granted. The object of the law was to encourage restitution when wrong had been done, and to remind the wrong-doer that the Divine displeasure had to be averted, as well as compensation given to the victim of injustice.

"There was one other case in which a trespass-offering was required. If a man committed adultery with his slave, the crime was not to be punished by the death of both, as was the law when both were free; but there was to be a scourging, not of the woman only, as our version has it, but perhaps of both, or still more probably of the man only, and then he was to bring a trespass-offering and to be forgiven. This assurance of pardon, apart from any guarantee of repentance for a real crime, stands alone in the Jewish law: its exceptional position would justify us, I think, in passing it over in a general estimate of the efficacy and results of animal sacrifice. Perhaps we ought to regard the provision as primarily intended not to provide atonement and secure pardon, but as one of the numerous arrangements by which the Mosaic system endeavoured to soften and to elevate the condition of the slave. It is clear that the relation of a master to his slaves involved the same evils in the early ages of the world that it involves now; and the Jewish lawgiver, unable to break down the atrocious system by the force of mere authority, so regulated it as to diminish its hardships, and gradually to develop a recognition of the indestructible right to personal freedom of every man who has not been guilty of a crime. The scourging was the physical penalty of the offence; the trespass-offering reminded the wrong-doer that he had both violated the rights of another and provoked the anger of God. But the difficulty of this case I frankly admit.

"Speaking generally, neither sin-offering nor trespass-offering could, when offered by an individual, assure forgiveness to the guilty for any sins committed either against God or man. They removed ceremonial defilement which had been unavoidably, involuntarily, or unconsciously incurred; but provided no atonement and secured no pardon for intentional violation of even ceremonial precepts. They gave rest to the conscience for unconscious trifling with holy things, or neglecting to aid in the administration of justice; but provided no atonement and secured no pardon for breaking solemn vows, or disregarding the sanctity of an oath. They gave assurance of God's forgiveness when, through ignorance, God's claims on property had not been satisfied, and this only on condition that more was consecrated to Him on the discovery of the offence than the law originally required; but provided no atonement and secured no pardon for intentional sacrilege. In certain special cases of injustice they obtained God's mercy when the wrong had been actually undone by voluntary restitution to the injured, and the shame of public confession had been voluntarily endured; but provided no atonement and secured no pardon for the innumerable sins against God or against man which cannot actually be undone by subsequent acts of reparation. The only moral offences which God forgave on the mere offering of a sacrifice, were offences freely acknowledged, offences not symbolically but actually atoned for and cancelled by voluntary restitution. God forgave only when by the voluntary act of the guilty the victim of injustice no longer suffered from the crime. If, when a man had told a lie, or committed a sensual sin, or intentionally neglected any religious duty, he had been directed to procure a sacrifice — no instruction, however clear, however authoritative, however solemn, to the effect that apart from interior repentance and trust in the Divine mercy the sacrifice would be unavailing, could have prevented men coming to regard the mere ceremonial act as an easy means of blotting out the moral offence. Iniquity would have been established by a law. The moral sense of the nation would have been enfeebled and paralysed by the natural influence of its religious institutions."

The ceremonial of the great Day of Atonement is illustrated on pages 196-201.

[1] Fourth edition. Edinburgh: T. & T. Clark, 1864. Vol. ii. 317-392.
[2] Second edition. London: Hodder and Stoughton, 1871.
[3] Pp. 186-204.

## *Note F*

It would be worth while to trace the direct influence of Isaiah liii. on the mind of our Lord Himself and of His first disciples. St. Matthew [1] recognises in the miracles of our Lord the fulfilment of Isaiah liii. 4. St. Mark [2] recognises in His crucifixion between two thieves the fulfilment of Isaiah liii. 12. St. Luke [3] represents our Lord as saying that "this that is written of Me must yet be accomplished, And He was numbered among the transgressors." [4] St. John [5] finds in the unbelief of the Jews the fulfilment of Isaiah liii. i. Philip [6] finds the eunuch reading Isaiah liii. 7, and "he began at the same scripture, and preached unto him Jesus." St. Paul [7] finds in, "Who hath believed our report?" [8] an anticipation of His own sorrowful experience — "They have not all obeyed the gospel." In his First Epistle to the Corinthians, his statement that "Christ died for our sins, according to the scriptures," [9] looks like a direct allusion to Isaiah liii. 5, 6, 8. A passage of some length in St. Peter [10] is partly a quotation and partly a paraphrase of Isaiah liii. 5, 6.

[1] Matt. viii. 17.
[2] Mark xv. 28.
[3] Luke xxii. 37.
[4] Isa. liii. 12.

[5] John xii. 38.
[6] Acts viii. 32.
[7] Rom. x. 16.
[8] Isa. liii. i.

[9] 1 Cor. xv. 3.
[10] 1 Pet, ii. 22-25.

## *Note G*

The Rev. Stopford Brooke, in the first of the two sermons on the Atonement contained in his *Freedom in the Church of England*, [1] has given an explanation of our Lord's cry on the cross, which, if it could be sustained, would go far to invalidate the argument of Lectures ii. and iii. The explanation is of a kind to be extremely attractive to many devout persons who shrink from the expiatory theory of the Atonement.

Mr. Brooke begins by laying down the principle that "this cry of Christ's, as all His acts, was at once individual and universal; was the cry of a man and the cry of humanity." [2] As the "cry of a man" — "a personal utterance," he speaks of its exquisite truth to human nature, [3] and calls special attention to "the way in which, unconsciously, He identified His suffering with that of another man," by making the words of an ancient Jewish psalmist the expression of His sorrow. [4] As I find no clear explanation in the earlier pages of the sermon of what it was that forced this personal cry from our Lord, I am obliged to look for it later on, and in pages 38, 39, there is the following passage: "During those awful hours Christ was, as perfect man, and sensitive in proportion to His perfect humanity, face to face with death, and with death accompanied with torture, with loneliness, with undeserved bitterness of enemies, with the sense of wrong. It was impossible for Him not to realise that that which had nailed Him there was the sinfulness of man. It was impossible for Him not to feel that all this pain and misery and death itself which He was suffering was caused on earth by sin, and that these things were the judgment of God on account of sin. But at the same time He must have also felt that He Himself was sinless. No consciousness of personal sin, no remorse passed across His soul. He was suffering the natural penalties of sin, and yet He knew that He did not deserve them, and feeling this — feeling at one with God in spirit, and yet enduring the consequences of man's evil — how could the cry help coming to His lips, 'My God, My God, why hast Thou forsaken Me?' This was the personal cry, and this we reverently suppose its cause."

I submit that the explanation is inadequate. If this is all, the cry may be marked by its "exquisite truth to human nature," but it is not true to the character of Christ or to the facts of the spiritual universe. Could *Christ* have felt, even for a moment, that the sufferings inflicted upon Him by the hands of lawless men, the physical anguish of the cross, the public scorn to which he was exposed, were in any sense the sign that God had forsaken Him? Had He not said to His disciples, "Blessed are ye when men shall revile you and persecute;...rejoice and be exceeding glad, for great is your reward in heaven: for so persecuted they the prophets which were before you"? [5] Had He not also told them that the world would hate them as it hated Him; and that in hating Him men had hated the Father also? [6] It is true that when great trouble has come upon a man, other men have been very apt to suppose that the sufferer is the special object of God's anger. But this is what Mr. Brooke, in his second sermon on the Atonement in the same volume, justly calls the world's "stupid maxim." Mr. Brooke continues: "Suffering does *not* always prove God's anger;" [7] and Christ knew that His own suffering did not prove God's anger. He knew it, on the cross, as perfectly as He had ever known it. The world's "stupid maxim," which too often perverts our thoughts of the sufferings of others, and which sometimes perverts our thoughts of our own sufferings, had no place in the mind and heart of Christ. Such an utterance as that on the cross — had it been the result of the kind of suffering by which, as a personal cry, Mr. Brooke accounts for it — would have been altogether inconsistent with the normal character of our Lord.

But the cry was also *"the cry of humanity,"* the cry of One who "felt Himself then as the impersonation of the whole race, who spoke to God and acted before God as the whole of humanity in one man." [8] Mr. Brooke conceives Christ as *passing through the channel* of His personal sorrow away from it altogether, and identifying Himself with the same sorrow as felt by all mankind. What men in all ages had felt when trials like His own had come upon them, what, apart from Himself, men in all future ages would feel under the strain of similar trials, came into the soul of Christ through His intense sympathy with mankind. "Into the whole sense of this vast human suffering, Christ, losing the consciousness of Himself and of His own pain, through the intensity of His sympathy with us, threw Himself — and so realising it as His own, offered it up to the pity and love of God, and cried, as the expression of all this sorrow of mankind to God, 'My God, My God, why hast Thou forsaken *Me*, forsaken man?'" [9]

This is an intelligible hypothesis, but as it stands it is imperfect, and Mr. Brooke himself supplies its imperfection a page or two later; but in completing the hypothesis he destroys it. He thinks it necessary, indeed, to qualify even this half of his theory as soon as he has stated it. "We must carefully distinguish the feeling of being forsaken from the reality." Man has *felt* that he was abandoned by God; but in reality God has never abandoned him. Christ, he alleges, recognised this, "even when by self-forgetfulness he had thrown Himself completely into the feeling of the race, and suffered through sympathy with its pain." Hence He said, "*My* God, *My* God, why hast Thou forsaken Me?" Mr. Brooke describes these words as "a paradox."

I should prefer an interpretation of them which rendered it unnecessary to regard them thus. The sense of the entire withdrawal of the light and joy of God's presence, whatever its cause, whether it was the psychological result, according to Mr. Brooke's theory, of an intense sympathy with the feeling of having been forsaken by God which had been the supreme sorrow of mankind, or whether it was the direct result of an actual suspension of the free personal manifestation of the Divine presence to the soul of Christ, is perfectly consistent with the continuance of that deep relationship to God which no loss of the consciousness of God's presence could destroy.

I object to Mr. Brooke's explanation because it makes our Lord's cry unreal. According to this explanation, God had neither forsaken Christ Himself, nor had God ever forsaken humanity; and therefore (1) the cry expresses, not what was really true of Christ Himself, but only what through His sympathy with men seemed for the moment to become true of Himself; and (2) the feeling with which Christ sympathised was in itself false. Man had *felt* that he was abandoned by God, but God had never really abandoned him. *Why should Christ have endorsed a false inference which human weakness had drawn from the pain and misery of human life?*

But Mr. Brooke perceived very clearly, that in affirming that Christ had this deep sympathy with the *suffering* of the race, he was affirming only half the truth which is implicated in the conception of our Lord as "the representative Man;" and therefore he completes the explanation by adding that Christ "realised through His own Death the sense of the death and pain and woe of all the world, and, *with it,* the Sin of all the world as their cause. He lost all thought of self in awful realisation of the Sin of the whole world." [10] But if so, how was it that He "cried to God as the voice of all humanity, 'My God, My God, why hast Thou forsaken Me, forsaken man?'" [11] Realising the sin of the world, should we not have expected Christ to utter an acknowledgment that God might justly forsake, or had justly forsaken, man?

On Mr. Brooke's conception of our Lord's relationship to the race, it is absolutely necessary to conceive of our Lord as realising on the cross the sins of men as well as their sorrows; and if He realised their sins, He must have had present to Him so vividly the terrible cause of man's sense of separation from God, that the cry becomes quite unintelligible as the cry of the representative of the race.

While unable to accept his explanation of these mysterious and awful words, I am too thankful for every recognition of the real objective value of our Lord's Death not to acknowledge that Mr. Brooke's theory includes the objective element very distinctly, though, as I venture to think, in an incomplete form.

The following passage [12] is practically a statement of that side of the theory which I have endeavoured to illustrate in Lecture x. "There in Christ all humanity was concentrated; there all humanity suffered and sacrificed itself; there all humanity reconciled itself to God; there God saw all humanity die to sin, and reconciled Himself to it; there all humanity conquered death in a last struggle with it; there the whole race united itself to the life of God, for Christ was not only a man. He was humanity. All the past of mankind had brought Him to this hour; all the future of mankind was anticipated and held in Him in that hour; all the present of mankind centered in Him there."

[1] London: H, S. King and Co. Second edition, 1871.
[2] Page 30.
[3] Page 31.
[4] Pp. 31, 32.

[5] Matt. v. 11, 12.
[6] John xv. 18-23.
[7] Page 49.
[8] Page 35.
[9] Pp. 35, 36.

[10] Page 60. The italics and capitals are not Mr. Brooke's.
[11] Page 40.
[12] Page 29.

## Note H

It is not quite clear that in any passage in the New Testament the preposition ὑπέρ *necessarily* conveys the idea of substitution as distinguished from the idea of representation. Representation, indeed, in many cases implies substitution, but the two ideas are not identical: practically, the representative may often be spoken of as a substitute, but not always. When St. Paul says, "Now then we are ambassadors for Christ (ὑπέρ χριστοῦ), as though God did beseech you by us: we pray you in Christ's stead (ὑπέρ χριστοῦ) be ye reconciled to God," [1] he speaks of himself as Christ's representative, and in representing Christ he takes Christ's place. This is a case in which representation may be said to include substitution. Christ does not "beseech," Paul does. Again, when he writes to Philemon concerning Onesimus, "whom I would have retained with me, that in thy stead (ὑπέρ σοῦ) he might have ministered unto me," Onesimus is regarded as the representative of Philemon, and this involves the substitution of the service of Philemon for that of Onesimus. Philemon cannot minister to Paul; Onesimus ministers in his place. But when St. Paul, writing to the Cormthians, says, "The love of Christ constraineth us, because we thus judged that [if] one died for all (ὑπέρ πάντων) then all died," it is not clear that representation is equivalent to substitution. For St. Paul's precise meaning seems to be, not that Christ died in our stead, so that His Death takes the place of ours, and renders it unnecessary for us to die — although when His Death is considered under other aspects this is true — but that we died *in Him*. If the idea of substitution as distinguished from representation had been in his mind, he would not have written "[if] one died for all, then all *died*," but [if] one died for all, then all were *delivered from the necessity of dying*.

That ὑπέρ may be so used as to be practically equivalent to ἀντί, is certain. It is so used in two of the passages which I have just quoted, but it may be fairly contended that it is so used in the New Testament only when representation necessarily carries with it the idea of substitution. Its ordinary meaning is "on behalf of," or "for the benefit of;" and those passages in which Christ is said to have died "for us" can only be alleged in support of the vicarious or substitutionary character of His Death, because if His Death had not that character, it is impossible to see how it could have secured for us the kind of benefits attributed to it.

Winer gives among the meanings of ὑπέρ with the genitive, "For the most part, one who acts on behalf of another, represents him. [2] Hence ὑπέρ is sometimes nearly equivalent to ἀντί instead, *loco*, Phil. 13." [3] But in a note he adds, "Still, in doctrinal passages relating to Christ's death [4] it is not justifiable to render vTrep rjfiatv and the like rigorously by "instead of," merely on account of such parallel passages as Matt. xx. 28. Ἀντί is the more definite of the two prepositions. Ὑπέρ signifies merely *for*, for men, for their deliver-

ance, leaving undetermined the precise sense in which Christ died *for* them.
[5]

Meyer, discussing the force of ὑπέρ in Rom. v. 6, says "that Paul did not intend by ὑπέρ to convey the meaning *instead of,* is shown partly by the fact that while he indeed sometimes exchanges it for the synonymous περί, [6] he does not once use instead of it the unambiguous ἀντί, [7] which must nevertheless have suggested itself to him most naturally; and partly by the fact that with ὑπέρ as well as with περί he puts not invariably the genitive of the person, but sometimes that of the *thing* (ἁμαρτιῶν), in which case it would be impossible to explain the preposition by *instead of.* [8] It is true that he has certainly regarded the Death of Jesus as an act furnishing the *satisfactio vicaria,* as is clear from the fact that this bloody death was accounted by him as an expiatory sacrifice. [9] Comp. ἀντίλυτρον in I Tim. ii. 6; but *in no passage* has he expressed the substitutionary relation *through the preposition.* On the contrary, his constant conception is this: the sacrificial Death of Jesus, taking the place of the punishment of men, and satisfying Divine justice, took place as such *in commodum* (ὑπέρ, περί) *of men,* or — which is the same thing — on *account of their sins* (*in gratiam*), in order to expiate them (περί, or ὑπέρ ἁμαρτιῶν). This we hold against Flatt, Olshausen, Winzer, Reithmayr, Bisping, who take ὑπέρ as *loco.* That ὑπέρ must at least be understood as *loco* in Gal. iii. 13; 2 Cor. V. 14 (notwithstanding ver. 15); i Pet. iii. 18 (Rückert, Fritzsche, Philippi), is not correct. [10]

Dr. F. C. Baur, while recognising the fact that ὑπέρ *by itself* does not carry the idea of substitution, goes very far beyond Meyer in conceding or rather maintaining that the preposition may sometimes, and that it actually does, imply substitution. Dr. Crawford [11] gives the following extract from F. C, Baur's posthumous work: [12] "As the death of Christ in relation to God is an act of *satisfaction,* so in relation to man it is *substitutionary* (*stellvertretend*). That Christ died ὑπέρ ἡμῶν, is the expression most commonly used by Paul to indicate the significance of His Death for men. From the preposition ὑπέρ by itself, the notion of *substitution* cannot indeed be inferred; *but just as little can the notion be excluded from it.* The two notions, that which was done for men, and that which was done in their stead, pass over into each other. Among the many places in which it is said of Christ that He died διὰ τὰ παραπτώματα ἡμῶν, or περί τῶν ἁμαρτιῶν ἡμῶν, or ὑπέρ τῶν ἁμαρτιῶν ἡμῶν, [13] the passage in 2 Cor. V. 15 contains most distinctly the notion of *substitution.* The Apostle draws from the proposition, εἷς ὑπέρ πάντων ἀπεθανεν, the immediate inference, ἆρα οἱ πάντες ἀπεθανον. Christ not merely died *for them,* but also *in their stead,* as the one in the place of many, — who, even because He died for them and in their stead, did not themselves actually die, but are only regarded as dead in Him their substitute. What happened to Christ happened objectively to all. [14] The idea in this passage is that of a union of Christ with us, effected by means of the principle of love [?], in virtue of which union, that which He has done for us is just the same as if we had done it ourselves; as He in His death has identified Himself with us, and in dying for us has put Himself into our place, so we must also think ourselves [?] into His place and regard ourselves as dead with Him. This mutual oneness of being, in which the one lives in the other, in which we are crucified with Christ, because He was crucified for us, and we live in Him because He lives in us, [15] is the genuine Pauline notion of substitution. This, therefore, is also the correct meaning of the preposition ὑπέρ. It is not the vague general 'for,' which may stand in all possible relations, but it expresses the inmost immediate entering (Eingehen) into another, and putting oneself in his place."

[1] 2 Cor. v. 20.
[2] I Tim. ii. 6; Cor. v. 15.
[3] See in particular, Eurip. *Alcest.* 700; Thuc. i. 141; Polyb. iii. 76.
[4] Gal. iii. 13; Rom. v. 6-8; xiv. 15; i Pet; iii. 18, etc.
[5] Winer's *Grammar of the New Testament Idiom.* Masson's Trans, p. 401.
[6] Gal. i, 4; like Matt, xxvi. 20; Mark xiv. 25.
[7] Matt. xx. 28.
[8] Rom. viii. 3; 1 Cor. xv. 3.
[9] Rom. iii. 25; Eph. v. 2; Steiger on 1 Pet, p. 342, seq.

[10] *Commentary on Epistle to Romans,* Vol. i. p. 231. Edinburgh: T. & T. Clark, 1873.
[11] *The Doctrine of Holy Scripture respecting the Atonement.* Edinburgh and London: Blackwood & Sons, 1871. Pp. 473, 474.
[12] *Neutestamentliche Theologie.* Pp. 158, 159.
[13] Rom. iv. 25; V. 6; viii. 3; Gal. i. 4; i Cor. xv. 3.
[14] This seems a somewhat different conception of the passage from that in the previous sentence, and it is a much truer conception. [R. W. D.]
[15] Gal. ii. 20.

## *Note I*

No doubt St. Peter's thought, if it were fully developed, would amount to this: — "You are falsely accused of committing sins of which you are innocent, and you suffer: it is better for you to suffer for sins of which you are innocent, than for sins of which you are guilty, for it was thus that Christ suffered." But the manner in which this thought is expressed is not the less startling; for although in a previous sentence he had said, "They speak evil of you as evil doers," and had spoken of the false accusations that were brought against good men, the sentence immediately preceding the phrase, "Christ also once suffered for sins" (κρέιττον γαρ ἀγαθοποιοῦνας, εἰ θέλει τὸ θέλημα τοῦ Θεοῦ, πάσχειν, ἢ κακοποιοῦντας), prepares us for some such sequence as on ὅτι καὶ χριστὸς ἀγαθοποιῶν ἔπαθε. But to have written this, true as it is, would have been contrary to the Apostle's habit of thought.

## Note J

I do not imagine that what is said is an exhaustive explanation of I Pet. i. 17-19. That the conception of the whole passage is sacrificial, is obvious: the blood of Christ has the power of the blood of "a lamb without spot," and had redeemed them from their "vain conversation," But St. Peter doubtless believed with St. Paul, and there are some intimations of it in this epistle — that the Death of Christ was the death of sin. The heathen were to *yield themselves to God as those that were alive from the dead,* because in the Death of Christ sin died. This, however, in no way enfeebles — perhaps it strengthens — the force of the argument derived from this passage for an objective Atonement.

## Note K

Cremer's articles [1] on Ἱλάσκομαι and Ἱλασμός, are extremely interesting and able.

Dr. Bushnell, in his *Vicarious Sacrifice,* [2] tries very hard to eliminate the idea of Expiation from the Old Testament as well as the New. In an article on *The "Moral View" of the Atonement,* which appeared in the *British Quarterly Review,* October, 1866, I endeavoured to reply to his argument. His first two points are of inconsiderable importance, the rest appear to require discussion. I do not know that I have anything to add to the following passages extracted from the article. [3]

"Thirdly, he objects that 'the original of the word *atone,* or *make atonement,* in the Hebrew Scriptures, carries no such idea of expiation. It simply speaks of *covering,* or *making cover* for sin, and is sufficiently answered by anything which removes it, hides it from the sight, brings it into a state of reconciliation, where the impeachment of it is gone.... Everything turns here, manifestly, on the meaning of the original Hebrew word; and as the root or symbol of this word means simply *to cover,* we can see for ourselves that while it might be applied as a figure, to denote a covering by expiation, it can certainly as well and as naturally be applied to anything which hides or takes away transgression." But if the word is almost uniformly used in. a connection which shows that the 'covering' was effected by 'expiation,' it is to no purpose to urge that it can 'as well and as naturally be applied to anything which hides or takes away transgression.' Can he give us any instance in which atonement can possibly mean the awakening of repentance in the wrong-doer?

"The true explanation of the word is that it means originally to 'cover;' that in relation to sin it always means so to cover it as to avert the *penalty* due to it; and that this covering is almost always effected by expiation. It is, without exception, an objective effect that is said to be accomplished by atonement.

"The fourth point is that atonements are accordingly said to be made where the very idea of expiation is excluded, and sometimes where there is in fact no sacrifice at all.'

"He instances first the atonements which were made for the sanctifying of the altar. The altar could not sin; and, therefore, no expiation could be made for its sin. But the ceremony of making an atonement for the altar, and indeed for 'the holy place' itself, was repeated every year on the great Day of Atonement, and the reason of the ceremony is given in Lev. xvi. 16: 'He shall make an atonement for the holy place because of the uncleanness of *the children of Israel,* and because of their transgressions in all their sins.' Kurtz gives a very just interpretation of the ritual when he says that, 'having been erected in the midst of the sinful nation, they might be regarded as having been contaminated and defiled by the impurity of the atmosphere that surrounded them.' The sanctification of the altar, 'in men's feeling,' was the result of the atonement for the sins which had defiled it.

"The other case, where expiation is excluded because there is no sacrifice,' is that of the intercession of Moses, who, when the people had sinned by making and worshipping the golden calf, said, 'Now I will go up unto the Lord, peradventure I shall make an atonement for your sins.' No more fatal illustration could have been alleged on behalf of the theory it is quoted to support.

"For (1), according to the 'moral view,' Moses should have preached to the people, to bring them to a better mind: instead of this, he went up into the mount, to pray to God. Plainly he must have thought that the immediate object of atonement was not to make men better, but to avert God's displeasure. (2) Did Dr. Bushnell forget the sublime spirit of self-sacrifice which was in the heart of the great legislator when he went back into the solitudes of Sinai to meet God? 'Yet now, if thou wilt forgive their sin,' he exclaimed, 'and if not, blot me, I pray thee, out of thy book;' anticipating the passionate exclamation of St. Paul, 'I could wish myself accursed from Christ for my brethren, my kinsmen according to the flesh.' It is clear that the immediate purpose of Moses was to obtain Divine pardon for the sins which the people had already committed, not to keep them from sin in the time to come; and it is even possible that when he spoke to them of 'atonement,' he was meditating an appeal to God that he might himself be punished in their stead. In any case, he was endeavouring to 'cover' the sin; not by leading the idolaters to repentance, but by interposing something, — perhaps his own vicarious intercession merely — between the anger of God and the guilt of the people.

"Fifthly, — 'It is a great point that expiations or expiatory sacrifices are certainly not offered where we should expect them to be, if they are offered at all.' He instances again the case of the golden calf, also the mutiny which followed the judgment of Korah, and the reformations of Jonah and of Ezra. 'In all such cases,' he says, 'and they are many, we look for expiation, and do not find it; and what is quite as remarkable, there is no case to be found where God's anger in a day of guilt and fear is placated, or ever attempted to be, by a clearly expiatory sacrifice.'

"The reference to the popular discontent which followed the destruction of Korah, Dathan, and Abiram, is singularly infelicitous. 'Moses said unto Aaron, Take a censer and put fire thereon from off the altar, and put on incense, and go quickly into the congregation, and make an atonement for them.' Dr. Bushnell says, 'It is never supposed that there is any such thing as expiation by incense.' But (1) what was the object of the act which Moses suggested? To use Dr. Bushnell's language, 'no one supposes that it was intended to touch the hearts of the people.' 'There is wrath gone out from the Lord; *the plague is begun;*' and Aaron's direct and sole purpose was to appeal to the Divine mercy, and to avert the wrath against the whole nation, which threatened to 'consume them as in a moment.' If there was no 'expiation,' there was certainly not 'such a working on the bad mind of sin as...reconciles it to God.' 'The effect' was not what Dr. Bushnell declares the effect of atonement to be, 'wholly subjective, being a change wrought in all the principles of life and character, and dispositions of the soul.' And (2) the fire is distinctly stated to have been taken *'from the altar.'* The burning incense was thus connected with the ritual of expiation.

"It is, however, perfectly true that the Jewish law did not provide for the expiation by sacrifice of definite moral offences, strictly so called. This act of Aaron's stands alone, so far as we remember, in Old Testament history. It was the natural impulse of a moment of agony, and the spirit in which the appeal was made to the Divine mercy was a reason for the Divine response to it: no such use either of incense or of sacrifices was contemplated in the Levitical institutions.

"We shall have occasion to speak of the great annual atonement in reply to another passage in Dr. Bushnell's treatise; but apart from that ceremonial, prescribed for a particular day once a year, the Jewish sacrifices did not profess to atone for violations of the moral law. Only involuntary ceremonial offences, which were but the symbols of real moral transgressions, could be expiated by sacrifices which were but the symbols of the real atonement for sin. Had it been otherwise, the worst and most fatal consequences would have followed. If when an individual or the whole nation had committed any moral offence, or intentionally violated any ceremonial law, the Levitical system had provided a ritual of atonement, nothing could have prevented the external act from being regarded as a means, divinely appointed, for cancelling the guilt. No exhortations about the necessity of repentance would have any practical effect. 'The moral sense of the nation would have been enfeebled and paralysed by the natural influence of its religious institutions.' When, therefore. Dr. Bushnell says that 'expiatory sacrifices are certainly not offered where he should expect them to be,' he shows that he has failed to recognize a most remarkable proof of the profound wisdom of the Mosaic legislation. In such cases as he instances — cases of gross moral offences —

expiatory sacrifices were not offered, because they were not prescribed: to have prescribed them would have been to inflict the gravest injury on the moral life of the people.

"Sixthly — 'The requirement of the heart, as a condition necessary to acceptance in the sacrifice, is a very strong presumptive evidence that no idea of expiation belonged to sacrifice. At first, nothing appears to be said of the spirit in which the offering is to be made, though it is not to be supposed that it was ever accepted, in any but a merely ritual and ceremonial sense, unless coupled unconsciously or implicitly with a true feeling of repentance.'

"A closer investigation of the Jewish sacrificial system would have led to the cancelling not only of these two sentences, but of the four or five paragraphs which follow them. For (1) it is a fact which any one may verify for himself, that though four books of the Pentateuch are almost filled with ritualistic laws, there is not a single line to remind the man who brings a sin-offering to the priest that its atoning efficacy will depend upon 'the spirit' in which the offering is made. (2) The offences which could be expiated by sacrifices were not, generally speaking, such as could be thought of 'unconsciously or implicitly with a true feeling of repentance;' and in the special cases in which acts of injustice were atoned for by 'trespass-offerings,' the wrong had actually been undone by voluntary restitution to the injured person, and the shame of public confession had been voluntarily endured, before the sacrifice was presented. (3) The denunciations of the prophets, directed against the hypocrisy and formalism of the Jewish people, were not intended to show that ceremonial atonements could not expiate involuntary ceremonial offences unless there was a right 'spirit' in the offerer. Isaiah, Jeremiah, Amos, and Micah insist upon the great moral duties which the nation had neglected, denounce the moral offences of which the kings, priests, and commonalty were guilty, and in the very spirit of the ancient legislation maintain that no ritualistic services can compensate for disobeying the moral law.

"A singular use is made of Saul's haste to offer sacrifices at the commencement of his campaign against the Philistines, and his sparing of the spoil taken from Agag.

"'We find that Saul, an overgrown child of superstition, offers a sacrifice on two several occasions in his own way, disregarding God's appointed way, and even His special command. In the first instance, because, in going to battle, he wants to "make supplication to the Lord;" and in the second, because, having gained a victory, he wants to honour God in a grand ovation of sacrifice. Whereupon Samuel meets him in sharp rebuke, saying, "Hath the Lord as great delight in burnt-offerings and sacrifices as in obeying the voice of the Lord?   Behold (this appears to be an already accepted proverb), to obey is better than sacrifice, and to hearken than the fat of rams.'"

"Surely this does not prove that 'the spirit' in which the offering was made was essential to whatever expiatory effect the sin offerings were supposed to produce. For (1) it is not said that Saul offered or intended to offer any 'sin-offerings' at all. (2) Saul committed, in the first instance, a moral offence in not waiting till Samuel came. As Samuel had told the king to wait for his coming, Saul was guilty of impatience and distrust by precipitately offering the sacrifice before the prophet's arrival. It was of the greatest importance that the first human monarch of the elect nation should recognize God as the true invisible King, under whose authority he reigned

("Ere Saul they chose,
God was their king, and God they durst depose");

but Saul was about to attack the Philistines without the Divine directions which Samuel would have given him. 'He disregarded,' as Dr. Bushnell says, 'God's special command,' and did not merely fail to offer his sacrifices in the right 'spirit.' In the second instance, Saul had already disobeyed 'the voice of the Lord,' in preserving the spoil which he had been told to destroy. Samuel does not condemn him for being about to sacrifice 'the sheep and oxen,' without 'the requirement of the heart,' which was 'a condition necessary to acceptance in the sacrifices,' but for rebellion and 'stubbornness.'

"Dr. Bushnell's seventh point, that it was not the death, but the blood, which was the significant element in the Jewish sacrifice, and that as 'the blood is the life, so it is life-giving; a symbol of God's inward purifying and regenerating baptism in the remission of sins,' has already been answered. Even if it be true that this was the meaning of the sprinkling of the blood of the victim, it only shows that after the death had expiated guilt, and so averted penalty, the removal of the interior pollution was still necessary.

"Eighthly — It is maintained that 'the passover sacrifice has certainly nothing of expiation in it,' and that as the 'Christian Supper which commemorates our Lord's Death is the continuance of this ceremony,' it is unlikely that the Death of Christ was expiatory. This argument we can afford to let go: to discuss it, would carry us far beyond the space to which the present article must be limited; but that there was an expiatory value in the blood of the paschal lamb, is confessed by some who deny that it was properly a sin-offering.

"Ninthly — Dr. Bushnell cannot believe that the sacrifices were associated with 'notions of penal sanction for sin,' because all 'the most joyous and grandest' religious festivals were 'celebrated in rivers of blood.' But (1) why should not the Jews rejoice when their sins had been atoned for; and especially when by 'burnt-offerings,' between which and 'offerings for sin' Dr. Bushnell makes no distinction, 'they had surrendered themselves afresh to God'? Nehemiah and Ezra checked the grief occasioned by the reading of the law, and charged the people, at the very time they were distressed by their long neglect, to 'go their way, eat the fat, and drink the sweet, and send portions to them for whom nothing is provided.' (2) The day on which the annual atonement was effected, was not a day of gladness; there were no 'processions of music and songs of praise;' but the people were to afflict their souls.

240

"Finally, it is alleged that 'where the rite of sacrifice bears a look of expiation, and the instances are taken as facts of expiation, a closer examination shows in every case that the impression is not supported by the transaction.'

"The sacrifice of Job for his sins is the single historical example on which Dr. Bushnell relies, and as we believe that in the 'burnt-offerings' of patriarchal times, the expiatory idea, if present at all, was exceedingly obscure, we do not take any exception to the paragraph in which it is contended that this was at most a supplicatory offering.

"We cannot extract, nor indeed is it necessary that we should, Dr. Bushnell's account of the solemnities of the Day of Atonement. A single paragraph in which, under the influence of the fundamental mistake of his whole argument, he implies that what is intended to produce a moral effect upon man cannot at the same time be expiatory before God, will adequately represent his account of these remarkable ceremonies.

"'We shall be struck in the review of them, *not with any discovery of an expiatory element,* but with the fact that everything is ordered with such a manifestly artistic study and skill, to beget, in minds too crude for the reflective modes of exercise, a whole set of impressions answering to those of the Christian doctrine of salvation, the holiness of God, the uncleanness and deep guilt of sin, and the faith of God's forgiving mercy.'

"Expiation, as defined by Dr. Pye Smith, 'denotes anything that may supply an *adequate reason* for exempting the criminal from the penalty due;' and it admits of proof that expiation was the most conspicuous and sometimes the only idea of all the 'sin-offerings' and 'trespass-offerings' of the Mosaic legislation. The subjective effect was secured by the presentation of an objective atonement.

"Dr. Bushnell discovers no 'expiatory element' in the service on the great Day of Atonement; but what was a Jew likely to discover in it? If the 'moral view' had been suggested to a devout worshipper in the tabernacle or the temple, we can imagine him giving some such reply as this: — 'What atonement is, I know. More than once, ignorantly and unintentionally, I have broken the precepts of the law, and when I discovered my offence, I was troubled by fear of the Divine displeasure. I brought a kid of the goats to the priest, and he offered it as a "sin-offering," — it was an expiation for the transgression I did not mean to commit; when it was offered, my involuntary offence was blotted out. But I have been guilty of sins innumerable, for which I could not offer any expiation. For my ungoverned anger, for my selfishness, for my want of pity for the poor, for the ingratitude of my heart to Jehovah for all His goodness to me, the law permits me to bring no sacrifice. If my lesser offences can only be forgiven when the priest has atoned for them, these greater sins must surely need atonement too. My case is that of the whole nation. We have all sinned and done wickedly; and though we have expiated involuntary transgressions, for our worst crimes no expiation has been made. But, year by year, we call to mind all our iniquities and we "afflict

241

our souls." We assemble before the holy place, and sacrifices are slain for us all. They are called "sin-offerings," — the very name which is given to the atonements for our inferior transgressions of the law. We cannot indeed believe, that if one man must bring a goat to expiate an unintentional breach of one of God's lighter precepts, these two goats can expiate all the great offences of which all the people have been guilty; and yet these two goats are also a "sin-offering." Over the head of one of them the high priest confesses "all the iniquities of the children of Israel, and all their transgressions in all their sins." Surely I am to think of the sacrifices offered for the nation as I think of the sacrifices which I have offered for myself: when the annual atonement is made, I may look to God to pardon me. God means me to think of all my sins as expiated by the death of the goat that is slain, and as removed from me, "far as the east is from the west," by the goat that is driven into the wilderness. No promise, indeed, is given that when the day is over all our iniquities shall be forgiven; and in this the law of the great Day of Atonement is unlike the laws which direct us how to atone individually for our ceremonial offences. The reason of the difference is plain, for in other cases a full expiation is made: in this case there is only the form of an expiation. But it is just because I see on this great day what exactly corresponds to the common atonements for ceremonial transgressions, that I dare to trust in the Divine mercy, and to hope that God will pardon all my sins. It is only a form; it has no real atoning power; and this prevents me sometimes from finding perfect peace. But God means that I should think of my worst sins as expiated, and though sometimes "heart and flesh fail" when I remember my transgressions, I will believe that He is willing to forgive them all.'

"Our imaginary Jew's account is, we think, truer to the genius of the Levitical institutions, and to the ritual of the Day of Atonement itself, than Dr. Bushnell's; nor would the Jew be at all perplexed by the suggestion that the goat by which the people are to be personally cleansed themselves, suffers no death or dying pain at all, as their substitute; but having their sins all put upon his head by the priest's confession, is turned loose alive, and driven off into the wilderness, so to signify the deportation or clean removal of their guiltiness.' It is expressly said that the *two* goats constituted the sin-offering: they cannot be severed. The one is sent off into the wilderness as a visible sign that the sins confessed over him are utterly removed, because the other has first been put to death.

"The idea of a real expiation cannot be separated from the sin-offerings for individual and ceremonial offences; the idea of a symbolic expiation cannot be separated from the sacrifices annually offered for the sins of the whole people. The institutions of Judaism, as well as the explicit teaching of Christ and the Apostles protest against the theory of an Atonement from which the expiatory idea is excluded.'"

[1] Biblico-Theological Lexicon.  [2] Page 425, seq.  [3] Page 442, seq.

## Note L

The question whether St. Paul had received a supernatural revelation, which he was commissioned to make known to mankind, and the question whether his writings are inspired, are quite distinct. Revelation and inspiration are very far from being identical. The Jewish nation at Sinai received a revelation from heaven. To the crowds that listened to the Sermon on the Mount, God Himself, in the person of our Lord Jesus Christ, directly revealed His thought and will. But in neither case were those who received the revelation "inspired." That inspiration is the condition of receiving certain forms of Divine revelation, is true; but Divine revelations are possible without it. Those persons to whom the theory of inspiration is involved in great difficulty, and to whom the doctrine that the writings of the New Testament are in any sense inspired writings is especially perplexing, may perhaps find a temporary foothold for faith in distinguishing between revelations which in ways unknown to us may have been made to St. Paul and the inspiration which is claimed for his epistles. In our times many persons must find their way from doubt to faith by postponing the question of inspiration until they have settled some other controversies of more immediate interest. The question of inspiration is one for those who have already arrived at a personal knowledge of the Lord Jesus Christ as the Son of God and Saviour of mankind, rather than for those who are still doubting whether He has a right to claim the perfect homage and perfect trust of the human race. The subject is discussed incidentally and popularly in *The Ultimate Principles of Protestantism*, [1] by the author of these Lectures.

[1] London: Hodder & Stoughton. 1874.

## Note M

The argument in Galatians iii. is immediately directed against those who were looking to the Jewish law for justification, and the point of it consists in the demonstration that the law, instead of justifying men, revealed their sin, and declared that because of sin they were under the curse; Christ brought deliverance from the curse by being made a curse for us. But it was not for the Jews alone that Christ died; nor did He die merely to exhaust the formal penalty which avenged transgression of the Jewish law. The Jewish constitution bore witness to the enduring order of the kingdom of God. The moral precepts of the Jewish law were but the temporary and imperfect expression of the precepts of that eternal Law of Righteousness which can never receive adequate expression in definite commandments; and its penalties were the visible symbols and prophecies of the final revelation of the righteous judgment of God. The Death of Christ, while satisfying the merely external conditions of the temporary law, also satisfied deeper and more august necessities; otherwise it could have had no universal or lasting significance. Hence in this very epistle St. Paul writes that Christ "gave Himself" — not merely for those transgressions which were formally forbidden and formally condemned by the Jewish law, but — "for our sins" — for our transgressions of that other and higher law of which the Jewish law was but a shadow. And He "gave himself for our sins" — not merely that He might redeem us from a formal curse, but — "that He might deliver us from this present evil world," [1] separating us now and for ever from that moral chaos out of which no Divine order can arise, and which is ultimately to perish. He effected this not merely by the moral and spiritual forces which act directly on the heart and conscience, but by giving Himself "for our sins." He endured the penalty of sin for us, that He might lift us out of the "world," which was disorganized by sin and exposed to the wrath of God. Later on in the epistle the Apostle appropriates Christ's great act of self-sacrifice to himself: He "loved me and gave Himself for me;" [2] and later still he expresses his sense of the infinite worth and power of the Death of Christ, by exclaiming, "God forbid that I should glory, save in the *cross* of our Lord Jesus Christ, by whom the world has been crucified to me and I unto the world." [3] The recognition of the unique function of the Death of Christ in human redemption is a golden cord woven into the very texture of the epistle.

[1] Gal. i. 4. | [2] Ibid. ii. 20. | [3] Ibid. vi. 14.

## *Note N*

It would be difficult to find in any Christian commentator or theologian a clearer and firmer apprehension of St. Paul's conception of Justification *at a single point* than that which is given in a very interesting treatise written by a Jewish rabbi at Leghorn. [1] St. Paul's doctrine of Justification is practically destructive of the "moral theory" of the Atonement; for if we were justified through the Death of Christ only because the Death of Christ makes us better men, the Pauline theory of Justification would have to be re-cast. The following passages from *Morale Juive et Morale Chrétienne,* [2] strengthen the argument in the text.

"Christians of every sect, of every party, of every shade, are agreed on one point — that in the judgment of St. Paul, the great lawgiver, the great moralist of Christianity, faith justifies without works...But the principle so stated appeared so confounding, so opposed to the noblest instincts of the human heart, so contrary to that emotional morality which Christianity preached, that it was very soon limited and qualified. While Protestantism, true to logic and to reason, boldly drew from the principle all that it involves, and proclaimed that works of morality are useless and pernicious, faith being the only condition of salvation, Catholicism on the contrary, since it was ruled by an external, social political authority, which is at once a government, an administrative system, and a police, shrunk with alarm from these revolutionary conclusions, this moral licentiousness, and it understood the "works" of St. Paul in their most restricted sense, that is to say, as the *works of the law,* as Mosaic practices, and it declared against the Protestants, in the Council of Trent, the necessity of good works. This was a return to the ancient Hebraic morality, it was to contradict at every point the Apostle of the Gentiles, it was to diminish considerably the importance and efficacy of redemption.

"Thus you see Protestants use the same language against the Catholics as Paul employs against the Pharisees and Judaizing Christians, and they place the Catholics on the same level as the Jews. *'The Catholic doctors,'* said Mosheim, *'confound the law with the gospel,' and represent eternal happiness as the reward of good works.'* Is this the true meaning and the real intention of St. Paul? This is the ground upon which the great dispute between the Catholics and Protestants began, as we have before said. For ourselves, the doctrine of St. Paul is exactly that which reason and independent criticism has ascribed to him by the mouth of Protestants. The following passages and expressions of St. Paul are explicit on this point. He gives us as an example of his principle, Abraham, Abraham justified not by works, but by faith. [3] Now the works of Abraham, 'which are not weighed in the balance by God,' according to St. Paul, were not, that I am aware of, *the works of the law,* which was not yet given, but in the strictest sense moral works — charity, justice, hospitality, the love of men, virtue, and monotheism spread among the Gentiles. And yet Abraham was not justified by his works, but simply by his faith. Would St. Paul speak thus if he were thinking only of the works of the law? Further, I say that if the example chosen by Paul is one of the most conclusive, the phrases which accompany it, the consequences which he draws from it, are in their turn not less decisive. 'For what saith the scripture? Abraham believed God, and it was counted unto him for righteousness. Now to him that worketh is the reward not reckoned of grace, but of debt.' [4] Here then every title to recompense, every meritorious work, is declared worthless. But this is not all. 'But to him that worketh not, but believeth on Him that justifieth the ungodly, his faith is counted for righteousness.' [5] No doubt about his meaning is possible. Without works, and however sinful, faith alone in Him who justifies the guilty is sufficient for salvation. Do we desire more proof? Paul goes on to say: "Even as David also describeth the blessedness of the man unto whom God imputeth righteousness without works, saying, Blessed are they whose iniquities are forgiven, and whose sins are covered. Blessed is the man to whom the Lord will not impute sin." [6] That is to say, according to the meaning given by Paul to these words of David, the grace of faith brings with it the pardon of iniquities, the imputation of righteousness; and in Rom. iii. 26 the ground of glorying is placed not in the *law of works, but in the law of faith.* Likewise in the Epistle to the Galatians [7] we learn that man is not justified by the *works of the law* (no distinction being made between different kinds of works), but solely by faith in Jesus Christ. It is true that in the Epistle to the Romans [8] the Apostle declares that *the law is not made void through faith,* but on the contrary it is *established*. It is also true that in the Epistle to the Galatians [9] he exhorts them *not to sin;* but it is because in the first place he was imitating the language of the Master, who saw in Christianity only what was spiritual and eternal in the reality and substance of the ancient law; and, further, because he was conscious himself of all the danger of his principles, because he saw all the possible consequences, and the immorality that might be introduced into the world under the cover of proclaiming that faith is the sole virtue which justifies. Again, I say, if he condemns immorality, if he is not willing to accord all the liberty that faith admits of, it is for some reason of expediency, and for some secondary consideration. For we know very well that it is not in the name of truth, justice, and absolute virtue, that Paul does not admit immorality under the empire of faith; but it is because faith, being perfectly able to forgive all vice and crime, it would be very unfitting to make it a party to sin, an instrument of evil, to make, as he says, *Christ the instrument of sin.* See how far Christianity was obliged to descend to find a support for morality after having taken away from it its ancient and natural foundation, the law."

[1] *Morale Juive et Morale Chrétienne.* Par E. Benamozegh. Paris. Michel l.evy, 1867.

[2] pp. 48-53.
[3] Rom. iv. 1-4.
[4] Ibid. iv. 3, 4.
[5] Ibid. iv. 5.

[6] Ibid. iv. 6-8.
[7] Gal. ii. 16.
[8] Rom. iii. 30.
[9] Gal. ii. 17.

## *Note O*

To interpret 2 Cor. v. 19, as meaning that God in Christ was subduing the hostility of men, and so reconciling them to Himself, is to force upon the words a sense which goes very far to destroy the coherence of the whole passage in which they occur, and is to disregard what may be described as the idiom of apostolic thought. The phrase "not imputing to them their trespasses" is in direct apposition to "God was reconciling the world to Himself." The appeal, "Be ye reconciled to God," is based on the fact that God had already reconciled Himself — as we should say — to mankind.

Our use of the word misleads us. When we speak of a man being "reconciled" to another, we always mean that the person who has received a real or imaginary offence ceases to be angry with the offender; and so the Apostle's phrase, "God was reconciling the world to Himself," naturally conveys the impression that God was removing the antagonism with which the world regarded Him. But καταλλάσσω really means the re-establishing of friendly relations between those who have been antagonistic; and it is by no means implied that the antagonism exists in the person who is the direct object of the active verb, or who, if the passive is used, is said to be reconciled. This is

246

very clear in the case of the cognate διαλλάσσω in Matt. v. 24. Our Lord supposes that a man who has brought his gift to the altar remembers that his brother has some cause of complaint against him: the man is to leave his gift before the altar, and to go to his brother and "be reconciled" to him (πρῶτον διαλλάγηθι τῷ ἀδελφῷ σου). According to the idiom of our own language, we should say that it is the man who has something against his brother who must "be reconciled;" but our Lord puts it the other way. The man *against* whom his brother has a complaint is to be "reconciled." For a man to "be reconciled" to another may therefore mean — not the removal of antagonism on *his* part — but the removal of antagonism on the part of the person to whom he is reconciled. The word means, as I have said, the re-establishment of friendly relations between persons who have been at variance: on which side the antagonism exists is not to be determined by the word itself or by its grammatical construction. A may reconcile B to himself — not by the removal of the antagonism of B: there may be no antagonism in B to remove, and the whole process may consist in the removal of A's own antagonism. God reconciled the world to Himself— changed His relation of antagonism to the world into a relation of friendship — by sending His Son "to be the propitiation for our sins.' His own love for the world moved Him to do this; but until He did it there was antagonism, which, according to the apostolic thought, would have ultimately issued in "wrath."

Cremer's articles on καταλλάσσω and καταλλαγή are very valuable, and he strongly supports the view contended for in this note. He defines the word as meaning "to exchange; then, like διαλλάσσειν, καταλλάσσω = συναλλάσσειν = to reconcile,..... both in one-sided and mutual enmity. In the former case the context must show on which side is the active enmity." [1] The whole article deserves careful study.

[1] Cremer: *Biblico-Theological Lexicon of New Testament Greek*. T. & T. Clark. 1872.

## *Note P*

"He made Him to be sin for us who knew no sin," — and was morally incapable of knowing sin (μὴ γνόντα ἁμαρτίαν) — "that we might become the righteousness of God in Him." [1] it is illegitimate to play fast and loose with the word "sin" in this passage, and to say that in one clause it means "sin," and in the other a "sin-offering." When St. Paul says that Christ, who could have no personal consciousness of *sin*, was made *sin* for us, the word should be taken in the same sense in both clauses. But how was it possible for God to make Christ sin for us? Are we to suppose that St. Paul meant that by a Divine fiction the sins of the world were imputed to Christ, and that so by imputation He became a *sinner,* and suffered in our stead? This is virtually to change "sin" into "sinners," and is no more legitimate than to change "sin" into "sin-offering." God made Christ "*sin* for us," not a "sin-offering," not a "sinner." This is what St. Paul affirms. The sentence is intensely rhetorical; literally, it was impossible that God should make Christ "sin." But the rhetoric stands for something, and it is our duty to try to find out the actual fact which rendered possible such a conception of Christ's Death as this.

Great light is thrown on the whole passage by the closing words. The ultimate end of Christ's redemptive work is that "we may become the righteousness of God in [Christ]." Righteousness is conceived — not as a mere quality of the redeemed, but as their very substance and life. It is no longer separable from them, even in idea. This is the consummation of our holiness. Had we not been saved, *sin* would at last have become something more than a mere quality of our nature; it would have become our very self; it would have become inseparable from us, even in idea. Not until there is a complete identification between the soul and sin, does God finally abandon us. While our true self can in any way be distinguished from the sin that is in us, He clings to us and works for our redemption. When sin and self become inseparable, then God deals with us as He deals with sin; He cannot do otherwise. He withdraws Himself from us, and His withdrawal is a mortal blow — a blow which, on one theory of the future of the impenitent, inflicts endless torment, which is what is commonly understood by "the second death;" and which on another theory inflicts agony so sharp and terrible, that it ends in the exhaustion and destruction of the life of the soul. God made Christ sin for us; withdrew from Him, as He must otherwise have withdrawn from us had *we* become sin, and this withdrawal brought with it the Death which atoned for sin. This seems to have been St. Paul's idea in this passage. I say again that the passage is intensely rhetorical; the conception is rhetorical as well as the expression; but what is of importance to the argument of these Lectures, is that no such rhetorical conception of the Death of Christ is possible to those who reject the vicarious or representative theory of His sufferings.

[1] Cor. v. 21.

## *Note Q*

The idea of Merit, as distinguished from that of Satisfaction, altogether obliterates the unique significance which Christ and His Apostles attached to His Death. His act in humbling Himself to become man was a moral act of infinite worth; and on the hypothesis that Atonement was effected by merit, the Incarnation — apart from the Death of Christ — would have been a sufficient Atonement for sin.

## *Note R*

"It is not clear to us that either Dr. Bushnell or Dr. Young believes in what is commonly understood by the Divine forgiveness. Their theory of the constitution of the spiritual universe leaves no place for it. 'In the very act, in the very moment of evil,' according to Dr. Young, 'the real penalty descends irresistibly, and *in the very amount* which is deserved. The sin insures, because it is its own punishment.' 'Punishment or reward, visible or invisible, or both, dispenses itself, and in the amount in which either is merited.' This is surely 'rectilineal justice.' But he also says, 'It can readily be shown that rectilineal justice, in the sense of apportioning exact desert, neither less nor more, is not an attribute of God at all' 'He does not need to be, and He is not just, in the human, rectilineal sense at all."

"What, then, are we to believe? Can the penalties of sin be remitted, averted, or not? Are we in the power of the 'spiritual laws' which 'never slumber and are never defrauded for a moment,' whose 'dire sanction' 'there is no evading,' from whose 'retributive awards' there is no escape, which infallibly and inevitably dispense 'punishment or reward' 'in the amount in which either is merited'? Or are we in the good hands of Him who is 'more and better than merely just, and acts on the ground of pure mercy'? 'Ever and ever,' says Dr. Young, elsewhere, 'justice inflicts an inevitable penalty, and expects the completest satisfaction.' And yet 'the whole course of the world, from the creation till now, and the manifest system of Divine providence towards the good and towards the bad, are right in the face of rectilineal justice.

"Into such irreconcilable contradictions is an able man betrayed when he constructs a theory which begins by affirming the independent and immutable authority of the eternal Law of Righteousness, and then denies the necessity of an Atonement as a condition of Divine pardon. Abelard was more consistent. He rejected the idea of expiation; but he also maintained that the Divine will is the fountain of moral law.

"A reconciliation of these apparently conflicting statements is attempted in the following passage, which states very concisely the theory of redemption which is offered to us in place of that which is commonly received in the Church: — 'There is no such attribute in God [as rectilineal justice]. But the inevitable punishment of moral evil, always and everywhere, is certain nevertheless. The justice of the universe, in this sense, is a tremendous fact, an eternal and necessary fact, which even God could not set aside. There is an irresistible, a real force, springing out of the essential constitution, whereby sin punishes itself. This is the fixed law of the moral universe, a law in perfect harmony with the eternal will, and which never is, and never can be broken. God's mercy in our Lord Jesus Christ does not in the least set aside this justice; what it does is to remove and render non-existent the only ground on which the claim of justice stands. Instead of arbitrarily withdrawing the criminal from punishment, it destroys in his soul that evil which is the only cause and reason of punishment, and which being removed, punishment cease of itself."

"Again, we ask, Does God forgive? Or does He simply change the condition of a man so that he does not need forgiveness?

"We further deny that Dr. Young is entitled to affirm that his theory does not represent God as "arbitrarily withdrawing the criminal from punishment." If sin is not merely "the only cause and reason of punishment," but, as is elsewhere maintained, "its *own* punishment," — the moral disorder and tendency to evil which every act of transgression increases being the worst consequence of disobeying the Divine precepts — is not the punishment, after all, "arbitrarily withdrawn," if God by a supernatural interference restores the harmony and purity of the soul?

"No natural law was violated when, at the Divine word, Lazarus, after he had been dead four days, left his sepulchre and came back to Bethany; for his resurrection was not an abnormal result of the common forces of the universe whose regular action constitutes the "order of nature;" it was the immediate effect of a volition which is above all natural law. But is the Divine will superior to the laws of the spiritual universe? Does it move in a region where their obligation does not bind? Is it absolutely free to dissolve the connection between sin and its penalty? This passage of Dr. Young's alleviates no difficulty and creates new confusion." [1]

[1] *British Quarterly Review,* October, 1866, pp. 423-425.

## *Note S*

"Not then because He was from the Father was He called the *First-born*" [as from the Father He is called the *Only-begotten*] "but because in Him the creation came to be; and as before the creation He was the Son, through whom was the creation, so also before He was called the First-born of the whole creation, not the less was the Word Himself with God, and the Word was God." [1]

"For it is evident to all, that neither for Himself, as being a creature, nor as having any connection according to substance with the whole creation, has He been called *First-born* of it; but because the Word, when at the beginning He framed the creatures, condescended to things generate, that it might be possible for them to come to be. For they could not have endured His untemporal nature, and His splendour from the Father, unless condescending by the Father's love for man. He had supported them and taken hold of them and brought them into substance; and next *because by this condescension of the Word, the creation, too, is made a son through Him,* that He might be in all respects *First-born* of it," &c. [2]

Athanasius also speaks of Christ as the "Offspring from the Father, in whom the whole creation is created and adopted into sonship." [3]

In a note, Dr. Newman says Athanasius "considers that 'first-born' is mainly a title connected with the Incarnation, and also connected with our Lord's office at the creation...In each economy it has the same meaning; it belongs to. Him as the type, idea, or rule, on which the creature was made, or new-

250

made, and the life by which it is sustained." He also quotes Augustine as saying, "Whatever God was about to make in the creature, was already in the Word, nor would be in the things were it not in the Word."

To develop this idea of Christ's relation to the universe would require a volume rather than a note. The creation of all things by and in Christ appears to be the necessary postulate of a true conception of the Incarnation; and the theory of the Incarnation also requires that man should be regarded as the crown and flower of the creation — in whom, under Christ, the creation finds its completest expression.

[1] Athanasius: *Select Treatises*, page 370. Translated by J. H. Newman. Oxford, J. H. Parker. 1844.
[2] Athanasius: *Select Treatises*, page 372. Translated by J. H. Newman. Oxford, J. H. Parker. 1844.
[3] Ibid, 413.

## *Note T*

The following passages from a Jewish Rabbi will be read with interest. What he affirms is a fiction, is verified in the consciousness of the Church: —

"The Hebraism of the Rabbis contained in its doctrine an idea that was very natural, very common, which it was hardly necessary to inculcate, but one which was needed to control some practices touching man after his death. Already the Bible, and the Hebrew prophets, greatly heightening the value of life, had said on innumerable occasions that the law, virtue, and God's commandments end at the gates of the tomb, that the dead no longer praise the Lord, that the sepulchre sends forth no hymn of gratitude; passages which men have wished to interpret in a materialistic sense, but on which, as we see, orthodox Hebraism put quite a different meaning. Pharisaism formulated them in one general expression the terms of which have a peculiar importance for those who would enter into the true meaning of very many passages in Christian writers, and more especially in Paul.

"The Pharisees said: 'With the dead there is freedom' (verse of the Psalms). When a man dies he is freed from the commandments. Is it not incredible "i This is the one circle in which Paul's words and thoughts incessantly turn, in a thousand passages where the freedom of the dead is in question; this is the origin, this the ground of one of the boldest and most remarkable fictions that have ever sprung from human imagination — a fiction, the effects of which surpassed calculation. Paul would have the faithful identify themselves with Christ, believe themselves condemned, crucified, and dead in their flesh with Him. By virtue of this death which they share with Him, they gain a freedom more precious than any other, freedom from the Law. Will a man after death be still subject to the Law? Can the Law stretch forth its sceptre beyond the tomb? Can it exact from a dead man the fulfilment of its customs, rites, and ceremonies? Again, to touch upon another point which will be raised in the words of Paul himself, what is the Kabbalistic doctrine with regard to the expiation of original sin, spiritual regeneration? Does it not set forth the Law or death as the only means of making amends for the first sin? 'Then, said Paul, of these two methods we have chosen the latter. We died, died completely with Jesus; we are in Him, and He in us; He died for the whole world. He crucified in himself our sinful flesh; He has fulfilled all the law for us in dying on the cross.' Behold us then returned, perfectly alive, into the precious freedom of spoiless spirits, and no longer can a dead man be taxed with the non-fulfilment of the Law. Have we exaggerated the ideas and expressions of Paul? Hear what he himself says. 'Our flesh,' says he, 'is counted as dead if Christ be in us.' 'He that is dead is freed from sin.' [1]

"But this is a far more important passage: 'Know ye not brethren for I speak to them that know the law' — that is to say, to those who are not ignorant of the Pharisaic ideas with reference to the duration of its observance — 'how that the law hath dominion over a man as long as he liveth?' [2]

"And after quoting the example of the woman who is free to marry after the death of her husband, [3] so, says he, my brethren, 'ye are also become dead to the law by the body of Christ; that ye should be married to another, even to him who is raised from the dead.' [4] 'For when we were in the flesh, the motions of sins, which were by the law, did work in our members; [5] but now we are delivered from the law, having died [here we follow the more trustworthy rendering of Diodati] to that wherein we were held. 'Nay more, the sin of Adam, which, as the Kabbalists and Paul hold, called forth the law, is expiated by the death of Jesus. 'He dies and is buried, and so are his disciples with Him.' [6] 'Our flesh has been condemned to suffer for all in Jesus. There is therefore now no condemnation for those who are in Jesus, who walk not after the flesh, but after the spirit.... For what the law could not do' (give complete liberty, at the same time expiating the old sin), 'in that it was weak in the flesh, God has done in sending his own Son in the likeness of sinful flesh, and for sin; and He has condemned sin in the flesh, that the righteousness of the law might be fulfilled in us.' [7]

"We will not further multiply quotations. A mere perusal of Paul's writings will make us better acquainted with the spirit which dictated them than isolated fragments. But the most prominent feature throughout is the strange abuse which is made there of what is simply and solely a fiction, and the conclusion which is drawn thence with a coolness almost incredible — the abolition of the Law. But in this tomb wherein you would bury the Law, in this quiescence which you demand in the dead, do you not see the death and annihilation of something else too— even of morality itself? Do you not fear to see this "dead man" release himself from the restraints of virtue and from moral obligations, as well as ceremonial ordinances? Do you not fear lest these members, which are said to be completely dead and buried, should refuse to discharge the holiest duties, and lest the spirit on returning into its native liberty should imagine that there is no yoke to lay upon the flesh by which it is surrounded, but which is already dead and crucified in Jesus? But the fiction goes further still: this believer, dead and buried with Jesus, rises again with Him; with Him our flesh too is considered to have undergone resurrection. We died to the Law that we might be another's, even His who has raised us from the dead; and Jesus, our brother, is the first-born of the dead. There is no room here for doubt. For Jesus, and for His disciples after Him, the era of the resurrection, the renovation of the world, the resurrection of the dead, was just beginning, and for the successors of Jesus, it had already commenced in their Master's person, in His body which had risen from the tomb alive, and had become 'the first-born of the dead.' But it is the resemblance to the doctrines then extant that gives to this fiction its exceptional importance. What did Resurrection mean for the Pharisees? Undoubtedly their conception not only comprised the bodies of mankind called to a new life, and endowed with greater perfection of powers and constitution, but included also all nature in a universal renovation, in a Palingenesis which was to change the world's outward semblance; and indeed the comparison of this doctrine, with its imitations in ancient and modern times, would be a task both curious and instructive.

"Though unanimous on this point, the Pharisaic school was divided as to the epoch of the era of the resurrection and its relation to the Messianic era. In the minds of the one party these two eras were identical and united in one and the same epoch, and the Messiah was not only destined to install Israel in an era of prosperity, safety, and liberty, but also to give the signal for the renovation and the regeneration of nature, in which the most solemn and most startling phenomenon would be the resurrection of the body.

"Others believed that the course of events would be entirely different. Throwing back to the furthest limits of finite ages the era of the resurrection, they anticipated nothing in the advent of the Messiah but a mere social transformation, in which nature's laws would remain unimpaired, where life would go its ordinary round: or, to sum up all in the formula of the text, 'Nothing will change except slavery into freedom.'

"It is unnecessary to state to which of these two schools Christianity adheres. For it no difference, no interval, no distinction between the Messianic era and that of the resurrection is possible, and while the contrary doctrine definitely prevailed in Judaism, the identity of the two epochs alone found support and sympathy in the heart of Christianity. This prime difference gave rise to a secondary one. Notwithstanding that the Pharisees extended to its utmost limits the reign of the Law, they arrested its power at the threshold of the resurrection. Corresponding to the complete change which was to take place in the physical constitution, corresponding to the new laws, created by new physical relations, which were to govern the stars, the suns, and the worlds in their orbits, a new Law, too, called into being by new social relations, was to supersede the ancient religious law. In this new world, on this new earth, in the midst of new beings, and amid new relations, God's thought, God's law, remaining still unchanged in essence, with the very end that it might be permanent, would have varied in its applications, just as it varies here on earth and in the actual universe, with different conditions, beings, and relations, according to the world, sun, or star in which it acts. [8]

"Here lie the origin and the true meaning of that crowd of arguments, propositions, and parables, where the idea of a new Law, of a new covenant, of repealed prohibitions, breaks through images and allegories, weapons with which Jewish orthodoxy has been so unduly attacked, and which Christian polemics have incessantly brought against the Rabbis. These were the same ideas which among the Jewish Christians led them to affirm the abolition of the Law; just as, almost universally, everything which has subsequently become a weapon in the hands of Christianity when established, was a force and creative power in primitive Christianity. Nothing is more simple, nothing more inevitable, after all that preceded, than this abolition of the Law. In the mind of the first Christians the era of the Messiah was absolutely identical with the era of the resurrection, and since the latter had already commenced with the resurrection of Christ, the first-born of the dead, and the entire Church was looking for the near and immediate destruction and renovation of the world, the first conclusion that would be drawn would be that the Law of Moses was about to give place to another Law more in harmony with the semi-spiritual state of the new community. In vain was this expectation proved false day after day, in vain did the real resurrection ever recede into the far distance, in vain did impatience prey upon their hearts, as we see it did by the Epistles. What matters it? Substitute still, in place of the true resurrection its shadow, its image, a resurrection entirely imaginary; teach that the believer, having died with Jesus, is raised with Him, that the sovereignty of the resurrection and the age of the Palingenesis have prevailed down from the resurrection of Jesus, and the abolition of the Law can still make its way." [9]

[1] Rom. vi. 7.
[2] Ibid. vii. 1.
[3] Ibid. vii. 4.
[4] Ibid. vii. 5.
[5] Ibid. vi. 7.
[6] Ibid. vii. 4.
[7] Ibid. viii. 1-4.
[8] In the system of the doctors, especially of the Kabbalists, the Law governs all worlds, from the most distant stars to the smallest atom. There is no star, no world, no angel, which does not observe it, each in his own way. God Himself is the chief observer of the Law.
[9] E. Benamozegh: *Morale Juive et Morale Chrétienne*. Paris, 1867. Pp. 62-70.

www.ingramcontent.com/pod-product-compliance
Lightning Source LLC
Chambersburg PA
CBHW031944240626
47153CB00003B/851